# Taking SIDES

## Clashing Views on Controversial Issues in American History Volume II Reconstruction to the Present

Sixth Edition

# Taking SIDES

## Clashing Views on Controversial Issues in American History

## Volume II

## Reconstruction to the Present

Sixth Edition

Edited, Selected, and with Introductions by

**Larry Madaras**
*Howard Community College*

and

**James M. SoRelle**
*Baylor University*

The Dushkin Publishing Group, Inc.

*To Maggie and Cindy*

**Photo Acknowledgments**

Part 1 Library of Congress
Part 2 Solomon D. Butcher Collection/Nebraska State Historical Society
Part 3 National Archives
Part 4 Library of Congress

**Cover Art Acknowledgment**

Charles Vitelli



Manufactured in the United States of America

Sixth Edition

10 9 8 7 6 5 4 3 2 1

**Library of Congress Cataloging-in-Publication Data**

Main entry under title:
Taking sides: clashing views on controversial issues in American history, volume 2, reconstruction to the present/edited, selected, and with introductions by Larry Madaras and James M. SoRelle.—6th ed.
Includes bibliographical references and index.
1. United States—History. 2. United States—Historiography. I. Madaras, Larry, *comp.* II. SoRelle, James M., *comp.*
E178.6.T35 973—dc20
1-56134-327-7 94-48862

*The Dushkin Publishing Group, Inc.*

# PREFACE

The success of the past five editions of *Taking Sides: Clashing Views on Controversial Issues in American History* has encouraged us to remain faithful to its original objectives, methods, and format. Our aim has been to create an effective instrument to enhance classroom learning and to foster critical thinking. Historical facts presented in a vacuum are of little value to the educational process. For students, whose search for historical truth often concentrates on *when* something happened rather than on *why*, and on specific events rather than on the *significance* of those events, *Taking Sides* is designed to offer an interesting and valuable departure. The understanding that the reader arrives at based on the evidence that emerges from the clash of views encourages the reader to view history as an *interpretive* discipline, not one of rote memorization.

As in previous editions, the issues are arranged in chronological order and can be easily incorporated into any American history survey course. Each issue has an issue *introduction*, which sets the stage for the debate that follows in the pro and con selections and provides historical and methodological background to the problem that the issue examines. Each issue concludes with a *postscript*, which ties the readings together, briefly mentions alternative interpretations, and supplies detailed *suggestions for further reading* for the student who wishes to pursue the topics raised in the issue.

**Changes to this edition** In this edition we have continued our efforts to move beyond the traditionally ethnocentric and male-oriented focus of American history, both in terms of the issues and the authors selected to represent the clashing viewpoints. This edition depicts a society that benefited from the presence of Native Americans, African Americans, and women of various racial and ethnic origins. With this in mind, we present six entirely new issues: *Was Reconstruction a Success?* (Issue 1); *Were Immigrants to the United States "Uprooted"?* (Issue 4); *Did Booker T. Washington's Philosophy and Actions Betray the Interests of African Americans?* (Issue 7); *Were the Progressives Imperialists?* (Issue 8); *Was Woodrow Wilson a Naive Idealist?* (Issue 9); and *Will History Forgive Richard Nixon?* (Issue 17). Although Issue 4 is new, the NO reading has been retained from the previous edition because of its effectiveness. In addition, for the issues on South Vietnam (Issue 15) and Martin Luther King, Jr. (Issue 16), one reading has been changed to gain a fresh perspective. In all, there are 13 new selections.

**A word to the instructor** An *Instructor's Manual With Test Questions* (multiple-choice and essay) is available through the publisher for the instructor using *Taking Sides* in the classroom. And a general guidebook, *Using Taking Sides* *in the Classroom,* which discusses methods and techniques for integrating the pro-con approach into any classroom setting, is also available.

**Acknowledgments** Many individuals have contributed to the successful completion of this edition. We appreciate the evaluations submitted to The Dushkin Publishing Group by those who have used *Taking Sides* in the classroom. Special thanks to those who responded with specific suggestions for this edition:

Jack Devine
Stockton State College

William P. Dionisio
Sacramento City College

Lawrence H. Douglas
Plymouth State College

John Whitney Evans
College of Saint Scholastica

James O. Farmer
University of South Carolina, Aiken

Maria-Christina García
Texas A & M University

Gail Greenwood
Mission College

Richard P. Guidorizzi
Iona College

Carol Hammond
University of North Texas

Ted M. Kluz
Auburn University, Montgomery

Joseph R. Mitchell
Howard Community College

Joseph T. Moore
Montclair State College

Kristine A. Norvell
Moberly Area Community College

Elliot Pasternack
Middlesex County College

Kenneth E. Peters
University of South Carolina, Columbia

Bradley Reynolds
California State University, Northridge

Neil Sapper
Amarillo College

Carol Silvey
Southwest Missouri State University

Paul Simon
Xavier University

H. Micheal Tarver
Bowling Green State University

We are particularly indebted to Maggie Cullen, Cindy SoRelle, Barry A. Crouch, Virginia Kirk, Joseph and Helen Mitchell, and Jean Soto, who shared their ideas for changes, pointed us toward potentially useful historical works, and provided significant editorial assistance. Sandy Rohwein and Miriam Wilson (Howard Community College) performed indispensable typing duties connected with this project. Finally, we are sincerely grateful for the commitment, encouragement, and patience provided over the years by Mimi Egan, publisher for the Taking Sides series, and we appreciate the work of David Dean, administrative editor, David Brackley, copy editor, and the entire staff of The Dushkin Publishing Group.

Larry Madaras
Howard Community College

James M. SoRelle
Baylor University

# CONTENTS IN BRIEF

# CONTENTS

government. Professor of history Carl N. Degler maintains that the American labor movement reacted conservatively to the radical organizational changes brought about in the economic system by big business.

---

**ISSUE 4. Were Immigrants to the United States "Uprooted"?** **72**

**YES: Oscar Handlin,** from *The Uprooted: The Epic Story of the Great Migrations That Made the American People,* 2d ed. **74**

**NO: John Bodnar,** from *The Transplanted: A History of Immigrants in Urban America* **83**

Pulitzer Prize–winning historian Oscar Handlin insists that immigrants to the United States were alienated from the cultural traditions of their homelands. Associate professor of history John Bodnar maintains that various immigrant groups retained, modified, and transformed their Old World cultures in the New World.

---

*PART 2 THE RESPONSE TO INDUSTRIALISM* **95**

**ISSUE 5. Did the Westward Movement Transform the Traditional Roles of Women in the Late Nineteenth Century?** **96**

**YES: Sandra L. Myres,** from *Westering Women and the Frontier Experience 1800–1915* **98**

**NO: Christine Stansell,** from "Women on the Great Plains 1865–1890," *Women's Studies* **110**

Professor of history Sandra L. Myres (1933–1991) argues that first- and second-generation women, though not revolutionary, often took jobs outside the home. According to professor of history Christine Stansell, women on the Great Plains were not able to create networks of female friendships and consequently endured lonely lives.

---

**ISSUE 6. Was City Government in Late Nineteenth-Century America a "Conspicuous Failure"?** **120**

**YES: Ernest S. Griffith,** from *A History of American City Government: The Conspicuous Failure, 1870–1900* **122**

**NO: Jon C. Teaford,** from *The Unheralded Triumph: City Government in America, 1860–1900* **131**

Professor of political science and political economy Ernest S. Griffith (1896–1981) argues that the city governments that were controlled by the political bosses represented a betrayal of the public trust. Professor of history Jon C. Teaford argues that municipal governments in the late nineteenth century achieved remarkable success in dealing with the challenges presented by rapid urbanization.

---

**ISSUE 7. Did Booker T. Washington's Philosophy and Actions Betray the Interests of African Americans?** **142**

**YES: W. E. B. Du Bois,** from *The Souls of Black Folk* **144**

**NO: Louis R. Harlan,** from "Booker T. Washington and the Politics of Accommodation," in John Hope Franklin and August Meier, eds., *Black Leaders of the Twentieth Century* **152**

W. E. B. Du Bois, a founding member of the National Organization for the Advancement of Colored People, argues that Booker T. Washington failed to articulate the legitimate demands of African Americans for full civil and political rights. Professor of history Louis R. Harlan portrays Washington as a political realist whose policies and actions were designed to benefit black society as a whole.

---

*PART 3 FROM PROSPERITY THROUGH WORLD WAR II* **165**

**ISSUE 8. Were the Progressives Imperialists?** **166**

**YES: William Appleman Williams,** from *The Tragedy of American Diplomacy,* 2d ed. **168**

**NO: Barton J. Bernstein and Franklin A. Leib,** from "Progressive Republican Senators and American Imperialism, 1898–1916: A Reappraisal," *Mid-America: An Historical Review* **178**

Diplomatic historian William Appleman Williams argues that Progressive politicians supported an imperialistic foreign policy that subverted the American commitment to the ideal of self-determination for the peoples of other nations. Historians Barton J. Bernstein and Franklin A. Leib conclude that Progressive Republicans in the U.S. Senate were not committed to an aggressive imperialistic foreign policy.

---

**ISSUE 9. Was Woodrow Wilson a Naive Idealist?** **190**

**YES: Henry Kissinger,** from *Diplomacy* **192**

Sherna Berger Gluck, a lecturer in oral history, argues that the wartime experiences of women produced rising expectations that fueled the new women's consciousness movement. Professor of American studies Elaine Tyler May insists that World War II reinforced sex segregation in the American workforce.

---



Professor of history McGeorge Bundy maintains that President Truman wisely dropped the atomic bomb in order to end the war as quickly as possible. Professor of history Martin J. Sherwin argues that dropping the atomic bomb was an unnecessary act.

---



Conservative social critic Charles Murray argues that the Great Society's programs actually contributed to the plight of U.S. inner cities. Joseph A. Califano, Jr., a former aide to President Lyndon Johnson, maintains that the Great Society programs brought about many positive revolutionary changes.

---



Military analyst Harry G. Summers, Jr., attributes the United States' failure in Southeast Asia to a strategic blunder on the part of President Lyndon

# INTRODUCTION

## The Study of History

Larry Madaras
James M. SoRelle

In a pluralistic society such as ours, the study of history is bound to be a complex process. How an event is interpreted depends not only on the existing evidence but also on the perspective of the interpretor. Consequently, understanding history presupposes the evaluation of information, a task that often leads to conflicting conclusions. An understanding of history, then, requires the acceptance of the idea of historical relativism. Relativism means that redefinition of our past is always possible and desirable. History shifts, changes, and grows with new and different evidence and interpretations. As is the case with the law and even medicine, beliefs that were unquestioned 100 or 200 years ago have been discredited or discarded since.

Relativism, then, encourages revisionism. There is a maxim that "the past must remain useful to the present." Historian Carl Becker argued that every generation should examine history for itself, thus assuring constant scrutiny of our collective experience through new perspectives. History, consequently, does not remain static, in part because historians cannot avoid being influenced by the times in which they live. Almost all historians commit themselves to revising the views of other historians, synthesizing theories into macrointerpretations, or revising the revisionists.

### SCHOOLS OF THOUGHT

Three predominant schools of thought have emerged in American history since the first graduate seminars in history were given at the Johns Hopkins University in Baltimore in the 1870s. The *progressive* school dominated the professional field in the first half of the twentieth century. Influenced by the reform currents of Populism, progressivism, and the New Deal, these historians explored the social and economic forces that energized America. The progressive scholars tended to view the past in terms of conflicts between groups, and they sympathized with the underdog.

The post–World War II period witnessed the emergence of a new group of historians who viewed the conflict thesis as overly simplistic. Writing against the backdrop of the cold war, these *neoconservative* or *consensus* historians argued that Americans possess a shared set of values and that the areas of agreement within the nation's basic democratic and capitalistic framework were more important than the areas of disagreement.

In the 1960s, however, the civil rights movement, women's liberation, and the student rebellion (with its condemnation of the war in Vietnam) fragmented the consensus of values upon which historians and social scientists of the 1950s centered their interpretations. This turmoil set the stage for the emergence of another group of scholars. *New Left* historians began to reinterpret the past once again. They emphasized the significance of conflict in American history, and they resurrected interest in those groups ignored by the consensus school. In addition, New Left historians critiqued the expansionist policies of the United States and emphasized the difficulties confronted by Native Americans, African Americans, women, and urban workers in gaining full citizenship status.

Progressive, consensus, and New Left history is still being written. The most recent generation of scholars, however, focuses upon social history. Their primary concern is to discover what the lives of "ordinary Americans" were really like. These new social historians employ previously overlooked court and church documents, house deeds and tax records, letters and diaries, photographs, and census data to reconstruct the everyday lives of average Americans. Some employ new methodologies such as quantification (enhanced by advancing computer technology) and oral history, while others borrow from the disciplines of political science, economics, sociology, anthropology, and psychology for their historical investigations.

The proliferation of historical approaches, which are reflected in the issues debated in this book, has had mixed results. On the one hand, historians have become so specialized in their respective time periods and methodological styles that it is difficult to synthesize the recent scholarship into a comprehensive text for the general reader. On the other hand, historians know more about the American past than at any other time in history. They dare to ask new questions or ones that previously were considered to be germane only to scholars in other social sciences. Although there is little agreement about the answers to these questions, the methods employed and issues explored make the "new history" a very exciting field to study.

The topics that follow represent a variety of perspectives and approaches. Each of these controversial issues can be studied for its individual importance to American history. Taken as a group, they interact with one another to illustrate larger historical themes. When grouped thematically, the issues reveal continuing motifs in the development of American history.

## ECONOMIC QUESTIONS

Issues 2 and 3 explore the dynamics of the modern American economy through investigations of the nineteenth-century entrepreneurs and labor organizations, respectively. Issue 2 evaluates the contributions of post–Civil War entrepreneurial giants. Were these industrial leaders "robber barons," as portrayed by contemporary critics and many history texts? John Tipple believes that industrialists like Cornelius Vanderbilt and John D. Rockefeller undermined American institutions and individualistic values by rendering them impotent in their pursuit of wealth. In contrast, Alfred D. Chandler, Jr., characterizes those businessmen as organizational and marketing innovators who created huge corporations that stimulated the rise of a national urban economy.

The majority of modern-day historians argue that the American labor movement traditionally has been more conservative than its European counterpart. According to Carl N. Degler in Issue 3, American workers accepted capitalism and reacted conservatively to changes in the nation's economic system that were brought about by the rise of big business. Bruce Laurie disagrees. Through an examination of the Knights of Labor, Laurie argues that this union espoused an American radical tradition that was outside the political consensus of the Gilded Age. Ideologically, says Laurie, the Knights of Labor occupied a middle way "between the individualistic libertarianism of bourgeois America and the collectivism of working-class socialists."

## POLITICAL REFORMS AND THE STATUS QUO

Issue 6 assesses the nature of urban government in the late nineteenth century. Ernest S. Griffith views these governments as "conspicuous failures" because they were unable to cope effectively with the numerous problems associated with the evolution of the industrial city. Jon C. Teaford takes a more positive look at the late-nineteenth-century city. He argues that scholars have traditionally overlooked the remarkable accomplishments of municipal governments in the late nineteenth century despite major obstacles.

In the 1920s the Ku Klux Klan emerged as the leading anti-Catholic, anti-immigrant, antiforeign, pro-Americanism group in the nation. In Issue 10 David H. Bennett takes the traditional position that the Klan was a reactionary organization that was prone to violence and unwilling to accept the cultural and social changes of the decade. Stanley Coben, taking a more sympathetic view, sees the Klan less as a nativist group and more as a pressure group. Exhibiting real concerns about the changing moral standards in their communities, many Klan members entered politics and attempted to enforce the older, Victorian moral standards.

The Great Depression of the 1930s remains one of the most traumatic events in U.S. history. The characteristics of that decade are deeply etched in American folk memory, but the remedies that were applied to these social and economic ills—known collectively as the New Deal—are not easy to evaluate. In Issue 11, William E. Leuchtenburg contends that the New Deal extended the power of the national government in order to humanize the worst features of American capitalism. Gary Dean Best, on the other hand, criticizes the New Deal from a 1990s conservative perspective. In his view, the Roosevelt administration prolonged the depression and retarded the recovery. Because New Deal agencies were antibusiness, they overregulated the economy and did not allow the free enterprise system to work out of the depression.

The 1960s was an era of great turmoil. President Lyndon B. Johnson hoped to be remembered as the president who extended the New Deal reforms of the 1930s to the bottom third of the population. So controversial were Johnson's domestic reforms that some members of the Bush administration blamed the Los Angeles riots in the spring of 1992 on the Great Society. In Issue 14, Charles Murray argues along this line. Not only did the retraining, anticrime, and welfare programs of the Great Society not work, says Murray, but they also contributed to the worsening plight of U.S. inner cities today. But Joseph A. Califano maintains that the 1960s reforms brought about positive revolutionary changes in the areas of civil rights, education, health care, the environment, and consumer protection.

Because he was forced to resign the presidency to avoid impeachment proceedings resulting from his role in the Watergate scandal, Richard Nixon remains a controversial political figure. How will Nixon, who died in the spring of 1994, be remembered? In Issue 17, Professor Joan Hoff-Wilson downplays the significance of the Watergate scandal as well as foreign policy accomplishments in assessing Nixon's legacy. Instead, she argues, Nixon should be applauded for his domestic accomplishments of reorganizing the executive branch of the federal government and implementing important civil rights, welfare, and economic planning programs. Stanley I. Kutler disagrees with these revisionist treatments of the former president, insisting that Nixon was a crass, cynical, narrow-minded politician who unnecessarily prolonged the Vietnam War to ensure his reelection and who implemented domestic reforms only to outflank his liberal opponents.

## THE OUTSIDERS: BLACKS, IMMIGRANTS, AND WOMEN

Perhaps no period of American history has been subject to more myth-making than the era of Reconstruction. In the first issue in the book, Professor Kenneth Stampp argues that radical reconstruction after the Civil War succeeded economically, by consolidating the position of industrial capitalism; politically, by producing the most democratic governments the South had ever seen; and socially, by promoting ratification of the Fourteenth and Fifteenth Amendments, which gave African Americans the promise of equal rights. On the other hand, Professor Eric Foner, while recognizing some of the accomplishments of the Reconstruction era, argues that it failed to secure civil, political, and economic rights for southern blacks or to establish the Republican party as a permanent force in the South.

One of the most controversial figures in American history was the early twentieth-century African American leader Booker T. Washington. Was Washington too accommodating toward white values and goals and too accepting of the political disfranchisement and social segregation that took away the basic freedoms that African Americans earned after their emancipation from slavery? In Issue 7, the black intellectual and social critic W. E. B. Du Bois argues the case against Washington's ideology and policies, but Louis R. Harlan maintains that there were two Washingtons. He argues that Booker T. Washington, while publicly assuring whites that he accepted segregation, fought active and bitter battles behind the scenes to advance the political, economic, and educational opportunities for African Americans. Washington, then, was a political realist whose long-range goals of progress toward equality was a practical response to the climate of the times in which he lived.

Issue 16 discusses the role of Martin Luther King, Jr., in the civil rights struggles of the 1950s and 1960s. Did the civil rights movement depend on King's leadership for its success? Vincent Harding believes that King outlined a visionary hope for humankind in the years following the passage of the Voting Rights Act by directing his concern to the problems of the poor and to public criticism of the war in Vietnam. Clayborne Carson, on the other hand, reflects the views of many younger black scholars who themselves were participants in the battle for black equality. Carson argues that the successes in this struggle depended upon mass activism, not the actions of a single leader.

Massive immigration to the United States in the late nineteenth and early twentieth centuries introduced widespread changes in American society. Moreover, the presence of increasing numbers of immigrants from southern and eastern Europe, many of them Catholics and Jews, seemed to threaten native-born citizens, most of whom were Protestant and of northern and western European ancestry. Asian immigrants, mainly from China or Japan, added to nativist fears. In Issue 4, Oscar Handlin argues that the immigrants were alienated from their Old World cultures as they adjusted to an unfamiliar and often hostile environment. John Bodnar, on the other hand, shows how various immigrant groups from southern and eastern Europe retained, modified, and at times transformed their Old World cultures in response to the urban and industrial setting of the United States.

In the past two decades scholars have devoted a considerable amount of attention to the field of women's history. Even traditional topics such as westward expansion now include African Americans, Hispanics, and Native Americans as part of the story. In Issue 5, Christine Stansell examines westering women and concludes that women became more oppressed than usual as they moved west. In her view, the women of the West became isolated from family and friends and were forced to endure lives of drudgery and loneliness, often within the context of unhappy marriages. Sandra L. Myres gives a more upbeat interpretation of westering women. She sees the frontier as a liberating force for both sexes. Westering women did not just stay home and raise a family; they often worked as teachers and nurses as well as in nontraditional occupations such as physicians, lawyers, ranchers, shopkeepers, and salespersons.

Scholars disagree over whether or not World War II liberated American women. In Issue 12, Elaine Tyler May insists that no permanent changes took place in spite of the nontraditional jobs in factories and government offices that were held by women during the war. In May's view, the wartime emergency reinforced the sex segregation of the workforce and underscored women's tasks as homemakers, women, and mothers. Sherna Berger Gluck, however, sees World War II as a turning point for American women. Although she recognizes that most women lost their industrial jobs after World War II ended, Gluck focuses upon the *process* of change rather than the *degree* of change. From this perspective, women's wartime work experiences produced rising expectations that transformed their concepts of themselves as women and fueled a new consciousness movement.

## THE UNITED STATES AND THE WORLD

As the United States developed a preeminent position in world affairs, the nation's politicians were forced to consider the proper relationship between their country and the rest of the world. To what extent, many asked, should the United States seek to expand its political, economic, or moral influence around the world? This was a particularly intriguing question for the Progressives of the early twentieth century, most of whom were more interested in domestic reforms than foreign policy. Issue 8 examines the level of international involvement of this group. The late New Left historian William Appleman Williams insisted that the Progressives' desires to improve American society and efforts to reform underdeveloped countries abroad amounted to a clear case of imperialism. Barton J. Bernstein and Franklin A. Leib counter with evidence that most Progressive reformers opposed U.S. economic interests abroad and generally tried to avoid military intervention.

One Progressive president, Woodrow Wilson, spent the better part of his two terms in office addressing international problems, but scholars have reached no consensus regarding the effectiveness of his leadership. In Issue 9, former secretary of state Henry Kissinger maintains that President Wilson used World War I to enforce moral principles of international diplomacy, which has made it difficult for the presidents who followed him to develop a coherent, well-reasoned foreign policy based upon the national interest. William Carleton, however, views Wilson as a true internationalist who understood much better than his narrow-minded nationalist opponents the new international role that the United States would play in world affairs.

The decision to drop the atomic bomb to end World War II, the subject of Issue 13, demonstrates how history affects one of the most important foreign policy decisions in the twentieth century. Could the United States have avoided the use of nuclear weapons? McGeorge Bundy argues that President Truman ordered the use of the atomic bomb to end the war as quickly as possible. Use of the bomb, continues Bundy, shortened the war because it brought the Russians into the Pacific a week ahead of schedule and gave the Japanese emperor leverage to pressure the Japanese military to surrender. Martin J. Sherwin understands why the bomb was dropped but concludes that it was unnecessary. Other options, such as awaiting a Soviet declaration of war, continuing conventional air bombings and naval blockades, or modifying the policy of unconditional surrender, were ruled out because the atomic bomb seemed to be the simplest solution.

No discussion of American foreign policy is complete without some consideration of the Vietnam War. Issue 15 considers whether or not the United States could have prevented the fall of South Vietnam to the Communists. Harry G. Summers argues that a formal declaration of war would have mobilized American public opinion to support the government's military policy, thereby producing the necessary will to win. George C. Herring, however, believes that American policymakers exaggerated the strategic importance of Vietnam for over a decade and deluded themselves about America's invincibility.

## CONCLUSION

The process of historical study should rely more on thinking than on memorizing data. Once the basics of who, what, when, and where are determined, historical thinking shifts to a higher gear. Analysis, comparison and contrast, evaluation, and explanation take command. These skills not only increase our knowledge of the past but they also provide general tools for the comprehension of all the topics about which human beings think.

The diversity of a pluralistic society, however, creates some obstacles to comprehending the past. The spectrum of differing opinions on any particular subject eliminates the possibility of quick and easy answers. In the final analysis, conclusions often are built through a synthesis of several different interpretations, but even then, they may be partial and tentative.

The study of history in a pluralistic society allows each citizen the opportunity to reach independent conclusions about the past. Since most, if not all, historical issues affect the present and future, understanding the past becomes necessary if society is to progress. Many of today's problems have a direct connection with the past. Additionally, other contemporary issues may lack obvious direct antecedents, but historical investigation can provide illuminating analogies. At first, it may appear confusing to read and to think about opposing historical views, but the survival of our democratic society depends on such critical thinking by acute and discerning minds.

# PART 1

# Reconstruction, Immigration, and the Industrial Revolution

*Deep and bitter wounds were left in the American nation as a result of the Civil War. Reconstruction was a period of further turmoil as the political institutions of the South were redesigned.*

*Economic expansion and the seemingly unlimited resources available in postbellum America offered great opportunity and created new political, social, and economic challenges. Political freedom and economic opportunity provided incentives for immigration to America. The need for cheap labor to run the machinery of the industrial revolution created an atmosphere for potential exploitation that was intensified by the concentration of wealth in the hands of a few capitalists. The labor movement took root, with some elements calling for an overthrow of the capitalist system, while others sought to establish political power within the existing system. Strains began to develop between immigrant and native-born workers as well as between workers and owners.*

# ISSUE 1

## Was Reconstruction a Success?

**YES: Kenneth M. Stampp,** from *The Era of Reconstruction, 1865–1877* (Alfred A. Knopf, 1965)

**NO: Eric Foner,** from *Reconstruction: America's Unfinished Revolution, 1863–1877* (Harper & Row, 1988)

### ISSUE SUMMARY

**YES:** Kenneth M. Stampp, a professor emeritus of history, argues that the period of Reconstruction after the Civil War succeeded economically, by consolidating the position of industrial capitalism; politically, by producing the most democratic governments the South had ever seen; and socially, by promoting ratification of the Fourteen and Fifteenth Amendments, which gave African Americans the promise of equal rights.

**NO:** Professor of history Eric Foner admits that radical rule produced a number of accomplishments, but he maintains that it failed to secure civil, political, and economic rights for southern blacks or to establish the Republican party as a permanent force in the South.

Given the complex political, economic, and social issues that America's leaders were forced to address in the post–Civil War years, it is not surprising that the era of Reconstruction (1865–1877) is shrouded in controversy. For the better part of the century following the war, historians typically characterized Reconstruction as a total failure that had proved detrimental to all Americans—northerners and southerners, whites and blacks. According to this traditional interpretation, a vengeful Congress, dominated by radical Republicans, imposed military rule upon the southern states. Carpetbaggers from the North, along with traitorous white scalawags and their black accomplices in the South, established coalition governments that rewrote state constitutions, raised taxes, looted state treasuries, and disenfranchised former Confederates while extending the ballot to the freedmen. This era finally ended in 1877, when courageous southern white Democrats successfully "redeemed" their region from "Negro rule" by toppling the Republican state governments.

This portrait of Reconstruction dominated the historical profession until the 1960s. One reason for this is that white historians (both northerners and southerners) who wrote about this period operated from two basic assumptions: (1) the South was perfectly capable of solving its own problems without federal government interference; and (2) the former slaves were intellectually inferior to whites and incapable of running a government (much less one in which some whites would be their subordinates). African American historians, such as W. E. B. Du Bois, wrote several essays and books that challenged this negative portrayal of Reconstruction, but their works were seldom taken seriously in the academic world and were rarely read by the general public. Still, these black historians foreshadowed the acceptance of revisionist interpretations of Reconstruction, which coincided with the successes of the civil rights movement (or "Second Reconstruction") in the 1960s.

Revisionist historians identified a number of accomplishments of the Republican state governments in the South and their supporters in Washington, D.C. For example, revisionists argued that the state constitutions written during Reconstruction were the most democratic documents that the South had seen up to that time. While taxes increased in the southern states, the revenues generated by these levies financed the rebuilding and expansion of the South's railroad network, the creation of a number of social service institutions, and the establishment of a public school system that benefited African Americans as well as whites. At the federal level, Reconstruction achieved the ratification of the Fourteenth and Fifteenth Amendments, which extended significant privileges of citizenship to African Americans, both North and South. Revisionists also placed the charges of corruption that were leveled by traditionalists against the Republican regimes in the South in a more appropriate context by insisting that political corruption was a *national* malady in the second half of the nineteenth century. Finally, revisionist historians sharply attacked the notion that African Americans dominated the reconstructed governments of the South. They pointed out that there were no black governors, only 2 black senators, and 15 black congressmen during this period. In no southern state did blacks control both houses of the legislature.

Kenneth M. Stampp's 1965 book *The Era of Reconstruction, 1865–1877*, is a classic statement of the revisionist viewpoint. Published a century after the end of the Civil War, this work offered a more balanced appraisal of Reconstruction and, in fact, emphasized the successes of the period of Republican rule in the South. In the excerpt that follows, Stampp admits the shortcomings of radical rule but insists that the Republican state governments chalked up a number of positive accomplishments during Reconstruction.

More recently, a third group of historians, the postrevisionists, have challenged the validity of the term *radical* as applied to the Reconstruction era by both traditional and revisionist historians. Eric Foner's essay represents an example of this postrevisionist approach. Although he recognizes a number of positive accomplishments, Foner concludes that Reconstruction must be judged a failure, part of an "unfinished revolution" initiated at the close of the Civil War. A number of forces, says Foner, conspired to eradicate the idealistic goal of full freedom for African Americans and the more pragmatic desire to establish an effective presence in the South for the Republican party.

**YES**

## Kenneth M. Stampp

# THE ERA OF RECONSTRUCTION, 1865–1877

### RADICAL RULE IN THE SOUTH

When Lord Bryce, in the 1880's, wrote *The American Commonwealth,* he commented at length on the southern state governments created under the radical plan of reconstruction. What he had to say about them was not remarkable for its originality, but a few passages are worth quoting to give the flavor of the approaching historical consensus. "Such a Saturnalia of robbery and jobbery has seldom been seen in any civilized country.... The position of these [radical] adventurers was like that of a Roman provincial governor in the latter days of the Republic.... [All] voting power lay with those who were wholly unfit for citizenship, and had no interest as taxpayers, in good government.... [Since] the legislatures were reckless and corrupt, the judges for the most part subservient, the Federal military officers bound to support what purported to be the constitutional authorities of the State, Congress distant and little inclined to listen to the complaints of those whom it distrusted as rebels, greed was unchecked and roguery unabashed." In drawing this unpleasant picture Lord Bryce anticipated the generalizations of the Dunningites, as did many others.

Each of the eleven states of the former Confederacy, during all or part of the decade between 1867 and 1877, fell under the control of the radical Republicans. Tennessee was the first to be captured by them—indeed, it never had a Johnson government—but it was also the first to be lost. Tennessee was "redeemed," as southern white Democrats liked to call their return to power, as early as 1869. The last three states to be redeemed were South Carolina, Florida, and Louisiana, where the radical regimes lasted until the spring of 1877....

The first step in the organization of new southern state governments, as required by the reconstruction acts, was the election of delegates to conventions to frame new state constitutions. Since these conventions were controlled by the radicals, since they were the first political bodies in the South to contain Negroes, white conservatives subjected them to violent denunciation. They contemptuously called them "black and tan conventions"; they described the delegates as "baboons, monkeys, mules," or "ragamuffins and jailbirds." The South Carolina convention, according to a local newspaper, was the "maddest, most infamous revolution in history."

Yet, the invectives notwithstanding, there was nothing mad and little revolutionary about the work of these conventions. In fact, one of the most significant observations to be made about them is that the delegates showed little interest in experimentation. For the most part the radicals wrote orthodox state constitutions, borrowing heavily from the previous constitutions and from those of other states. To find fault with the way these southern constitutions were drawn is to find fault with the way most new state constitutions have been drawn; to criticize their basic political structure is to criticize the basic political structure of all the states. They were neither original nor unique. There was no inclination to test, say, the unicameral legislature, or novel executive or judicial systems.

Nor did the conventions attempt radical experiments in the field of social or economic policy. Since land reform had been defeated in Congress, a few delegates tried to achieve it through state action. The South Carolina convention provided for the creation of a commission to purchase land for sale to Negroes. In Louisiana, some Negro delegates proposed that when planters sold their estates purchases of more than 150 acres be prohibited. One white scalawag suggested a double tax on uncultivated land. A few delegates in other states advocated various policies designed to force the breakup of large estates. But these and all other attacks upon landed property were easily defeated.

As for the freedmen, the new constitutions proclaimed the equality of all men by quoting or paraphrasing the Declaration of Independence. Negroes were given the same civil and political rights as white men. "The equality of all persons before the law," proclaimed the Arkansas constitution, "is recognized and shall ever remain inviolate; nor shall any citizen ever be deprived of any right, privilege, or immunity, nor exempted from any burden or duty, on account of race, color, or previous condition." But on the subject of the social relations of Negroes and whites, most of the radical constitutions were evasive. South Carolina provided that its public schools were to be open to all "without regard to race or color," but only the state university actually made an attempt at integration. The Louisiana constitution declared: "There shall be no separate schools or institutions of learning established exclusively for any race by the State of Louisiana." In New Orleans from 1871 to 1877 about one third of the public schools were integrated, and white resistance was remarkably mild; but elsewhere in Louisiana segregation was the rule. Outside of South Carolina and Louisiana the radicals made no explicit constitutional provision for social integration. The Mississippi convention first defeated a proposal that segregated schools be required, then defeated a proposal that they be prohibited; the result was that the new constitution ignored the issue altogether. The only reference to segregation in it was a vague statement that "the rights of all citizens to travel upon public conveyances shall not be infringed upon, nor in any manner abridged in this state." But whether or not this clause prohibited segregation in public transportation is far from clear.

Yet, though the new constitutions were essentially conservative documents, they did accomplish some modest reforms, most of which were long overdue. In general, they eliminated certain undemocratic features of the old constitutions, for example, the inequitable systems of legislative apportionment that had discriminated against the interior regions of Virginia, North Carolina, and South Carolina. In the states of the Southeast, many offices that had previously been appointive were now made elective, and county government was taken out of the hands of local oligarchies. The rights of women were enlarged, tax systems were made more equitable, penal codes were reformed, and the number of crimes punishable by death was reduced. Most of the constitutions provided for substantial improvements in the state systems of public education and in the facilities for the care of the physically and mentally handicapped and of the poor.

In South Carolina, according to the historians of reconstruction in that state, the radical convention was an orderly body which accomplished its work with reasonable dispatch. It produced a constitution "as good as any other constitution that state has ever had"—good enough to remain in force for nearly two decades after the white Democrats regained control. This was, in fact, the state's first really democratic constitution; for, in addition to removing distinctions based on race, it provided for manhood suffrage, abolished property qualifications for officeholding, gave the voters the power for the first time to select the governor and other state officers, and transferred the election of presidential electors from the legislature to the voters. Another important provision related to public education: unlike the previous constitution, "the fundamental law of the state carried the obligation of universal education" and aimed at "the creation of a school system like that of Northern states." Other reforms included an extension of women's rights, adoption of the state's first divorce law, strengthening of the state's fiscal power, revision of the tax system, and modernization of the judiciary and of county government.

The responsible behavior of South Carolina's radical constitutional convention was in striking contrast to the angry and irresponsible criticism of the Democrats. Chiefly because of its provisions for racial equality, they ridiculed the new constitution as "the work of sixty-odd negroes, many of them ignorant and depraved, together with fifty white men, outcasts of Northern society, and Southern renegades, betrayers of their race and country." Specifically, the Democrats charged that manhood suffrage was designed to further the ambitions of "mean whites"; that Negro suffrage would bring ruin to the state; that the judicial reforms were "repugnant to our customs and habits of thought"; and that the public school requirements were "a fruitful source of peculant corruption." In spite of this fanciful criticism by a party whose chief appeal was to racial bigotry, the work of the radical convention was ratified by a majority of nearly three to one.

At the time that the new constitutions were ratified, elections were held for state officers and legislators. After the elections, when Congress approved of the constitutions, political power was transferred from the military to the new civil governments. Thus began the era of radical government in the South—an era which, according to tradition, produced some of the worst state administrations in American history. Some of the southern radical regimes earned their evil reputations, others did not; but viewed collectively, there was much in the record they made to justify severe criticism. To say that they were not always models of efficiency and integrity would be something of an understatement. "The great impediment of the Republican party in this state," wrote a Tennessee radical, "is the incompetence of its leaders.... After the war the loyal people in many counties had no competent men to be judges, lawyers or political leaders." Indeed, all of the radical governments suffered more or less from the incompetence of some, the dishonesty of a few, and above all the inexperience of most of the officeholders....

Meanwhile, the credit of some of the southern states was impaired as public debts mounted. In Florida the state debt increased from $524,000 in 1868 to $5,621,000 in 1874. In South Carolina a legislative committee reported that between 1868 and 1871 the state debt had increased from $5,403,000 to $15,768,000, but another committee insisted that it had increased to $29,159,000. By 1872 the debts of the eleven states of the former Confederacy had increased by approximately $132,000,000. The burden on taxpayers grew apace. Between 1860 and 1870 South Carolina's tax rate more than doubled, while property values declined by more than fifty per cent. In Tennessee a radical reported that during the first three years after the war taxes had increased sevenfold, though property had declined in value by one third. Throughout the South the tax burden was four times as great in 1870 as it had been in 1860. Such rates, complained many southern landholders, were confiscatory; and, indeed, taxes and other adversities of the postwar years forced some of them to sell all or part of their lands. Sympathy for South Carolina's planter aristocracy caused a northern conservative to ask: "When before did mankind behold the spectacle of a rich, high-spirited, cultivated, self-governed people suddenly cast down, bereft of their possessions, and put under the feet of the slaves they had held in bondage for centuries?"

High taxes, mounting debts, corruption, extravagance, and waste, however, do not constitute the complete record of the radical regimes. Moreover, to stop with a mere description of their misdeeds would be to leave all the crucial questions unanswered—to distort the picture and to view it without perspective. For example, if some of these governments contained an uncommonly large number of inexperienced or incompetent officeholders, if much of their support came from an untutored electorate, there was an obvious reason for this. Howard K. Beale, in a critique of various reconstruction legends, observed that the political rulers of the ante-bellum South "had fastened ignorance or inexperience on millions of whites as well as Negroes and that it was this ignorance and inexperience that caused trouble when Radicals were in power.... Wealthy Southerners... seldom recognized the need for general education of even the *white* masses." Even in 1865 the men who won control of the Johnson governments showed little disposition to adopt the needed reforms. In South Carolina the Johnsonians did almost nothing to establish a system of public education, and at the time that the radicals came to power only one eighth of the white children of school age were attending school. The Negroes, of course, had been ignored entirely. It was probably no coincidence that the radicals made their poorest record in South Carolina, the state which had done the least for education and whose prewar government had been the least democratic.

As for the corruption of the radical governments, this phenomenon can be understood only when it is related to the times and to conditions throughout the country. One must remember that the administrations of President Grant set the moral tone for American government at all levels, national, state, and local. The best-remembered episodes of the Grant era are its numerous scandals—the Crédit Mobilier and the Whiskey Ring being the most spectacular of them—involving members of Congress as well as men in high administration circles. There were, moreover, singularly corrupt Republican machines in control of various northern states, including Massachusetts, New York, and Pennsylvania. But corruption was not a phenomenon peculiar to Republicans of the Gilded Age, as the incredible operations of the so-called Tweed Ring in New York City will testify. Indeed, the thefts of public funds by this organization of white Tammany Democrats surpassed the total thefts in all the southern states combined....

Most of the debt increases in the southern states resulted not from the thefts and extravagance of radical legislators but from the grants and guarantees they gave to railroad promoters, among whom were always some native white Democrats. In Florida more than sixty per cent of the debt incurred by the radical regime was in the form of railroad guarantee bonds. In North Carolina the radical government, prodded by the carpetbagger Milton S. Littlefield, a skilled lobbyist, issued millions of dollars of railroad bonds. Among those who benefited were many of the state's "best citizens," including George W. Swepson, a local business promoter and Democrat. Most of Alabama's reconstruction debt —$18,000,000 out of $20,500,000—was in the form of state bonds issued to subsidize railroad construction, for which the state obtained liens upon railroad property. When one measure for state aid was before the Alabama legislature, many Democrats were among the lobbyists working for its passage. Yet, complained a radical, the Democrats who expect to profit from the bill "will use the argument that the Republican party had a majority in the Legislature, and will falsely, but hopefully, charge it upon Republicans as a partisan crime against the state."

Indeed, all of the southern states, except Mississippi, used state credit to finance the rebuilding and expansion of their railroads, for private sources of credit were inadequate. This policy had been developed before the war; it was continued under the Johnsonians; and in some cases when the Democrats overthrew the radicals there was no decline in the state's generosity to the railroads. While the radicals controlled the southern legislatures, not only they but many members of the Democratic minority as well voted for railroad bond issues. According to an historian of reconstruction in Louisiana, "Such measures were supported by members of both parties, often introduced by Democrats, in every case supported by a large majority of Democrats in both houses." The subservience of many postwar southern legislatures to the demands of railroad and other business promoters is in some respects less shocking than pathetic. For it expressed a kind of blind faith shared by many Southerners of both parties that railroad building and industrialization would swiftly solve all of their section's problems. No price seemed too high for such a miracle.

In several states, for obviously partisan reasons, the actual increase in the size of the public debt was grossly exaggerated. In Mississippi, for example, there was a durable legend among white Democrats that the radicals had added $20,000,000 to the state debt, when, in fact, they added only $500,000. Mississippi radicals had guarded against extravagance by inserting a clause in the constitution of 1868 prohibiting the pledging of state funds to aid private corporations —a clause which the conservatives, incidentally, had opposed. In Alabama, apart from railroad bonds secured by railroad property, the radicals added only $2,500,000 to the state debt. They did not leave a debt of $30,000,000 as conservatives claimed. In most other states, when loans to the railroads are subtracted, the increases in state debts for which the radicals were responsible appear far less staggering.

As for taxes, one of the positive achievements of many of the radical governments was the adoption of more equitable tax systems which put a heavier burden upon the planters. Before the war the southern state governments had performed few public services and the tax burden on the landed class had been negligible; hence the vehement protests of the landholders were sometimes as much against radical tax policies as against the alleged waste of taxpayers' money. The restoration governments often brought with them a return to the old inequitable fiscal systems. In Mississippi the subsequent claim of the conservatives that they had reduced the tax burden the radicals had placed upon property holders was quite misleading. The conservatives did lower the state property tax, but, as a consequence, they found it necessary to shift various services and administrative burdens from the state to the counties. This led to an increase in the cost of county government, an increase in the rate of county taxes, and a net increase in total taxes, state and county, that Mississippi property holders had to pay.

As a matter of fact, taxes, government expenditures, and public debts were bound to increase in the southern states during the postwar years no matter who controlled them. For there was no way to escape the staggering job of physical reconstruction—the repair of public buildings, bridges, and roads—and costs had started to go up under the Johnson governments before the radicals came to power. So far from the expenditures of the reconstruction era being totally lost in waste and fraud, much of this physical reconstruction was accomplished while the radicals were in office. They expanded the state railroad systems, increased public services, and provided public school systems—in some states for the first time. Since schools and other public services were now provided for Negroes as well as for whites, a considerable increase in the cost of state government could hardly have been avoided. In Florida between 1869 and 1873 the number of children enrolled in the public schools trebled; in South Carolina between 1868 and 1876 the number increased from 30,000 to 123,000. The economies achieved by some of the restoration governments came at the expense of the schools and various state institutions such as hospitals for the insane. The southern propertied classes had always been reluctant to tax themselves to support education or state hospitals, and in many cases the budget-cutting of the conservatives simply strangled them.

Thus radical rule, in spite of its shortcomings, was by no means synonymous with incompetence and corruption; far too many carpetbagger, scalawag, and Negro politicians made creditable records to warrant such a generalization. Moreover, conditions were improving in the final years of reconstruction. In South Carolina the last radical administration, that of the carpetbagger Governor Daniel H. Chamberlain, was dedicated to reform; in Florida "the financial steadiness of the state government increased toward the end of Republican rule." In Mississippi the radicals made a remarkably good record. The first radical governor, James L. Alcorn, a scalawag, was a man of complete integrity; the second, Adelbert Ames, a carpetbagger, was honest, able, and sincerely devoted to protecting the rights of the Negroes. Mississippi radicals, according to Vernon L. Wharton, established a system of public education far better than any the state had known before; reorganized the state judiciary and adopted a new code of laws; renovated public buildings and constructed new ones, including state hospitals at Natchez and Vicksburg; and provided better state asylums for the blind, deaf, and dumb. The radicals, Wharton concludes, gave Mississippi "a government of greatly expanded functions at a cost that was low in comparison with that of almost any other state." No major political scandal occurred in Mississippi during the years of radical rule—indeed, it was the best governed state in the postwar South. Yet white conservatives attacked the radical regime in Mississippi as violently as they did in South Carolina, which suggests that their basic grievance was not corruption but race policy.

Finally, granting all their mistakes, the radical governments were by far the most democratic the South had ever known. They were the only governments in southern history to extend to Negroes complete civil and political equality, and to try to protect them in the enjoyment of the rights they were granted. The overthrow of these governments was hardly a victory for political democracy, for the conservatives who "redeemed" the South tried to relegate poor men, Negro and white, once more to political obscurity. Near the end of the nineteenth century another battle for political democracy would have to be waged; but this time it would be, for the most part, a more limited version—for whites only. As for the Negroes, they would have to struggle for another century to regain what they had won—and then lost—in the years of radical reconstruction....

## TRIUMPH OF THE CONSERVATIVES

During the state and presidential elections of 1876, when violence broke out in South Carolina, Florida, and Louisiana, President Grant would do nothing more than issue a sanctimonious proclamation. Indeed, when the outcome of that election was in dispute, Republicans had to bargain hard with southern Democrats in order to secure the peaceful inauguration of Rutherford B. Hayes. In one last sectional compromise, that of 1877, the Republicans promised to remove the remaining federal troops in the South, to be fair to Southerners in the distribution of federal patronage, and to vote funds for a number of southern internal improvements. In return, southern Democrats agreed to acquiesce in the inauguration of Hayes and to deal fairly with the Negroes.

The Compromise of 1877 signified the final end of radical reconstruction, for with the removal of federal troops, the last of the radical regimes collapsed. Soon after his inauguration President Hayes made a goodwill tour of the South. Conservative Democratic leaders, such as Governor Wade Hampton of South Carolina, greeted him cordially and assured him that peace and racial harmony now reigned in the South. Hayes tried hard to believe it, because he hoped so much that it was true.

"What is the President's Southern policy?" asked ex-Governor Chamberlain of South Carolina. Judged by its results, "it consists in the abandonment of Southern Republicans, and especially the colored race, to the control and rule not only of the Democratic party, but of that class at the South which regarded slavery as a Divine Institution, which waged four years of destructive war for its perpetuation, which steadily opposed citizenship and suffrage for the negro—in a word, a class whose traditions, principles, and history are opposed to every step and feature of what Republicans call our national progress since 1860."

It was in the 1870's, then, and not in 1865, that the idealism of the antislavery crusade finally died. Along with the loss of the idealism that had been one of the prime motivating forces behind radical reconstruction, the practical considerations also lost their relevance. Whereas in 1865 the urban middle classes still regarded the agrarian South and West as a serious threat, by the 1870's their position was consolidated and their power supreme. By then the leaders of business enterprise had so far penetrated the Democratic party and had so much influence among the so-called "redeemers" of the South that they no longer equated Republican political defeat with economic disaster. Samuel J. Tilden, the Democratic presidential candidate in 1876, was a wealthy, conservative New York corporation lawyer, thoroughly "sound" on monetary, banking, and fiscal policy, in no respect unfriendly to business interests. Whichever way the presidential election of 1876 had gone, these interests could hardly have lost. Grover Cleveland, the only Democrat elected President between James Buchanan before the Civil War and Woodrow Wilson in the twentieth century, was also "sound" and conservative on all the economic issues of his day.

As for the Republican party, it too felt more secure than it had before. In 1865 it was still uncertain whether this party, born of crisis, could survive in a reunited, peaceful Union in which the slavery issue was resolved. But by the 1870's the party was firmly established, had an efficient, powerful, amply endowed organization, and had the unswerving support of a mass of loyal voters. True, the Republicans lost the congressional elections of 1874 and almost lost the presidency in 1876, but this could be attributed to the depression and abnormal conditions. Normally, in order to exist as a major national party, Republicans no longer needed the votes of southern Negroes. The reason for this was that during and since the war they had won control of the Old Northwest, once a stronghold of agrarianism and copperheadism. Indeed, a significant chapter in the history of reconstruction is the political and economic reconstruction of this flourishing region. The Civil War, the identification of the Republican party with nationalism and patriotism, the veteran vote, the Homestead Act, and federal appropriations for internal improvements all helped to make the states of the Old Northwest Republican strongholds. Moreover, the westward advance of the industrial revolution —the growth of urban centers such as Cleveland, Detroit, and Chicago—identified powerful economic groups in the Old Northwest with the industrial interests of the Northeast.

How these western states voted in the eleven presidential elections between 1868 and 1908 is significant when it is remembered that they had consistently gone Democratic before the Civil War. In eight elections the Old Northwest went Republican unanimously. Of the seven states in this region, Indiana voted Democratic three times, Illinois and Wisconsin once, the rest never. Thus, with the Old Northwest made safe for the Republican party, the political motive for radical reconstruction vanished, and practical Republicans could afford to abandon the southern Negro. With the decline of the idealism and the disappearance of the realistic political and economic considerations that had supported it, radical reconstruction came to an end.

* * *

Viewing radical reconstruction with its three chief motivating forces in mind, are we to call it a success or a failure? Insofar as its purpose was to consolidate the position of American industrial capitalism, it was doubtless a striking success. During the last three decades of the nineteenth century, social and economic reformers subjected irresponsible business entrepreneurs to constant attack, but they won no significant victories. In fact, they met constant defeat, climaxed by the failure of the Populists in the 1890's. With William McKinley, the conservative son of an Ohio industrialist, installed in power in 1897, American capitalism rode to the end of the nineteenth century with its power uncurbed and its supremacy not yet effectively challenged. Above all, the conservative Democratic leaders of the New South were no longer enemies but allies.

Politically, radical reconstruction was also a success. Even though Republicans failed in their effort to establish an effective and durable organization in the South, they nevertheless emerged from the era of reconstruction in a powerful position. Most of their subsequent political victories were narrow; sometimes they lost a congressional campaign. But until Wilson's election in 1912, only once, in 1892, did the Democrats win control of the presidency and both houses of Congress simultaneously. And if conservative Republican Congressmen counted almost no Southerners in their caucus, they found a large number of southern Democrats remarkably easy to work with. The coalition of northern Republicans and southern Dixiecrats, so powerful in recent Congresses, was an important fact of American political life as early as the 1880's. The coalition had to be an informal one and had to endure a great deal of partisan rhetoric, but it was real nonetheless.

Finally, we come to the idealistic aim of the radicals to make southern society more democratic, especially to make the emancipation of the Negroes something more than an empty gesture. In the short run this was their greatest failure. In the rural South the basic socioeconomic pattern was not destroyed, for share-cropping replaced the antebellum slave-plantation system. Most of the upper-class large landowners survived the ordeal of war and reconstruction, and the mass of Negroes remained a dependent, propertyless peasantry. After reconstruction, in spite of the Fourteenth and Fifteenth Amendments, the Negroes were denied equal civil and political rights. In 1883 the Supreme Court invalidated the Civil Rights Act of 1875; in 1894 Congress repealed the Force Acts; and in 1896 the Supreme Court sanctioned social segregation if Negroes were provided "equal" accommodations. Thus Negroes were denied federal protection, and by the end of the nineteenth century the Republican party had nearly forgotten them. In place of slavery a caste system reduced Negroes to an inferior type of citizenship; social segregation gave them inferior educational and recreational facilities; and a pattern of so-called "race etiquette" forced them to pay deference to all white men. Negroes, in short, were only half emancipated.

Still, no one could quite forget that the Fourteenth and Fifteenth Amendments were now part of the federal Constitution. As a result, Negroes could no longer be deprived of the right to vote, except by extralegal coercion or by some devious subterfuge. They could not be deprived of equal civil rights, except by deceit. They could not be segregated in public places, except by the spurious argument that this did not in fact deprive them of the equal protection of the laws. Thus Negroes were no longer denied equality by the plain language of the law, as they had been before radical reconstruction, but only by coercion, by subterfuge, by deceit, and by spurious legalisms. For a time, of course, the denial of equality was as effective one way as the other; but when it was sanctioned by the laws of the Johnson governments and approved by the federal government, there was no hope. When, however, state-imposed discrimination was, in effect, an evasion of the supreme law of the land, the odds, in the long run, were on the side of the Negro.

The Fourteenth and Fifteenth Amendments, which could have been adopted only under the conditions of radical reconstruction, make the blunders of that era, tragic though they were, dwindle into insignificance. For if it was worth four years of civil war to save the Union, it was worth a few years of radical reconstruction to give the American Negro the ultimate promise of equal civil and political rights.

# NO

**Eric Foner**

## THE RIVER HAS ITS BEND

Thus, in the words of W. E. B. Du Bois, "the slave went free; stood a brief moment in the sun; then moved back again toward slavery." The magnitude of the Redeemer counterrevolution underscored both the scope of the transformation Reconstruction had assayed and the consequences of its failure. To be sure, the era of emancipation and Republican rule did not lack enduring accomplishments. The tide of change rose and then receded, but it left behind an altered landscape. The freedmen's political and civil equality proved transitory, but the autonomous black family and a network of religious and social institutions survived the end of Reconstruction. Nor could the seeds of educational progress planted then be entirely uprooted. While wholly inadequate for pupils of both races, schooling under the Redeemers represented a distinct advance over the days when blacks were excluded altogether from a share in public services.

If blacks failed to achieve the economic independence envisioned in the aftermath of the Civil War, Reconstruction closed off even more oppressive alternatives than the Redeemers' New South. The post-Reconstruction labor system embodied neither a return to the closely supervised gang labor of antebellum days, nor the complete dispossession and immobilization of the black labor force and coercive apprenticeship systems envisioned by white Southerners in 1865 and 1866. Nor were blacks, as in twentieth-century South Africa, barred from citizenship, herded into labor reserves, or prohibited by law from moving from one part of the country to another. As illustrated by the small but growing number of black landowners, businessmen, and professionals, the doors of economic opportunity that had opened could never be completely closed. Without Reconstruction, moreover, it is difficult to imagine the establishment of a framework of legal rights enshrined in the Constitution that, while flagrantly violated after 1877, created a vehicle for future federal intervention in Southern affairs. As a result of this unprecedented redefinition of the American body politic, the South's racial system remained regional rather than national, an outcome of great importance when economic opportunities at last opened in the North.

From Eric Foner, *Reconstruction: America's Unfinished Revolution, 1863–1877* (Harper & Row, 1988).  Notes omitted.

Nonetheless, whether measured by the dreams inspired by emancipation or the more limited goals of securing blacks' rights as citizens and free laborers, and establishing an enduring Republican presence in the South, Reconstruction can only be judged a failure. Among the host of explanations for this outcome, a few seem especially significant. Events far beyond the control of Southern Republicans—the nature of the national credit and banking systems, the depression of the 1870s, the stagnation of world demand for cotton—severely limited the prospects for far-reaching economic change. The early rejection of federally sponsored land reform left in place a planter class far weaker and less affluent than before the war, but still able to bring its prestige and experience to bear against Reconstruction. Factionalism and corruption, although hardly confined to Southern Republicans, undermined their claim to legitimacy and made it difficult for them to respond effectively to attacks by resolute opponents. The failure to develop an effective long-term appeal to white voters made it increasingly difficult for Republicans to combat the racial politics of the Redeemers. None of these factors, however, would have proved decisive without the campaign of violence that turned the electoral tide in many parts of the South, and the weakening of Northern resolve, itself a consequence of social and political changes that undermined the free labor and egalitarian precepts at the heart of Reconstruction policy.

For historians, hindsight can be a treacherous ally. Enabling us to trace the hidden patterns of past events, it beguiles us with the mirage of inevitability, the assumption that different outcomes lay beyond the limits of the possible. Certainly, the history of other plantation societies offers little reason for optimism that emancipation could have given rise to a prosperous, egalitarian South, or even one that escaped a pattern of colonial underdevelopment. Nor do the prospects for the expansion of scalawag support—essential for Southern Republicanism's long-term survival—appear in retrospect to have been anything but bleak. Outside the mountains and other enclaves of wartime Unionism, the Civil War generation of white Southerners was always likely to view the Republican party as an alien embodiment of wartime defeat and black equality. And the nation lacked not simply the will but the modern bureaucratic machinery to oversee Southern affairs in any permanent way. Perhaps the remarkable thing about Reconstruction was not that it failed, but that it was attempted at all and survived as long as it did. Yet one can, I think, imagine alternative scenarios and modest successes: the Republican party establishing itself as a permanent fixture on the Southern landscape, the North summoning the resolve to insist that the Constitution must be respected. As the experiences of Readjuster Virginia and Populist-Republican North Carolina suggest, even Redemption did not entirely foreclose the possibility of biracial politics, thus raising the question of how Southern life might have been affected had Deep South blacks enjoyed genuine political freedoms when the Populist movement swept the white counties in the 1890s.

Here, however, we enter the realm of the purely speculative. What remains certain is that Reconstruction failed, and that for blacks its failure was a disaster whose magnitude cannot be obscured by the genuine accomplishments that did endure. For the nation as a whole, the collapse of Reconstruction was a tragedy that deeply affected the course of its future development. If racism contributed to the undoing of Reconstruction, by the same token Reconstruction's demise and the emergence of blacks as a disenfranchised class of dependent laborers greatly facilitated racism's further spread, until by the early twentieth century it had become more deeply embedded in the nation's culture and politics than at any time since the beginning of the antislavery crusade and perhaps in our entire history. The removal of a significant portion of the nation's laboring population from public life shifted the center of gravity of American politics to the right, complicating the tasks of reformers for generations to come. Long into the twentieth century, the South remained a one-party region under the control of a reactionary ruling elite who used the same violence and fraud that had helped defeat Reconstruction to stifle internal dissent. An enduring consequence of Reconstruction's failure, the Solid South helped define the contours of American politics and weaken the prospects not simply of change in racial matters but of progressive legislation in many other realms.

The men and women who had spearheaded the effort to remake Southern society scattered down innumerable byways after the end of Reconstruction. Some relied on federal patronage to earn a livelihood. The unfortunate Marshall Twitchell, armless after his near-murder in 1876, was appointed U.S. consul at Kingston, Ontario, where he died in 1905. Some fifty relatives and friends of the Louisiana Returning Board that had helped make Hayes President received positions at the New Orleans Custom House, and Stephen Packard was awarded the consulship at Liverpool—compensation for surrendering his claim to the governorship. John Eaton, who coordinated freedmen's affairs for General Grant during the war and subsequently took an active role in Tennessee Reconstruction, served as federal commissioner of education from 1870 to 1886, and organized a public school system in Puerto Rico after the island's conquest in the Spanish-American War. Most carpetbaggers returned to the North, often finding there the financial success that had eluded them in the South. Davis Tillson, head of Georgia's Freedman's Bureau immediately after the war, earned a fortune in the Maine granite business. Former South Carolina Gov. Robert K. Scott returned to Napoleon, Ohio, where he became a successful real estate agent—"a most fitting occupation" in view of his involvement in land commission speculations. Less happy was the fate of his scalawag successor, Franklin J. Moses, Jr., who drifted north, served prison terms for petty crimes, and died in a Massachusetts rooming house in 1906.

Republican governors who had won reputations as moderates by courting white Democratic support and seeking to limit blacks' political influence found the Redeemer South remarkably forgiving. Henry C. Warmoth became a successful sugar planter and remained in Louisiana until his death in 1931. James L. Alcorn retired to his Mississippi plantation, "presiding over a Delta domain in a style befitting a prince" and holding various local offices. He remained a Republican, but told one Northern visitor that Democratic rule had produced "good fellowship" between the races. Even Rufus Bullock, who fled Georgia accused of every kind of venality, soon reentered Atlanta society, serving, among other things, as president of the city's chamber of commerce. Daniel H. Chamberlain left South Carolina in 1877 to launch a successful New York City law practice, but was well received on his numerous visits to the state. In retrospect, Chamberlain altered his opinion of Reconstruction: a "frightful experiment" that sought to "lift a backward or inferior race" to political equality, it had inevitably produced "shocking and unbearable misgovernment." "Governor Chamberlain," commented a Charleston newspaper, "has lived and learned."

Not all white Republicans, however, abandoned Reconstruction ideals. In 1890, a group of reformers, philanthropists, and religious leaders gathered at the Lake Mohonk Conference on the Negro Question, chaired by former President Hayes. Amid a chorus of advice that blacks eschew political involvement and concentrate on educational and economic progress and remedying their own character deficiencies, former North Carolina Judge Albion W. Tourgée, again living in the North, voiced the one discordant note. There was no "Negro problem," Tourgée observed, but rather a "white" one, since "the hate, the oppression, the injustice, are all on our side." The following year, Tourgée established the National Citizens' Rights Association, a short-lived forerunner of the National Association for the Advancement of Colored People, devoted to challenging the numerous injustices afflicting Southern blacks. Adelbert Ames, who left Mississippi in 1875 to join his father's Minnesota flour-milling business and who later settled in Massachusetts, continued to defend his Reconstruction record. In 1894 he chided Brown University President E. Benjamin Andrews for writing that Mississippi during his governorship had incurred a debt of $20 million. The actual figure, Ames pointed out, was less than 3 percent of that amount, and he found it difficult to understand how Andrews had made "a $19,500,000 error in a $20,000,000 statement." Ames lived to his ninety-eighth year, never abandoning the conviction that "caste is the curse of the world." Another Mississippi carpetbagger, Massachusetts-born teacher and legislator Henry Warren, published his autobiography in 1914, still hoping that one day, "possibly in the present century," America would live up to the ideal of "equal political rights for all without regard to race."

For some, the Reconstruction experience became a springboard to lifetimes of social reform. The white voters of Winn Parish in Louisiana's hill country expressed their enduring radicalism by supporting the Populists in the 1890s, Socialism in 1912, and later their native son Huey Long. Among the female veterans of freedmen's education, Cornelia Hancock founded Philadelphia's Children's Aid Society, Abby May became prominent in the Massachusetts women's suffrage movement, Ellen Collins turned her attention to New York City housing reform, and Josephine Shaw Lowell became a supporter of the labor movement and principal founder of New York's Consumer League. Louis F. Post, a New Jersey-born carpetbagger who took stenographic notes for South Carolina's legislature in the early 1870s, became a follower of Henry George, attended the founding meeting of the NAACP, and as Woodrow Wilson's Assistant Secretary of Labor, sought to mitigate the 1919 Red Scare and prevent the deportation of foreign-born radicals. And Texas scalawag editor Albert Parsons became a nationally known Chicago labor reformer and anarchist, whose speeches drew comparisons between the plight of Southern blacks and Northern industrial workers, and between the aristocracy resting on slavery the Civil War had destroyed and the new oligarchy based on the exploitation of industrial labor it had helped to create. Having survived the perils of Texas Reconstruction, Parsons met his death on the Illinois gallows after being wrongfully convicted of complicity in the Haymarket bombing of 1886.

Like their white counterparts, many black veterans of Reconstruction survived on federal patronage after the coming of "home rule." P. B. S. Pinchback and Blanche K. Bruce held a series of such posts and later moved to Washington, D.C., where they entered the city's privileged black society. Richard T. Greener, during Reconstruction a professor at the University of South Carolina, combined a career in law, journalism, and education with various government appointments, including a stint as American commercial agent at Vladivostok. Long after the destruction of his low country political machine by disenfranchisement, Robert Smalls served as customs collector for the port of Beaufort, dying there in 1915. Mifflin Gibbs held positions ranging from register of Little Rock's land office to American consul at Madagascar. Other black leaders left the political arena entirely to devote themselves to religious and educational work, emigration projects, or personal advancement. Robert G. Fitzgerald continued to teach in North Carolina until his death in 1919; Edward Shaw of Memphis concentrated on activities among black Masons and the AME Church; Richard H. Cain served as president of a black college in Waco, Texas; and Francis L. Cardozo went on to become principal of a Washington, D.C., high school. Aaron A. Bradley, the militant spokesman for Georgia's lowcountry freedmen, helped publicize the Kansas Exodus and died in St. Louis in 1881, while Henry M. Turner, ordained an AME bishop in 1880, emerged as the late nineteenth century's most prominent advocate of black emigration to Africa. Former Atlanta councilman William Finch prospered as a tailor. Alabama Congressman Jeremiah Haralson engaged in coal mining in Colorado, where he was reported "killed by wild beasts."

Other Reconstruction leaders found, in the words of a black lawyer, that "the tallest tree... suffers most in a storm." Former South Carolina Congressman and Lieut. Gov. Alonzo J. Ransier died in poverty in 1882, having been employed during his last years as a night watchman at the Charleston Custom House and as a city street sweeper. Robert B. Elliott, the state's most brilliant political organizer, found himself "utterly unable to earn a living owing to the severe ostracism and mean prejudice of my political opponents." He died in 1884 after moving to New Orleans and struggling to survive as a lawyer. James T. Rapier died penniless in 1883, having dispersed his considerable wealth among black schools, churches, and emigration organizations. Most local leaders sank into obscurity, disappearing entirely from the historical record. Although some of their children achieved distinction, none of Reconstruction's black officials created a family political dynasty—one indication of how Redemption aborted the development of the South's black political leadership. If their descendants moved ahead, it was through business, the arts, or the professions. T. Thomas Fortune, editor of the New York *Age*, was the son of Florida officeholder Emanuel Fortune; Harlem Renaissance writer Jean Toomer, the grandson of Pinchback; renowned jazz pianist Fletcher Henderson, the grandson of an official who had served in South Carolina's constitutional convention and legislature.

By the turn of the century, as soldiers from North and South joined to take up the "white man's burden" in the Spanish-American War, Reconstruction was widely viewed as little more than a regrettable detour on the road to reunion. To the bulk of the white South, it had become axiomatic that Reconstruction had been a time of "savage tyranny" that "accomplished not one useful result, and left behind it, not one pleasant recollection." Black suffrage, wrote Joseph Le Conte, who had fled South Carolina for a professorship at the University of California to avoid teaching black students, was now seen by "all thoughtful men" as "the greatest political crime ever perpetrated by any people." In more sober language, many Northerners, including surviving architects of Congressional policy, concurred in these judgments. "Years of thinking and observation" had convinced O. O. Howard "that the restoration of their lands to the planters provided for [a] future better for the negroes." John Sherman's recollections recorded a similar change of heart: "After this long lapse of time I am convinced that Mr. Johnson's scheme of reorganization was wise and judicious.... It is unfortunate that it had not the sanction of Congress."

This rewriting of Reconstruction's history was accorded scholarly legitimacy —to its everlasting shame—by the nation's fraternity of professional historians. Early in the twentieth century a group of young Southern scholars gathered at Columbia University to study the Reconstruction era under the guidance of Professors John W. Burgess and William A. Dunning. Blacks, their mentors taught, were "children" utterly incapable of appreciating the freedom that had been thrust upon them. The North did "a monstrous thing" in granting them suffrage, for "a black skin means membership in a race of men which has never of itself succeeded in subjecting passion to reason, has never, therefore, created any civilization of any kind." No political order could survive in the South unless founded on the principle of racial inequality. The students' works on individual Southern states echoed these sentiments. Reconstruction, concluded the study of North Carolina, was an attempt by "selfish politicians, backed by the federal government... to Africanize the State and deprive the people through misrule and oppression of most that life held dear." The views of the Dunning School shaped historical writing for generations, and achieved wide popularity through D. W. Griffith's film *Birth of a Nation* (which glorified the Ku Klux Klan and had its premiere at the White House during Woodrow Wilson's Presidency), James Ford Rhodes's popular multivolume chronicle of the Civil War era, and the national best-seller *The Tragic Era* by Claude G. Bowers. Southern whites, wrote Bowers, "literally were put to the torture" by "emissaries of hate" who inflamed "the negroes' egotism" and even inspired "lustful assaults" by blacks upon white womanhood.

Few interpretations of history have had such far-reaching consequences as this image of Reconstruction. As Francis B. Simkins, a South Carolina-born historian, noted during the 1930s, "the alleged horrors of Reconstruction" did much to freeze the mind of the white South in unalterable opposition to outside pressures for social change and to any thought of breaching Democratic ascendancy, eliminating segregation, or restoring suffrage to disenfranchised blacks. They also justified Northern indifference to the nullification of the Fourteenth and Fifteenth Amendments. Apart from a few white dissenters like Simkins, it was left to black writers to challenge the prevailing orthodoxy. In the early years of this century, none did so more tirelessly than former Mississippi Congressman John R. Lynch, then living in Chicago, who published a series of devastating critiques of the racial biases and historical errors of Rhodes and Bowers. "I do not hesitate to assert," he wrote, "that the Southern Reconstruction Governments were the best governments those States ever had." In 1917, Lynch voiced the hope that "a fair, just, and impartial historian will, some day, write a history covering the Reconstruction period, [giving] the actual facts of what took place."

Only in the family traditions and collective folk memories of the black community did a different version of Reconstruction survive. Growing up in the 1920s, Pauli Murray was "never allowed to forget" that she walked in "proud shoes" because her grandfather, Robert G. Fitzgerald, had "fought for freedom" in the Union Army and then enlisted as a teacher in the "second war" against the powerlessness and ignorance inherited from slavery. When the Works Progress Administration sent agents into the black belt during the Great Depression to interview former slaves, they found Reconstruction remembered for its disappointments and betrayals, but also as a time of hope, possibility, and accomplishment. Bitterness still lingered over the federal government's failure to distribute land or protect blacks' civil and political rights. "The Yankees helped free us, so they say," declared eighty-one-year old former slave Thomas Hall, "but they let us be put back in slavery again." Yet coupled with this disillusionment were proud, vivid recollections of a time when "the colored used to hold office." Some pulled from their shelves dusty scrapbooks of clippings from Reconstruction newspapers; others could still recount the names of local black leaders. "They made pretty fair officers," remarked one elderly freedman; "I thought them was good times in the country," said another. Younger blacks spoke of being taught by their parents "about the old times, mostly about the Reconstruction, and the Ku Klux." "I know folks think the books tell the truth, but they shore don't," one eighty-eight-year old former slave told the WPA.

For some blacks, such memories helped to keep alive the aspirations of the Reconstruction era. "This here used to be a good county," said Arkansas freedman Boston Blackwell, "but I tell you it sure is tough now. I think it's wrong—exactly wrong that we can't vote now." "I does believe that the negro ought to be given more privileges in voting," echoed Taby Jones, born a slave in South Carolina in 1850, "because they went through the reconstruction period with banners flying." For others, Reconstruction inspired optimism that better times lay ahead. "The Bible says, 'What has been will be again'," said Alabama sharecropper Ned Cobb. Born in 1885, Cobb never cast a vote in his entire life, yet he never forgot that outsiders had once taken up the black cause—an indispensable source of hope for one conscious of his own weakness in the face of overwhelming and hostile local power. When radical Northerners ventured South in the 1930s to help organize black agricultural workers, Cobb seemed almost to have been waiting for them: "The whites came down to bring emancipation, and left before it was over.... Now they've come to finish the job." The legacy of Reconstruction affected the 1930s revival of black militancy in other ways as well. Two leaders of the Alabama Share Croppers Union, Ralph and Thomas Gray, claimed to be descended from a Reconstruction legislator. (Like many nineteenth-century predecessors, Ralph Gray paid with his life for challenging the South's social order—he was killed in a shootout with a posse while guarding a union meeting.)

Twenty more years elapsed before another generation of black Southerners launched the final challenge to the racial system of the New South. A few participants in the civil rights movement thought of themselves as following a path blazed after the Civil War. Discussing the reasons for his involvement, one black Mississippian spoke of the time when "a few Negroes was admitted into the government of the State of Mississippi and to the United States." Reconstruction's legacy was also evident in the actions of federal judge Frank Johnson, who fought a twelve-year battle for racial justice with Alabama Gov. George Wallace. Johnson hailed from Winston County, a center of Civil War Unionism, and his great-grandfather had served as a Republican sheriff during Reconstruction. By this time, however, the Reconstruction generation had passed from the scene and even within the black community, memories of the period had all but disappeared. Yet the institutions created or consolidated after the Civil War—the black family, school, and church—provided the base from which the modern civil rights revolution sprang. And for its legal strategy, the movement returned to the laws and amendments of Reconstruction.

"The river has its bend, and the longest road must terminate." Rev. Peter Randolph, a former slave, wrote these words as the dark night of injustice settled over the South. Nearly a century elapsed before the nation again attempted to come to terms with the implications of emancipation and the political and social agenda of Reconstruction. In many ways, it has yet to do so.

# POSTSCRIPT

## Was Reconstruction a Success?

In *Nothing But Freedom: Emancipation and Its Legacy* (Louisiana State University Press, 1984), Foner compares the treatment of American freedmen with those who were newly emancipated in Haiti and the British West Indies. Only in the United States, he claims, were the former slaves given voting and economic rights. Although these rights had been stripped away from the majority of black southerners by 1900, Reconstruction had, nevertheless, created a legacy of freedom that inspired succeeding generations of African Americans.

C. Vann Woodward, the dean of southern historians, is less sanguine about the potential for success presented by the Reconstruction proposals. Despite all the successes enumerated by the revisionists, Woodward concludes that the experiment failed. In "Reconstruction: A Counterfactual Playback," an essay in his thought-provoking *The Future of the Past* (Oxford University Press, 1988), Woodward argues that former slaves were as poorly treated in the United States as they were in other countries. He also believes that the confiscation of former plantations and the redistribution of land to the former slaves would have failed in the same way that the Homestead Act of 1862 failed to generate equal distribution of government lands to poor white settlers. Finally, Woodward claims that reformers who worked with African Americans during Reconstruction failed because their goals were out of touch with the realities of the late nineteenth century.

Thomas Holt's *Black Over White: Negro Political Leadership in South Carolina During Reconstruction* (University of Illinois Press, 1977) is representative of state and local studies that employ modern social science methodology to yield new perspectives. While critical of white Republican leaders, Holt (who is African American) also blames the failure of Reconstruction in South Carolina on freeborn mulatto politicians, whose background distanced them economically, socially, and culturally from the masses of freedmen. Consequently, these political leaders failed to develop a clear and unifying ideology to challenge white South Carolinians who wanted to restore white supremacy.

The study of the Reconstruction period benefits from an extensive bibliography. Traditional accounts of Reconstruction include William Archibald Dunning's *Reconstruction, Political and Economic, 1865–1877* (Harper & Brothers, 1907); Claude Bowers's *The Tragic Era: The Revolution After Lincoln* (Riverside Press, 1929); and E. Merton Coulter's *The South During Reconstruction, 1865–1877* (Louisiana State University Press, 1947), which is considered by many to be the last major work written from the Dunning (or traditional) point of view. Early revisionist views are presented in W. E. B. Du Bois, *Black Reconstruction in America: An Essay Toward a History of the Part Which*

*Black Folk Played in the Attempt to Reconstruct Democracy in America, 1860–1880* (Harcourt, Brace, 1935), which is a Marxist analysis of Reconstruction, and John Hope Franklin, *Reconstruction: After the Civil War* (University of Chicago Press, 1961). Foner's *Reconstruction: America's Unfinished Revolution, 1863–1877* (Harper & Row, 1988) includes a complete bibliography on the subject. Briefer overviews are available in Forrest G. Wood, *The Era of Reconstruction, 1863–1877* (Harlan Davidson, 1975) and Michael Perman, *Emancipation and Reconstruction, 1862–1879* (Harlan Davidson, 1987). One well-written study of a specific episode from the Reconstruction years is Willie Lee Rose's *Rehearsal for Reconstruction: The Port Royal Experiment* (Bobbs-Merrill, 1964), which describes the failed effort at land reform in the sea islands of South Carolina. Richard Nelson Current's *Those Terrible Carpetbaggers: A Reinterpretation* (Oxford University Press, 1988) is a superb challenge to the traditional view of those much-maligned Reconstruction participants. Finally, for collections of interpretive essays on various aspects of the Reconstruction experience, see Staughton Lynd, ed., *Reconstruction* (Harper & Row, 1967); Seth M. Scheiner, ed., *Reconstruction: A Tragic Era?* (Holt, Rinehart & Winston, 1968); and Edwin C. Rozwenc, ed., *Reconstruction in the South*, 2d ed. (D. C. Heath, 1972).

# ISSUE 2

## Were Nineteenth-Century Entrepreneurs Robber Barons?

**YES: John Tipple,** from "Big Businessmen and a New Economy," in H. Wayne Morgan, ed., *The Gilded Age* (Syracuse University Press, 1970)

**NO: Alfred D. Chandler, Jr.,** from "The Beginnings of 'Big Business' in American Industry," *Business History Review* (Spring 1959)

### ISSUE SUMMARY

**YES:** Professor of history John Tipple characterizes big businessmen of the late nineteenth century as destructive forces whose power and greed undermined the nation's traditional institutions and values.

**NO:** Professor of business history Alfred D. Chandler, Jr., concludes that American entrepreneurs were organizational and marketing innovators whose creation of great industrial corporations strengthened the country's economy by sparking the growth of a national urban market.

Between 1860 and 1914 the United States was transformed from a country of farms, small towns, and modest manufacturing concerns to a modern nation dominated by large cities and factories. During those years the population tripled, and the nation experienced astounding urban growth. A new proletariat emerged to provide the necessary labor for the country's developing factory system. Between the Civil War and World War I, the value of manufactured goods in the United States increased 12-fold, and the capital invested in industrial pursuits multiplied 22 times. In addition, the application of new machinery and scientific methods to agriculture produced abundant yields of wheat, corn, and other foodstuffs, despite the decline in the number of farmers.

Why did this industrial revolution occur in the United States during the last quarter of the nineteenth century? What factors contributed to the rapid pace of American industrialization? In answering these questions, historians often point to the first half of the 1800s and the significance of the "transportation revolution," which produced better roads, canals, and railroads to move people and goods more efficiently and cheaply from one point to another. Technological improvements such as the Bessemer process, refrigeration, electricity, and the telephone also made their mark in the nation's "Machine Age." Government cooperation with business, large-scale immigration from Europe and Asia, and the availability of foreign capital for industrial investments provided still other underpinnings for this industrial growth. Finally, American industrialization depended upon a number of individuals in the United States who were willing to organize and finance the nation's industrial base for the sake of anticipated profits. These, of course, were the entrepreneurs.

American public attitudes have reflected a schizophrenic quality as regards the activities of the industrial leaders of the late nineteenth century. Were these entrepreneurs "robber barons" who employed any means necessary to enrich themselves at the expense of their competitors? Or were they "captains of industry" whose shrewd and innovative leadership brought order out of industrial chaos and generated great fortunes that enriched the public welfare through the workings of various philanthropic agencies that these leaders established? Although the "robber baron" stereotype emerged as early as the 1870s, it probably gained its widest acceptance in the 1930s. In the midst of the Great Depression, as many critics were proclaiming the apparent failure of American capitalism, Matthew Josephson published *The Robber Barons* (1934), in which he bitterly condemned the ruthless and occasionally violent methods of industrialists such as John D. Rockefeller and Jay Gould. Since the 1930s, however, some historians, including Allan Nevins, Alfred D. Chandler, Jr., and Maury Klein, have sought to revise the negative assessments offered by earlier generations of scholars. In the hands of these "business historians," the late nineteenth-century businessmen have become "industrial statesmen" who skillfully oversaw the process of raising the United States to a prominent position among the nations of the world. The following essays reveal the divergence of scholarly opinion as it applies to these American entrepreneurs.

John Tipple points out that the public antipathy expressed toward big businessmen like Rockefeller and Andrew Carnegie stemmed from their association with huge corporations whose existence challenged traditional American values. This adverse public opinion was well deserved, says Tipple, because the business magnates frequently behaved recklessly and unethically (if not illegally) in order to amass their great fortunes.

Alfred D. Chandler, Jr., on the other hand, sees the operations of the entrepreneurs as essential to the economic expansion of the country. These business executives, he concludes, developed innovative organizational and marketing strategies that promoted the growth of the nation's urban market economy.

# YES

## John Tipple

# BIG BUSINESSMEN AND A NEW ECONOMY

It is more than coincidence that the beginning of the Robber Baron legend, the portrayal of the big businessman as a warlike brigand cheating and plundering his way to millions, was contemporaneous with the inauguration of the corporation as the major instrument of business control in the United States. After the Civil War, the large corporation began to dominate the American economic scene. In those same years, Charles Francis Adams, Jr., launched his first assault against the "Erie robbers," and his brother, Henry Adams, warned of the day when great corporations, "swaying power such as has never in the world's history been trusted in the hands of mere private citizens," would be controlled by one man or combinations of men who would use these new leviathans to become masters of the nation.

Such dangerous potentialities were not recognizable prior to the Civil War because the majority of businesses operated as local enterprises, usually as individual proprietorships, partnerships, or as small closed corporations in which ownership and control were almost invariably synonymous. Under most circumstances, the power and influence of the businessman were limited to the immediate environs of operation and seldom extended beyond state boundaries. Equally important, there existed among most businessmen of prewar days a nearly universal desire and a practical necessity for community esteem. This governed their conduct, kept their ventures well within the limits of individual liability, and tended to restrain irresponsible profiteering. Antebellum criticisms of the businessman therefore were few and sporadic. Disapproval usually focused on the speculator or stock gambler, and was often inspired by an agrarian distrust of big-city ways.

The bloody struggles of the Civil War helped bring about revolutionary changes in economic and political life. War needs created almost insatiable demands for goods—arms, munitions, clothing—and offered some manufacturers unsurpassed opportunities to make fortunes. More important, the stimulus of massive military demands alerted entrepreneurs to new concepts of the power and possibilities of large-scale enterprise: "The great operations of war, the handling of large masses of men, the influence of discipline, the

From John Tipple, "Big Businessmen and a New Economy," in H. Wayne Morgan, ed., *The Gilded Age* (Syracuse University Press, 1970), pp. 13–22, 26–30.  Notes omitted.

lavish expenditure of unprecedented sums of money, the immense financial operations, the possibilities of effective cooperation, were lessons not likely to be lost on men quick to receive and apply all new ideas." Though the war prevented general economic expansion, the new ideas were profitably applied to the peacetime economy.

With the rich resources of the trans-Mississippi West open to private exploitation, the businessman had singular opportunities to become wealthy. Before him spread an immense untapped continent whose riches were his virtually for the taking; new means to turn these resources to profitable account were at hand. A host of new inventions and discoveries, the application of science to industry, and improved methods of transportation and communication were ready to assist the businessman. But all these aids would have been valueless without effective means to put them to work. The practical agency to meet these unprecedented entrepreneurial demands on capital and management proved to be the corporation. The stockholding system provided immense capital beyond the reach of any individual, and the corporate hierarchy presented a feasible solution to the greatly augmented problems of management.

The corporation was no novelty. It had served political as well as economic purposes in seventeenth-century America; as an instrumentality of business its use antedated the discovery of this continent. Seldom before in American history, however, had the corporation been used on such a large scale. From a relatively passive creature of legalistic capitalism, it was transformed by fusion with techniques into a dynamic system spearheading economic expansion.

The impact of the newborn corporation on American society was almost cataclysmic. In the first few decades of its existence the modern corporate system enabled the nation to develop more wealth more rapidly than in any period since the discovery. But it also menaced hallowed economic theories and usages, threatening to ride like a great tidal wave over the traditional democratic social and political beliefs. Its size alone was sufficient to change fundamental social and economic relationships. Of the newly formed United States Steel Corporation an awed commentator wrote at the turn of the century: "It receives and expends more money every year than any but the very greatest of the world's national governments; its debt is larger than that of many of the lesser nations of Europe; it absolutely controls the destinies of a population nearly as large as that of Maryland or Nebraska, and indirectly influences twice that number." Moreover, this concentrated economic power normally gravitated into the hands of a few, raising up a corporate ruling class with great economic authority....

The dedicated businessman could make money on an unprecedented scale. Though John D. Rockefeller never quite became a billionaire, his fortune in 1892 reportedly amounted to $815,647,796.89. Andrew Carnegie did nearly as well. The profits from his industrial empire in the decade 1889 to 1899 averaged about $7,500,000 a year and, in 1900 alone, amounted to $40,000,000. In the following year he sold out his interest for several hundred million dollars. Such fortunes, exceptional even for those days, emphasized the wealth available to the big businessman. In 1892, two New York newspapers engaged in a heated contest to count the number of American millionaires, the

*World* uncovering 3,045 and the *Tribune* raising it to 4,047. Regardless of the exact total, millionaires were becoming fairly common. By 1900, for instance, the Senate alone counted twenty-five millionaires among its members, most of them the well-paid agents of big business—a notorious fact that led some suspicious folk to dub that august body the "Rich Man's Club" and the "House of Dollars."

This sudden leap of big businessmen into new positions of wealth and power caught the public eye. To Americans accustomed to thinking primarily of individuals, the big businessman stood out as the conspicuous symbol of corporate power—his popular image encompassing not only his personal attributes and failings but combining also the more amorphous and impersonal aspects of the business organization by which he had climbed to fortune. Just as the diminutive Andrew Carnegie came to represent the entire steel-making complex of men and decisions which bore his name, so the lean, ascetic John D. Rockefeller personified Standard Oil, and the prominent nose and rotund figure of J. P. Morgan signified the whole of Wall Street with its thousands of operators, its ethical flaws, and its business virtues.

Big businessmen were usually attacked not for personal failings, though they had them as well as the lion's share of wealth, but as the recognizable heads of large corporations. When Carnegie and Rockefeller gave up business careers and became private citizens, the rancor against them almost ceased. Instead of being censured for past actions, which had been widely and vehemently criticized, they were praised as benefactors and good citizens. Public castigation of the steel trust was shifted from "Little Andy" to the broader shoulders of Charles Schwab. The odium of monopoly which had surrounded his father was inherited by John D. Rockefeller, Jr. Only as the active and directive heads of great corporations, and not as subordinates or members of a business elite, were big businessmen branded "Robber Barons" and indicted for alleged crimes against society.

If the big businessman was not resented as an individual but as a power symbol wielding the might of the great corporation, the provocative question arises of why there was such resentment against the corporation. The answer is that the large industrial corporation was an anomaly in nineteenth-century America. There was no place for it among existing institutions and no sanction for it in traditional American values....

What was to be done with such a monster? Either the corporation had to be made to conform to American institutions and principles or those institutions and principles had to be changed to accommodate the corporation. This was the dilemma first seriously confronted by Americans during the Gilded Age, and the issue that set off the great movement of introspection and reform which activated the American people for the next fifty years.

Most flagrantly apparent was the destructive effect of the large corporation upon free competition and equal opportunity. According to the accepted theory, which was a projection of the doctrines of liberal democracy into the economic sphere, the ideal economy—the only one, in fact, sanctioned by nature—was made up of freely competing individuals operating in a market unrestricted by man but fairly ruled by the inexorable forces of natural law. The ideal polity was achieved by bargaining among free and equal individuals under the benevolent eye of nature. It was assumed that, in economic affairs, impartial rivalry between individual entrepreneurs and free competition would automatically serve the best interests of society by preventing anyone from getting more than his fair share of the wealth.

In early nineteenth-century America, this self-regulating mechanism seemed to work. Where businesses and factories were small, prices and output, wages and profits, rose and fell according to supply and demand. Every man appeared to have equal opportunity to compete with every other man. Even after the war, the individual businessman was forced, in the interests of self-preservation, to observe the common rules of competition. Ordinarily his share of the market was too small to permit any attempt at price control unless he joined with others in a pool, a trade association, or another rudimentary price-fixing agreement. The average businessman eschewed trade agreements, not out of theoretical considerations, but for the practical reason that such coalitions did not work very well, often suffering from mutual distrust and the pursuit of centrifugal aims.

But what was true in a world of individual proprietors and workers was not necessarily correct for the corporation. It possessed greater unity of control and a larger share of the market and could either dictate prices or combine successfully with other corporations in monopolistic schemes. By bringing to bear superior economic force which to a great extent invalidated the tenets of the free market, the large organization put the big businessman in the favored position of operating in an economy dedicated to the idea of freely competing individuals, yet left him unhampered by the ordinary restrictions. Under such auspicious circumstances, he soon outdistanced unorganized rivals in the race for wealth.

This unfair advantage did not go unchallenged. As the earliest of the large corporations in the United States, the railroads were the first to come under concentrated attack. The immense extension of railways after 1865, and the crucial nature of their operations as common carriers, exposed their activities to public scrutiny and subjected their mistakes or misdeeds to considerable publicity. Popular resentment against the railroads in the early 1870's grew hottest in the farming states of the Midwest, but indignant reports from all over the country accused railroads of using monopoly power against equal opportunity.

A most frequent criticism, common to both East and West, was that railway superintendents and managers showed unreasonable favoritism by discriminating between persons and places, offering rate concessions to large shippers, charging more for short than long hauls, and giving preferential treatment to large corporations in the form of secret rebates and drawbacks. That these preferential rates might sometimes have been forced upon the railroads by pressure from business made little difference. The popular consensus was that this elaborate system of special rates denied the little man equal opportunity with the rich and influential, breaking the connection between individual merit and success. The ultimate effect extended further monopoly by preventing free competition among businesses where railway transportation was an important factor.

The Standard Oil Company seemed to be the outstanding example of a monopoly propagated in this manner, the charge being that the determining factor behind Rockefeller's spectacular conquest of the oil business had been this railway practice of secrecy and favoritism which had aided his company and ruined others. By collecting rebates on their own shipments and drawbacks on those of competitors, Standard had gained virtual control of oil transportation. It then could regulate the prices of crude oil, with the detrimental result, so Henry Demarest Lloyd charged, that by 1881, though the company produced only one-fiftieth of the nation's petroleum, Standard refined nine-tenths of the oil produced in the United States and dictated the price of all of it.

As the whipping boy among trusts, Standard undoubtedly got more than its share of criticism, yet by contemporary standards of competition, the corporation was fairly adjudged a monopoly. Through the testimony of H. H. Rogers, an executive of the company, The Hepburn Committee in 1879 was able to establish that 90 to 95 percent of all the refiners in the country acted in harmony with Standard Oil. In 1886, the monopolistic proclivities of the oil trust were attested to by the Cullom Committee:

> It is well understood in commercial circles that the Standard Oil Company brooks no competition; that its settled policy and firm determination is to crush out all who may be rash enough to enter the field against it; that it hesitates at nothing in the accomplishment of this purpose, in which it has been remarkably successful, and that it fitly represents the acme and perfection of corporate greed in its fullest development.

Similar convictions were expressed by a New York senate committee before which Rockefeller and other executives testified in 1888. Four years later, in 1892, the Supreme Court of Ohio declared that the object of the Standard Oil Company was "to establish a virtual monopoly of the business of producing petroleum, and of manufacturing, refining and dealing in it and all its products, throughout the entire country, and by which it might not merely control the production, but the price, at its pleasure."

These findings were reaffirmed by new investigations. In 1902, the United States Industrial Commission reported that Standard, through its control of pipe lines, practically fixed the price of crude oil. In 1907, the commissioner of corporations supported and amplified this conclusion. The company might fall short of an absolute monopoly, the commissioner pointed out, but its intentions were monopolistic. In 1911, the United States Supreme Court confirmed this allegation, observing that "no disinterested mind" could survey the history of the Standard Oil combination from 1870 onward "without being irresistibly driven to the conclusion that the very genius for commercial development and organization... soon begot an intent and purpose... to drive others from the field and to exclude them from their right to trade and thus accomplish the mastery which was the end in view."

Far from regarding the intricate system of business combination he had developed as a monster to be cured or destroyed, a big businessman such as Rockefeller looked proudly upon his creation as a marvel of beneficence, an extraordinary and distinctive expression of American genius. And Carnegie contended "not evil, but good" had come from the phenomenal development of the corporation. He and others pointed out that the world obtained goods and commodities of excellent quality at prices which earlier generations would have considered incredibly cheap. The poor enjoyed what the richest could never before have afforded.

The big businessman supported his actions as being entirely in keeping with the business requisites of the day. Rather than engaging in a conscious conspiracy to undermine equal opportunity, he had sought only the immediate and practical rewards of successful enterprise, rationalizing business conduct on the pragmatic level of profit and loss.

Instead of deliberately blocking free competition, big businessmen maintained that their actions were only natural responses to immutable law. Charles E. Perkins, president of the Chicago, Burlington and Quincy Railroad Company, denied deliberate misuses of power in establishing rates, and claimed that the price of railroad transportation, like all other prices, adjusted itself. Discriminatory practices were viewed as part of an inevitable conflict between buyer and seller, a necessary result of competition. The payment of rebates and drawbacks was simply one method of meeting the market. In answer to the accusation that the railroads had made "important discriminations" in favor of Standard Oil, an executive of that company replied: "It may be frankly stated at the outset that the Standard Oil Company has at all times within the limits of fairness and with due regard for the laws ought to secure the most advantageous freight rates and routes possible." Rockefeller went on record as saying that Standard had received rebates from the railroads prior to 1880, because it was simply the railroads' way of doing business. Each shipper made the best bargain he could, hoping to outdo his competitor.

Furthermore, Rockefeller claimed this traffic was more profitable to the railroads than to the Standard Oil Company, stating that whatever advantage the oil company gained was passed on in lower costs to the consumer. Just as his company later justified certain alleged misdemeanors as being typical of the sharp practices prevailing in the oil fields in the early days, so Rockefeller exonerated the whole system of rebates and drawbacks on the grounds that everybody was doing it, concluding cynically that those who objected on principle did so only because they were not benefiting from it.

Yet despite his public rationalizations, the big businessman's attitude toward competition was ambivalent. He lauded it as economic theory, but denied it in practical actions. Theoretically, there was no such thing as an absolute monopoly; there was always the threat of latent competition. Whenever a trust exacted too much, competitors would automatically appear. Competition as a natural law would survive the trusts. "It is here; we cannot evade it," declaimed Carnegie. "And while the law may be sometimes hard for the individual, it is best for the race, because it insures the survival of the fittest in every department."

In practical matters, however, the big businessman acted as if the law had long since become outmoded, if not extinct. Progressive opinion in the business world heralded the growing monopolistic trend as a sign of economic maturity. Increased concentration in capital and industry was defended as necessary and inevitable. Monopolistic practices in general were upheld in business circles on the grounds that they prevented disastrous competition. In the long run they benefited, rather than plundered, the public by maintaining reasonable rates and prices. "There seems to be a great readiness in the public mind to take alarm at these phenomena of growth, there might rather seem to be reason for public congratulation," announced Professor William Graham Sumner of Yale. "We want to be provided with things abundantly and cheaply; that means that we want increased economic power. All these enterprises are efforts to satisfy that want, and they promise to do it." Many big businessmen believed that, practically at least, the trust proved the superiority of combination over competition....

In condemning trusts as "dangerous to Republican institutions" and in branding corporate leaders as Robber Barons "opposed to free institutions and free commerce between the states as were the feudal barons of the middle ages," aroused Americans of the Gilded Age had clearly seized upon the major issue. They had somehow recognized that American society with its individualistic traditions was engaged in a life-and-death struggle with the organized forces of dissolution.

The once-welcome business and industrial concentration threatened the foundations of the nation. There was more individual power than ever, but those who wielded it were few and formidable. Charles Francis Adams, Jr., denounced these "modern potentates for the autocratic misuse of that power":

> The system of corporate life and corporate power, as applied to industrial development, is yet in its infancy.... It is a new power, for which our language contains no name. We know what aristocracy, autocracy, democracy are; but we have no word to express government by monied corporations.... It remains to be seen what the next phase in this process of gradual development will be. History never quite repeats itself, and... the old familiar enemies may even now confront us, though arrayed in such a modern garb that no suspicion is excited.... As the Erie ring represents the combination of the corporation and the hired proletariat of a great city; as Vanderbilt embodies the autocratic power of Caesarism introduced into corporate life, and neither alone can obtain complete control of the government of the State, it, perhaps, only remains for the coming man to carry the combination of elements one step in advance, and put Caesarism at once in control of the corporation and of the proletariat, to bring our vaunted institutions within the rule of all historic precedent.

Yet the public already sensed that something had gone wrong with American institutions and values. With less understanding than Adams, they felt that somehow the old rules had been broken. Behind their growing animosity to the big businessman was the feeling that in some way he cheated his countrymen. The belief was becoming fairly common that extreme wealth was incompatible with honesty. "The great cities," Walt Whitman wrote in 1871, "reek with respectable as much as non-respectable robbery and scoundrelism." There were undoubtedly moral men of wealth, but many Americans agreed with Thomas A. Bland, who in *How to Grow Rich* suggested: "In all history, ancient and modern, the examples of men of honest lives and generous hearts who have become rich... is so rare as to be exceedingly exceptional, and even these have invariably profited largely... by the labor of others."

Very revealing in this regard was the portrayal of the big businessman in contemporary fiction. Socialist writers naturally depicted him as a "criminal of greed" or an "economic monster" who with other "business animals" preyed upon the life of the nation. Oddly enough, however, in an age when the corporation made unprecedented achievements in production and organization to the enrichment of countless people, when material success was widely favored as a legitimate goal, scarcely a single major novelist presented the big businessman as a hero or even in a favorable light. Except at the hands of a few hack writers, the business or industrial leader was consistently portrayed as powerful and capable, but nonetheless an enemy of American society. This may have reflected the bias of the aesthetic or creative temperament against the pragmatic money-maker, but the big businessman was in disfavor with most of American society.

In the popular mind, the vices of lying and stealing were legendarily associated with Wall Street. The big businessmen who dominated "the street" were regarded by some as the ethical counterparts of the pirate and buccaneer. By the simple devices of "stock-watering" or the issuance of fictitious securities not backed by capital assets, speculators were generally believed to have stolen millions of dollars from the American people. In the opinion of the more jaundiced, the men of Wall Street had barely escaped prison bars. "If the details of the great reorganization and trustification deals put through since 1885 could be laid bare," contended Thomas W. Lawson, a financier turned critic, "eight out of ten of our most successful stock-jobbing financiers would be in a fair way to get into State or federal prisons."

The iniquity of Wall Street was not merely legendary, but had firm basis in fact. Though not all speculators were swindlers nor all speculation gambling, only a small number of the stock exchange transactions were unquestionably of an investment character. The vast majority were virtually gambling. Many corporations, although offering huge blocks of stock to the public, issued only the vaguest and most ambiguous summary of assets and liabilities. While this was not iniquitous in itself, secrecy too often cloaked fraud.

The men at the top who had used the corporate device to make millions did not see it this way at all. They justified their millions on the ground that they had fairly earned it. Cornelius Vanderbilt, at the age of eighty-one, boasted that he had made a million dollars for every year of his life, but added that it had been worth "three times that to the people of the United States." Others shared his belief. In *The Railroad and the Farmer,* Edward Atkinson made practically the same statement, asserting that the gigantic fortune of the older Vanderbilt was but a small fraction of what the country gained from the development of the railway system under his genius. The Reverend Julian M. Sturtevant of Illinois College also envisioned the Vanderbilts and Astors of the world as "laborers of gigantic strength, and they must have their reward and compensation for the use of their capital." Carnegie maintained that great riches were no crime. "Under our present conditions the millionaire who toils on is the cheapest article which the community secures at the price it pays for him, namely, his shelter, clothing, and food."

Most Americans, however, did not so readily accept this evaluation. Some recognized that the big businessman in pursuing private ends had served national prosperity—the majority felt that he had taken extravagant profits entirely out of proportion to the economic services he had rendered. Rockefeller's millions were thought to be typical of the fortunes made by Robber Barons, representing "the relentless, aggressive, irresistible seizure of a particular opportunity, the magnitude of which... was due simply to the magnitude of the country and the immensity of the stream of its prosperous industrial life." The feeling was general that the great fortunes of all the big business magnates—Vanderbilt, Gould, Harriman, Stanford, Carnegie, Morgan, and the rest—represented special privilege which had enabled them to turn the abundant natural resources and multitudinous advantages offered by a growing nation into a private preserve for their own profit.

The public at large was not clearly aware of it, but the chief instrument of special privilege was the corporation. Though public franchises and political favoritism played a large part in the aggrandizement of the Robber Barons, in the money-making world of late nineteenth-century America special privilege invariably meant corporate privilege. The corporation enabled Vanderbilt to unify his railroads while making large speculative profits on the side. The same device made it possible for men like Rockefeller to create and combine private enterprises embodying new technological and financial techniques while diverting enormous profits to themselves. The corporation was the constructive power behind the building of the cross-country railroads, but it was also the destructive instrument used by Jay Gould, Tom Scott, Collis P. Huntington, and others to convert them into quick money-making machines with no regard for their obligations as public carriers.

The problem remained of establishing the relationship of big businessmen to the corporation. Judging by their conduct, they were not fully cognizant of the tremendous power placed in their hands by the corporation with single men controlling "thousands of men, tens of millions of revenue, and hundreds of millions of capital." Or they wilfully exerted this prodigious force for private benefit regardless of consequences to the nation or ideals. Unhappily, most of those labeled Robber Baron by their contemporaries fell into the latter category. Cornelius Vanderbilt held the law in contempt. Except where his own interests were involved, he had little regard for the consequences of his actions, manipulating and watering every corporate property he captured. One year after he took over the New York Central railroad, he increased the capitalization by $23,000,000, almost every cent of which represented inside profits for himself and friends. When admonished that some of his transactions were forbidden by law, he supposedly roared, "Law! What do I care about the law? Hain't I got the power?" He confirmed this attitude in testimony before the committee on railroads of the New York State Assembly in 1869. But Vanderbilt's methods were in no way exceptional. Most of the biggest businessmen made their millions in similar fashion. Twenty-four who because of notoriety and conspicuous power might be regarded as "typical" Robber Barons combined the role of promoter with that of entrepreneur. Stock manipulation along with corporate consolidation was probably the easiest way to wealth that ever existed in the United States. The exuberance with which promoters threw themselves into it proved that they were well aware of its golden possibilities.

As a consequence of these reckless corporate maneuverings, however, public opinion turned against the big businessman. While from a corporate point of view the conduct of the money-makers was often legal, although ethically dubious, the public often felt cheated. Puzzled and disenchanted by the way things had turned out, they questioned the way every millionaire got his money, and were quite ready to believe that a crime was behind every great fortune. While its exact nature escaped them, they felt they had been robbed. The classic statement of this feeling of outrage appeared in the Populist platform of 1892: "The fruits of the toil of millions are boldly stolen to build up colossal fortunes for a few, unprecedented in the history of mankind; and the possessors of these, in turn, despise the Republic and endanger liberty."

The inchoate charges were basically accurate: too much wealth was being selfishly appropriated by a few. By the irresponsible use of the corporation, essentially a supralegal abstraction above the traditional laws of the land, they were undermining individualistic institutions and values. Big businessmen like John D. Rockefeller were attacked as Robber Barons because they were correctly identified as destroyers, the insurgent vanguard of the corporate revolution.

# NO

Alfred D. Chandler, Jr.

## THE BEGINNINGS OF "BIG BUSINESS" IN AMERICAN INDUSTRY

Between the depression of the 1870's and the beginning of the twentieth century, American industry underwent a significant transformation. In the 1870's, the major industries serviced an agrarian economy. Except for a few companies equipping the rapidly expanding railroad network, the leading industrial firms processed agricultural products and provided farmers with food and clothing. These firms tended to be small, and bought their raw materials and sold their finished goods locally. Where they manufactured for a market more than a few miles away from the factory, they bought and sold through commissioned agents who handled the business of several other similar firms.

By the beginning of the twentieth century, many more companies were making producers' goods, to be used in industry rather than on the farm or by the ultimate consumer. Most of the major industries had become dominated by a few large enterprises. These great industrial corporations no longer purchased and sold through agents, but had their own nation-wide buying and marketing organizations. Many, primarily those in the extractive industries, had come to control their own raw materials. In other words, the business economy had become industrial. Major industries were dominated by a few firms that had become great, vertically integrated, centralized enterprises.

In the terms of the economist and sociologist a significant sector of American industry had become bureaucratic, in the sense that business decisions were made within large hierarchical structures. Externally, oligopoly was prevalent, the decision-makers being as much concerned with the actions of the few other large firms in the industry as with over-all changes in markets, sources of supplies, and technological improvements.

These basic changes came only after the railroads had created a national market. The railroad network, in turn, had grown swiftly primarily because of the near desperate requirements for efficient transportation created by the movement of population westward after 1815. Except for the

Excerpted from Alfred D. Chandler, Jr., "The Beginnings of 'Big Business' in American Industry," *Business History Review,* vol. 35 (Spring 1959).  Notes omitted.

Atlantic seaboard between Boston and Washington, the construction of the American railroads was stimulated almost wholly by the demand for better transportation to move crops, to bring farmers supplies, and to open up new territories to commercial agriculture.

By greatly expanding the scope of the agrarian economy, the railroads quickened the growth of the older commercial centers, such as New York, Philadelphia, Cincinnati, Cleveland, and St. Louis, and helped create new cities like Chicago, Indianapolis, Atlanta, Kansas City, Dallas, and the Twin Cities. This rapid urban expansion intensified the demand for the products of the older consumer goods industries—particularly those which processed the crops of the farmer and planter into food, stimulants, and clothing.

At the same time, railroad construction developed the first large market in this country for producers' goods. Except for the making of relatively few textile machines, steamboat engines, and ordnance, the iron and nonferrous manufacturers had before 1850 concentrated on providing metals and simple tools for merchants and farmers. Even textile machinery was usually made by the cloth manufacturers themselves. However, by 1860, only a decade after beginning America's first major railroad construction boom, railroad companies had already replaced the blacksmiths as the primary market for iron products, and had become far and away the most important market for the heavy engineering industries. By then, too, the locomotive was competing with the Connecticut brass industry as a major consumer of copper. More than this, the railroads, with their huge capital outlay, their fixed operating costs, the large size of their labor and management force, and the technical complexity of their operations, pioneered in the new ways of oligopolistic competition and large-scale, professionalized, bureaucratized management.

The new nation-wide market created by the construction of the railroad network became an increasingly urban one. From 1850 on, if not before, urban areas were growing more rapidly than rural ones. In the four decades from 1840 to 1880 the proportion of urban population rose from 11 per cent to 28 per cent of the total population, or about 4 per cent a decade. In the two decades from 1880 to 1900 it grew from 28 per cent to 40 per cent or an increase of 6 per cent a decade. Was this new urban and national market, then, the primary stimulant for business innovation and change, and for the coming of big business to American industry?

## CHANGES IN THE CONSUMERS' GOODS INDUSTRIES

The industries first to become dominated by great business enterprises were those making consumer goods, the majority of which were processed from products grown on the farm and sold in the urban markets. Consolidation and centralization in the consumers' goods industries were well under way by 1893. The unit that appeared was one which integrated within a single business organization the major economic processes: production or purchasing of raw materials, manufacturing, distribution, and finance.

Such vertically integrated organizations came in two quite different ways. Where the product tended to be somewhat new in kind and especially fitted for the urban market, its makers created their businesses by first building large marketing and then purchasing organizations. This technique appears to have been true of the manufacturers or distributors of fresh meat, cigarettes, high-grade flour, bananas, harvesters, sewing machines, and typewriters. Where the products were established staple items, horizontal combination tended to precede vertical integration. In the sugar, salt, leather, whiskey, glucose, starch, biscuit, kerosene, fertilizer, and rubber industries a large number of small manufacturers first combined into large business units and then created their marketing and buying organizations. For a number of reasons the makers of the newer types of products found the older outlets less satisfactory and felt more of a need for direct marketing than did the manufacturers of the long-established goods.

### Integration via the Creation of Marketing Organization

The story of the changes and the possible reasons behind them can be more clearly understood by examining briefly the experience of a few innovating firms. First, consider the experience of companies that grew large through the creation of a nation-wide marketing and distributing organization. Here the story of Gustavus F. Swift and his brother Edwin is a significant one. Gustavus F. Swift, an Easterner, came relatively late to the Chicago meat-packing business. Possibly because he was from Massachusetts, he appreciated the potential market for fresh western meat in the eastern cities. For after the Civil War, Boston, New York, Philadelphia, and other cities were rapidly outrunning their local meat supply. At the same time, great herds of cattle were gathering on the western plains. Swift saw the possibilities of connecting the new market with the new source of supply by the use of the refrigerated railroad car. In 1878, shortly after his first experimental shipment of refrigerated meat, he formed a partnership with his younger brother, Edwin, to market fresh western meat in the eastern cities.

For the next decade, Swift struggled hard to carry out his plans, the essence of which was the creation, during the 1880's, of the nation-wide distributing and marketing organization built around a network of branch houses. Each "house" had its storage plant and its own marketing organization. The latter included outlets in major towns and cities, often managed by Swift's own salaried representatives. In marketing the product, Swift had to break down, through advertising and other means, the prejudices against eating meat killed more than a thousand miles away and many weeks earlier. At the same time he had to combat boycotts of local butchers and the concerted efforts of the National Butchers' Protective Association to prevent the sale of his meat in the urban markets.

To make effective use of the branch house network, the company soon began to market products other than beef. The "full line" soon came to include lamb, mutton, pork, and, some time later, poultry, eggs, and dairy products. The growing distributing organization soon demanded an increase in supply. So between 1888 and 1892, the Swifts set up meat-packing establishments in Kansas City, Omaha, and St. Louis, and, after the depression of the 1890's, three more in St. Joseph, St. Paul, and Ft. Worth. At the same time, the company systematized the buying of its cattle and other products at the stockyards. In the 1890's, too, Swift began a concerted effort to make more profitable use of by-products.

Before the end of the 1890's, then, Swift had effectively fashioned a great, vertically integrated organization. The major departments—marketing, processing, purchasing, and accounting—were all tightly controlled from the central office in Chicago. A report of the Commissioner of Corporations published in 1905 makes clear the reason for such control:

> Differences in quality of animals and of their products are so great that the closest supervision of the Central Office is necessary to enforce the exercise of skill and sound judgement on the part of the agents who buy the stock, and the agents who sell the meat. With this object, the branches of the Selling and Accounting Department of those packing companies which have charge of the purchasing, killing, and dressing and selling of fresh meat, are organized in the most extensive and thorough manner. The Central Office is in constant telegraphic correspondence with the distributing houses, with a view to adjusting the supply of meat and the price as nearly as possible to the demand.

As this statement suggests, the other meat packers followed Swift's example. To compete effectively, Armour, Morris, Cudahy, and Schwarzschild & Sulzberger had to build up similar integrated organizations. Those that did not follow the Swift model were destined to remain small local companies. Thus by the middle of the 1890's, the meat-packing industry, with the rapid growth of these great vertically integrated firms had become oligopolistic (the "Big Five" had the major share of the market) and bureaucratic; each of the five had its many departments and several levels of management.

This story has parallels in other industries processing agricultural products. In tobacco, James B. Duke was the first to appreciate the growing market for the cigarette, a new product which was sold almost wholly in the cities. However, after he had applied machinery to the manufacture of cigarettes, production soon outran supply. Duke then concentrated on expanding the market through extensive advertising and the creation of a national and then world-wide selling organization. In 1884, he left Durham, North Carolina, for New York City, where he set up factories, sales, and administrative offices. New York was closer to his major urban markets, and was the more logical place to manage an international advertising campaign than Durham. While he was building his marketing department, Duke was also creating the network of warehouses and buyers in the tobacco-growing areas of the country.

In 1890, he merged his company with five smaller competitors in the cigarette business to form the American Tobacco Company. By 1895 the activities of these firms had been consolidated into the manufacturing, marketing, purchasing, and finance departments of the single operating structure Duke had earlier fashioned. Duke next undertook development of a full line by handling all types of smoking and chewing tobacco. By the end of the century, his company completely dominated the tobacco business. Only two other firms, R. J. Reynolds & Company and P. Lorillard & Company had been able to build up comparable vertically integrated organizations. When they merged with American Tobacco they continued to retain their separate operating organizations. When the 1911 antitrust decree split these and other units off from the American company, the tobacco industry had become, like the meat-packing business, oligopolistic, and its dominant firms bureaucratic.

What Duke and Swift did for their industries, James S. Bell of the Washburn-Crosby Company did during these same years in the making and selling of high-grade flour to the urban bakeries and housewives, and Andrew J. Preston achieved in growing, transporting, and selling another new product for the urban market, the banana. Like Swift and Duke, both these men made their major innovations in marketing, and then went on to create large-scale, departmentalized, vertically integrated structures.

The innovators in new consumer durables followed much the same pattern. Both Cyrus McCormick, pioneer harvester manufacturer, and William Clark, the business brains of the Singer Sewing Machine Company, first sold through commissioned agents. Clark soon discovered that salaried men, working out of branch offices, could more effectively and at less cost display, demonstrate, and service sewing machines than could the agents. Just as important, the branch offices were able to provide the customer with essential credit. McCormick, while retaining the dealer to handle the final sales, came to appreciate the need for a strong selling and distributing organization, with warehouses, servicing facilities, and a large salaried force, to stand behind the dealer. So in the years following the Civil War, both McCormick and Singer Sewing Machine Company concentrated on building up national and then world-wide marketing departments. As they purchased their raw materials from a few industrial companies rather than from a mass of farmers, their purchasing departments were smaller, and required less attention than those in the firms processing farmers' products. But the net result was the creation of a very similar type of organization.

### Integration via Horizontal Combination

In those industries making more standard goods, the creation of marketing organizations usually followed large-scale combinations of a number of small manufacturing firms. For these small firms, the coming of the railroad had in many cases enlarged their markets but simultaneously brought them for the first time into competition with many other companies. Most of these firms appear to have expanded production in order to take advantage of the new markets. As a result, their industries became plagued with overproduction and excess capacity; that is, continued production at full capacity threatened to drop prices below the cost of production. So in the 1880's and early 1890's, many small manufacturers in the leather, sugar, salt, distilling and other corn products, linseed and cotton oil, biscuit, petroleum, fertilizer and rubber boot and glove industries, joined in large horizontal combinations.

In most of these industries, combination was followed by consolidation and vertical integration, and the pattern was comparatively consistent. First, the new combinations concentrated their manufacturing activities in locations more advantageously situated to meet the new growing urban demands. Next they systematized and standardized their manufacturing processes. Then, except in the case of sugar and corn products (glucose and starch), the combinations began to build large distributing and smaller purchasing departments. In so doing, many dropped their initial efforts to buy out competitors or to drive them out of business by price-cutting. Instead they concentrated on the creation of a more efficient flow from the producers of their raw materials to the ultimate consumer, and of the development and maintenance of markets through brand names and advertising. Since the large majority of these combinations began as regional groupings, most industries came to have more than one great firm. Only oil, sugar, and corn products remained long dominated by a single company. By World War I, partly because of the dissolutions under the Sherman Act, these industries had also become oligopolistic, and their leading firms vertically integrated.

Specific illustrations help to make these generalizations more precise. The best-known is the story of the oil industry, but equally illustrative is the experience of the leading distilling, baking, and rubber companies.

The first permanent combination in the whiskey industry came in 1887 when a large number of Midwestern distillers, operating more than 80 small plants, formed the Distillers' and Cattle Feeders' Trust. Like other trusts, it adopted the more satisfactory legal form of a holding company shortly after New Jersey in 1889 passed the general incorporation law for holding companies. The major efforts of the Distillers Company were, first, to concentrate production in a relatively few plants. By 1895 only 21 were operating. The managers maintained that the large volume per plant permitted by such concentration would mean lower costs, and also that the location of few plants more advantageously in relation to supply and marketing would still reduce expenses further. However, the company kept the price of whiskey up, and since the cost of setting up a distillery was small, it soon had competition from small local plants. The company's answer was to purchase the new competitors and to cut prices. This strategy proved so expensive that the enterprise was unable to survive the depression of the 1890's.

Shortly before going into receivership in 1896, the Distillers Company had begun to think more about marketing. In 1895, it had planned to spend a million dollars to build up a distributing and selling organization in the Urban East—the company's largest market. In 1898, through the purchase of the Standard Distilling & Distributing Company and the Spirits Distributing Company, it did acquire a marketing organization based in New York City. In 1903, the marketing and manufacturing units were combined into a single operating organization under the direction of the Distillers Securities Company. At the same time, the company's president announced plans to concentrate on the development of brand names and specialties, particularly through advertising and packaging. By the early years of the twentieth century, then, the Distillers Company had become a vertically integrated, departmentalized, centralized operating organization, competing in the modern manner, more through advertising and product differentiation than price.

The experience of the biscuit industry is even more explicit. The National Biscuit Company came into being in 1898 as a merger of three regional combinations: The New York Biscuit Company formed in 1890, the American Biscuit and Manufacturing Company, and the United States Biscuit Company founded a little later. Its initial objective was to control price and production, but as in the case of the Distillers Company, this strategy proved too expensive. The

Annual Report for 1901 suggests why National Biscuit shifted its basic policies:

> This Company is four years old and it may be of interest to shortly review its history.... When the company started, it was an aggregation of plants. It is now an organized business. When we look back over the four years, we find that a radical change has been wrought in our methods of business. In the past, the managers of large merchandising corporations have found it necessary, for success, to control or limit competition. So when this company started, it was thought that we must control competition, and that to do this we must either fight competition or buy it. The first meant a ruinous war of prices, and a great loss of profit; the second, a constantly increasing capitalization. Experience soon proved to us that, instead of bringing success, either of those courses, if persevered in, must bring disaster. This led us to reflect whether it was necessary to control competition.... we soon satisfied ourselves that within the Company itself we must look for success.
>
> We turned our attention and bent our energies to improving the internal management of our business, to getting full benefit from purchasing our raw materials in large quantities, to economizing the expenses of manufacture, to systematizing and rendering more effective our selling department; and above all things and before all things to improve the quality of our goods and the condition in which they should reach the customer.
>
> It became the settled policy of this Company to buy out no competition....

In concentrating on distribution, the company first changed its policy from selling in bulk to wholesalers to marketing small packages to retailers. It developed the various "Uneeda Biscuit" brands, which immediately became popular. "The next point," the same Annual Report continued, "was to reach the customer. Thinking we had something that the customer wanted, we had to advise the customer of its existence. We did this by extensive advertising." This new packaging and advertising not only quickly created a profitable business, but also required the building of a sizable marketing organization. Since flour could be quickly and easily purchased in quantity from large milling firms, the purchasing requirements were less complex, and so the company needed a smaller purchasing organization. On the other hand, it spent much energy after 1901 in improving plant layout and manufacturing processes in order to cut production costs and to improve and standardize quality. Throughout the first decade of its history, National Biscuit continued the policy of "centralizing" manufacturing operations, particularly in its great New York and Chicago plants.

In the rubber boot, shoe, and glove industries, the story is much the same. Expansion of manufacturing facilities and increasing competition as early as 1874, led to the formation, by several leading firms, of the Associated Rubber Shoe Companies—an organization for setting price and production schedules through its board of directors. This company continued until 1886. Its successor, the Rubber Boot and Shoe Company, which lasted only a year, attempted, besides controlling prices and production, to handle marketing, which had always been done by commissioned agents. After five years of uncontrolled competition, four of the five firms that had organized the selling company again combined, this time with the assistance of a large rubber importer, Charles A. Flint. The resulting United States Rubber Company came, by

1898, to control 75 per cent of the nation's rubber boot, shoe, and glove output.

At first the new company remained a decentralized holding company. Each constituent company retained its corporate identity with much freedom of action, including the purchasing of raw materials and the selling of finished products, which was done, as before, through jobbers. The central office's concern was primarily with controlling price and production schedules. Very soon, however, the company began, in the words of the 1896 Annual Report, a policy of "perfecting consolidation of purchasing, selling, and manufacturing." This was to be accomplished in four ways. First, as the 1895 Annual Report had pointed out, the managers agreed "so far as practicable, to consolidate the purchasing of all supplies of raw materials for the various manufacturies into one single buying agency, believing that the purchase of large quantities of goods can be made at more advantageous figures than the buying of small isolated lots." The second new "general policy" was "to undertake to reduce the number of brands of goods manufactured, and to consolidate the manufacturing of the remaining brands in those factories which have demonstrated superior facilities for production or advantageous labor conditions. This course was for the purpose of utilizing the most efficient instruments of production and closing those that were inefficient and unprofitable." The third policy was to consolidate sales through the formation of a "Selling Department," which was to handle all goods made by the constituent companies in order to achieve "economy in the distribution expense." Selling was now to be handled by a central office in the New York City headquarters, with branch offices throughout the United States and Europe. Of the three great new departments, actually manufacturing was the slowest to be fully consolidated and centralized. Finally, the treasurer's office at headquarters began to obtain accurate data on profit and loss through the institution of uniform, centralized cost accounting.

Thus United States Rubber, National Biscuit, and the Distillers Securities Company soon came to have organizational structures paralleling those of Swift and American Tobacco. By the first decade of the twentieth century, the leading firms in many consumers' goods industries had become departmentalized and centralized. This was the organizational concomitant to vertical integration. Each major function, manufacturing, sales, purchasing, and finance, became managed by a single and separate department head, usually a vice president, who, assisted by a director or a manager, had full authority and responsibility for the activities of his unit. These departmental chiefs, with the president, coordinated and evaluated the work of the different functional units, and made policy for the company as a whole. In coordinating, appraising, and policy-making, the president and the vice presidents in charge of departments came to rely more and more on the accounting and statistical information, usually provided by the finance department, on costs, output, purchases, and sales. . . .

## CONCLUSION: THE BASIC INNOVATIONS

The middle of the first decade of the new century might be said to mark the end of an era. By 1903, the great merger movement was almost over, and by then the metals industries and those processing agricultural products had developed patterns of internal organization and external competition which were to remain. In those years, too, leading chemical, electrical, rubber, power machinery and implement companies had initiated their "full line" policy, and had instituted the earliest formal research and development departments created in this country. In this decade also, electricity was becoming for the first time a significant source of industrial power, and the automobile was just beginning to revolutionize American transportation. From 1903 on, the new generators of power and the new technologies appear to have become the dominant stimuli to innovation in American industry, and such innovations were primarily those which created new products and processes. Changes in organizational methods and marketing techniques were largely responses to technological advances.

This seems much less true of the changes during the 20 to 25 years before 1903. In that period, the basic innovations were more in the creation of new forms of organization and new ways of marketing. The great modern corporation, carrying on the major industrial processes, namely, purchasing, and often production of materials and parts, manufacturing, marketing, and finance —all within the same organizational structure —had its beginnings in that period. Such organizations hardly existed, outside of the railroads, before the 1880's. By 1900 they had become the basic business unit in American industry.

Each of these major processes became managed by a corporate department, and all were coordinated and supervised from a central office. Of the departments, marketing was the most significant. The creation of nation-wide distributing and selling organizations was the initial step in the growth of many larger consumer goods companies. Mergers in both the consumer and producer goods industries were almost always followed by the formation of a centralized sales department.

The consolidation of plants under a single manufacturing department usually accompanied or followed the formation of a national marketing organization. The creation of such a manufacturing department normally meant the concentration of production in fewer and larger plants, and such consolidation probably lowered unit costs and increased output per worker. The creation of such a department in turn led to the setting up of central traffic, purchasing, and often engineering organizations. Large-scale buying, more rational routing of raw materials and finished products, more systematic plant lay-out, and plant location in relation to materials and markets probably lowered costs still further. Certainly the creators of these organizations believed that it did. In the extractive and machinery industries integration went one step further. Here the motives for controlling raw materials or parts and components were defensive as well as designed to cut costs through providing a more efficient flow of materials from mine to market.

These great national industrial organizations required a large market to provide the volume necessary to support the increased overhead costs. Also, to be profitable, they needed careful coordination between the different functional departments. This coordination required a steady flow of accurate data on costs, sales, and on all purchasing, manufacturing, and marketing activities. As a result, the comptroller's office became an increasingly important department. In fact, one of the first moves after a combination by merger or purchase was to institute more effective and detailed accounting procedures. Also, the leading entrepreneurs of the period, men like Rockefeller, Carnegie, Swift, Duke, Preston, Clark, and the DuPonts, had to become, as had the railroad executives of an earlier generation, experts in reading and interpreting business statistics.

Consolidation and departmentalization meant that the leading industrial corporations became operating rather than holding companies, in the sense that the officers and managers of the companies were directly concerned with operating activities. In fact, of the 50 companies with the largest assets in 1909, only United States Steel, Amalgamated Copper, and one or two other copper companies remained purely holding companies. In most others, the central office included the heads of the major functional departments, usually the president, vice presidents, and sometimes a chairman of the board and one or two representatives of financial interests. These men made major policy and administrative decisions and evaluated the performance of the departments and the corporation as a whole. In the extractive industries a few companies, like Standard Oil (N.J.) and some of the metals companies, were partly holding and partly operating companies. At Standard Oil nearly all important decisions were made in the central headquarters, at 26 Broadway, which housed not only the presidents of the subsidiaries but the powerful policy formulating and coordinating committees. But in some of the metals companies, the subsidiaries producing and transporting raw materials retained a large degree of autonomy.

The coming of the large vertically integrated, centralized, functionally departmentalized industrial organization altered the internal and external situations in which and about which business decisions were made. Information about markets, supplies, and operating performance as well as suggestions for action often had to come up through the several levels of the departmental hierarchies, while decisions and suggestions based on this data had to be transmitted down the same ladder for implementation. Executives on each level became increasingly specialists in one function—in sales, production, purchasing, or finance —and most remained in one department and so handled one function only for the major part of their business careers. Only he who climbed to the very top of the departmental ladder had a chance to see his own company as a single operating unit. Where a company's markets, sources of raw materials, and manufacturing processes remained relatively stable, as was true in the metals industries and in those processing agricultural goods, the nature of the business executive's work became increasingly routine and administrative.

When the internal situation had become bureaucratic, the external one tended to be oligopolistic. Vertical integration by one manufacturer forced others to follow. Thus, in a very short time, many American industries became dominated by a few large firms, with the smaller ones handling local and more specialized aspects of the business. Occasionally industries like oil, tobacco, and sugar, came to be controlled by one company, but in most cases legal action by the federal government in the years after 1900 turned monopolistic industries into oligopolistic ones.

Costs, rather than interfirm competition, began to determine prices. With better information on costs, supplies, and market conditions, the companies were able to determine price quite accurately on the basis of the desired return on investment. The managers of the different major companies had little to gain by cutting prices below an acceptable profit margin. On the other hand, if one firm set its prices excessively high, the other firms could increase their share of the market by selling at a lower price and still maintain a profit. They would, however, rarely cut to the point where this margin was eliminated. As a result, after 1900, price leadership, price umbrellas, and other evidences of oligopolistic competition became common in many American industries. To increase their share of the market and to improve their profit position, the large corporations therefore concerned themselves less with price and concentrated more on obtaining new customers by advertising, brand names, and product differentiations; on cutting costs through further improvement and integration of the manufacturing, marketing, and buying processes; and on developing more diversified lines of products.

The coming of the large vertically integrated corporation changed more than just the practices of American industrialists and their industries. The effect on the merchant, particularly the wholesaler, and on the financier, especially the investment banker, has been suggested here. The relation between the growth of these great industrial units and the rise of labor unions has often been pointed out. Certainly the regulation of the large corporation became one of the major political issues of these years, and the devices created to carry out such a regulation were significant innovations in American constitutional, legal, and political institutions. But an examination of such effects is beyond the scope of this paper.

**Reasons for the Basic Innovations**

One question remains to be reviewed. Why did the vertically integrated corporation come when it did, and in the way it did? The creation by nearly all the large firms of nation-wide selling and distributing organizations indicates the importance of the national market. It was necessary that the market be an increasingly urban one. The city took the largest share of the goods manufactured by the processors of agricultural products. The city, too, with its demands for construction materials, lighting, heating and many other facilities, provided the major market for the metals and other producers' goods industries after railroad construction slowed. Without the rapidly growing urban market there would have been little need and little opportunity for the coming of big business in American industry. And such a market could hardly have existed before the completion of a nation-wide railroad network.

What other reasons might there have been for the swift growth of the great industrial corporation? What about foreign markets? In some industries, particularly oil, the overseas trade may have been an important factor. However, in most businesses the domestic customers took the lion's share of the output, and in nearly all of them the move abroad appears to have come after the creation of the large corporation, and after such corporations had fashioned their domestic marketing organization.

What about the investor looking for profitable investments, and the promoter seeking new promotions? Financiers and promoters certainly had an impact on the changes after 1897, but again they seem primarily to have taken advantage of what had already proved successful. The industrialists themselves, rather than the financiers, initiated most of the major changes in business organization. Availability of capital and cooperation with the financier figured much less prominently in these industrial combinations and consolidations than had been the case with the earlier construction of the railroads and with the financing of the Civil War.

What about technological changes? Actually, except for electricity, the major innovations in the metals industries seem to have come before or after the years under study here. Most of the technological improvements in the agricultural processing industries appear to have been made to meet the demands of the new urban market. The great technological innovations that accompanied the development of electricity, the internal combustion engine, and industrial chemistry did have their beginning in these years, and were, indeed, to have a fundamental impact on the American business economy. Yet this impact was not to be really felt until after 1900.

What about the entrepreneurial talent? Certainly the best-known entrepreneurs of this period were those who helped to create the large industrial corporation. If, as Joseph A. Schumpeter suggests, "The defining characteristic [of the entrepreneur and his function] is simply the doing of new things, and doing things that are already done, in a new way (innovation)," Rockefeller, Carnegie, Frick, Swift, Duke, McCormick, the DuPonts, the Guggenheims, Coffin of General Electric, Preston of United Fruit, and Clark of Singer Sewing Machine were all major innovators of their time. And their innovations were not in technology, but rather in organization and in marketing. "Doing a new thing" is, to Schumpeter, a "creative response" to a new situation, and the situation to which these innovators responded appears to have been the rise of the national urban market.

# POSTSCRIPT

## Were Nineteenth-Century Entrepreneurs Robber Barons?

Regardless of whether American entrepreneurs are regarded as "captains of industry" or "robber barons," there is no doubt that they constituted a powerful elite and were responsible for defining the character of society in the Gilded Age. For many Americans, these businessmen represented the logical culmination of the country's attachment to laissez-faire economics and rugged individualism. In fact, it was not unusual at all for the nation's leading industrialists to be depicted as the real-life models for the "rags-to-riches" theme epitomized in the self-help novels of Horatio Alger. Closer examination of the lives of most of these entrepreneurs, however, reveals the mythical dimensions of this American ideal. Simply put, the typical business executive of the late nineteenth century did not rise up from humble circumstances, a product of the American rural tradition or the immigrant experience, as frequently claimed. Rather, most of these big businessmen (Andrew Carnegie may have been an exception) were of Anglo-Saxon origin and reared in a city by middle-class parents. On Sundays, they attended an Episcopal or Congregational Protestant Church. According to one survey, over half the leaders had attended college at a time when even the pursuit of a high school education was considered unusual. In other words, instead of having to pull themselves up by their own bootstraps from the bottom of the social heap, these individuals usually started their climb to success at the middle of the ladder or higher.

The reader may be surprised to learn that in spite of the massive influx of immigrants from Asia and southern and eastern Europe in the years 1880 to 1924, today's leaders are remarkably similar in their social and economic backgrounds to their nineteenth-century counterparts. A 1972 study by Thomas Dye listing the top 4,000 decisionmakers in corporate, governmental, and public-interest sectors of American life revealed that 90 percent were affluent, white, Anglo-Saxon males. There were only two African Americans in the whole group; there were no Native Americans, Hispanics, or Japanese Americans, and very few recognizable Irish, Italians, or Jews.

A useful contextual framework for examining the role of the American entrepreneur can be found in Thomas C. Cochran and William Miller, *The Age of Enterprise: A Social History of Industrial America*, rev. ed. (Harper & Row, 1961), and in Glenn Porter, *The Rise of Big Business, 1860–1910* (Harlan Davidson, 1973). Peter d'A. Jones, ed., *The Robber Barons Revisited* (D.C. Heath, 1968), has assembled an excellent collection of the major viewpoints on the "robber baron" thesis. For efforts to present the actions of the late nineteenth-century businessmen in a favorable light, see Allan Nevins, *A Study in Power: John D. Rockefeller, Industrialist and Philanthropist*, 2 vols. (Scribner's, 1953); Harold Livesay, *Andrew Carnegie and the Rise of Big Business* (Little, Brown, 1975); and Maury Klein, *The Life and Legend of Jay Gould* (Johns Hopkins University Press, 1986). Robert Sobel's *The Entrepreneurs: Explorations Within the American Business Tradition* (Weybright & Talley, 1974) presents sympathetic sketches of the builders of often neglected industries of the nineteenth and twentieth centuries. For a critique of Matthew Josephson, one of the architects of the "robber baron" thesis, see Maury Klein, "A Robber Historian," *Forbes* (October 26, 1987).

The works of Alfred D. Chandler, Jr., are vital to the understanding of American industrialization. Chandler almost singlehandedly reshaped the way in which historians write about American corporations. Instead of arguing about the morality of nineteenth-century businessmen, he employed organizational theories of decision-making borrowed from the sociologists and applied them to case studies of corporate America. See *Strategy and Structure: Chapters in the History of the American Industrial Enterprise* (MIT Press, 1962); *The Visible Hand: The Managerial Revolution in American Business* (Harvard University Press, 1977); and *Scale and Scope: The Dynamics of Industrial Capitalism* (Harvard University Press, 1990). Chandler's most important essays are collected in Thomas K. McCraw, ed., *The Essential Alfred Chandler: Essays Toward a Historical Theory of Big Business* (Harvard Business School Press, 1988). For an assessment of Chandler's approach and contributions, see Louis Galambos's "The Emerging Organizational Synthesis in Modern American History," *Business History Review* (Autumn 1970) and Thomas K. McCraw's "The Challenge of Alfred D. Chandler, Jr.: Retrospect and Prospect," *Reviews in American History* (March 1987).

# ISSUE 3

## Was the American Labor Movement Radical?

**YES: Bruce Laurie,** from *Artisans Into Workers: Labor in Nineteenth-Century America* (Hill & Wang, 1989)

**NO: Carl N. Degler,** from *Out of Our Past: The Forces That Shaped Modern America,* 3rd ed. (Harper & Row, 1984)

### ISSUE SUMMARY

**YES:** Professor of history Bruce Laurie argues that the Knights of Labor was a radical labor organization composed of skilled and unskilled workers that favored using governmental remedies to improve working conditions.

**NO:** Professor of history Carl N. Degler maintains that the American labor movement accepted capitalism and reacted conservatively to the radical organizational changes brought about in the economic system by big business.

The two major labor unions that developed in the late nineteenth century were the Knights of Labor and the American Federation of Labor. Because of the hostility toward labor unions, the Knights of Labor functioned for 12 years as a secret organization. Between 1879 and 1886 the Knights of Labor grew from 10,000 to 700,000 members. Idealistic in many of its aims, the union supported social reforms such as equal pay for men and women, prohibition of alcohol, and the abolition of convict and child labor. Economic reforms included the development of workers' cooperatives, public ownership of utilities, and a more moderate, eight-hour workday. The Knights declined after 1886 for several reasons. Although it was opposed to strikes, the union received a black eye (as did the whole labor movement) when it was blamed for the bombs that were thrown at the police during the Haymarket Square riot in Chicago. According to most historians, other reasons that are usually associated with the decline of the Knights include the failure of some cooperative businesses, conflict between skilled and unskilled workers, and, most importantly, competition from the American Federation of Labor. By 1890 the Knights's membership had dropped to 100,000. It died in 1917.

A number of skilled unions got together in 1896 and formed the American Federation of Labor (AFL). Samuel Gompers was elected its first president, and his philosophy permeated the AFL during his 37 years in office. He pushed for practical reforms—better hours, wages, and working conditions. Unlike the Knights, the AFL avoided associations with political parties, workers' cooperatives, unskilled workers, immigrants, and women. Decision-making power was in the hands of locals rather than the central board. Gompers was heavily criticized by his contemporaries, and later by historians, for his narrow craft unionism. But membership increased in spite of the depression of the 1890s from 190,000 to 500,000 by 1900, to 1,500,000 in 1904, and to 2,000,000 by the eve of World War I.

Gompers's cautiousness is best understood in the context of his times. The national and local governments were in the hands of men who were sympathetic to the rise of big business and hostile to the attempts of labor to organize. Whether it was the railroad strike of 1877, the Homestead steel strike of 1892, or the Pullman car strike of 1894, the pattern of repression was always the same. Companies would cut wages, workers would go out on strike, scab workers would be brought in, fights would break out, companies would receive court injunctions, and the police and state and federal militia would beat up the unionized workers. After a strike was broken, workers would lose their jobs or would accept pay cuts and longer workdays.

On the national level, Theodore Roosevelt became the first president to show any sympathy for the workers. As a police commissioner in New York City and later as governor of New York, Roosevelt observed firsthand the deplorable occupational and living conditions of the workers. Although he avoided recognition of the collective bargaining rights of labor unions, Roosevelt forced the anthracite coal owners in Pennsylvania to mediate before an arbitration board for an equitable settlement of a strike with the mine workers.

In 1905 a coalition of socialists and industrial unionists formed America's most radical labor union—the Industrial Workers of the World (IWW). There were frequent splits within this union and much talk of violence. But in practice, the IWW was more interested in organizing workers into industrial unions than in fighting, as were the earlier Knights of Labor and the later Congress of Industrial Organizations. Strikes were encouraged to improve the daily conditions of the workers through long-range goals, which included reducing the power of the capitalists by increasing the power of the workers.

In the first selection, Bruce Laurie maintains that even though they were not socialists, the Knights of Labor stood outside the consensus of laissez-faire politics in the Gilded Age. Composed of skilled and unskilled laborers, the Knights of Labor favored using governmental remedies to improve working conditions. In the second selection, Carl N. Degler argues that American workers accepted capitalism and, like business unionist Samuel Gompers, were interested in obtaining better hours, wages, and working conditions. Socialism was rejected, he argues, because workers believed they were achieving economic and social mobility under capitalism.

# YES

## Bruce Laurie

# THE RISE AND FALL OF THE KNIGHTS OF LABOR

Terence V. Powderly seized upon the immediate significance of employer recrimination. The firings and blacklists made "victims of hundreds of Knights of Labor, who left... [Pennsylvania] in all directions" with the gospel of Knighthood. The young machinist was in a good position to know. Powderly had spent the Long Depression out of work and on the move, finally getting a job in a Scranton railway shop near his place of birth on the eve of the 1877 riots. Within a year he would be elected Grand Master Workman of the Noble and Holy Order of the Knights of Labor.

Powderly was a bundle of contradictions. A wiry man of medium height with a walruslike mustache and deep-set eyes that squinted through a pince-nez, he cut a stately figure in his customary black broadcloth coat and starched white collar. The labor journalist John Swinton wrote that "English novelists take men of Powderly's look for poets, gondoliers, scullers, philosophers, and heroes crossed in love, but no one ever drew such a looking man as the leader of a million horny-fisted sons of toil." But a labor leader he was in spite of administrative skills and a social personality more suited to a small pulpit. Self-righteous and maddeningly thin-skinned, Powderly made enemies easily and turned against his best friends but was revered by those who knew him from afar. Some Knights named their sons after him, but he mistook such reverence for foolishness and wrote insulting letters to those who would even consider such a thing. He avoided the saloon and rough centers of working-class sociability. He was most at ease when he was alone, writing, gardening, and poring over his collection of rocks and geological specimens. The son of a Catholic, he spoke in evangelical idiom and abstained from liquor until he was forty-five. He served three terms (1878–84) as Greenback-Labor mayor of Scranton while leading a movement whose manifesto read like a political platform, but he loathed politics and clamped down hard on third-party talk within the Knights. "Our Order," he once said, "is above politics." He also believed the Order was above the class struggle. In his second autobiography his boast was: "Not once did I, during my fourteen years in the office of Grand Master Workman, order a strike." No one ever thought him or his organization easy to fathom.

Powderly spent his formative years in small-town America. He was the eleventh of twelve children born to Irish immigrants Terence and Margery Powderly, who arrived in the United States in 1826 and settled briefly in Ogdensburg, New York, where Terence toiled as a day laborer for local miners and farmers. Three years later in the midst of the coal boom in eastern Pennsylvania, Terence moved his family to Carbondale and took a job at a colliery. Fifteen years with pick and shovel paid off; in 1845 he opened a mine of his own. By the time his son Terence was born in 1849, the family had achieved a stake in society, and judging from his father's election to the town council two years later, some prominence as well. The Powderlys were secure enough to keep their son at school until age thirteen, and sufficiently connected to arrange a job for him with a local railroad. Young Powderly rose quickly from switch tender to brakeman and might have made engineer, the pinnacle of railway work, had his father not convinced James Dickson, master mechanic at the Delaware and Hudson shop, to take him on as a machinist's apprentice. Young Powderly spent an enjoyable three years learning the craft and developing a deep respect for his teacher. Family connections again opened the way upward when in 1869 Powderly's father importuned William Scranton, paternalistic owner of the Delaware, Lackawanna, and Western, to hire his son. The wealthy railway man and the budding machinist got on famously. Scranton dropped by the shop floor for friendly chats and probably fancied arranging a romance with his daughter. He also shielded Powderly from the wrath of foreman James Dawson, who once and possibly twice wanted to fire him. Powderly never quite forgot the patronage of Scranton or Dickson. He remembered both men as model bosses whose benefactions gave the lie to those who believed in the inevitability of class strife.

Dawson made an 1873 firing stick, possibly because of the onset of hard times, and Powderly found himself in a fruitless search for work in upstate New York and as far afield as the Mississippi Valley. "Only the man who stands utterly alone, friendless, moneyless, ill-clad, shirtless, and hungry," he would later recall, "can know what it is to be a real tramp. The experience was mine, through no fault of my own." He came close to being hired on no fewer than four occasions but was turned down at the last minute because of a blacklist circulated among repair shops by the vindictive Dawson. The want and isolation of these years reinforced a growing conviction of the need for some form of organization, something that offered fellowship and security. Powderly had taken a step in that direction in 1871 or 1872 upon joining the Machinists' and Blacksmiths' International Union, if only because it offered a life insurance plan and other benefits. Within a year he was elected president of his union lodge and in 1874 was its delegate at an antimonopoly convention in Philadelphia, hometown of the Knights of Labor. There he met William Fennimore, an early member of the Knights, who inducted him into the Order.

The Knights were still in their infancy when Powderly became a member. Founded five years earlier by a group of Philadelphia garment cutters, the Order had only a few assemblies in 1872, all of them in the Quaker City. "It was difficult," wrote the labor reformer George McNeill, "to find earnest and active members" willing to risk the infamy of the blacklist. Widespread fears of detection by employers, paired with the fact that charter members belonged to fraternal orders with clandestine traditions, led to a policy of secrecy. The Order was not referred to by name in public before 1882. Members learned of meetings by word of mouth or symbolic announcements scribbled on sidewalks or published in the labor press. The notation

$$8\ ^{329}/_{14}$$

meant that Local Assembly 14 would meet on March 29 at 8 p.m. The meaning of these signs was soon clear to greater numbers of workers in and around Philadelphia. The Knights were part of the great expansion of unionism that accompanied the eight-hour movement beginning in the summer of 1872. Over the next eighteen months scores of local assemblies emerged in Philadelphia and some were established in the coalfields north and east of the city. At least forty assemblies met in Philadelphia by late 1873, but the growth was short-lived. The panic brought down about half the lodges and those that survived probably lost as many members as they gained, a pattern that would plague the Knights for years in good times and bad. Few new lodges were founded in Philadelphia during the depression but hundreds took root elsewhere, so that by 1877 there were some 500 assemblies with about 6,000 members. The economic recovery of 1877 through 1880 saw the membership rise to just under 30,000 and the number of assemblies increase to over 1,600.

The Knights had no national officers until the Reading convention of 1878. Before that the Order relied on a foundation of local assemblies and district assemblies. Local assemblies had at least ten members and covered wards or neighborhoods in urban places and counties in rural areas. The locals elected delegates to district assemblies, which typically represented entire cities or larger political units. There were equal proportions of urban and rural assemblies before the precipitous membership decline after 1886, but in that year, since urban locals were larger, two-thirds of the members were from the cities. Lodges with a plurality of workers from a single craft were known as trade assemblies, while those with members representing several different occupations were called mixed assemblies. Mixed assemblies were established by the Knights and favored by Powderly and his supporters to lessen the divisiveness of craft unionism. In their view, mixed assemblies promoted brotherhood and broader social identity. There were two deviations from this structural pattern. State assemblies were authorized in sparsely settled regions in 1883, and workers in the same trade were occasionally permitted to form district and national trade assemblies. The historic Reading convention had also established the General Assembly, a yearly congress of delegates elected at the local level, and a panel of national officers, headed by the Grand Master Workman, who formed the General Executive Board, which carried out policy made by the General Assembly and managed daily affairs.

Membership in the Knights was open to all manual workers. Bankers, stockbrokers, and lawyers—individuals historically associated with idleness and parasitism—were barred, along with liquor dealers, gamblers, and others thought to abet vice and corruption; merchants and manufacturers could join, if just, morally upright, and sympathetic to Knighthood; indeed some did hold Knight cards. Middle-class Knights usually hailed from what Norman Ware called the "last frontier of semi-itinerant craftsmen and small shopkeepers." Local Assembly 3184 in Onekama, Michigan, said a local observer, included "a number of our best citizens," as did numerous backwoods assemblies. But the middle classes of urban America, where social lines were more sharply drawn, did not join and left the Knights to wage earners.

Even before the runaway expansion of the mid-1880s, the Order cast a wide net. Its magic lay in a comprehensive program that offered a little something for just about everyone. West Coast workers, enraged by the presence of Chinese labor, responded enthusiastically to Knight organizers promising to end importation of the hated "coolies." Powderly's ethnic lineage and work for the Land League appealed to Irish workmen. Socialists found the Knights an attractive alternative to craft unions. Unskilled workers, long scorned by the labor movement, finally found a place to hang their hats.

The broad sweep of Knighthood was manifested in its platform and preamble adopted at Reading. Though amended from time to time, the Reading platform reflected the guiding values of the brotherhood. It included such essentials of bread-and-butter unionism as the eight-hour day, abolition of contract and convict labor, and the establishment of government bureaus of labor statistics along with loftier demands for social reform in the name of the "producing masses." The reference to producers, labor's traditional self-description, was the thread that tied the Knights to the revivalistic radicalism of the 1840s. "The recent alarming development and aggression of aggregated wealth," the preamble read, "will inevitably lead to the pauperization and hopeless degradation of the toiling masses" unless checked by a counterforce that honored the "divine injunction, 'In the sweat of thy brow shalt thou eat bread.'" It comes as no surprise, therefore, that Knighthood evoked such venerable pieties as the repeal of "all laws that do not bear equally upon capital and labor" and the establishment of "co-operative institutions, productive and distributive." Trade unionism remained strongly identified with social reform.

But it is inaccurate to insist, as some writers have, that the Reading platform represented old wine in new bottles. For just as time improves the vintage, so did it transform the radical tradition. Several Reading planks suggest that the Knights looked forward as well as backward and adapted radicalism to the contingencies of the new industrial order. The Knights reflected the latest thinking on monetary reform by endorsing Greenbackism, a scheme that would have government-owned banks issue paper money convertible into interest-bearing bonds. They also demanded government regulation of the "health and safety of those engaged in mining, manufacturing, and building pursuits," and by the 1880s called for public ownership of the railways and telegraphs. Insofar as Greenbackism and health and safety regulations vested government with powers never contemplated by antebellum radicals, the Knights assumed the mantle of latter-day pioneers extending the frontiers of radicalism. Such demands not only pushed the Knights beyond early radicalism but also outside the political consensus of the Gilded Age. Neither mainstream political party, in lockstep retreat from the active government of the Civil War years, was likely to nationalize the banks and railways or redistribute the plantation lands of the old Confederacy. Yet the Knights never did formally endorse a labor party or establish their own political organization. National leaders demurred and steadfastly refused to draw the Order into the political fray, even though many were Greenbackers. There were decided limits to the politics of Gilded Age radicals.

Late radicalism also put forth contradictory proposals calculated to ease labor's travail in the routine relations between employee and employer. Its goal, enshrined in the Reading platform and reiterated in print and oratory, was the "abolition of wage slavery" through cooperative production and land reform. While both measures would erase the invidious distinction between labor and capital, in the short run workers could expect a continuation of the naked social combat prevalent in postwar America. That troubling prospect lay behind the Reading plank calling for the "substitution of arbitration for strikes." This was not unique to the Knights or entirely na¨$DIve. During Reconstruction and the Gilded Age labor leaders in the United States, and in England for that matter, first turned to arbitration, which was understood to mean negotiations and not third-party interventions. The National Labor Union considered work stoppages to be a "last resort," and beginning in the late 1870s several national craft unions adopted constitutional provisions that greatly restricted the ability of local unions to declare strikes. The founding fathers of the Knights continued to believe in the policy of the NLU while applying it in a flexible way. Uriah Stephens and James L. Wright, founding members of the Order in Philadelphia, preached social pacification but that did not stop them from sharing rostrums with Marxists in the Eight Hour League during the early 1870s or condoning work stoppages when all else failed. Nor did the Reading men believe arbitration would come easily. Their own plank recommended it "wherever and whenever employers and employees are willing to meet on equitable grounds." Problems arose not because of the no-strike policy but because some leaders and members of the rank and file alike would raise it to a dogma, refusing to believe it would take more than professions of good faith or unilateral declaration of peaceful intentions to call off the class war.

In ideological terms, Knighthood may be seen as a middle ground between the individualistic libertarianism of bourgeois America and the collectivism of working-class socialists. Like the former, Knights affirmed the sanctity of private property even as they reviled its excessive accumulation and decried acquisitive individualism. Theirs was an older ethic rooted in the perfectionism of the evangelical church, a popular position that defamed corporate capital as the "anti-Christ" and imagined a "new Pentecost" in which "every man shall have according to his needs." They tied this moral outlook to the well-being of the work group, proclaiming "an injury to one is the concern of all." But they were not socialists despite their collectivist language and the recognition of the need for more forceful government—the demands for public ownership of financial and transportation institutions—reflected in the Reading platform. Knights repudiated the public control of modern socialism along with its doctrine of irreconcilable conflict between labor and capital. "I curse the word class," said Powderly. To him, as to most early Knights, wage earners were "producers," capitalists were "accumulators" and "monopolists," and his movement aimed to abolish "wage slavery," not overthrow capitalism. Here was a language and outlook any antebellum radical would have easily understood.

How do we explain the endurance of this ideology? Radicalism, after all, remained the language of North American labor long after European workmen learned more modern social vocabularies. Part of this American peculiarity lies in the fact that radicalism went unrivaled longer in the United States than in Europe, where theories such as Marxism had more exposure after 1850. American workers were hardly aware of Marx as late as 1870, but even if revolutionary socialism had had wider currency, it is doubtful that it would have gained a wider following. Gilded Age Marxists lectured to a working class weaned on a creed that denied the basic proposition of revolutionary socialism regarding the seizure and exercise of state power. The old republican axiom that reliance on government corrupted the body politic flew in the face of Marxism. At the same time, the Civil War invigorated the language of radicalism. The war had been fought squarely on radical terms for the preservation of "free labor" against an odious "slave power." To Northern workingmen it was a heroic time, to be sure, but it also postponed the struggle against "wage slavery." Long after Appomattox they continued to respond to labor journalists and politicians who spoke of taking the war to the "Vicksburgs of Labor's enemies." This would suggest yet another answer to the old question first asked by the German sociologist Werner Sombart: "Why is there no socialism in the United States?" Socialism, it would seem, was so weak because radicalism was so strong.

Demographic factors and occupational mobility also replenished radicalism. As Herbert Gutman observed, "many persons new to the urban-industrial world would not settle easily into a factory-centered civilization." A good portion of newcomers were not only immigrants but former farmers and villagers reared on radicalism. The traditional antimonopolistic instincts of rural America that fueled the Granger and Alliance movements also found an outlet in Knighthood. On the other hand, opportunities for social advancement in the city were still available for rural-urban migrant and longtime urban dweller alike. Workers who did set up on their own did not always turn their backs on those they had left behind. Uriah Stephens and fellow Knight founder Robert McCloskey ran a garment store in Philadelphia; Arsene Sauva, the militant New York Knight, owned a tailor shop that was also a meeting place for neighborhood radicals; and the New Haven publisher Alexander Troup was one of numerous small printers in the Order. Much like the Fall River job printer John Keogh, small employers did not think of themselves as capitalists. Asked by a Senate investigator if he ran his "own business" as he "please[d]," Keogh answered, "Yes, but I do not consider myself a capitalist." Neither did scores of other former workers who continued to identify with their class of origin and its radical sensibility.

Life on the job could also soften ruder aspects of work and restore faith in radicalism's belief that differences between employer and employee could be resolved. The trade unionist, labor politician, and amateur writer Martin Foran captured as much in his 1886 novel *The Other Side.* Richard Arbyght, its protagonist, is a farm-bred lad who, like Foran himself, completes a cooper's apprenticeship but faces tragedy when his father is robbed and murdered by a rogue who later becomes Richard's employer. A better future is possible when Richard recovers the stolen money, marries well, and goes into business for himself to produce an unnamed but "useful commodity." He is a humane and considerate employer, a radical's dream, who welcomes unionism and on top of this offers his hands a profit-sharing plan. Real life sometimes imitated this bit of popular art even in the bare-fisted labor relations of the Gilded Age. Terre Haute railway promoter Riley McKeon struck the pose of the fraternal paternalistic, the fair boss loyal to workman and community, and for a time, he was accepted in just this way. His admirers included the youthful Eugene Debs, a member of the local lodge of the Brotherhood of Locomotive Firemen in the mid-1870s. In the aftermath of the 1877 railway strikes, which Debs loudly condemned as fellow lodgemen walked picket lines, McKeon lent him $1,000 to rebuild BLF headquarters and consorted with other business leaders to guarantee Debs's bond as treasurer of the brotherhood. McKeon would later back Debs's first bid for elective office. That Debs had a more generous patron in McKeon than Powderly had in William Scranton matters less than the larger implications of such relationships. Any employer who willingly shared profits with workers or lent a hand to those in need could surely be persuaded to go a step further by enlisting in the crusade to terminate "wage slavery."

Radicalism became the touchstone of Knighthood's movement culture. Soon after the first local assembly appeared in 1869, and fully a decade before the advent of paid organizers, recruiters appeared in the guise of "sojourners." Later joined by workers fired after the railway strikes in 1877, sojourners took to the field with the zeal of missionaries, albeit clandestine ones with a slightly different scripture. Their initiates went through a lengthy ceremony packed with rite and ritual of the Order meticulously spelled out in the *Adelphon Kruptos.* Each inductee signed his name to a card, or had to learn to do so, before being escorted into a room to clasp hands with brothers in a symbolic circle of unity and pledge himself to "heaven ordained labor" and to "defend the life, interest, and reputation, and family of all true members." Other publications used symbols to convey a more explicit political message. The traditional symbol of the Order was a triangle whose corners symbolized "Secrecy, Obedience, and Mutual Assistance." A Knight journalist reinterpreted the "full pyramid" to represent what "labor earns." A heavy black line drawn through its center stood for the "unholy part taken by the fiend's hired men, the usurers, the bloodsuckers, who don't work—who live by the sweat of other men's brows." Stump speakers hammered home similar themes. Larger local assemblies published their own organs to supplement the *Journal of United Labor,* official voice of the Order. Fellow lodgers organized poetry clubs and theater groups along with singing societies and brass bands that performed after meetings were adjourned and provided entertainment at official functions. Picnics and dinners were especially popular. Years after Henry Ward Beecher's vulgar sermon on the railway strikers in 1877, lodges continued to hold "Bread and Water Beecher Banquets" and guest speakers still attacked the arrogant cleric. A Michigan Knight chided the "pot-bellied millionaires who eat Porterhouse steaks, drink champagne, smoke 15 cent cigars, who will ride out with their wives, or more likely other people's wives," a reference to Beecher's scandalous love affair with Elizabeth Tilton, the wife of a prominent reform editor.

Much like antebellum radicals, Knights promoted total abstinence. The drinker was seen as a social dependent, a servile and irresponsible soul who brought disrepute to his class and poverty to his family. But he was not to be scorned or punished, or indeed used as an excuse to outlaw liquor sales. Powderly deplored prohibitionists who "patronized labor" and would "regulate our appetite for liquor... [and] everything else." Knights, like the antebellum Washingtonians, practiced voluntarism and used the moral suasion of the group to rehabilitate the problem drinker. Lecturers and columnists stressed the baleful effects of drink and lodges barred spirits from official functions, meetings, and even picnics. Members helped brothers overcome their habit and were duty-bound to report cases of backsliding. Unreconstructed drinkers and wayward members charged with "conduct unbecoming a Knight" answered to courts of lodgemen. One-time offenders usually got off lightly; recidivists were fined or dismissed.

This spirit of mutuality also gained expression in cooperative stores and workshops. Ambitious plans for producer and consumer cooperatives funded and coordinated by the Executive Board never panned out. Indecisive leadership, a mark of Powderly's rule, produced only a single cooperative of much importance, a mine that soon failed. Equally damaging was Powderly's appointment of John Samuel to head the Co-operative Board. Samuel resisted using funds in the national coffers for local projects, which threw assemblies back on their own resources. Lean budgets hampered progress, for as Powderly noted in 1884, "to be successful... *capital* is required. The workingmen who have a little capital cling to it, and hold aloof from cooperation, those who have no capital cannot embark in it." Local assemblies still persisted and by the early 1880s many ran cooperatives that turned out light consumer goods and supplied fuel and groceries to their members at a discount.

No movement culture, however, remains static. None was more variable than Knighthood, if only because it had a longer history, more time to change, than any predecessor. The Order underwent a transition of sorts in 1882 following the hotly disputed decision to abandon secrecy and reform the ritual in response to criticism by the Catholic Church. Meetings lost much of their mystical aura and induction ceremonies became a bit bland. Loyalty and cohesion may have suffered some, but reformed Knighthood also brought compensations. Partly as a result of operating in the open, interest picked up and membership in the Knights climbed to nearly 100,000 by 1884 from about 40,000 in 1882. Larger lodges erected spacious meeting halls, established newspapers, and printed their own propaganda. Rallies and demonstrations grew larger and members grew more aggressive at the workplace, which exacerbated inherent tensions with national officers; differences, however, were usually settled without much ill will. Through the early stirrings of militancy, the Order maintained a balance between the practical concerns of unionism and the ideals of labor reform. It was the mounting class conflict from 1884 through 1886, commonly known as the Great Upheaval, that would upset this delicate balance.

Between 1880 and 1884... the number of work stoppages fluctuated around 450 a year, rose to 645 in 1885, and soared to over 1,400 in 1886–87. Nearly half the strikes in 1880–82 were the spontaneous actions of nonunion workers. By 1883 and increasingly thereafter more and more were called by unions, so that by 1888 two-thirds enjoyed official sanction. For the Knights' part, the most significant of these centered on the railways of the Southwest. Twice in 1884, in May and August, local assemblies along Jay Gould's Union Pacific fought off wage cuts and firings. The following spring brought two more victories against Gould lines, first the Wabash and then the Missouri, Kansas, and Texas. The Wabash strike was supported by a boycott of Gould rolling stock that was ordered by the General Executive Board. The disdainful "robber baron" who was said to have bragged that he "could hire one half of the working class to kill the other half" had been humiliated. "No such victory," wrote the St. Louis *Chronicle* in amazement, "has ever been secured in this nation or any other."

The rash of strikes brought great numbers of new members into the Order. From July 1, 1885, to June 30, 1886, alone, the number of district assemblies jumped from 48,800 to over 11,000, and the 6,200 added in this short time surpassed the growth in the previous sixteen years. Membership swelled from a respectable 110,000 in July 1885 to an all-time high of nearly 750,000 a year later. "Never in history," exulted John Swinton, "has there been such a spectacle as the march of the Knights of Labor at the present time." That national and some district leaders did not share Swinton's enthusiasm is easily understood. Many officials were unnerved by the deluge of raw recruits ignorant of Knighthood. They especially feared expansion triggered by strikes that swept in militants with no higher objective than improving wages and conditions. As early as 1880 Powderly had been deeply concerned about the appeal of work stoppages, warning the General Assembly that "the remedy... lie [sic] not in the suicidal strike, but... in thorough, effective organization." He became alarmed when in 1882 rosters lengthened in the midst of a slight upturn in strike activity. "The tidal wave of strikes," said the jittery Powderly, flowed directly from "exaggerated reports of the strength of the Order." "Such a course," he believed, "may lead men into the Order... but by a path that leads them out again... as soon as they become deceived and lose confidence." Alarm turned into panic when in the floodtide of March 1886 Powderly ordered a forty-day moratorium on admissions. "The majority of the newcomers," he would later explain, were not of the "quality the Order had sought in the past."

Who were these newcomers? A fair number were skilled workers, labor aristocrats from the old handicrafts and newer industrial sectors who had different union backgrounds. Most were either first-time unionists or dual unionists who held membership in existing craft unions. Others had been expelled from craft unions for scabbing, working under scale, or other infractions. Most of the new members, however, were semiskilled and unskilled workers customarily excluded from craft unions and theretofore a minority within the Knights. As May Day 1886 approached, membership in the Knights resembled a pyramid: skilled workers of American birth at the peak and an expanding base of semiskilled and unskilled workers largely Irish, German, and English in origin. Even Polish immigrants, a small but growing group of "new immigrants," rushed into the Knights.

# NO

## Carl N. Degler

# OUT OF OUR PAST

### THE WORKERS' RESPONSE

To say that the labor movement was affected by the industrialization of the postwar years is an understatement; the fact is, industrial capitalism created the labor movement. Not deliberately, to be sure, but in the same way that a blister is the consequence of a rubbing shoe. Unions were labor's protection against the forces of industrialization as the blister is the body's against the irritation of the shoe. The factory and all it implied confronted the workingman with a challenge to his existence as a man, and the worker's response was the labor union.

There were labor unions in America before 1865, but, as industry was only emerging in those years, so the organizations of workers were correspondingly weak. In the course of years after Appomattox, however, when industry began to hit a new and giant stride, the tempo of unionization also stepped up. It was in these decades, after many years of false starts and utopian ambitions, that the American labor movement assumed its modern shape.

Perhaps the outstanding and enduring characteristic of organized labor in the United States has been its elemental conservatism, the fantasies of some employers to the contrary notwithstanding. Indeed, it might be said that all labor unions, at bottom, are conservative by virtue of their being essentially reactions against a developing capitalism. Though an established capitalist society views itself as anything but subversive, in the days of its becoming and seen against the perspective of the previous age, capitalism as an ideology is radically subversive, undermining and destroying many of the cherished institutions of the functioning society. This dissolving process of capitalism is seen more clearly in Europe than in America because there the time span is greater. But, as will appear later, organized labor in the United States was as much a conservative response to the challenge of capitalism as was the European trade union movement.

Viewed very broadly, the history of modern capitalism might be summarized as the freeing of the three factors of production—land, labor, and capital—from the web of tradition in which medieval society held them. If capitalism was to function, it was necessary that this liberating process take place. Only when these basic factors are free to be bought and sold according to the dictates of the profit motive can the immense production which capitalism promises be realized. An employer, for example, had to be free to dismiss labor when the balance sheet required it, without being compelled to retain workers because society or custom demanded it. Serfdom, with its requirement that the peasant could not be taken from the land, was an anachronistic institution if capitalism was to become the economic ideology of society. Conversely, an employer needed to be unrestricted in his freedom to hire labor or else production could not expand in accordance with the market. Guild restrictions which limited apprenticeships were therefore obstacles to the achievement of a free capitalism.

The alienability of the three factors of production was achieved slowly and unevenly after the close of the Middle Ages. By the nineteenth century in most nations of the West, land had become absolutely alienable—it could be bought and sold at will. With the growth of banking, the development of trustworthy monetary standards, and finally the gold standard in the nineteenth century, money or capital also became freely exchangeable. Gradually, over the span of some two centuries, the innovating demands of capitalism stripped from labor the social controls in which medieval and mercantilistic government had clothed it. Serfdom as an obstacle to the free movement of labor was gradually done away with; statutes of laborers and apprenticeships which fixed wages, hours, and terms of employment also fell into disuse or suffered outright repeal. To avoid government interference in the setting of wage rates, the English Poor Law of 1834 made it clear that the dole to the unemployed was always to be lower than the going rate for unskilled labor. Thus supply and demand would be the determinant of wage levels. Both the common law and the Combination Acts in the early nineteenth century in England sought to ensure the operation of a free market in labor by declaring trade unions to be restraints on trade.

Like land and capital, then, labor was being reduced to a commodity, freely accessible, freely alienable, free to flow where demand was high. The classical economists of the nineteenth century analyzed this long historical process, neatly put it together, and called it the natural laws of economics.

To a large extent, this historical development constituted an improvement in the worker's status, since medieval and mercantilist controls over labor had been more onerous than protective. Nevertheless, something was lost by the dissolution of the ancient social ties which fitted the worker into a larger social matrix. Under the old relationship, the worker belonged in society; he enjoyed a definite if not a high status; he had a place. Now he was an individual, alone; his status was up to him to establish; his urge for community with society at large had no definite avenue of expression. Society and labor alike had been atomized in pursuit of an individualist economy. Herein lay the radical character of the capitalist ideology.

That the workingman sensed the radical change and objected to it is evident from what some American labor leaders said about their unions. Without rejecting the new freedom which labor enjoyed, John Mitchell, of the Mine Workers, pointed out that the union "stands for fraternity, complete and absolute." Samuel Gompers' eulogy of the social microcosm which was the trade union has the same ring. "A hundred times we have said it," he wrote, "and we say it again, that trade unionism contains within itself the potentialities of working class regeneration." The union is a training ground for democracy and provides "daily object lessons in ideal justice; it breathes into the working classes the spirit of unity"; but above all, it affords that needed sense of community. The labor union "provides a field for noble comradeship, for deeds of loyalty, for self-sacrifice beneficial to one's fellow-workers." In the trade union, in short, the workers could obtain another variety of that sense of community, of comradeship, as Gompers put it, which the acid of individualistic capitalism had dissolved.

And there was another objection to the transformation of labor into an exchangeable commodity. The theoretical justification for the conversion of the factors of production into commodities is that the maximum amount of goods can be produced under such a regime. The increased production is deemed desirable because it would insure greater amounts of goods for human consumption and therefore a better life for all. Unfortunately for the theory, however, labor cannot be separated from the men who provide it. To make labor a commodity is to make the men who provide labor commodities also. Thus one is left with the absurdity of turning men into commodities in order to give men a better life!...

Seen in this light, the trade union movement stands out as a truly conservative force. Almost instinctively, the workers joined labor unions in order to preserve their humanity and social character against the excessively individualistic doctrines of industrial capitalism. Eventually, the workers' organizations succeeded in halting the drive to the atomized society which capitalism demanded, and in doing so, far from destroying the system, compelled it to be humane as well as productive.

The essential conservatism of the labor movement is to be seen in particular as well as in general. The organizations of American labor that triumphed or at least survived in the course of industrialization were conspicuous for their acceptance of the private property, profit-oriented society. They evinced little of the radical, anticapitalist ideology and rhetoric so common among European trade unions. Part of the reason for this was the simple fact that all Americans—including workers—were incipient capitalists waiting for "the break." But at bottom it would seem that the conservatism of American labor in this sense is the result of the same forces which inhibited the growth of socialism and other radical anticapitalist ideologies. This question will be dealt with at some length at the end of this chapter.

"The overshadowing problem of the American labor movement," an eminent labor historian has written, "has always been the problem of staying organized. No other labor movement has ever had to contend with the fragility so characteristic of American labor organizations." So true has this been that even today the United States ranks below Italy and Austria in percentage of workers organized (about 25 per cent as compared, for instance, with Sweden's 90 per cent). In such an atmosphere, the history of organized labor in America has been both painful and conservative. Of the two major national organizations of workers which developed in the latter half of the nineteenth century, only the cautious, restrictive, pragmatic American Federation of Labor [A.F. of L.] lived into the twentieth century. The other, the Knights of Labor, once the more powerful and promising, as well as the less accommodating in goals and aspirations, succumbed to Selig Perlman's disease of fragility.

Founded in 1869, the Noble Order of the Knights of Labor recorded its greatest successes in the 1880's, when its membership rolls carried 700,000 names. As the A.F. of L. was later to define the term for Americans, the Knights did not seem to constitute a legitimate trade union at all. Anyone who worked, except liquor dealers, bankers, lawyers, and physicians, could join, and some thousands of women workers and Negroes were members in good standing of this brotherhood of toilers. But the crucial deviation of the Knights from the more orthodox approach to labor organization was its belief in worker-owned producers' co-operatives, which were intended to make each worker his own employer. In this way, the order felt, the degrading dependence of the worker upon the employer would be eliminated. "There is no good reason," Terence V. Powderly, Grand Master Workman of the order, told his followers, "why labor cannot, through co-operation, own and operate mines, factories and railroads."

In this respect the order repudiated the direction in which the America of its time was moving. It expressed the small-shopkeeper mentality which dominated the thinking of many American workers, despite the obvious trend in the economy toward the big and the impersonal. As the General Assembly of 1884 put it, "our Order contemplates a radical change, while Trades' Unions... accept the industrial system as it is, and endeavor to adapt themselves to it. The attitude of our Order to the existing industrial system is necessarily one of war." Though the order called this attitude "radical," a more accurate term, in view of the times, would have been "conservative" or "reactionary."

In practice, however, the Knights presented no more of a threat to capitalism than any other trade union. Indeed, their avowed opposition to the strike meant that labor's most potent weapon was only reluctantly drawn from the scabbard. The Constitution of 1884 said, "Strikes at best afford only temporary relief"; members should learn to depend on education, co-operation, and political action to attain "the abolition of the wage system."

Though the order officially joined in political activity and Grand Master Workman Powderly was at one time mayor of Scranton, its forays into politics accomplished little. The experience was not lost on shrewd Samuel Gompers, whose American Federation of Labor studiously eschewed any alignments with political parties, practicing instead the more neutral course of "rewarding friends and punishing enemies."

In a farewell letter in 1893, Powderly realistically diagnosed the ills of his moribund order, but offered no cure: "Teacher of important and much-needed reforms, she has been obliged to practice differently from her teachings. Advocating arbitration and conciliation as first steps in labor disputes she has been forced to take upon her shoulders the responsibilities of the aggressor first and, when hope of arbitrating and conciliation failed, to beg of the opposing side to do what we should have applied for in the first instance. Advising against strikes we have been in the midst of them. While not a political party we have been forced into the attitude of taking political action."

For all its fumblings, ineptitude, and excessive idealism, the Knights did organize more workers on a national scale than had ever been done before. At once premature and reactionary, it nonetheless planted the seeds of industrial unionism which, while temporarily overshadowed by the successful craft organization of the A.F. of L., ultimately bore fruit in the C.I.O. [Committee for Industrial Organization]. Moreover, its idealism, symbolized in its admission of Negroes and women, and more in tune with the mid-twentieth century than the late nineteenth, signified its commitment to the ideals of the democratic tradition. For these reasons the Knights were a transitional type of unionism, somewhere between the utopianism of the 1830's and the pragmatism of the A.F. of L. It seemed to take time for labor institutions to fit the American temper.

In the course of his long leadership of the American Federation of Labor, Samuel Gompers welcomed many opportunities to define the purposes of his beloved organization....

"The trade unions are the business organizations of the wage-earners," Gompers explained in 1906, "to attend to the business of the wage-earners." Later he expressed it more tersely: "The trade union is not a Sunday school. It is an organization of wage-earners, dealing with economic, social, political and moral questions." As Gompers' crossing of swords with Hillquit demonstrated, there was no need or place for theories. "I saw," the labor leader wrote years later, in looking back on his early life in the labor movement, "the danger of entangling alliances with intellectuals who did not understand that to experiment with the labor movement was to experiment with human life.... I saw that the betterment of workingmen must come primarily through workingmen."

In an age of big business, Samuel Gompers made trade unionism a business, and his reward was the survival of his Federation. In a country with a heterogeneous population of unskilled immigrants, reviled and feared Negroes, and native workers, he cautiously confined his fragile organization to the more skilled workers and the more acceptable elements in the population. The result was a narrow but lasting structure.

Though never ceasing to ask for "more," the A.F. of L. presented no threat to capitalism. "Labor Unions are *for* the workingman, but against no one," John Mitchell of the United Mine Workers pointed out. "They are not hostile to employers, not inimical to the interests of the general public.... There is no necessary hostility between labor and capital," he concluded. Remorselessly pressed by Morris Hillquit as Gompers was, he still refused to admit that the labor movement was, as Hillquit put it, "conducted against the interests of the employing people." Rather, Gompers insisted, "It is conducted for the interests of the employing people." And the rapid expansion of the American economy bore witness to the fact that the Federation was a friend and not an enemy of industrial capitalism. Its very adaptability to the American scene—its conservative ideology, if it was an ideology at all—as Selig Perlman has observed, contained the key to its success. "The unionism of the American Federation of Labor 'fitted'... because it recognized the virtually inalterable conservatism of the American community as regards private property and private initiative in economic life."

This narrow conception of the proper character of trade unionism—job consciousness, craft unionism, lack of interest in organizing the unskilled, the eschewing of political activity—which Gompers and his Federation worked out for the American worker continued to dominate organized labor until the earthquake of the depression cracked the mold and the Committee for Industrial Organization issued forth.

## NOBODY HERE BUT US CAPITALISTS

"By any simple interpretation of the Marxist formula," commented Socialist Norman Thomas in 1950, "the United States, by all odds the greatest industrial nation and that in which capitalism is most advanced, should have had long ere this is a very strong socialist movement if not a socialist revolution. Actually," he correctly observed, "in no advanced western nation is organized socialism so weak." Nor was this the first time Socialists had wondered about this. Over eighty years ago, in the high noon of European socialism, Marxist theoretician Werner Sombart impatiently put a similar question: *"Warum gibt es in den Vereinigten Staaten keinen Sozialismus?"*

The failure of the American working class to become seriously interested in socialism in this period or later is one of the prominent signs of the political and economic conservatism of American labor and, by extension, of the American people as a whole. This failure is especially noteworthy when one recalls that in industrialized countries the world over—Japan, Italy, Germany, Belgium, to mention only a few—a Socialist movement has been a "normal" concomitant of industrialization. Even newly opened countries like Australia and New Zealand have Labour parties. Rather than ask, as Americans are wont to do, why these countries have nurtured such frank repudiators of traditional capitalism, it is the American deviation from the general pattern which demands explanation.

In large part, the explanation lies in the relative weakness of class consciousness among Americans. Historically, socialism is the gospel of the *class-conscious* working class, of the workingmen who feel themselves bound to their status for life and their children after them. It is not accidental, therefore, that the major successes of modern socialism are in Europe, where class lines have been clearly and tightly drawn since time immemorial, and where the possibility of upward social movement has been severely restricted in practice if not in law. Americans may from time to time have exhibited class consciousness and even class hatred, but such attitudes have not persisted, nor have they been typical. As Matthew Arnold observed in 1888, "it is indubitable that rich men are regarded" in America "with less envy and hatred than rich men in Europe." A labor leader like Terence Powderly was convinced that America was without classes. "No matter how much we may say about classes and class distinction, there are no classes in the United States.... I have always refused to admit that we have classes in our country just as I have refused to admit that the labor of a man's hand or brain is a commodity." And there was a long line of commentators on American society, running back at least to Crèvecoeur, to illustrate the prevalence of Powderly's belief.

The weakness of American class consciousness is doubtless to be attributed, at least in part, to the fluidity of the social structure. Matthew Arnold, for example, accounted for the relative absence of class hatred on such grounds, as did such very different foreign observers as Werner Sombart and Lord Bryce. The British union officials of the Mosely Commission, it will be recalled, were convinced of the superior opportunities for success enjoyed by American workers. Stephan Thernstrom in his study of Newburyport gave some measure of the opportunities for economic improvement among the working class when he reported that all but 5 per cent of those unskilled workers who persisted from 1850 to 1900 ended the period with either property or an improvement in occupational status.

Men who are hoping to move upward on the social scale, and for whom there is some chance that they can do so, do not identify themselves with their present class. "In worn-out, king-ridden Europe, men stay where they are born," immigrant Charles O'Conor, who became an ornament of the New York bar, contended in 1869. "But in America a man is accounted a failure, and certainly ought to be, who has not risen about his father's station in life." So long as Horatio Alger means anything to Americans, Karl Marx will be just another German philosopher.

The political history of the United States also contributed to the failure of socialism. In Europe, because the franchise came slowly and late to the worker, he often found himself first an industrial worker and only later a voter. It was perfectly natural, in such a context, for him to vote according to his economic interests and to join a political party avowedly dedicated to those class interests. The situation was quite different in America, however, for political democracy came to America prior to the Industrial Revolution. By the time the industrial transformation was getting under way after 1865, all adult males could vote and, for the most part, they had already chosen their political affiliations without reference to their economic class; they were Republicans or Democrats first and workers only second —a separation between politics and economics which has become traditional in America. "In the main," wrote Lord Bryce about the United States of the 1880's, "political questions proper have held the first place in a voter's mind and questions affecting his class second." Thus, when it came to voting, workers registered their convictions as citizens, not as workingmen. (In our own day, there have been several notable failures of labor leaders to swing their labor vote, such as John L. Lewis' attempt in 1940 and the C.I.O.'s in 1950 against Senator Taft and the inability of union leaders to be sure they could hold their members to support Hubert Humphrey in the Presidential election of 1968.) To most workers, the Socialist party appeared as merely a third party in a country where such parties are political last resorts.

Nor did socialism in America gain much support from the great influx of immigration. It is true that many Germans came to this country as convinced Socialists and thus swelled the party's numbers, but they also served to pin the stigma of "alien" upon the movement. Even more important was the fact that the very heterogeneity of the labor force, as a result of immigration, often made animosities between ethnic groups more important to the worker than class antagonism. It must have seemed to many workers that socialism, with its central concern for class and its denial of ethnic antagonism, was not dealing with the realities of economic life.

In the final reckoning, however, the failure of socialism in America is to be attributed to the success of capitalism. The expanding economy provided opportunities for all, no matter how meager they might appear or actually be at times. Though the rich certainly seemed to get richer at a prodigious rate, the poor, at least, did not get poorer—and often got richer. Studies of real wages between 1865 and 1900 bear this out. Though prices rose, wages generally rose faster, so that there was a net gain in average income for workers during the last decades of the century. The increase in real wages in the first fifteen years of the twentieth century was negligible—but, significantly, there was no decline. The high wages and relatively good standard of living of the American worker were patent as far as the twenty-three British labor leaders of the Mosely Commission were concerned. The American is a "better educated, better housed, better clothed and more energetic man than his British brother," concluded the sponsor, Alfred Mosely, a businessman himself.

But America challenged socialism on other grounds than mere material things. Some years ago an obscure Socialist, Leon Samson, undertook to account for the failure of socialism to win the allegiance of the American working class; his psychological explanation merits attention because it illuminates the influence exercised by the American Dream. Americanism, Samson observes, is not so much a tradition as it is a doctrine; it is "what socialism is to a socialist." Americanism to the American is a body of ideas like "democracy, liberty, opportunity, to all of which the American adheres rationalistically much as a socialist adheres to his socialism—because it does him good, because it gives him work, because, so he thinks, it guarantees him happiness. America has thus served as a substitute for socialism."

Socialism has been unable to make headway with Americans, Samson goes on, because "every concept in socialism has its substitutive counterconcept in Americanism." As Marxism holds out the prospect of a classless society, so does Americanism. The opportunities for talent and the better material life which socialism promised for the future were already available in America and constituted the image in which America was beheld throughout the world. The freedom and equality which the oppressed proletariat of Europe craved were a reality in America—or at least sufficiently so to blunt the cutting edge of the Socialist appeal. Even the sense of mission, of being in step with the processes of history, which unquestionably was one of the appeals of socialism, was also a part of the American Dream. Have not all Americans cherished their country as a model for the world? Was not this the "last, best hope of earth"? Was not God on the side of America, as history, according to Marx, was on the side of socialism and the proletariat?

Over a century ago, Alexis de Tocqueville predicted a mighty struggle for the minds of men between two giants of Russia and the United States. In the ideologies of socialism and the American Dream, his forecast has been unexpectedly fulfilled.

# POSTSCRIPT

## Was the American Labor Movement Radical?

Laurie presents a sophisticated analysis of how the Knights of Labor traced its values back to the republican ideology of the generation of the Founding Fathers in the late eighteenth century. The Knights embraced a unified conception of work and culture that extolled the virtues of individual hard work, love of family, and love of country.

Membership in the Knights was open to all manual workers. Excluded were bankers, lawyers, stockbrokers, gamblers, and liquor dealers—individuals who were associated with idleness and corruption. Merchants and manufacturers could join if they did not exploit workers. Terence V. Powderly, long-time leader of the Knights, distinguished between *producers,* who were the wage earners of society, and *capitalists,* who were the accumulators and monopolists. The Knights were accepting a variety of workers at its peak, before the Haymarket Square riot in 1886. Most of the new members came from the ranks of the semiskilled and unskilled workers.

Laurie argues that, in ideological terms, the Knights occupied "a middle ground between the individualistic libertarianism of bourgeois America and the collectivism of working-class socialists." The Knights were to the left of the two parties that existed in the Gilded Age in that they advocated a more activist national government. Still, as Laurie points out, few Knights were socialists because most Americans, including the early radicals, believed the old republican adage that an overdependency on government corrupted the body politic.

Degler takes a different approach to this issue. In his view, the real radicals were the industrialists who created a more mature system of capitalism. Labor was merely fashioning a conservative response to the radical changes brought about by big business. The inability of the Knights of Labor to accept the changes in the industrial system led to its demise, according to Degler. Its place was taken by the American Federation of Labor, whose long-time leader Samuel Gompers was famous for his acceptance of the wage system and American capitalism. The American Federation of Labor adopted practical goals, striving to improve the lot of the workers by negotiating for better hours, wages, and working conditions.

Degler argues that socialism failed in America because Americans lacked a working-class consciousness due to their prevailing belief in real mobility. Also, a labor party failed to emerge because Americans developed their commitment to the two-party system before the issues of the Industrial Revolution came to the forefront. The influx of immigrants from a variety of countries created a heterogeneous labor force, and animosities between rival ethnic groups appeared more real than class antagonisms.

For the past two decades historians have begun to study the social and cultural environment of the American working class. The approach is modeled after E.P. Thompson's highly influential and sophisticated Marxist analysis *The Making of the English Working Class* (1963), which is the capstone of an earlier generation of British and French social historians. The father of the "new labor history" in the United States is the late Herbert G. Gutman, whose collections of essays in *Work, Culture and Society* (Alfred A. Knopf, 1976) and *Power and Culture: Essays on the American Working Class* (Pantheon Books, 1987) are the starting points for every student of the period. Gutman was the first to discuss American workers as a group separate from the organized union movement. Gutman's distinction between preindustrial and industrial values laid the groundwork for a whole generation of scholars who have engaged in case studies of both union and nonunion workers in both urban and rural areas of America. Such works have proliferated in recent years, and students should sample the following collections of articles: Daniel J. Lieb, ed., *The Labor History Reader* (University of Illinois Press, 1985); Charles Stephenson and Robert Asher, eds., *Life and Labor: Dimensions of American Working Class History* (State University of New York Press, 1986); and Milton Cantor, ed., *American Working Class Culture: Explorations in American Labor and Social History* (Greenwood Press, 1979).

The question of why the United States never developed a major socialist movement or labor party has been the subject of much speculation. A good starting point is John H. Laslett and Seymour Martin Lipset, eds., *Failure of a Dream: Essays in the History of American Socialism* (Doubleday, 1974). Political scientist Theodore J. Lowi argues that the U.S. political system of federalism prevented a socialist movement in "Why Is There No Socialism in the United States?" *Society* (January/February 1985). Finally, see historian Eric Foner's "Why Has There Been No Socialist Transformation in Any Advanced Capitalist Society?" *History Workshop* (Spring 1984).

There are a number of general histories worth consulting. Three old-school histories that are sympathetic to labor are Foster Rhea Dulles, *Labor in America* (Crowell, 1960); Henry Pelling, *American Labor* (University of Chicago Press, 1960); and Joseph A. Rayback, *A History of American Labor* (Macmillan, 1959). The three most important "new-school" labor histories are Bruce Laurie, *Artisans Into Workers: Labor in Nineteenth-Century America* (Hill & Wang, 1989); James R. Green, *The World of the Worker: Labor in Twentieth-Century America* (Hill & Wang, 1980); and Leon Fink, *Workingmen's Democracy: The Knights of Labor and American Politics* (University of Illinois Press, 1983).

Two journals devote entire issues to the American labor movement. Brian Greenberg has edited "Labor History and Public History" for the fall 1989 issue of *The Public Historian*, while Leon Fink and others have written interpretative essays in the February 1982 edition of *Social Education*.

# ISSUE 4

## Were Immigrants to the United States "Uprooted"?

**YES: Oscar Handlin,** from *The Uprooted: The Epic Story of the Great Migrations That Made the American People,* 2d ed. (Little, Brown, 1973)

**NO: John Bodnar,** from *The Transplanted: A History of Immigrants in Urban America* (Indiana University Press, 1985)

### ISSUE SUMMARY

**YES:** Pulitzer Prize–winning historian Oscar Handlin insists that immigrants to the United States in the late nineteenth century were alienated from the cultural traditions of the homelands they had left as well as from those of their adopted country.

**NO:** Associate professor of history John Bodnar maintains that various immigrant groups retained, modified, and transformed their Old World cultures in response to urban/industrial America in the years between 1880 and 1920.

Immigration has been one of the most powerful forces shaping the development of the United States since at least the early seventeenth century. In fact, it should not be overlooked that even the ancestors of the country's Native American population were migrants to this "New World" some 37,000 years ago. There can be little doubt that the United States is a nation of immigrants, a reality reenforced by the motto "E Pluribus Unum" (one out of many), which is used on the Great Seal of the United States and on several U.S. coins.

The history of immigration to the United States can be organized into four major periods of activity: 1607–1830, 1830–1890, 1890–1924, and 1968 to the present. During the first period, the seventeenth and early eighteenth centuries, there was a growing number of European migrants who arrived in North America mostly from the British Isles, as well as several million Africans who were forced to migrate to colonial America as a consequence of the Atlantic slave trade. While increased numbers of non-English immigrants arrived in America in the eighteenth century, it was not until the nineteenth century that large numbers of immigrants from other northern and western European countries, as well as from China, arrived and created significant population diversity. Two European groups predominated during this second major period: as a result of the potato famine, large numbers of Irish Catholics emigrated in the 1850s; and, for a variety of religious, political, and economic reasons, so did many Germans. Chinese immigration increased, and these immigrants found work in low-paying service industries, such as laundries and restaurants, and as railroad construction workers.

The Industrial Revolution of the late nineteenth century sparked a third wave of immigration. Immigrants by the millions began pouring into the United States attracted by the unskilled factory jobs that were becoming more abundant. Migration was encouraged by various companies whose agents distributed handbills throughout Europe advertising the ready availability of good paying jobs in America. This phase of immigration, however, represented something of a departure from previous ones as most of these "new immigrants" came from southern and eastern Europe. This flood continued until World War I, after which mounting xenophobia culminated in the passage by Congress in 1924 of the National Origins Act, which restricted the number of immigrants into the country to 150,000 annually, and which placed quotas on the number of immigrants permitted from each foreign country.

In the aftermath of World War II, restrictions were eased for several groups, especially those who survived the Nazi death camps or who sought asylum in the United States in the wake of the aggressive movement into Eastern Europe by the Soviet Union after the war. But restrictions against Asians and Africans were not lifted until the Immigration Reform Act of 1965, which set in motion a fourth phase of immigration history. In contrast to earlier migrations, the newest groups have come from countries in Latin America and Asia.

Efforts to curb immigration to the United States reflect an anxiety and ambivalence that many Americans have long held with regard to "foreigners." Anxious to benefit from the labor of these newcomers but still hesitant to accept the immigrants as full-fledged citizens entitled to the same rights and privileges as native-born residents, Americans have on a number of occasions discovered that they had an "immigrant problem." Harsh anti-immigrant sentiment based on prejudicial attitudes toward race, ethnicity, or religion have periodically boiled over into violence and calls for legislation to restrict immigration.

What effect did these kinds of attitudes have on those who migrated to the United States in search of a life better than the one they experienced in their native lands? What happened to their Old World customs and traditions? How fully did immigrants assimilate into the new culture they encountered in the United States? Was the United States, in fact, a melting pot for immigrants, as some have suggested?

In the following readings, Oscar Handlin argues that the immigrants were uprooted from their Old World cultures as they attempted to adjust to an unfamiliar and often hostile environment in the United States. John Bodnar substantially modifies Handlin's view, explaining that while immigrants in the years between 1880 and 1920 were sucked into an economic system dominated by the worldwide industrial revolution, they maintained a substantial amount of their Old World cultures through tight-knit family systems.

# YES

## Oscar Handlin

# THE SHOCK OF ALIENATION

As the passing years widened the distance, the land the immigrants had left acquired charm and beauty. Present problems blurred those they had left unsolved behind; and in the haze of memory it seemed to these people they had formerly been free of present dissatisfactions. It was as if the Old World became a great mirror into which they looked to see right all that was wrong with the New. The landscape was prettier, the neighbors more friendly, and religion more efficacious; in the frequent crises when they reached the limits of their capacities, the wistful reflection came: *This would not have happened there.*

The real contacts were, however, disappointing. The requests—that back there a mass be said, or a wise one consulted, or a religious medal be sent over—those were gestures full of hope. But the responses were inadequate; like all else they shrank in the crossing. The immigrants wrote, but the replies, when they came, were dull, even trite in their mechanical phrases, or so it seemed to those who somehow expected these messages to evoke the emotions that had gone into their own painfully composed letters. Too often the eagerly attended envelopes proved to be only empty husks, the inner contents valueless. After the long wait before the postman came, the sheets of garbled writing were inevitably below expectations. There was a trying sameness to the complaints of hard times, to the repetitious petty quarrels; and before long there was impatience with the directness with which the formal greeting led into the everlasting requests for aid.

This last was a sore point with the immigrants. The friends and relatives who had stayed behind could not get it out of their heads that in America the streets were paved with gold. *Send me for a coat... There is a piece of land here and if only you would send, we could buy it... Our daughter could be married, but we have not enough for a dowry... We are ashamed, everyone else gets... much more frequently than we.* Implicit in these solicitations was the judgment that the going-away had been a desertion, that unfulfilled obligations still remained, and that the village could claim assistance as a right from its departed members.

From the United States it seemed there was no comprehension, back there, of the difficulties of settlement. It was exasperating by sacrifices to scrape together the remittances and to receive in return a catalogue of new needs, as if there were not needs enough in the New World too. The immigrants never shook off the sense of obligation to help; but they did come to regard their Old Countrymen as the kind of people who depended on help. The trouble with the Europeans was, they could not stand on their own feet.

The cousin green off the boat earned the same negative appraisal. Though he be a product of the homeland, yet here he cut a pitiable figure; awkward manners, rude clothes, and a thoroughgoing ineptitude in the new situation were his most prominent characteristics. The older settler found the welcome almost frozen on his lips in the face of such backwardness.

In every real contact the grandeur of the village faded; it did not match the immigrants' vision of it and it did not stand up in a comparison with America. When the picture came, the assembled family looked at it beneath the light. This was indeed the church, but it had not been remembered so; and the depressing contrast took some of the joy out of remembering.

The photograph did not lie. There it was, a low building set against the dusty road, weather-beaten and making a candid display of its ill-repair. But the recollections did not lie either. As if it had been yesterday that they passed through those doors, they could recall the sense of spaciousness and elevation that sight of the structure had always aroused.

Both impressions were true, but irreconcilable. The mental image and the paper representation did not jibe because the one had been formed out of the standards and values of the Old Country, while the other was viewed in the light of the standards and values of the New. And it was the same with every other retrospective contact. Eagerly the immigrants continued to look back across the Atlantic in search of the satisfactions of fellowship. But the search was not rewarded. Having become Americans, they were no longer villagers. Though they might willingly assume the former obligations and recognize the former responsibilities, they could not recapture the former points of view or hold to the former judgments. They had seen too much, experienced too much to be again members of the community. It was a vain mission on which they continued to dispatch the letters; these people, once separated, would never belong again.

* * *

Their home now was a country in which they had not been born. Their place in society they had established for themselves through the hardships of crossing and settlement. The process had changed them, had altered the most intimate aspects of their lives. Every effort to cling to inherited ways of acting and thinking had led into a subtle adjustment by which those ways were given a new American form. No longer Europeans, could the immigrants then say that they belonged in America? The answer depended upon the conceptions held by other citizens of the United States of the character of the nation and of the role of the newcomers within it.

In the early nineteenth century, those already established on this side of the ocean regarded immigration as a positive good. When travel by sea became safe after the general peace of 1815 and the first fresh arrivals trickled in, there was a general disposition to welcome the movement. The favorable attitude persisted even when the tide mounted to the flood levels of the 1840's and 1850's. The man off the boat was then accepted without question or condition.

The approval of unlimited additions to the original population came easily to Americans who were conscious of the youth of their country. Standing at the edge of an immense continent, they were moved by the challenge of empty land almost endless in its extension. Here was room enough, and more, for all who would bend their energies to its exploitation. The shortage was of labor and not of acres; every pair of extra hands increased the value of the abundant resources and widened opportunities for everyone.

The youth of the nation also justified the indiscriminate admission of whatever foreigners came to these shores. There was high faith in the destiny of the Republic, assurance that its future history would justify the Revolution and the separation from Great Britain. The society and the culture that would emerge in this territory would surpass those of the Old World because they would not slavishly imitate the outmoded forms and the anachronistic traditions that constricted men in Europe. The United States would move in new directions of its own because its people were a new people.

There was consequently a vigorous insistence that this country was not simply an English colony become independent. It was a nation unique in its origins, produced by the mixture of many different types out of which had come an altogether fresh amalgam, the American. The ebullient citizens who believed and argued that their language, their literature, their art, and their polity were distinctive and original also believed and argued that their population had not been derived from a single source but had rather acquired its peculiar characteristics from the blending of a variety of strains.

There was confidence that the process would continue. The national type had not been fixed by its given antecedents; it was emerging from the experience of life on a new continent. Since the quality of men was determined not by the conditions surrounding their birth, but by the environment within which they passed their lives, it was pointless to select among them. All would come with minds and spirits fresh for new impressions; and being in America would make Americans of them. Therefore it was best to admit freely everyone who wished to make a home here. The United States would then be a great smelting pot, great enough so that there was room for all who voluntarily entered; and the nation that would ultimately be cast from the crucible would be all the richer for the diversity of the elements that went into the molten mixture.

The legislation of most of the nineteenth century reflected this receptive attitude. The United States made no effort actively to induce anyone to immigrate, but neither did it put any bars in the way of their coming. Occasional laws in the four decades after 1819 set up shipping regulations in the hope of improving the conditions of the passage. In practice, the provisions that specified the minimum quantities of food and the maximum number of passengers each vessel could carry were easily evaded. Yet the intent of those statutes was to protect the travelers and to remove harsh conditions that might discourage the newcomers.

Nor were state laws any more restrictive in design. The seaports, troubled by the burdens of poor relief, secured the enactment of measures to safeguard their treasuries against such charges. Sometimes the form was a bond to guarantee that the immigrant would not become at once dependent upon public support; sometimes it was a small tax applied to defray the costs of charity. In either case there was no desire to limit entry into the country; and none of these steps had any discernible effect upon the volume of admissions.

Once landed, the newcomer found himself equal in condition to the natives. Within a short period he could be naturalized and acquire all the privileges of a citizen. In some places, indeed, he could vote before the oath in court so transformed his status. In the eyes of society, even earlier than in the eyes of the law, he was an American. . . .

* * *

As the nineteenth century moved into its last quarter, a note of petulance crept into the comments of some Americans who thought about this aspect of the development of their culture. It was a long time now that the melting pot had been simmering, but the end product seemed no closer than before. The experience of life in the United States had not broken down the separateness of the elements mixed into it; each seemed to retain its own identity. Almost a half-century after the great immigration of Irish and Germans, these people had not become indistinguishable from other Americans; they were still recognizably Irish and German. Yet even then, newer waves of newcomers were beating against the Atlantic shore. Was there any prospect that all these multitudes would ever be assimilated, would ever be Americanized?

A generation earlier such questions would not have been asked. Americans of the first half of the century had assumed that any man who subjected himself to the American environment was being Americanized. Since the New World was ultimately to be occupied by a New Man, no mere derivative of any extant stock, but different from and superior to all, there had been no fixed standards of national character against which to measure the behavior of newcomers. The nationality of the new Republic had been supposed fluid, only just evolving; there had been room for infinite variation because diversity rather than uniformity had been normal.

The expression of doubts that some parts of the population might not become fully American implied the existence of a settled criterion of what was American. There had been a time when the society had recognized no distinction among citizens but that between the native and the foreign-born, and that distinction had carried no imputation of superiority or inferiority. Now there were attempts to distinguish among the natives between those who really belonged and those who did not, to separate out those who were born in the United States but whose immigrant parentage cut them off from the truly indigenous folk.

It was difficult to draw the line, however. The census differentiated after 1880 between natives and native-born of foreign parents. But that was an inadequate line of division; it provided no means of social recognition and offered no basis on which the *true Americans* could draw together, identify themselves as such.

Through these years there was a half-conscious quest among some Americans for a term that would describe those whose ancestors were in the United States before the great migrations. Where the New Englanders were, they called themselves Yankees, a word that often came to mean non-Irish or non-Canadian. But Yankee was simply a local designation and did not take in the whole of the old stock. In any case, there was no satisfaction to such a title. Its holders were one group among many, without any distinctive claim to Americanism, cut off from other desirable peoples prominent in the country's past. Only the discovery of common antecedents could eliminate the separations among the really American.

But to find a common denominator, it was necessary to go back a long way. Actually no single discovery was completely satisfactory. Some writers, in time, referred to the civilization of the United States as Anglo-Saxon. By projecting its origins back to early Britain, they implied that their own culture was always English in derivation, and made foreigners of the descendants of Irishmen and Germans, to say nothing of the later arrivals. Other men preferred a variant and achieved the same exclusion by referring to themselves as "the English-speaking people," a title which assumed there was a unity and uniqueness to the clan which settled the home island, the dominions, and the United States. Still others relied upon a somewhat broader appellation. They talked of themselves as Teutonic and argued that what was distinctively American originated in the forests of Germany; in this view, only the folk whose ancestors had experienced the freedom of tribal self-government and the liberation of the Protestant Reformation were fully American.

These terms had absolutely no historical justification. They nevertheless achieved a wide currency in the thinking of the last decades of the nineteenth century. Whatever particular phrase might serve the purpose of a particular author or speaker, all expressed the conviction that some hereditary element had given form to American culture. The conclusion was inescapable: to be Americanized, the immigrants must conform to the American way of life completely defined in advance of their landing.

* * *

There were two counts to the indictment that the immigrants were not so conforming. They were, first, accused of their poverty. Many benevolent citizens, distressed by the miserable conditions in the districts inhabited by the laboring people, were reluctant to believe that such social flaws were indigenous to the New World. It was tempting, rather, to ascribe them to the defects of the newcomers, to improvidence, slovenliness, and ignorance rather than to inability to earn a living wage.

Indeed to those whose homes were uptown the ghettos were altogether alien territory associated with filth and vice and crime. It did not seem possible that men could lead a decent existence in such quarters. The good vicar on a philanthropic tour was shocked by the moral dangers of the dark unlighted hallway. His mind rushed to the defense of the respectable young girl: *Whatever her wishes may be, she can do nothing—shame prevents her from crying out.* The intention of the reformer was to improve housing, but the summation nevertheless was, *You cannot make an American citizen out of a slum.*

The newcomers were also accused of congregating together in their own groups and of an unwillingness to mix with outsiders. The foreign-born flocked to the great cities and stubbornly refused to spread out as farmers over the countryside; that alone was offensive to a society which still retained an ideal of rusticity. But even the Germans in Wisconsin and the Scandinavians in Minnesota held aloofly to themselves. Everywhere, the strangers persisted in their strangeness and willfully stood apart from American life. A prominent educator sounded the warning: *Our task is to break up their settlements, to assimilate and amalgamate these people and to implant in them the Anglo-Saxon conception of righteousness, law, and order.*

It was no simple matter to meet this challenge. The older residents were quick to criticize the separateness of the immigrant but hesitant when he made a move to narrow the distance. The householders of Fifth Avenue or Beacon Street or Nob Hill could readily perceive the evils of the slums but they were not inclined to welcome as a neighbor the former denizen of the East Side or the North End or the Latin Quarter who had acquired the means to get away. Among Protestants there was much concern over the growth of Catholic, Jewish, and Orthodox religious organizations, but there was no eagerness at all to provoke a mass conversion that might crowd the earlier churches with a host of poor foreigners. When the population of its neighborhood changed, the parish was less likely to try to attract the newcomers than to close or sell its building and move to some other section.

Indeed there was a fundamental ambiguity to the thinking of those who talked about "assimilation" in these years. They had arrived at their own view that American culture was fixed, formed from its origins, by shutting out the great mass of immigrants who were not English or at least not Teutonic. Now it was expected that those excluded people would alter themselves to earn their portion in Americanism. That process could only come about by increasing the contacts between the older and the newer inhabitants, by sharing jobs, churches, residences. Yet in practice, the man who thought himself an Anglo-Saxon found proximity to the other folk just come to the United States uncomfortable and distasteful and, in his own life, sought to increase rather than to lessen the gap between his position and theirs.

There was an escape from the horns of this unpleasant dilemma. It was tempting to resolve the difficulty by arguing that the differences between Americans on the one hand and Italians or Jews or Poles on the other were so deep as to admit of no conciliation. If these other stocks were cut off by their own innate nature, by the qualities of their heredity, then the original breed was justified both in asserting the fixity of its own character and in holding off from contact with the aliens....

The fear of everything alien instilled by the First World War brought to fullest flower the seeds of racist thinking. Three enormously popular books by an anthropologist, a eugenist, and a historian revealed to hundreds of thousands of horrified Nordics how their great race had been contaminated by contact with lesser breeds, dwarfed in stature, twisted in mentality, and ruthless in the pursuit of their own self-interest.

These ideas passed commonly in the language of the time. No doubt many Americans who spoke in the bitter terms of race used the words in a figurative sense or in some other way qualified their acceptance of the harsh doctrine. After all, they still recognized the validity of the American tradition of equal and open opportunities, of the Christian tradition of the brotherhood of man. Yet, if they were sometimes troubled by the contradiction, nevertheless enough of them believed fully the racist conceptions so that five million could become members of the Ku Klux Klan in the early 1920's....

* * *

The activities of the Klan were an immediate threat to the immigrants and were resisted as such. But there was also a wider import to the movement. This was evidence, at last become visible, that the newcomers were among the excluded. The judgment at which the proponents of assimilation had only hinted, about which the racist thinkers had written obliquely, the Klan brought to the open. The hurt came from the fact that the mouthings of the Kleagle were not eccentricities, but only extreme statements of beliefs long on the margin of acceptance by many Americans. To the foreign-born this was demonstration of what they already suspected, that they would remain as alienated from the New World as they had become from the Old.

Much earlier the pressure of their separateness had begun to disturb the immigrants. As soon as the conception of Americanization had acquired the connotation of conformity with existing patterns, the whole way of group life of the newcomers was questioned. Their adjustment had depended upon their ability as individuals in a free society to adapt themselves to their environment through what forms they chose. The demand by their critics that the adjustment take a predetermined course seemed to question their right, as they were, to a place in American society.

Not that these people concerned themselves with theories of nationalism, but in practice the hostility of the "natives" provoked unsettling doubts about the propriety of the most innocent actions. The peasant who had become a Polish Falcon or a Son of Italy, in his own view, was acting as an American; this was not a step he could have taken at home. To subscribe to a newspaper was the act of a citizen of the New World, not of the Old, even if the journal was one of the thousand published by 1920 in languages other than English. When the immigrants heard their societies and their press described as un-American they could only conclude that they had somehow become involved in an existence that belonged neither in the old land nor in the new.

Yet the road of conformity was also barred to them. There were matters in which they wished to be like others, undistinguished from anyone else, but they never hit upon the means of becoming so. There was no pride in the surname, which in Europe had been little used, and many a new arrival was willing enough to make a change, suitable to the new country. But August Björkegren was not much better off when he called himself Burke, nor the Blumberg who became Kelly. The Lithuanians and Slovenes who moved into the Pennsylvania mining fields often endowed themselves with nomenclature of the older settlers, of the Irish and Italians there before them. In truth, these people found it difficult to know what were the "American" forms they were expected to take on.

What they did know was that they had not succeeded, that they had not established themselves to the extent that they could expect to be treated as if they belonged where they were.

If he was an alien, and poor, and in many ways helpless, still he was human, and it rankled when his dignity as a person was disregarded. He felt an undertone of acrimony in every contact with an official. Men in uniform always found him unworthy of respect; the bullying police made capital of his fear of the law; the postmen made sport of the foreign writing on his letters; the streetcar conductors laughed at his groping requests for directions. Always he was patronized as an object of charity, or almost so.

His particular enemies were the officials charged with his special oversight. When misfortune drove him to seek assistance or when government regulations brought them to inspect his home, he encountered the social workers, made ruthless in the disregard of his sentiments by the certainty of their own benevolent intentions. Confident of their personal and social superiority and armed with the ideology of the sociologists who had trained them, the emissaries of the public and private agencies were bent on improving the immigrant to a point at which he would no longer recognize himself.

The man who had dealings with the social workers was often sullen and unco-operative; he disliked the necessity of becoming a case, of revealing his dependence to strangers. He was also suspicious, feared there would be no understanding of his own way of life or of his problems; and he was resentful, because the powerful outsiders were judging him by superficial standards of their own. The starched young gentleman from the settlement house took stock from the middle of the kitchen. Were there framed pictures on the walls? Was there a piano, books? He made a note for the report: *This family is not yet Americanized; they are still eating Italian food.*

The services are valuable, but taking them is degrading. It is a fine thing to learn the language of the country; but one must be treated as a child to do so. *We keep saying all the time, This is a desk, this is a door. I know it is a desk and a door. What for keep saying it all the time? My teacher is a very nice young lady, very young. She does not understand what I want to talk about or know about.*

The most anguished conflicts come from the refusal of the immigrants to see the logic of their poverty. In the office it seems reasonable enough: people incapable of supporting themselves would be better off with someone to take care of them. It is more efficient to institutionalize the destitute than to allow them, with the aid of charity, to mismanage their homes. But the ignorant poor insist on clinging to their families, threaten suicide at the mention of the Society's refuge, or even of the hospital. What help the woman gets, she is still not satisfied. Back comes the ungrateful letter. *I don't ask you to put me in a poorhouse where I have to cry for my children. I don't ask you to put them in a home and eat somebody else's bread. I can't live here without them. I am so sick for them. I could live at home and spare good eats for them. What good did you give me to send me to the poorhouse? You only want people to live like you but I will not listen to you no more.*

A few dedicated social workers, mostly women, learned to understand the values in the immigrants' own lives. In some states, as the second generation became prominent in politics, government agencies came to co-operate with and protect the newcomers. But these were rare exceptions. They scarcely softened the rule experience everywhere taught the foreign-born, that they were expected to do what they could not do—to live like others.

For the children it was not so difficult. They at least were natives and could learn how to conform; to them the settlement house was not always a threat, but sometimes an opportunity. Indeed they could adopt entire the assumption that national character was long since fixed, only seek for their own group a special place within it. Some justified their Americanism by discovery of a colonial past; within the educated second generation there began a tortuous quest for eighteenth-century antecedents that might give them a portion in American civilization in its narrower connotation. Others sought to gain a sense of participation by separating themselves from later or lower elements in the population; they became involved in agitation against the Orientals, the Negroes, and the newest immigrants, as if thus to draw closer to the truly native. Either course implied a rejection of their parents who had themselves once been green off the boat and could boast of no New World antecedents.

* * *

The old folk knew then they would not come to belong, not through their own experience nor through their offspring. The only adjustment they had been able to make to life in the United States had been one that involved the separateness of their group, one that increased their awareness of the differences between themselves and the rest of the society. In that adjustment they had always suffered from the consciousness they were strangers. The demand that they assimilate, that they surrender their separateness, condemned them always to be outsiders. In practice, the free structure of American life permitted them with few restraints to go their own way, but under the shadow of a consciousness that they would never belong. They had thus completed their alienation from the culture to which they had come, as from that which they had left.

# NO

John Bodnar

# THE TRANSPLANTED: A HISTORY OF IMMIGRANTS IN URBAN AMERICA

## INTRODUCTION

The people who moved to American cities and industrial towns during the first century of American capitalism have been chronicled and described by an abundant number of scholars, novelists, journalists, and other writers and have been ascribed an array of characteristics. Often their flight to America has been seen as the act of desperate individuals fleeing poverty and disorder only to be further weakened by back-breaking labor and inhospitable cities in America. Their fate was one of a life in insulated ethnic ghettos, continual struggle, and an eventual but precarious attachment to the new economy. Others have celebrated these humble newcomers as bearers of proud, long-established traditions which helped to organize their lives amidst the vagaries of the industrial city and served as a context in which they organized their transition, rather successfully, to a new land. A third school of thought has advanced the argument that these newcomers were aspiring individuals whose ties to tradition were loosened in their homelands and who moved to America eager for opportunity, advancement, and all the rewards of capitalism. In this final framework, immigrants moved from tradition-bound peasants to modern, acquisitive individuals.

Most previous descriptions of immigrants assume that the immigrant experience was a common experience shared equally by all; the transition to capitalism is either entirely difficult, conducted entirely within the confines of a traditional but apparently adaptive culture, or entirely rewarding over a given period of time. But even the most cursory glance at an immigrant community or stream will suggest that not all newcomers behaved in a similar fashion, that varying degrees of commitment to an assortment of cultures and ideologies were evident, and that not everyone faced identical experiences. Some individuals pursued modern forms of life and livelihood while others valued more traditional patterns. Workers existed who championed socialism and others died for their attachment to Catholicism. Some immigrants came to America and acquired large fortunes, and many more simply went to work every day with no appreciable gain. What they actually shared in common was a need to confront a new economic order and provide for their own welfare and that of their kin or household group. They all did this but they did so in different ways and with divergent results....

In essence neither immigration nor capitalism as it emerged in the United States would have been possible without each other. Prior to the 1830s American economic growth was extremely slow as little investment in material capital took place and technology advanced slowly. A virtual absence of productivity-raising activity characterized the nation and small populations, low levels of per capita income, and primitive technologies of transportation and communications existed. By 1840, however, this picture was changing as economic growth and output per capita were showing signs of increasing. Stimulated by a growing foreign demand for American staples, the economy began to expand and offer greater incentives for investments in material capital, inventions, and acquisition of skills, and, of course, inexpensive labor. Manufacturing sectors grew and stimulated the growth of cities. Dependent upon economies of scale, manufacturers had to locate where transportation routes facilitated the acquisitions of raw materials and the presence of population concentrations could easily meet demands for larger supplies of labor. American population growth led to expanded markets which made possible the exploitation of economies of large-scale production. These economies were realized from specialization and the division of labor within firms and from increased specialization among firms as well as technological innovation. Slowly the merchant capitalism which predominated prior to the Civil War gave way to an industrial capitalism which rationalized production under the factory system and looked for an ever-increasing supply of labor to fill the growing number of simple tasks it created and keep labor costs somewhat depressed. By 1870 the United States had a manufacturing output equal to that of France and Germany combined. By 1913 American manufacturing output equaled that of France, Germany and the United Kingdom, and it was the chief producer of foodstuffs in the world. In 1870 over one-half of all workers were farmers or farm laborers. Forty years later over two-thirds were industrial toilers, many of whom had come from regions as diverse as Japan, Mexico, Ireland, Germany, and Italy.

Immigrants were quite important to the entire industrial transformation. Without European immigration to America, for instance, it has been estimated that wages in Eastern industries would have been 11 percent higher than they were in 1910. Immigrants also brought a sizable body of skills and knowledge which were absolutely indispensable for the growth of some industries, and the presence of a large pool of unskilled labor attracted further investment. Additionally, the fact that the cost of rearing and training a huge labor force was largely borne outside the United States allowed for even greater levels of investment and growth. Without immigration in the first century of American capitalism, the United States work force would have been only 70 percent of what it was by 1940.

Finally, by going beyond vague dichotomies of preindustrial immigrants and American culture and looking precisely at the specific points of contact between capitalism as both an economic system and a way of life and specific categories of newcomers, the entire scope of immigration history is rescued from a model of understanding which has dominated scholarly and popular understanding for decades. Whether immigrants were upwardly mobile achievers or dispirited peasants, they were always assumed to move in a linear progression from a premodern, holistic community to a modern, atomistic one. Such a framework presented immigration as a clash of cultures. But if the entire experience is broken down into innumerable points of contact between various categories and beliefs, what emerges is a clearer portrait of the process of social change stimulated almost incessantly by the changing imperatives of the marketplace and the diverse responses of human beings themselves. Their response, conditioned by their social station, familial status, and ideological orientation, becomes a variable itself helping to structure not only their own life path but even somewhat the all-embracing economic system. Ordinary individuals were rescued from the status of victims; they are not simply manipulated by leaders, their class standing, or their culture, but active participants in a historical drama whose outcome is anything but predictable. This view further accentuates a process hidden from sight in previous accounts. Immigrants now are no longer confronting an amorphous mass called America or modern society but specific leaders and ideologies which evoke acceptance, resistance, and divergent paths into the capitalist economy. Agents of tradition preaching ethnic culture, conservatism, and religious devotion appear alongside champions of assimilation, education, and even worker militancy. Spokesmen for what Fernand Braudel calls the "material life," the old routines handed down from time immemorial, compete against advocates of modernization and protest. Occasionally an ideology of tradition will be used in the service of social change. The point is that instead of linear progression, immigrants faced a continual dynamic between economy and society, between class and culture. It was in the swirl of this interaction and competition that ordinary individuals had to sort out options, listen to all the prophets, and arrive at decisions of their own in the best manner they could. Inevitably the results were mixed. Some fared better than others; some stayed in America and others returned home. Immigrants existed who became radicals and others worshiped the ethic of entrepreneurship. Some did not even care either way. In many cases decisions were incomplete and imprecise. These were after all neither heroes nor villains but ordinary people. Life for them as for us was never clear-cut. What was ultimately important amidst the political and economic currents of their times was not only how they adapted to it all but what if anything endured in their lives and brought it order and stability....

## THE CULTURE OF EVERYDAY LIFE

Immigrant people by definition related to capitalism and its attendant social order in complex and often ingenious ways which have often been misunderstood. Generally, this process of understanding and adjusting was carried on in two broad categories. In reality two immigrant Americas existed. One consisted largely of workers with menial jobs. The other, a smaller component, held essentially positions which pursued personal gain and leadership. Immigrants did not enter a common mass called America but adapted to two separate but related worlds which might be termed broadly working class and middle class.

These two components were represented everywhere. Middle-class supporters of capitalism could be found among commercial farmers in Mexico, Sicily, or Hungary, entrepreneurs within immigrant groups, or industrialists in all American cities. They wielded relatively more power than most of their contemporaries, enjoyed extensive reinforcement from loyal supporters in political and public life including government officials, educators and even reformers and placed a high value on individual freedom, personal gain, political power, and an improved future. Below them, although far more numerous, stood millions of ordinary people whose perspective was considerably more circumscribed. They were not immune to the satisfaction to be derived from personal gain or political power but could not realistically indulge in such pursuits for too long a period of time. Their power to influence public affairs and their supporters in public institutions were minimal. Tied considerably more to the concerns of family and communal welfare, they focused daily activities, in the words of folklorist Henry Glassie, "in the place where people are in control of their own destinies." These public and private spheres were not totally separate and, indeed, were part of a common system, but one was substantially more expansive, confident, and less circumscribed than the other.

Somewhere in time and space all individuals meet the larger structural realities of their existence and construct a relationship upon a system of ideas, values, and behavior which collectively gives meaning to their world and provides a foundation upon which they can act and survive. Collectively their thought and action are manifestations of a consciousness, a mentality, and ultimately a culture. Immigrants, who were after all common men and women, could not completely understand what was taking place as capitalism entered their world. They were not fully aware of the sweeping political and economic decisions and transitions which were altering the nineteenth and twentieth centuries. In lieu of a comprehensive understanding of social and historical change, they fashioned their own explanations for what they could feel and sense. To give meaning to the realities and structures which now impinged upon them, they forged a culture, a constellation of behavioral and thought patterns which would offer them explanations, order, and a prescription for how to proceed with their lives. This culture was not a simple extension of their past, an embracement of the new order of capitalism, or simply an affirmation of a desire to become an American. It was nurtured not by any one reality such as their new status as workers but was produced from whatever resources were at hand: kinship networks, folklife, religion, socialism, unions. It was a product of both men and women, believers and non-believers, workers and entrepreneurs, leaders and followers. It was creative yet limited by available options. It drew from both a past and a present and continually confronted "the limits of what was possible." The demands of economic forces, social structures, political leaders, kin, and community were real and could not be ignored. Life paths and strategies were informed by knowledge from the past and estimates about the future but largely from the specific options of the present. Immigrants were free to choose but barely.

It must be made clear, however, that this culture of everyday life, while generated at the nexus of societal structures and subjective experience, was ultimately the product of a distinct inequality in the distribution of power and resources within the system of capitalism. It would be convenient to call this a culture of the working class but it was not tied that simply to the means of production or the workplace and was not simply the prerogative of laborers. It was also tied to traditional culture, although it was certainly not entirely ethnic or premodern. Its core was a fixation upon the needs of the family-household for both laborers and entrepreneurs and the proximate community. The relative lack of resources and of a comprehensive knowledge of vast social economic change forced immigrants (and probably ordinary people in other places) to focus an inordinate amount of their lives in two areas. First, they had to devise explanations of their status in terms intelligible to themselves by drawing on folk thought, religion, ancestry, and similar devices close at hand. Second, they had to devote nearly all their attention to that portion of their world in which they actually could exert some power and influence: the family-household, the workplace, and the local neighborhood or community. They sought, in other words, a degree of meaning and control. Like peasants in the Pyrenees studied by Pierre Bourdieu, they forged a world view that allowed for safeguarding what was considered "essential" at all times. The alternative would have been a life completely out of their hands, entirely bewildering and completely orchestrated by industrialists, public institutions, and economic forces.

The thrust of almost all previous scholarship seeking to interpret the immigrant experience in urban America around considerations of ethnic culture or class has been much too narrow and has failed to make a crucial distinction between the content and foundation of immigrant mentalities. The content which drew from ethnic traditions and present realities seemed as much cultural as it was class-based. That is to say, the newcomers acted as workers but also remained tied to selected ethnic symbols and institutions which appeared to mute solely class concerns. But the basis for this preoccupation with familiar ways, as well as with working-class realities, was to be found in the placement of these ordinary people in the larger social structure of capitalism. Even traditional family and ethnic communities were a preoccupation ultimately not because they were familiar but because they represented somewhat manageable and understandable systems to people who possessed little control or understanding of the larger society. Because they possessed relatively less material and social influence, they were preoccupied with understanding and constructing life at very immediate levels. They did this in part because they were relatively powerless to affect the sweeping currents of their times but, ironically, in doing so they actually generated a degree of power and social control of their own and transcended a status as simply victims.

This pragmatic culture of everyday life accepted the world for what it was and what it was becoming and yet ceaselessly resisted the inevitable at numerous points of contact in the workplace, the classroom, the political hall, the church, and even at home. *Mentalité* for the immigrants was an amalgam of past and present, acceptance and resistance. Ordinary people could never live a life insulated from the actions of their social superiors, nor could they ever fully retreat from their present. Peasants responded to the whims of nobles, immigrants responded to the profit-seeking activities of commercial farmers or industrial capitalists. Since they could not control the direction of either elites or capital, they placed most of their priorities and focused most of their attention on the immediate, the attainable, the portion of their world in which they could exert some influence. This was true in "material life" and life under capitalism as well. By implication the culture of everyday life, shaped primarily by social status and unequal ownership of the means of production and informed by traditions and communal needs, always aspired to modest goals and was devoid of extremely radical or liberal impulses. The extent newcomers would go in either direction depended a great deal on the ability and impact of various leaders. And still ordinary people left their mark. Leaders constantly had to modify their ideology to effectively attract immigrant support. Peasants in the homelands could do little to dissuade the upper classes from promoting the spread of commercial agriculture. They did, however, force local elites to pay more for their farm labor by deciding to emigrate. Similarly, immigrants could not make decisions where to locate plants or invest large amounts of capital, but they could force industrialists to change personnel and wage policies by their transiency which stemmed from their private agendas. Some scholars might call this a form of class antagonism, but it also represented an effort to construct life strategies within available options.

Ultimately, then, the mentality and culture of most immigrants to urban America was a blend of past and present and centered on the immediate and the attainable. Institutions from the past such as the family-household were modified but retained; the actions of landed elites at home and industrial capitalists abroad forced them to confront a new market and social order which they accepted but somewhat on their own terms. They would move, several times, if they had to, and become wage laborers or even small entrepreneurs. They did so not because they were victimized by capitalism or embraced it but because they pursued the immediate goal of family-household welfare and industrial jobs which were very accessible. If they had the skills or capital, which some did, even a small business was not out of the question. Those that moved had eschewed any retreat into a fictitious peasant past or becoming large, commercial farmers, although many still dreamed of living on the land. Overall, however, for people in the middle, immigration made a great deal of sense. Barrington Moore, who has written about German workers in the early twentieth century, has suggested that they were consumed by practical issues, such as the possible inability of the breadwinner to earn a living. Secondary concerns did include injustice and unfair treatment at the workplace but basically their fears and hopes revolved around everyday life: getting enough to eat and having a home of one's own. They expressed hopes for a better future but were usually too busy making ends meet to do much about it. The pattern apparently transcended time and space.

Since capitalism was the central force which created these immigrants, it is still not possible to conclude they made an inevitable and smooth transition to a new way of life and a new culture. They were not one-dimensional beings rooted only to old ways of life or a new economy. They did not proceed simply from an ethnic world to a class world. Rather their consciousness and culture were continually grounded in several levels of status and culture prior to emigration and after arrival as well. It was tied simultaneously to the lower levels of tradition, household, and community as well as to the higher levels of capitalism, industrialization, and urbanization. Between the microscopic forces of daily life, often centering around ethnic communal and kinship ties, and the macroscopic world of economic change and urban growth stood the culture of everyday life. This was a culture not based exclusively on ethnicity, tradition, class, or progress. More precisely, it was a mediating culture which confronted all these factors. It was simultaneously turbulent and comforting: It looked forward and backward, although not very far in either direction. It could not hope to exert the influence on history that industrial capitalism did, but it was far from being simply reflexive. Depending on premigration experience and leadership in America, it could prepare the way for a transition to a working-class or a middle-class America but seldom did it lead to a complete embracement of any new order.

If the culture of everyday life dominated the lives of most American immigrants, it did not mean that all newcomers were alike. Even within similar ethnic aggregations, a preoccupation with the practical and the attainable did not create identical life strategies. Some manifested a sojourning orientation and planned to return home fortified in their ability to live off the land. Others came to stay and effectively exploited their skills and resources to establish careers and businesses in urban America. Still others never really made up their minds and simply worked from day to day. Divergent resources and orientations in the homeland, moreover, often led to varying rates of attainment and participation in the culture of capitalism; those who settled in higher social stations and were already further removed from "material life" prior to emigration began to move more purposefully toward the new culture of acquisitiveness and personal gain. The origins of inequality in urban America were not located solely in the industrial workplace, or the city, or even ethnic cultures. They were also rooted in the social structure of the homeland and immigrant stream. Such divisions, in fact, would fragment immigrant communities and insure that urban-ethnic enclaves and settlements would only exist temporarily. But fragmentation at the group level should not obscure the ties that most of the first generation had to the culture of everyday life and the need to take what was available and secure the welfare of those closest to them. Immigrants were generally part of the masses and the culture of the masses in the nineteenth and much of the twentieth century was not solely traditional, modern, or working class. It was a dynamic culture, constantly responding to changing needs and opportunities and grounded in a deep sense of pragmatism and mutual assistance. Fernand Braudel spoke of three levels of historic time: political, which was rapid and episodic; social, which was modulated by the slower pace of everyday life; geographical, where change was nearly imperceptible. Immigrants were closely preoccupied with social time and the realities of the immediate and the present, although the levels of time and culture were never completely separated.

The center of every life was to be found in the family-household and the proximate community. It was here that past values and present realities were reconciled, examined on an intelligible scale, evaluated, and mediated. No other institution rivaled the family-household in its ability to filter the macrocosm and microcosm of time and space. Kinship and the household, of course, are not necessarily identical concepts and family and work need not be inextricably linked. The truth of the matter, however, was that during the first century of American capitalism they inevitably were. The family-household mobilized resources and socialized people. Even though capitalism entered the peasant household in the homeland and caused a shift from subsistence to market production, the transition was essentially one of function and not form. The linking of individuals to a wage rather than a household economy did not inevitably lead to a decline of the family-household. In the first century of industrial capitalism, the family-household continued to remain effective because supporting institutions of capitalism such as the state, public education, and even federally regulated unions had not yet become strong enough to fully penetrate the confines of private space.

Because of the continued viability of the family-household, the small community or urban neighborhood, usually built upon congeries of such units, continued to function and the culture of everyday life persisted. But this did not mean that private space was immune from public ritual and activity. Repeatedly, albeit episodically, the culture of everyday life was punctuated by "political time," by the rhetoric and ambitions of competing leaders. A new society and a new economy presented opportunities for newcomers with particular skills or resources to pursue power and middle-class status, to forsake the ambiguity of the culture of everyday life for the single-minded culture of power, wealth, and personal gain. Among all groups, not just among Japanese or Jewish entrepreneurs, this process of middle-class formation and pursuit of individual power took place to one extent or another.

While leaders emerged within all immigrant communities, they did not all advocate ideas and values consistent with the new order of capitalism or with each other. Many successful entrepreneurs advocated rapid Americanization and individual achievement. These leaders, such as Carl Schurz, A. P. Giannini, and Peter Rovnianek, were usually reinforced by the larger society which supported them and shared their faith. American political parties actually subsidized part of the ethnic press and further attempted to violate the boundaries of everyday life. Opposed to these accommodationists, however, were those who exhibited a stronger defense of tradition and communal values. They included clerics and fraternal leaders, were usually less tied to the new economy than politicians and entrepreneurs, and while not opposed to Americanization, were skeptical of rapid change, growing secularism, and the dangers inherent in a pluralistic society which threatened their elevated status. Irish Catholic prelates, for instance, could allow for Americanization but not accept public education in a society dominated by other cultures and religions. Advocates of religious authority and homeland causes, while often bitterly divided, were both ultimately defenders of the "everyday culture" in which they usually held prominent positions. Because they were tied closer to the culture of the masses, they generally exerted a stronger influence than leaders attached to external cultures such as trade unionists, socialists, educational reformers, or national political figures. . . .

But not all leaders or elites were equally effective. Ideology cannot be reduced to simple strategies advanced by the prominent to further their own interests nor does it simply flow from the top to the bottom of society. The rhetoric and symbols of leaders were most effective when they reflected to some extent the feeling and thought of ordinary people themselves. Educational reformers, socialists, some political figures, and even trade unionists often failed to realize this fully. Those that did, such as unionists who recruited ethnic organizers or editors who championed the cause of the homeland, were much more successful in mobilizing portions of the immigrant population. The Irish Land League, the rise of Catholic schools, the quest for German-language instruction, the rise of the United Mine Workers, and the cause of Russian Jews even in the 1890s illustrate how private issues could effectively enter public space. Religion, the homeland, and labor matters were probably the most debated issues. These matters concerned key elements of the past and present and of everyday culture; religion and labor especially had deep implications for a well-ordered family-household.

Immigrants not only influenced their leaders in an episodic fashion but resisted intervention into the only world they could control on an ongoing basis even while adjusting to a new economic order. They were not simply duped by a hegemonic culture. Neither the prominent within their groups nor the owners of the means of production were beyond their influence. Immigrant laymen fought to maintain control of churches, Italians practiced rituals in defiance of clerical authority, religious and ethnic schools were established to resist the culture of outsiders, laborers controlled production, left jobs they did not like and struck spontaneously in colorful, communal fashion if it suited their purposes. They never tired of assisting friends and relatives to find jobs and probably had as much as managers to do with shaping the informal system of employment recruitment which dominated American industry during the century before World War II. Leaders who urged newcomers to support extended schooling or various political parties usually made little headway unless they addressed the issues relating to the family-household and community that newcomers felt strongest about: homeownership, jobs, neighborhood services, steady work, and traditional beliefs.

Immigrants lived in scattered urban-ethnic enclaves which were heavily working class. But these settlements were neither structurally nor ideologically monolithic. Newcomers were tied to no single reality. The workplace, the church, the host society, the neighborhood, the political boss, and even the homeland all competed for their minds and bodies. On a larger level, industrial capitalism could not be stopped. But on the level of everyday life, where ordinary people could inject themselves into the dynamic of history, immigrants acquiesced, resisted, hoped, despaired, and ultimately fashioned a life the best they could. Transplanted by forces beyond their control, they were indeed children of capitalism. But like children everywhere they were more than simply replicas of their parents; independence and stubborn resistance explained their lives as much as their lineage. Their lives were not entirely of their own making, but they made sure that they had something to say about it.

# POSTSCRIPT

## Were Immigrants to the United States "Uprooted"?

Handlin has been recognized as the most influential scholar on immigration history since his doctoral dissertation won the Dunning Prize when he was only 26 years old. Published as *Boston's Immigrants: A Study in Acculturation* (Harvard University Press, 1941), this was the first study of immigration to integrate sociological concepts within a historical framework. A decade later, Handlin published *The Uprooted*, in which he combined the interdisciplinary framework with a personal narrative of the immigrants' history.

Bodnar's *The Transplanted*, while offering a contrasting metaphor for the immigration experience to the United States, shares with Handlin's work an attempt to present a general account of that experience, to portray the immigrants in a sympathetic light, and to employ an interdiscliplinary approach by borrowing concepts from the social sciences. As the foregoing essays reveal, however, Handlin and Bodnar differ in their perspectives about America's ethnic past. Handlin views the immigrants as people who were removed from their particular Old World cultures and who assimilated into the New World value system within two generations. In contrast, Bodnar argues that some first-generation immigrants may have shed their traditional cultures quickly upon arrival in the United States, but many more continued to maintain a lifestyle in their adopted homeland that focused upon the family household and the neighboring ethnic community.

*The Harvard Encyclopedia of American Ethnic Groups* (Harvard University Press, 1980), edited by Stephan Thernstrom and Oscar Handlin, is a valuable collection of articles on every ethnic group in the United States. Leonard Dinnerstein and David Reimers's *Ethnic Americans: A History of Immigration and Assimilation*, 2d ed. (Harper & Row, 1982) is a short but accurate text, while Joe R. Feagan's *Racial and Ethnic Relations*, 2d ed. (Prentice Hall, 1985) is a useful sociological text that examines the major ethnic groups through assimilationist and power-conflict models.

In the last generation, dozens of studies have focused on the experiences of particular immigrant groups in the United States. See, for example, Jack Chen, *The Chinese in America* (Harper & Row, 1980); Matt S. Meier and Feliciano Rivera, *The Chicanos: A History of Mexican Americans* (Hill & Wang, 1972); and Humbert Nelli, *Italians in Chicago, 1880–1930: A Study of Ethnic Mobility* (Oxford University Press, 1970). The reaction to the immigration of the late nineteenth century can be observed in John Higham's *Strangers in the Land: Patterns of American Nativism, 1860–1925* (Rutgers University Press, 1955), which is considered the best work on anti-immigrant prejudice in this time period.

# PART 2

# The Response to Industrialism

*The westward movement and the early pioneers who conquered the wilderness have become part of the folklore of American history. Since the conquering heroes were assumed to be white males, women were generally excluded from the story. Contemporary letters, diaries, and reminiscences, however, suggest that these westerning women put their stamp on the frontier not only as mothers, wives, and teachers, but also as lawyers, physicians, and shopkeepers.*

*With the growth of industry, urban problems became more acute. Improvements in water and sewerage, street cleaning, housing, mass transit, and fire and crime prevention developed slowly because the incredible population growth strained municipal services and urban governments had limited powers, which often fell under the control of political bosses.*

*At the end of the nineteenth century, the African American population began fighting for civil rights, political power, and integration into society. Spokespeople for the blacks, such as Booker T. Washington, began to emerge, but their often unclear agendas frequently touched off controversy among both black people and white people.*

# ISSUE 5

## Did the Westward Movement Transform the Traditional Roles of Women in the Late Nineteenth Century?

**YES: Sandra L. Myres,** from *Westering Women and the Frontier Experience 1800–1915* (University of New Mexico Press, 1982)

**NO: Christine Stansell,** from "Women on the Great Plains 1865–1890," *Women's Studies* (Alfred A. Knopf, 1986)

### ISSUE SUMMARY

**YES:** Professor of history Sandra L. Myres (1933–1991) argues that first- and second-generation women, though not revolutionary, often moved outside the home and worked as teachers, missionaries, doctors, lawyers, ranchers, miners, and businesspeople.

**NO:** According to professor of history Christine Stansell, women on the Great Plains were not able to create networks of female friendships and consequently endured lonely lives and loveless marriages.

In 1893 young historian Frederick Jackson Turner (1861–1932) delivered an address before the American Historical Association on "The Significance of the Frontier in American History." Turner's essay not only sent him from Wisconsin to Harvard, it became one of the most important essays ever written in American history. According to Turner's thesis, American civilization was unique and different from European civilization because the continent contained an abundance of land that was settled in four major waves of migration from 1607 through 1890. During this process the European heritage was shed, and the American characteristics of individualism, mobility, nationalism, and democracy developed.

This frontier theory of American history did not go unchallenged. Historians said that Turner's definition of the frontier was too vague and imprecise; he underestimated the cultural forces that came to the West from Europe and the eastern states; he neglected the forces of urbanization and industrialization in opening the West; he placed an undue emphasis on sectional developments and neglected class struggles for power; and, finally, his provincial view of American history prolonged the isolationist views of a nation that had become involved in world affairs in the twentieth century. By the time Turner died, his thesis had been widely discredited. Historians continued to write about the West, but new fields and new theories were competing for attention.

New historians have begun to question the traditional interpretation of western expansion. For example, the older historians believed that growth was good and automatically brought forth progress. New historians William Cronin, Patricia Limerick, and others have questioned this assumption in examining the disastrous ecological effects of American expansionism, such as the elimination of the American buffalo and the depletion of forests.

Until recently, most historians did not consider women part of western history. One scholar who searched 2,000 pages of Turner's work could find only one paragraph devoted to women. Men built the railroads, drove the cattle, led the military expeditions, and governed the territories. "Women," said one writer, "were invisible, few in number, and not important to the taming of the West."

When scholars did acknowledge the presence of women on the frontier, perceptons were usually based upon stereotypes that were created by male observers and that had become prevalent in American literature. According to Sandra L. Myres, there were three main images. The first image was that of a frightened, tearful woman who lived in a hostile environment and who was overworked and overbirthed, depressed and lonely, and resigned to a hard life and an early death. The second image, in contrast, was of a helpmate and a civilizer of the frontier who could fight Indians as well as take care of the cooking, cleaning, and rearing of the children. A third image of the westering woman was that of the "bad woman," who was more masculine than feminine in her behavior and who was "hefty, grotesque and mean with a pistol."

The proliferation of primary source materials since the early 1970s—letters, diaries, and memoirs written by frontierswomen—has led to a reassessment of the role of westering women. They are no longer what Joan Hoff Wilson once referred to as the "orphans of women's history." There are disagreements in interpretation, but they are based upon sound scholarships. One area where scholars disagree is over the following issue: Were the traditional roles of women changed by their participation in the westward movements of the nineteenth century?

In the first selection, Sandra L. Myres applies the Turner thesis to women in a positive fashion. Myres believes that first- and second-generation women often moved outside the home and worked as teachers, missionaries, doctors, lawyers, ranchers, miners, and businesspeople. In the second selection, Christine Stansell argues from a Marxist perspective. She claims that women on the Great Plains were torn from their eastern roots, isolated in their home environments, and forced to endure lonely lives and loveless marriages because they could not create networks of female friendships.

# YES

Sandra L. Myres

## WOMEN AS FRONTIER ENTREPRENEURS

The West offered challenges to women's skills and provided opportunities for them to develop and test new talents and to broaden the scope of their home and community activities. It also offered, for whatever reason, a significant degree of political participation. But did the West offer economic opportunity as well? Frederick Jackson Turner maintained that the West was a liberating influence in American life and that the frontier setting offered westering Americans, at least westering males, both economic and political opportunity. "So long as free land exists," he wrote in his famous essay on the significance of the frontier, "the opportunity for a competency exists and economic power secures political power." In recent years, a number of historians have attacked portions of Turner's frontier hypothesis and especially its relevance to westering women. Indeed, several radical feminist authors have maintained that the West exerted a regressive rather than a progressive influence on women's lives. These authors contended that women on the frontiers were forced into unfamiliar, demeaning roles, and that although women in the Western settlements continued to try to reinstate a culture of domesticity, their work as virtual hired hands prevented them either from returning to older, more familiar roles in the social structure or from creating positive new roles. Unable to "appropriate their new work to their own ends and advantage," the authors of one article concluded, frontier women "remained estranged from their function as able bodies."...

Writing from a somewhat different perspective, several historians questioned the application of Turner's thesis to women's frontier experiences and concluded that women did not share in the freedom and opportunities the West offered to men. The stereotype of American women as the "virtuous, religious, progenitor of democracy—the cornerstone of the family and society," one maintained, was a product of an agrarian mythology (and by implication a frontier mythology as well). He argued that it was not on the farm, or on the frontier, that women won political and legal rights, but rather in the city. "It was the city," he wrote, "which became the catalyst for all the aspirations of freedom and equality held by American women." The frontier influenced women as well as men, another historian agreed, but "If we accept Turner's

From Sandra L. Myres, *Westering Women and the Frontier Experience 1800–1915* (University of New Mexico Press, 1982).  Notes omitted.

own assumption that economic opportunity is what matters, and that the frontier was significant as the context within which economic opportunity occurred, then we must observe that for American women... opportunity began pretty much where the frontier left off." In a similar vein, another historian wrote that although there were independent Western women who may have been different from women in the urban East, industrialism and the city, not the Western farm, opened new avenues for women. The frontier, according to his interpretation, "strongly reinforced the traditional role of the sexes," and, he concluded, mill girls were likely to be "potentially far more 'revolutionary' than their rural, Western counterparts."

Yet despite arguments to the contrary, there is clear evidence that Western women did not confine themselves to purely traditional domestic and community concerns. It is true that most Western women were not revolutionary. Like Western men, they did not completely break with tradition nor, with very few exceptions, attempt radically to change women's lives and role in society. They did enlarge the scope of woman's place, however, and countered prevailing Eastern arguments about woman's sphere and the cult of true womanhood. Indeed, the ideals of true womanhood never really applied to a large number of women. As one historian has pointed out, at the very time that domesticity and true womanhood were being expounded as an American ideal, an increasing number of women were leaving their homes to become factory workers and wage earners. Factory work was obviously not available in frontier areas, but like many of their Eastern sisters, Western women were employed in a number of economic activities, and some of them engaged in new fields of endeavor outside what was considered their competency, skills, or proper sphere.

On the Western frontiers, as in other rural areas, much of women's work was tied to domestic manufacture. Historians have estimated that in the colonial period, when the United States was still predominantly rural, 60 to 75 percent of domestic manufacture, particularly in textiles, was carried out by women....

Such domestic manufacture continued on the Western frontiers for many years after it had ceased in the East. Although by the nineteenth century, factories were beginning to produce foodstuffs, clothing, and other goods previously provided by home production, frontier women continued to manufacture such items themselves because "neither the goods, nor the cash to obtain them were readily available." Long, and often primitive, transportation made factory goods scarce and therefore expensive, and few frontier families, at least during the first years of settlement, had extra money to purchase what the women could, and did, produce at home. It was the women, as one Iowa man recalled, who saw that "the garden [was] tended, the turkeys dressed, the deer flesh cured and the fat prepared for candles or culinary use, the wild fruits were garnered and preserved or dried, that the spinning and knitting was done and the clothing made." Such production was not considered gainful employment, of course, and female home manufacturers were rarely, if ever, listed by census takers as employed or working women. Yet such employment was essential to the family economy. Women, as one historian wrote, were "to their families what the factory was to an industrialized society;" they were "the key link in turning unusable raw materials into consumable finished goods."

Not only did women provide needed goods and services for their families, which otherwise would have had to be purchased, but they often exchanged the produce of such work for needed goods or for cash. Margaret Murray recalled that her mother "sold Butter Eggs & Beeswax & anything we could spare off the farm, [and] in the summer and fall we gathered Black Berries wild grapes & anything we raised on the farm that would bring money or exchange for groceries."...

Through these contributions some women came to exert a good deal of influence on the family decision-making process. "The women were not unaware" of their contributions, one reported, and were "quite capable of scoring a point on occasion when masculine attitudes became too bumptious." Some women were openly aggressive or even contradictory in opposing male decisions, while others worked more subtly and were "careful to maintain the idea of male superiority." For example, one woman bought some milk cows and began a small dairy business while her husband was away doing carpenter work, but when he returned, he sold the cows since such work "did not appeal to him." The woman, however, without raising a fuss, simply took some inheritance money and reinvested in cows and "eventually the family acquired hogs to help consume the milk... [and] stock raising ended as the family's main economic activity."

Often women's domestic skills became the basis for a profitable business. Cooks, seamstresses, and washerwomen were in demand, especially in the mining camps and in other areas where the population included a number of single men. Although such work was laborious, it was usually well paid, particularly during the early frontier period. "I know girls that is ritch," one woman reported, "just working out bie the month," while another wrote that wages for women's work were high, "$50 to $75 a month."...

Most of this type of work could be done at home, and women thus provided a small income for their families while they continued to carry out their household chores and care for their children within a familiar setting....

In frontier areas, women also served an important function as hotel and boardinghouse keepers. Women frequently boarded hired hands or seasonal workers. One California woman wrote that during the harvesting she had ten men in the family. "Washing and cooking for this crew," she reported, "takes me all the time...." A Texas woman recorded that her husband owned a cotton gin for twenty-two years, and "I had my part to play in this business as we boarded the hands and I did the cooking." Other women opened their homes to boarders or operated small hotels to provide an income for themselves or their families. Shortly after her husband died, Amelia Barr wrote, "I have opened my house last week for boarders and intend to take about eight steady boarders," and a Texas woman recalled that her grandmother "kept a boarding house" to support her family when her Unionist husband left for Mexico.

Boardinghouses varied in size and type of services provided. Some boarding establishments furnished only meals while others supplied both meals and lodging. Others offered a combination of services. A Kansas woman recorded that she had two lodgers for whom she provided breakfast and supper and two others who "cook their own food and lodge in our little hut." Most boarding establishments were relatively small operations. With limited space and cooking facilities, most women could not accommodate more than eight to ten boarders at a time, but a few attempted to run fairly substantial operations....

On the frontier, women were actively sought not only as wives but as contributors to the local economy. Many community builders believed that a few good women would not only help in civilizing and taming the frontier but would add to its economic development as well. The Western agents for R. G. Dun and Company (the forerunner of Dun and Bradstreet) certainly were aware of women's potential economic contributions and recommended "equality of economic opportunity when it came to finding credit endorsements." Indeed, according to one analysis of Denver credit ratings for the period 1859 to 1877, "women without collateral could usually get recommendations for credit where men could not, even when everything was equal except their sex."

However remunerative, domestic work was often boring as well as laborious, and it kept women confined within their domestic spaces. "There is something dull in sitting here day by day, planning this garment and making that, but that seems to be my destiny just now," mourned a young Nebraska girl who made a good living as a seamstress. "There does not seem to be much that a girl can do here." Other women, equally bored by dull work, tried to find an outlet for their energies and creative urges in quiltmaking, fancy sewing, or by adding artistic touches to their home manufactures. Texas pioneer Ella Bird-Dumont longed to be a sculptress but, denied the opportunity to study in her Panhandle home, she settled instead for creating beauty in the gloves and vests she made and sold to neighboring ranch hands and cowmen....

Some frontier women refused to subvert their artistic talents to the tasks of sewing, butter making, and other home chores. A number of women were able to combine pioneering and domestic tasks and at the same time open new avenues into the "life of the mind." By the nineteenth century, writing was considered a fairly respectable occupation for women, and a number of them combined the pen with homemaking and child care. According to a recent study, between 1784 and 1860 at least one hundred magazines, most of which were devoted to women's interests, were founded in the United States and provided a market for articles by and for women. Many of these articles were about what women knew best —homemaking and the domestic arts— but the journals also published poetry, essays, and short stories by women. Women also became increasingly active in writing books as well as articles. Of the 1150 novels by American authors published in the United States between 1830 and 1850, a large proportion (perhaps as many as one-third) were written by women. So successful were some of these works that Nathaniel Hawthorne felt compelled to complain to his publisher that "America is wholly given over to a damned mob of scribbling women...." Although many of the "damned mob" admittedly produced third and fourth-rate works, their books were nonetheless popular and brought their authoresses a good deal of attention as well as a source of income....

Aside from the arts, teaching was about the only profession open to respectable women in the nineteenth century.... [E]ducation was considered an extension of women's traditional roles as child rearers and moral and cultural guardians, and American education became increasingly feminized during the nineteenth century. As Catherine Beecher pointed out, teaching young children not only provided an essential service to the community, but it helped women prepare themselves for "the great purpose of a woman's life—the happy superintendence of a family." Beecher's advice did not go unheeded: a number of women taught school at one time or another.

Although most women teachers were single, some women continued at least part-time teaching after their marriage. Especially in Western communities where men were engaged in the "multitudes of other employments that will... lead to wealth" (as Beecher so bluntly wrote), educated women, whatever their marital status, were frequently urged to help begin schools and teach for a term or two. The scarcity of teachers and the desire of frontier dwellers to provide an education for their children led to many attempts to recruit young women from the East. "We want good female teachers, who could obtain constant employment and the best of wages," a Kansas settler wrote home to a New England newspaper; "we want them immediately, and they would do much good." Various Eastern groups attempted to respond to the demand. Catherine Beecher began a campaign to send women teachers to the West, warning that "Western children were growing up without the benefit of either a practical or a moral education." Beecher, and the Board of National Popular Education, formed in 1847, did recruit some teachers. The Board served as an agency for single teachers and provided job training as well as placement services, but the number of Eastern teachers provided by the group never approached the 90,000 young women Beecher believed were needed "if the tides of barbarism were to be pushed back." Far more helpful in recruiting teachers in the West than the actions of Eastern groups and agencies were the more practical solutions found by frontier residents who relied on the resources available and found local women with at least a modicum of education to fulfill the communities' educational needs....

Despite poor working conditions, rowdy pupils, low salaries, and increasing educational requirements, some women chose full-time, lifetime careers in teaching and were able to advance themselves professionally. Many young women took advantage of the more liberal educational opportunities available to them in Western colleges and universities to improve their academic skills and qualify them for better-paying and more professionally fulfilling jobs in the educational system. When the franchise was opened to Western women, elective school offices were opened to them as well, and in most Western states, women held posts as principals, superintendents, and served on state boards of education....

A number of women combined a desire to teach with religious zeal and entered the mission field. Indeed, for some women the principal motivation for going West was not family desires or economic betterment but an answer to a religious calling to minister to the Indians....

During the 1790s, the Second Awakening "spawned a whole family of state, regional, and national societies." Thus, by the beginning of the nineteenth century most denominations sponsored both foreign and home missions, and several interdenominational societies had been formed to carry the gospel to both the Indians and the white inhabitants of new Western settlements.

The boards which organized and controlled Western missions were made up entirely of men, and decisions about the establishment and conduct of the missions were made in the East, not in the West. Nonetheless, it was the missionaries in the field who were crucial to the success of the missionary effort, and women, living and working in the West, made important and significant contributions to mission work. At first a number of mission boards refused to allow women to enter the field, fearing the frontier and Indian villages too dangerous and unseemly a place for delicate females. Women filled with missionary ardor had to content themselves with fund-raising activities and quiet support of the mission effort. Eventually, however, mission boards actively recruited both married and single women to wash, cook, and clean at the mission stations and to assist the male missionaries in teaching in the mission schools, in evangelizing among the Indian women, and in other aspects of mission work. Between 1820 and 1850, a growing number of women joined missions in the trans-Appalachian West and in Indian Territory. As the frontier moved further West, new mission fields opened, and women became increasingly prominent in missionary work. They broadened the scope of their activities, preached as well as taught, and occasionally had full responsibility for the establishment and operation of mission schools and churches. A few were ordained to the regular ministry, in order, as one put it, "to add in some ways to her power to serve."...

Conservative and traditional in most of their views towards social progress and the role of women, the missionaries nonetheless helped broaden women's place within Western society and in the nation as a whole. Certainly they proved the ability of women to undertake successfully this strenuous and difficult calling. A number of them became strong advocates for improved education for women so that they could more effectively serve in the mission field, and their books about their mission life, their letters to newspapers and magazines, and their public speaking tours to raise funds provided a greater visibility for women as public rather than private participants in American life.

At the opposite end of the social scale from the missionaries were the practitioners of a very different, publically visible, but traditional and exclusively female occupation, the so-called soiled doves or ladies of the night. A great deal has been written about Western prostitutes; much of it, of a popular, and often sensational, nature, concentrated on such colorful characters as Poker Alice, Tit Bit, Big Nose Kate, and Rose of the Cimarron. These women were often portrayed as nice girls gone wrong, women of some character and experience who drank, gambled, and sold their favors but who still were of a basically honest nature and had "hearts of pure gold." Or they were pictured as women of "evil name and fame," depraved, vicious, and cruel "Cyprian sisters." Several recent and more scholarly studies have suggested that some girls entered the profession in order to advance themselves economically or to escape dull and dreary lives on isolated farms and ranches. Many were attracted by the bright lights and excitement of the mining camps and cattle towns and hoped to earn a little nest egg, meet a cowboy, farmer, or rancher, and eventually settle down to a respectable life. Others hoped to become economically independent and viewed prostitution as one of the few professions where women had some chance of financial success. As one Denver woman succinctly noted, "I went into the sporting life for business reasons and no other. It was a way for a woman in those days to make money and I made it." . . .

Brothel owners and operators and girls who worked in the better establishments generally scorned the dance hall and saloon girls who rented upstairs rooms over the taverns and the "crib" girls who sold their wares from small two-room establishments with a bedroom with a window on the street and a kitchen in the rear. At the bottom of the scale were the women who walked the streets and who were often ill and frequently subjected to cruel and violent treatment at the hands of both customers and law enforcement officials. But whatever their social or economic level—madame, parlor girl, saloon or crib girl, or streetwalker, their life was a hard one. Many committed suicide, died of disease and alcoholism, drifted away into other occupations or, among the more fortunate, found a husband or protector. One survey of prostitutes in the Kansas cattle towns found that the average age of these women was 23.1 years, and very few were over the age of thirty. Despite the legendary success of a few women, prostitution was neither an attractive nor a rewarding occupation.

Prostitution was a town or city occupation as were other more respectable occupations such as domestic service, hotel and boardinghouse management, and teaching. The economic opportunities for rural women, especially in frontier areas, were more limited. Yet a surprising number of farm and ranch women were able to turn their knowledge of domestic production and farm and ranch management into prosperous business enterprises. In addition to their domestic occupations such as cloth production, and chicken, egg, dairy, and butter businesses, many rural women actually ran the family farm. . . . [W]omen often had to take over farm management when the men were ill or incapacitated or were gone from home prospecting, fighting Indians, working in town for cash, or just wandering. This was particularly true in Mormon settlements where the men were often required to be gone for one or two years on missions for the church or were involved in other church activities. Meanwhile, the women stayed at home to "milk the cows, plant the crops, and care for the children." In many instances, women (non-Mormon as well as Mormon) provided most of the support for themselves and their families. Even when their menfolk remained at home, most rural women worked with their husbands during especially busy times of the year, and they thus came to have a good understanding of the various farm operations. Wrote one young Iowa farm girl, "I can't describe a thrashing floor so you understand but some day I can show you just how it was done. . . ." Such experience stood women in good stead when they were widowed or left alone and had to take over. In the East, single or widowed women probably would have relied on a father, brothers, or uncles to aid them, but in the West they had fewer of these support networks to draw on, hired help was scarce and expensive, and most simply took over and continued to operate the family farm until they remarried or retired and left the property to their children. . . .

A surprising number of Western women, both single and married, took up land in their own name. In the former Mexican states and territories, where Spanish rather than English law prevailed, married women could hold separate property in their own name, and many took advantage of the opportunity to purchase and adminster their own land. Indeed, Jane McManus Storms Cazneau applied for, and received, an empresario grant from the Mexican government. During the Texas Revolution she offered to borrow money against her landholdings. "As a female, I cannot bear arms for my adopted country," she wrote in 1835, "but if the interest I possess in her soil, will be a guarantee for any money, I will with joy contribute my mite to purchase arms for her brave defenders." In other former Mexican states other women, both of Mexican and English ancestry, owned farm and ranch property which they administered themselves.

Between 1800 and 1850, many changes occurred in the social, economic, and legal position of women, and a number of states and territories outside the former Mexican provinces passed more liberal laws governing women's property rights. As one legal historian pointed out, the number of women with a stake in society increased rapidly during this period, and the English common law, primarily geared to the needs of the landed gentry, no longer was satisfactory for American needs. In fact, he wrote, "the tangle of rules and practices was potentially an impediment to the speed and efficiency of the land market. The statutes spoke of rights of husband and wife, as if the real issue was the intimate relations between the sexes. But the real point of the statutes was to rationalize more cold-blooded matters, such as the rights of a creditor to collect debts out of land owned by husbands and wives, or both." In 1839, Mississippi made the first tentative reforms in the laws relating to married women's property, and other states and territories soon followed suit. By 1850, seventeen states, many of them in the West, had granted married women legal control over their property, while in Oregon, the Donation Land Law of 1850 allowed wives of settlers to claim a half-section (320 acres) in their own right. Most Western states' legal codes made some provision for women to purchase homestead land and own and operate businesses in their own name. Husbands sometimes took advantage of these laws to escape debts or bankruptcy by transferring property to the wife's name, but this device often backfired, for women, once in legal possession of the property, frequently refused to return it, assisted in its administration, and used their legal ownership as a weapon to force their husbands to comply with their wishes....

Whether ranchwomen confined themselves to more traditional roles or actively participated in ranch operations, they tended to become increasingly self-reliant and independent. According to Nannie Alderson, "the new country offered greater personal liberty than an old and settled one," and although she admitted that her years of ranch life never taught her any business sense, she nonetheless believed that Western ranch life instilled a good deal of self-reliance in women and children. This opinion was shared by a number of outside observers. The English visitor Anthony Trollope wrote in 1862 that ranchwomen were "sharp as nails and just as hard." They were rarely obedient to their menfolk, he reported, and "they know much more than they ought to. If Eve had been a ranchwoman, she would never have tempted Adam with an apple. She would have ordered him to make his [own] meal." This was particularly true of girls who grew up on Western farms and ranches. They were even more likely than their mothers to learn riding and roping skills, participate in ranch work, and understand business operations. According to one such young woman, "it is as beneficial for a woman as for a man to be independent," and, she continued, she knew of no reasons "why the judgement of women should not be as good as that of men if they gave the subject attention." In later life, many of these ranch girls assisted their husbands in the ranching business, operated ranches of their own, or turned their talents into careers in rodeo and wild west shows....

Some women turned their farm and ranch experience to the development of large-scale commercial agricultural enterprises, and others became very successful real estate investors. As early as 1742, a young frontiers-woman, Eliza Lucas, assumed management of her father's extensive Carolina estates and developed a profitable indigo market. Mention has already been made of Margaret Brent who managed not only her own lands but was executrix for Leonard Calvert's estate as well. These women established an early pattern for other women. By the late nineteenth century, a Western traveler commented on the number of "bright-minded women from other parts of the country" who were "engaged in real estate transactions in this country.... [I]t is not a rare thing," she continued, "for numbers of feminine speculators to attend the auction sales of land," and she estimated that of the sixty-five women teachers in the Los Angeles schools, "almost all own some land."...

In addition to real estate and commercial agriculture, Western women engaged in many other business and professional enterprises. A survey of the R. G. Dun and Company reports revealed a number of women in the Western states and territories owned and operated millinery shops, dressmaking establishments, grocery and dry goods stores, hotels and restaurants, and other similar establishments. For some, these enterprises served as a basis for other businesses or professions. For example, an Oregon woman, Bethenia Owens-Adair, opened a millinery shop in order to earn money for medical school, and other women reported that the income from their shops helped to underwrite real estate and mining investments. Two enterprising westering women purchased a supply of cloth and other dry goods which they sold from the back of their spring wagon to help pay their expenses to California.

Other women engaged in less-traditional businesses including manufacturing, mining, printing, and editing. Frontier women who had learned to "make-do" and who had devised various means to overcome shortages or unavailable goods applied for patents on various inventions, many of them developed out of their frontier experience. Most of these inventions were closely related to domestic and farm work—improvements for milk coolers, separators and churns, new types of wash tubs, quilting frames, beekeeping equipment, and new strains of farm and garden plants; but others, like Harriet Strong's patent for a "method and means for impounding debris and storing water," provided the basis for other businesses. Strong used her patents and her knowledge of engineering to develop an irrigation and water company in the San Gabriel Valley and became an expert on underground water storage and flood control....

Women were also employed as reporters and contributors for many Western journals and newspapers. After 1850, Ladies' Department columns began to appear in newspapers, often run by the editor's wife or one of the paper's more notable female contributors. Talented women journalists, however, also wrote regular columns or contributed articles on topics of general interest....

By the end of the nineteenth century, according to a recent survey, 1,238 women were engaged in printing and publication and another 1,127 were employed as compositors, linotype operators, and typesetters in eleven far-Western states. A separate study identified twenty-five women newspaper owners and editors in Missouri in the same period.

Western women were also active in other professions including medicine and law. Although these women faced many of the same obstacles and discriminations as Eastern professional women, they had less difficulty in establishing themselves and gaining recognition of their professional status.... [F]rontier women often had to render medical assistance and treatment, and many were recognized as professional or near-professional practitioners of the healing arts. In Mexican-American communities and in many Indian societies, women were believed to have special gifts as healers, and *curanderas* and medicine women were valued for their skills in treating illness and reducing pain. A number of women assisted their physician-husbands and sometimes substituted for them in emergencies. Midwifery and nursing were common occupations for frontier women, although these services rarely earned them monetary remuneration, and they were not acknowledged as gainfully employed in the census or other official documents. After Elizabeth Blackwell's successful assault on male domination of medicine in 1847, an increasing number of women attended medical school and became licensed physicians. In Utah, the Mormon community actively supported women's work in all aspects of medicine and dentistry and produced one of "the most remarkable groups of women doctors in American history." In 1873 Church leader Brigham Young suggested that women's classes be formed in Salt Lake City to study physiology and obstetrics and that "the Bishops see that such women be supported."...

Although Utah undoubtedly had the highest percentage of women actors, other Western states and territories also had a fairly high percentage of professional women. By 1893, a number of coeducational medical schools had been established in the West and enrolled a number of women—19 percent at the University of Michigan, 20 percent at the University of Oregon, and 31 percent at Kansas Medical School.

Women had more difficulty in obtaining legal training because of statutory prohibitions based on English common law which prohibited women from being called to the bar. Nonetheless, after 1870, a few women succeeded in winning admission to legal practice, and those who did frequently vied with each other for the honor of being named the first woman admitted to practice before their state bar or the first woman to try a case before a state supreme court....

Everywhere in the West, by the end of the nineteenth century, women were entering new professions and businesses and were finding new roles outside the recognized scope of woman's place. Many of these Western female entrepreneurs first learned business skills by assisting their husbands, but others learned because of necessity and gained economic and technical expertise through hard work and often bitter experience.... Other women were forced to become independent because of the absence or death of their husbands. Certainly some were reluctant capitalists and businesswomen, but others, often to their own amazement, found that they enjoyed earning their own livelihood and controlling their own lives, and they became enthusiastic entrepreneurs. "I am a great believer in the independence of women," one wrote. "I think married women should be allowed to go on with their career if they wish...." Another, the very successful California businesswoman Harriet Strong, advocated business and economic education for all women so that they would be prepared to assume management of their property if necessary. She hoped to organize a Ladies Business League of America and establish a series of business colleges and training schools to teach women the basic principles of economics and business management. It was not easy for women to succeed in business, she cautioned. "Whatever vocation a woman would enter, she must give it the same scientific study and hard work that a man would in order to make a success." Moreover, she warned:

> A woman needs to have five times as much ability as a man in order to do the same thing. She may be permitted to conduct her own ranch and be a success in a small business enterprise —yes, but let her go into the business of incorporating a large enterprise and bonding it, as a man would... and then see if the word does not go forth, "This woman is going too far; she must be put down."...

Whether the frontier provided a liberating experience and economic as well as social and political opportunities for women is still a question of much debate. Certainly there is some evidence that it did not. As noted at the beginning of this chapter, some historians have concluded, based on women's reminiscences, diaries, and letters, that the frontier did not offer as many opportunities for women as it did for men and that women often failed to take advantage of the frontier experience as a means of liberating themselves from constricting and sexist patterns of behavior. Yet these same reminiscences, diaries, and letters also contain evidence to support the contention that women on the frontiers modified existing norms and adopted flexible attitudes and experimental behavior patterns. For some these changes were easily made and enthusiastically accepted; for others they were reluctantly made and strongly resisted. What has perhaps confused the various interpretations of woman's place and the westering experience is that the *reality* of women's lives changed dramatically as a result of adaptation to frontier conditions while the public *image* remained relatively static. Image, myth, and stereotype were contrary to what women were actually experiencing and doing. The ideal for women in the late nineteenth century moved more and more toward a romanticized view of the wife, mother, and lady, if not of leisure, at least of withdrawn and demure refinement. If frontier necessity, practice, and even law recognized female economic and political independence, social custom and tradition ignored it. Despite a growing emphasis on women's rights, nineteenth-century writers overlooked—or at least chose not to draw attention to—Western life models on which other women might pattern their own lives. Temperance and suffrage rather than economic education and independence for women dominated the feminist literature, often to the detriment of effective women's rights. Women who did not marry or who effectively ran businesses or professional enterprises were often viewed as being not quite respectable or at least unfeminine no matter how efficiently they also ran their homes or carried on family responsibilities in addition to challenging male domination of the marketplace.

Yet women who survived the first or even the second wave of adjustment to frontier conditions and changed roles for women tended to ignore, or at least not slavishly strive toward, Eastern-dictated models of femininity or the ideal of true womanhood. These hardy and self-sufficient women stepped out of woman's place with few regrets. If they did not glory in their new freedom, they did express pride in their newfound talents and accomplishments. It was the later generations of Western women, those who no longer lived on a frontier, who began to emulate Eastern models of propriety and sought to perpetuate the myths of woman's proper sphere. Yet even these later generations betrayed their frontier heritage in their personal values and attitudes. This heritage was reflected in a survey in 1943 which showed that Western women, as compared to those in the North and the South, were far better educated, held a wider variety of jobs, and were more likely to continue working, were less prone to adhere to traditional religious and denominational beliefs, were more excited and more optimistic about their lives, were more open to change, and were more likely to approve equal standards for men and women. Thus, the westering experience continued to influence Western women's values and attitudes long after the passing of the frontier.

# NO

## Christine Stansell

# WOMEN ON THE GREAT PLAINS 1865–1890

In 1841, Catharine Beecher proudly attested to the power of her sex by quoting some of Tocqueville's observations on the position of American women. On his tour of 1831, Tocqueville had found Americans to be remarkably egalitarian in dividing social power between the sexes. In his opinion, their ability to institute democratic equality stemmed from a clearcut division of work and responsibilities: "in no country has such constant care been taken... to trace two clearly distinct lines of action for the two sexes, and to make them keep pace with the other, but in two pathways which are always different." In theory, men and women controlled separate "spheres" of life: women held sway in the home, while men attended to economic and political matters. Women were not unaware of the inequities in a trade-off between ascendancy in the domestic sphere and participation in society as a whole. Attached to the metaphorical bargain struck between the sexes was a clause ensuring that women, through "home influence," could also affect the course of nation-building. For Miss Beecher, domesticity was also imperial power "to American women, more than to any others on earth, is committed the exalted privilege of extending over the world those blessed influences, which are to renovate degraded man, and 'clothe all climes with beauty.' "

Yet despite Beecher's assertions to the contrary, by 1841 one masculine "line of action" was diverging dangerously from female influences. Increasing numbers of men were following a pathway which led them across the Mississippi to a land devoid of American women and American homes. In the twenty-odd years since the Santa Fe trade opened the Far West to American businessmen, only men, seeking profits in furs or trading, had gone beyond the western farmlands of the Mississippi Valley; no women participated in the first stages of American expansion. Consequently, by 1841 the West was in one sense a geographical incarnation of the masculine sphere, altogether untouched by "home influence." Although in theory American development preserved a heterosexually balanced democracy, in actuality, the West, new arena of political and economic growth, had become a man's world.

In 1841, the first Americans intending to settle in the trans-Mississippi region rather than only trap or trade began to migrate over the great overland

From Christine Stansell, "Women on the Great Plains 1865-1890," *Women's Studies*, vol. 4 (1976). Adapted from Christine Stansell, *City of Women: Sex and Class in New York, 1789–1860* (Alfred A. Knopf, 1986).  Notes omitted.

road to the coast. For the first time, women were present in the caravans, and in the next decades, thousands of women in families followed. Their wagon trains generally carried about one-half men, one-half women and children: a population with the capacity to reinstate a heterosexual culture. Only during the Gold Rush years, 1849–1852, were most of the emigrants once again male. Many of the forty-niners, however, chose to return East rather than to settle. In the aftermath of the Rush, the numerical balance of men and women was restored. By 1860, the sex ratio in frontier counties, including those settled on the Great Plains, was no different from the average sex ratio in the East.

Despite the heterosexual demography, however, the West in the years after 1840 still appeared to be masculine terrain. Everywhere, emigrants and travellers saw "such lots of men, but very few ladies and children." In mining camps, "representatives of the gentler sex were so conspicuous by their absence that in one camp a lady's bonnet and boots were exhibited for one dollar a look." Similarly, "the Great Plains in the early period was strictly a man's country." Even later, historians agree that "the Far West had a great preponderance of men over women," and that the absence of "mothers and wives to provide moral anchorage to the large male population" was a primary cause of its social ills. What accounts for the disparity between these observations and the bare facts of demography? In many frontier regions, women failed to reinstitute their own sphere. Without a cultural base of their own, they disappeared behind the masculine preoccupations and social structure which dominated the West. Despite their numbers, women were often invisible, not only in the first two decades of family settlement but in successive phases as well.

In this essay, I try to sketch out some ways of understanding how the fact of this masculine imperium affected women's experiences in the great trans-Mississippi migrations. The following pages are in no way a monograph but rather a collection of suggestions which I have developed through reading and teaching about the West, and which I hope will encourage others to begin investigating this neglected area. Western migration constituted a critical rite of passage in nineteenth century culture; its impact still reverberates a century later in our own "Western" novels, movies, and television serials. Women's relationship to this key area of the "American experience" has remained submerged and unquestioned. There are only a few secondary books on women in the West, and the two best-known works are simplistic and sentimental. Few writers or scholars have attempted to look at frontier women in the light of the newer interpretations of women's history which have evolved over the last four years. There are a wealth of questions to investigate and a wealth of sources to use. To demonstrate how new analyses can illuminate conventional teaching and lecture material, I have chosen one clearly defined area of "pioneer experience," settlers on the Great Plains from 1865–1890. . . .

Until after the Civil War, emigrants usually travelled over the Great Plains without a thought of stopping. Explorers, farmers, and travellers agreed that the dry grasslands of the "Great American Desert"—the Dakotas, western Kansas, and western Nebraska—were not suitable for lucrative cultivation. In the late

60's, however, western land-grant railroads attempting to boost profits from passenger fares and land sales by promoting settlement in the region launched an advertising campaign in America and Europe which portrayed the Plains as a new Eden of verdant grasslands, rich soil, and plenteous streams. The railroad propaganda influenced a shift in public opinion, but technological advances in wheat-growing and steadily expanding urban markets for crops were far more significant in attracting settlers from Europe and the Mississippi Valley to the region. Emigrants came to take advantage of opportunities for more land, more crops, and more profits.

Who decided to move to the new lands? In the prevailing American notions of family relations, decisions about breadwinning and family finances were more or less in the hands of the male. Of course, removal to the Plains was a significant matter, and it is doubtful that many husbands and fathers made a unilateral decision to pull up stakes. Unfortunately, no large body of evidence about the choice to migrate to the Plains has been found or, at least, utilized in scholarly studies. I have sampled, however, some of the more than seven hundred diaries of men and women travelling to California and Oregon twenty years earlier. These indicate that the man usually initiated a plan to emigrate, made the final decision, and to a greater or lesser degree imposed it on his family. Men's involvement with self-advancement in the working world provided them with a logical and obvious rationale for going West.

The everyday concerns of "woman's sphere," however, did not provide women with many reasons to move. In the system that Tocqueville praised and Beecher vaunted, women's work, social responsibilities, and very identities were based almost entirely in the home. Domesticity involved professionalized housekeeping, solicitous childrearing, and an assiduous maintenance of a proper moral and religious character in the family. Clearly, women could keep house better, literally and metaphorically, in "civilized" parts, where churches, kinfolk, and women friends supported them. The West held no promise of a happier family life or a more salutary moral atmosphere. On the contrary, it was notoriously destructive to those institutions and values which women held dear.

The Plains region was an especially arid prospect for the transplantation of womanly values. Lonely and crude frontier conditions prevailed into the 90's; in some areas, the sparse population actually declined with time: "following the great boom of the 80's, when the tide of migration began to recede, central Dakota and western Nebraska and Kansas presented anything but a land of occupied farms." The loneliness which women endured "must have been such as to crush the soul," according to one historian of the region. Another asserts that "without a doubt" the burden of the adverse conditions of Plains life—the aridity, treelessness, heat, perpetual wind, and deadening cold—fell upon the women. Almost without exception, others concur: "although the life of the frontier farmer was difficult special sympathy should go to his wife" ... "it is certain that many stayed until the prairie broke them in spirit or body while others fled from the monotonous terror of it." An observer who visited the Plains in the 50's found life there to be "peculiarly severe upon women and oxen." The duration as well as the severity of cultural disruption which Plains women experienced was perhaps without parallel in the history of nineteenth-century frontiers.

First of all, emigrant women did not move into homes like the ones they had left behind, but into sod huts, tarpaper shacks, and dugouts. Seldom as temporary as they planned to be, these crude structures still existed as late as the nineties. Most settlers lived in one room "soddies" for six or seven years: if luck left a little cash, they might move into a wooden shack. Thus a farmer's wife often spent years trying to keep clean a house made of dirt. The effort became especially disheartening in rainstorms, when leaking walls splattered mud over bedclothes and dishes: "in those trying times the mud floors were too swampy to walk upon and wives could cook only with an umbrella held over the stove; after they were over every stitch of clothing must be hung out to dry." Dry weather gave no respite from dirt, since dust and straw incessantly sifted down from the walls. Housekeeping as a profession in the sense that Catharine Beecher promulgated it was impossible under such circumstances. Soddies were so badly insulated that during the winter, water froze away from the stove. In summer, the paucity of light and air could be stifling.

Often there was simply no money available to build a decent house. Drought, grasshoppers, or unseasonable rains destroyed many of the harvests of the 80's and 90's. Even good crops did not necessarily change a family's living conditions, since debts and mortgages which had accrued during hard times could swallow up any profits. But in any case, home improvements were a low priority, and families often remained in soddies or shacks even when there was cash or credit to finance a frame house. The farmer usually earmarked his profits for reinvestment into the money-making outlay of better seeds, new stock, machinery, and tools. Farm machinery came first, labor-saving devices for women last: "there was a tendency for the new homesteader to buy new machinery to till broad acres and build new barns to house more stock and grain, while his wife went about the drudgery of household life in the old way in a little drab dwelling overshadowed by the splendour of machine farming." Washers and sewing machines graced some farms in the 80's, but "for the most part... the machine age did not greatly help woman. She continued to operate the churn, carry water, and run the washing machine—if she were fortunate enough to have one—and do her other work without the aid of horse power which her more fortunate husband began to apply in his harvesting, threshing, and planting."

Against such odds, women were unable to recreate the kinds of houses they had left. Nor could they reinstate the home as a venerated institution. A sod house was only a makeshift shelter; no effort of the will or imagination could fashion it into what one of its greatest defenders eulogized as "the fairest garden in the wide field of endeavour and achievement." There were other losses as well. Many feminine social activities in more settled farm communities revolved around the church, but with the exception of the European immigrant enclaves, churches were scarce on the Plains. At best, religious observance was makeshift; at worst, it was non-existent. Although "it is not to be supposed that only the ungodly came west," one historian noted, "there seemed to exist in some parts of the new settlements a spirit of apathy if not actual hostility toward religion." Circuit-riders and evangelical freelancers drew crowds during droughts and depressions, but during normal times, everyday piety was rare. Few families read the Bible, sang hymns, or prayed together: "when people heard that a family was religious, it was thought that the head of the household must be a minister."

Women were also unable to reconstitute the network of female friendships which had been an accustomed and sustaining part of daily life "back home." Long prairie winters kept everyone housebound for much of the year. During summers and warmer weather, however, men travelled to town to buy supplies and negotiate loans, and rode to nearby claims to deliver mail, borrow tools, or share news. "As soon as the storms let up, the men could get away from the isolation," wrote Mari Sandoz, Nebraska writer and daughter of a homesteader: "But not their women. They had only the wind and the cold and the problems of clothing, shelter, food, and fuel." On ordinary days men could escape, at least temporarily, "into the fields, the woods, or perhaps to the nearest saloon where there was warmth and companionship, but women had almost no excuses to leave. Neighbors lived too far apart to make casual visiting practicable; besides, a farmer could seldom spare a wagon team from field work to take a woman calling. Hamlin Garland, who moved to the Plains as a young boy, remembered that women visited less than in Wisconsin, his former home, since "the work on the new farms was never-ending": "I doubt if the women—any of them—got out into the fields or meadows long enough to enjoy the birds and the breezes."

In most respects, the patterns of life rarely accommodated women's needs. Plains society paid little mind to women, yet women were essential, not incidental, to its functioning. Without female labor, cash-crop agriculture could never have developed. A man could not farm alone, and hired help was almost impossible to come by. Ordinarily, a farmer could count only on his wife and children as extra hands. On the homestead, women's responsibilities as a farmhand, not as a home-maker or a mother, were of first priority. Women still cooked, sewed, and washed, but they also herded livestock and toted water for irrigation.

The ambitious farmer's need for the labor power of women and children often lent a utilitarian quality to relations between men and women. For the single settler, marriage was, at least in part, a matter of efficiency. Courtships were typically brief and frank. Molly Dorsey Sanford, a young unmarried homesteader in Nebraska territory, recorded in her diary over half a dozen proposals in a few years. Most of her suitors were strangers. One transient liked her cooking, another heard about a "hull lot of girls" at the Dorsey farm and came to try his luck, and an old man on the steamboat going to Nebraska proposed after an hour's acquaintance. Jules Sandoz, father of Mari Sandoz, married four times. Three wives fled before he found a woman who resigned herself to the emotionless regimen of his farm. Stolid and resilient, the fourth, Mari's mother, lived to a taciturn old age, but her daughter could not forget others of her mother's generation who had not survived their hasty marriages: "after her arrival the wife found that her husband seldom mentioned her in his letters or manuscripts save in connection with calamity. She sickened and left her work undone... so the pioneer could not plow or build or hunt. If his luck was exceedingly bad, she died and left him his home without a housekeeper until she could be replaced." With characteristic ambivalence, Sandoz added, "at first this seems a calloused, even a brutal attitude, but it was not so intended."

Instrumentality could also characterize other family relations. Jules Sandoz "never spoke well of anyone who might make his words an excuse for less prompt jumping when he commanded. This included his wife and children." Garland described himself and his fellows as "a Spartan lot. We did not believe in letting our wives and children know they were an important part of our contentment." Jules' wife "considered praise of her children as suspect as self praise would be." Preoccupied by her chores, she maintained only minimal relationships with her family and assigned the care of the younger children to Mari, the oldest daughter.

In the domestic ideology of the family, careful and attentive child-rearing was especially important. Unlike the stoic Mrs. Sandoz, the American women who emigrated were often openly disturbed and troubled by a situation in which mothering was only peripheral to a day's work, and keenly felt the absence of cultural support for correct child-rearing. Mrs. Dorsey, the mother of diarist Molly Sanford, continually worried that her children, exiled from civilization, would turn into barbarians. In towns like Indianapolis, the family's home, schools, churches, and mothers worked in concert. In Nebraska, a mother could count on few aids. The day the Dorseys reached their claim, Molly wrote, "Mother hardly enters into ecstasies... she no doubt realizes what it is to bring a young rising family away from the world... if the country would only fill up, if there were only schools or churches or even some society. We do not see women at all. All men, single, or bachelors, and one gets tired of them." Molly occasionally responded to her mother's anxiety by searching herself and her siblings for signs of mental degeneration, but Mrs. Dorsey's fears were never warranted. The children grew up healthy and dutiful: in Molly's words, "the wild outdoor life strengthens our physical faculties, and the privations, our powers of endurance." To her confident appraisal, however, she appended a cautionary note in her mother's mode: "so that we do not degenerate mentally, it is all right; Heaven help us." Mrs. Dorsey, however, could seldom be reassured. When a snake bit one of the children, "Poor Mother was perfectly prostrated... she sometimes feels wicked to think she is so far away from all help with her family." On her mother's fortieth birthday, Molly wrote, "I fear she is a little blue today. I do try so hard to keep cheerful. I don't know as it is hard work to keep myself so, but it is hard with her. She knows now that the children ought to be in school. We will have to do the teaching ourselves."...

As Mrs. Dorsey saw her ideas of child-rearing atrophy, she also witnessed a general attenuation of the womanliness which had been central to her own identity and sense of importance in the world. Her daughters particularly taxed her investment in an outmoded conception of womanhood. Molly, for instance, was pleased with her facility in learning traditionally male skills. "So it seems I can put my hand to almost anything," she wrote with pride after helping her father roof the house. Mrs. Dorsey regarded her daughter's expanding capacities in a different light. When Molly disguised herself as a man to do some chores, "it was very funny to all but Mother, who fears I am losing all the dignity I ever possessed." Molly was repentant but defensive: "I know I am getting demoralized, but I should be more so, to mope around and have no fun."

Mrs. Dorsey's partial failure to transmit her own values of womanhood to her daughter is emblematic of many difficulties of the first generation of woman settlers. Women could not keep their daughters out of men's clothes, their children in shoes, their family Bibles in use, or their houses clean; at every step, they failed to make manifest their traditions, values, and collective sensibility. It was perhaps the resistance of the Plains to the slightest feminine modification rather than the land itself which contributed to the legend of woman's fear of the empty prairies: "literature is filled with women's fear and distrust of the Plains... if one may judge by fiction, one must conclude that the Plains exerted a peculiarly appalling effect on women." The heroine of [O. E.] Rolvaag's *Giants in the Earth* echoed the experience of real women in her question to herself: "how will human beings be able to endure this place?... Why, there isn't even a thing that one can *hide behind!*" The desolation even affected women who passed through on their way to the coast. Sarah Royce remembered shrinking from the "chilling prospect" of her first night on the Plains on the Overland Trail: "surely there would be a few trees or a sheltering hillside.... No, only the level prairie.... Nothing indicated a place for us—a cozy nook, in which for the night we might be guarded."

Fright was not a rarity on the Plains. Both men and women knew the fear of droughts, blizzards, and accidental death. Yet the reported frequency of madness and suicide among women is one indication that [Everett] Dick may have been right in his contention that "the real burden... fell upon the wife and mother." Men's responsibilities required them to act upon their fears. If a blizzard hung in the air, they brought the cattle in; if crops failed, they renegotiated the mortgages and planned for the next season. In contrast, women could often do nothing in the face of calamity. "If hardships came," Sandoz wrote, "the women faced it at home. The results were tersely told by the items in the newspapers of the day. Only sheriff sales seem to have been more numerous than the items telling of trips to the insane asylum."

Men made themselves known in the acres of furrows they ploughed up from the grassland. Women, lacking the opportunities of a home, had few ways to make either the land or their neighbors aware of their presence. The inability of women to leave a mark on their surroundings is a persistent theme in Sandoz's memoirs. When Mari was a child, a woman killed herself and her three children with gopher poison and a filed down case knife. The neighbors agreed that "she had been plodding and silent for a long time," and a woman friend added sorrowfully, "If she could 'a had even a geranium, but in that cold shell of a shack...." In Sandoz's memory, the women of her mother's generation are shadows, "silent... always there, in the dark corner near the stove."

I have emphasized only one side of woman's experience on the Plains. For many, the years brought better times, better houses, and even neighbors. A second generation came to maturity: some were daughters like the strong farm women of Willa Cather's novels who managed to reclaim the land that had crushed their mothers. Yet the dark side of the lives of the first women on the Plains cannot be denied. Workers in an enterprise often not of their own making, their labor was essential to the farm, their womanhood irrelevant. Hamlin Garland's *Main Travelled Roads,* written in part as a condemnation of "the futility of woman's life on a farm," elicited this response from his mother: "you might have said more but I'm glad you didn't. Farmer's wives have enough to bear as it is."

# POSTSCRIPT

## Did the Westward Movement Transform the Traditional Roles of Women in the Late Nineteenth Century?

Stansell and Myres approach the issue of westering women from very different perspectives. Stansell adopts a radical feminist stance and argues that women who moved to the West regressed from the traditional cult of motherhood adhered to by middle-class eastern women who attended to the moral and physical needs of their homes and their children. Out on the frontier, says Stansell, women were isolated from their support systems of other women, and their marriages were often dominated by males who showed their wives neither love and affection nor respect. In short, Stansell paints a very grim picture of frontier life for women.

Myres, on the other hand, gives a much more upbeat portrayal of westering women than Stansell. Like Stansell, Myres uses many of the diaries and letters of middle-class white women as sources, but she also includes more materials on black, Hispanic, and Native American women (but not immigrant women), and she covers a broader time period. Myres sees frontier women as extremely active in business, manufacturing, agriculture, and the traditional teaching and nursing professions, many of which were carried on outside the home.

More than any other historian of the West, Myres has updated the Turner thesis and applied it to frontier women. She sees her book "not as women's history but as frontier history." In her preface, Myres criticizes both the "scissors and paste" historians who added women to the traditional accounts of the West and feminist writers like Stansell. "By isolating women from the social and cultural milieu in which they lived," says Myres, "such studies distorted the role of women on the frontier and often replaced old myths and stereotypes with new ones. Women were an important part of the frontier experience, but they must be viewed within the context of that experience, not isolated in pristine splendor or tacked on at the end of a chapter on the winning of the west."

A third study, Julie Roy Jeffrey's *Frontier Women: The Trans-Mississippi West 1840–1880* (Hill & Wang, 1979), falls between the Myres and Stansell interpretations in that it emphasizes the conservative behavior of western women. Jeffrey says in her introduction, "I hoped to find that pioneer women used the frontier as a means of liberating themselves from stereotypes and behaviors which I found constricting and sexist. I discovered they did not. More important, I discovered why they did not."

Overviews of the new western history are most easily sampled in the following essays: Larry McMurtry, "The Revisionists' Failure of Imagination: How the West Was Won or Lost," *The New Republic* (October 22, 1990); "The Old West: The New View of Frontier Life," *U.S. News and World Report* (May 21, 1990); Alan Brinkley, "The Western Historians: Don't Fence Them In," *The New York Times Book Review* (September 20, 1992); Brian W. Dippie, "The Winning of the West Reconsidered," *The Wilson Quarterly* (Summer 1990); John Mack Faragher, "Gunslingers and Bureaucrats: Some Unexpected Truths About the American West," *The New Republic* (December 14, 1992); Diane Stevenson, "The New Frontier," *The Nation* (September 14, 1992); and David Seal, "The New Custerism," *The Nation* (May 13, 1991).

Four major anthologies that sample the new western history are: William Cronin et al., *Under an Open Sky: Rethinking America's Western Past* (W. W. Norton, 1992); Patricia Nelson Limerick et al., *Trails: Toward a New Western History* (University of Kansas Press, 1991); Roger L. Nicholas, ed., *American Frontier and Western Issues: A Historiographical Review* (Greenwood Press, 1986); and Michael Malone, ed., *Historians and the American West* (University of Nebraska Press, 1983). These four readers deal with the environment, industrialization, Native Americans, African Americans, Hispanics, paintings, films, and other areas of the West neglected by Turner and his followers.

Each of the above anthologies contains historiographical essays that are replete with comprehensive bibliographies about western women by Katherine G. Morrissey, Peggy Pascoe, Glenda Riley and Sandra L. Myres. The most recent is Morrissey, "Engendering the West," in *Under an Open Sky*. The current scholarship on women has moved beyond literate white women who settled in the West and focuses upon minority women. Papers from the conferences held by the Coalition for Western Women's History and the Southwest Institute for Research on Women are published in Susan Armitage et al., eds., *The Women's West* (University of Oklahoma Press, 1987) and Lillian Schlissel et al., eds., *Western Women: Their Land, Their Lives* (University of New Mexico Press, 1988).

Students should contrast the old and new approaches to western history. The starting point remains Frederick Jackson Turner's widely reprinted address delivered to the American Historical Association in 1893 on "The Significance of the Frontier in American History." The Turner tradition can be found in the works of Ray Allen Billington, whose *Westward Expansion: A History of the American Frontier* (Macmillan, 1982) has been through five editions. Also see Billington's biography *Frederick Jackson Turner: Historian, Scholar, Teacher* (Oxford University Press, 1973) as well as his collected essays in *America's Frontier Heritage* (Holt, Rinehart & Winston, 1966).

The two best overviews of the new western history are Patricia Nelson Limericks's *The Legacy of Conquest: The Unbroken Part of the American West* (W. W. Norton, 1987) and Richard White's monumental *"It's Your Misfortune and None of My Own": A New History of the American West* (University of Oklahoma Press, 1992).

# ISSUE 6

## Was City Government in Late Nineteenth-Century America a "Conspicuous Failure"?

**YES: Ernest S. Griffith,** from *A History of American City Government: The Conspicuous Failure, 1870–1900* (National Civic League Press, 1974)

**NO: Jon C. Teaford,** from *The Unheralded Triumph: City Government in America, 1860–1900* (Johns Hopkins University Press, 1984)

### ISSUE SUMMARY

**YES:** Professor of political science and political economy Ernest S. Griffith (1896–1981) focuses upon illegal and unethical operations of the political machine and concludes that the governments controlled by the bosses represented a betrayal of the public trust.

**NO:** Professor of history Jon C. Teaford argues that scholars traditionally have overlooked the remarkable success municipal governments in the late nineteenth century achieved in dealing with the challenges presented by rapid urbanization.

During the late nineteenth century, American farmers based their grievances on revolutionary changes that had occurred in the post–Civil War United States. Specifically, they saw themselves as victims of an industrial wave that had swept over the nation and submerged their rural, agricultural world in the undertow. Indeed, the values, attitudes, and interests of all Americans were affected dramatically by the rapid urbanization that accompanied industrial growth. The result was the creation of the modern city with its coordinated network of economic development, which emphasized mass production and mass consumption.

In the years from 1860 to 1920, the number of urban residents in the United States increased much more rapidly than the national population as a whole. For example, the Census Bureau reported in 1920 that the United States housed 105,711,000 people, three times the number living in the country on the eve of the Civil War. Urban dwellers, however, increased ninefold during the same period. The number of "urban" places (incorporated towns with 2,500 or more residents, or unincorporated areas with at least 2,500 people per square mile) increased from 392 in 1860 to 2,722 by 1920. Cities with populations in excess of 100,000 increased from 9 in 1860 to 68 in 1920.

Reflecting many of the characteristics of "modern" America, these industrial cities produced a number of problems for the people who lived in them —problems associated with fire and police protection, sanitation, utilities, and a wide range of social services. These coincided with increased concerns over employment opportunities and demands for transportation and housing improvements. Typically, municipal government became the clearinghouse for such demands. What was the nature of city government in the late nineteenth-century United States? How effectively were American cities governed? To what extent did municipal leaders listen to and redress the grievances of urban dwellers? In light of James Lord Bryce's blunt statement in 1888 that city government in the United States was a "conspicuous failure," it is worthwhile to explore scholarly assessments of Bryce's conclusion.

Ernest S. Griffith surveys the nature of municipal government in the last three decades of the nineteenth century and concludes that city politics was consumed by a "cancer of corruption" that predominated in the years from 1880 to 1893. He identifies numerous factors that contributed to this unethical environment, as well as the disreputable and illegal lengths gone to that perpetuated the power of the bosses but prevented city government from operating in the true interest of the people.

Jon C. Teaford, on the other hand, complains that scholars like Griffith are too eager to condemn the activities of late nineteenth-century municipal governments without recognizing their accomplishments. While admitting numerous shortcomings, Teaford argues that American city dwellers enjoyed a higher standard of public services than any other urban residents in the world. Also, in contrast to the portrait of boss dominance presented by Griffith and others, Teaford claims that authority was widely distributed among various groups, which peacefully coexisted with one another. For Teaford, nineteenth-century cities failed to develop a political image but succeeded to a remarkable degree in meeting the needs of those dependent upon them.

# YES

Ernest S. Griffith

## THE CANCER OF CORRUPTION

### INTRODUCTION

Corruption may be defined as personal profit at the expense of the public—stealing and use of office for private gain, including the giving and taking of bribes outside of the law. More broadly defined, it is any antisocial conduct that uses government as an instrument. Its twilight zone is never the same from age to age, from community to community, or even from person to person....

Historically, the motivations of the electorate, the uses to which tax money and campaign contributions were put, the pressures of reward and punishment to which candidates and officeholders were subjected, were never very far from the gray zone in which the line between the corrupt and the ethical—or even the legal—had somehow to be drawn. Votes were "coin of the realm" in a democracy; office holding or power-wielding was secured by votes. They might be freely and intelligently given; they might be the result of propaganda, friendship, or pressure; they might be purchased by money or otherwise; they might be manufactured out of election frauds. Those who were members of the government, visible or invisible, were ultimately dependent on the voters for their opportunity to serve, for their livelihood, for the chance to steal or betray. These conditions existed in the late nineteenth century; with differing emphases they still exist today.

What, then, determined whether a late-nineteenth-century city government was corrupt or ethical, or something in between? Ethically speaking, the nadir of American city government was probably reached in the years between 1880 and 1893. Why and how? There was obviously no one answer. The time has long since passed when municipal reformers, not to mention historians, believed there was a single answer. There was present a highly complex situation—a *Gestalt,* or pattern—never identical in any two places, but bearing a family resemblance in most respects. The path to better municipal governance was long and difficult because of this very complexity. The story of the 1890's and of the Progressive Era of the first twelve or fifteen years of the twentieth century was the story of a thousand battles on a

From Ernest S. Griffith, *A History of American City Government: The Conspicuous Failure, 1870–1900* (National Civic League Press, 1974). 

thousand fronts—the unraveling of a refractory network of unsuitable charters and procedures, of a human nature that at times led to despair, of an economic order that put a premium on greed, of a social order of class and ethnic divisions reflected often in incompatible value systems—all infinitely complicated by rapidity of growth and population mobility. . . .

## PATRONAGE

[H]ow are we to account for the corrupt machine in the first place, and for what came to be its endemic character in American cities for two or three decades? This is part of a broader analysis, and will be undertaken presently. As always, in the end the legacy of a corrupt and corrupting regime was a malaise of suspicion, discouragement, and blunted ideals in society as a whole.

In examining the fact of corruption, it was obvious that the city—any city, good or bad—provided livelihood for scores, hundreds, even thousands of people directly employed. They would fight if their livelihood were threatened. There were also large numbers dependent upon the city for contracts, privileges, and immunities. Not as sharply defined, and often overlapping one or both of these categories, were persons who served as organizers, brokers, or instruments of these other two groups, and whose livelihoods therefore also depended upon the city. They, too, would fight to attain, keep, or augment this livelihood, and probably the sense of power (and occasionally the constructive achievements) that their positions carried with them. They were the "machine," the "ring," the "boss," the professional politician, the political lawyer. This is to say, for many people (as regards the city) employment, power, and access to those with power were matters of economic life or death for themselves and their families—and, if these same people were wholly self-seeking, to them the end justified the means.

First, consider the municipal employees. "To the victors belong the spoils"—the party faction and machine rewarded their own and punished the others. In 1889 the mayor of Los Angeles appointed all of his six sons to the police force, but this helped to defeat him in the next election. In the smaller cities, and in the larger ones before skills seemed essential, a change of administration or party was the signal for wholesale dismissals and wholesale patronage. This fact created the strongest incentive for those currently employed to work for the retention in power of those influential in their employment; that they had so worked constituted a logical basis for their dismissal; given the success of the opposing candidates. That the city might suffer in both processes was unimportant to those whose livelihood was at stake in the outcome of the struggle. Those involved, in many instances, would not even respect the position of school teacher, and could usually find ways and means to subvert the civil service laws when they emerged, in intent if not in formal ritual. In Brooklyn, for example, during the Daniel Whitney administration of 1885, only favored candidates were informed of the dates of the examinations in time to apply. Examinations were then leniently graded, to put it mildly. One illiterate received a grade of 97.5 per cent on a written test. About 1890, each member of the Boston city council received a certain number of tickets corresponding to his quota of men employed by the city. No one was eligible without such a ticket, and existing employees were discharged to make room if necessary.

## SALE OF PRIVILEGES AND IMMUNITIES

As regards the sale for cash of privileges and immunities, many politicians and officials did not stop with the twilight zone of liquor violations, gambling, and prostitution, but went on to exploit what would be regarded as crime in any language or society. Denver (incidentally, at least until the 1960's) was one of the worst. From the late 1880's until 1922, Lou Blonger, king of the city's underworld, held the police department in his grasp. For many of these years he had a direct line to the chief of police, and his orders were "law." Criminals were never molested if they operated outside the city limits, and often not within the limits, either. He contributed liberally to the campaign funds of both parties, those of the district attorneys being especially favored. Blonger was sent to jail in 1922 by Philip Van Cise, a district attorney who had refused his conditional campaign contribution of $25,000.

Yet, it was the insatiable appetite of men for liquor, sex, and the excitement and eternal hope of gambling that proved by all the odds the most refractory and the most corrupting day-to-day element....

The police of most cities, and the politicians and officials, took graft or campaign contributions from the liquor interests so that they would overlook violations of the law. Judging from extant material of the period, corruption by the liquor trade occurred more frequently than any other. Over and over again the question of enforcement of whatever laws existed was an issue at the polls. The fact was that, at this time, the trade did not want *any* regulation and resented all but the most nominal license fee, unless the license in effect granted a neighborhood semimonopoly, and increased profitability accordingly. It was prepared to fight and pay for its privileges. Council membership was literally jammed with saloon keepers, and Buffalo (1880) was not too exceptional in having a brewer as mayor. Apparently in one instance (in Nebraska), the liquor interests resorted to assassination of the clerk of the U.S. Federal Circuit Court in revenge for his part in the fight against them.

More clearly illegal, because here it was not a question of hours of sale but of its right to exist, was commercial gambling. State laws and even municipal ordinances were fairly usual in prohibiting it, but these laws were sustained neither by enforcement nor by public opinion. If the public opinion calling for enforcement was present, the requisite ethical standard was not there that would preclude the offering and accepting of the bribes that made the continuance of gambling possible—except for an occasional spasm of raids and reform.

Oklahoma City will serve as a case study. At one point gambling houses regularly paid one fine a month. Four-fifths of the businessmen refused to answer whether they would favor closing such joints; going on record either way would hurt their business. Citing District Attorney William T. Jerome's views of attempts to secure enforcement of this type of law, one writer commented: "The corrupt politician welcomes the puritan as an ally. He sees in laws that cannot and will not be permanently enforced a yearly revenue in money and in power."

The situation regarding commercialized vice was similar. Laws and ordinances forbidding brothels were on the statute books. Brothels existed in every large city and most of the smaller ones. Especially in the Western cities where men greatly outnumbered women, they appeared in large numbers, and the same might be said of the commercial centers and the seaport towns. A boss like Boies Penrose of Philadelphia patronized them. So, in fact, did a number of presumably otherwise respectable citizens. Many of this last group also drew rent from the brothels.

What this meant to the city government of a place like Seattle may be illustrated by an episode in 1892:

> The police department thought it had a vested property right in the collections from prostitutes and gamblers. The new mayor, Ronald, was waited on almost immediately by a group of high ranking police officers who asked him how much of a cut he wanted out of the monthly "pay off" for gambling and prostitution. "Not a cent! Moreover, there isn't going to be any collection or places that pay protection money," he said as he pounded the table. The committee patiently explained that it was "unofficial licensing," a very effective way to control crime. The mayor exploded again and one of the captains took out a revolver and dropped it on the table. "Somebody is going to get hurt—maybe." The mayor tried as hard as ever anyone could to clean up, but found it impossible. He was powerless because he had no real support. He resigned in less than a year.

For the depths of degradation into which the combination of lust and greed can sink a city government, one can only cite the example of Kansas City, where girls at the municipal farm were sold by the politicians (who of course pocketed the money) and sent to brothels in New Orleans....

Each city, as the pressures of urban living forced regulation, found itself under conflicting demands. The people as a whole probably wanted "nuisances" cleared up—unsanitary dwellings, cattle in the streets, sign encroachments, garbage left around, and a hundred other annoying matters—the counterpart in today's world of illegal parking. But to the particular person involved, there was an interest in leaving things as they were—an interest for which he was prepared to pay by a tip or a vote. Compulsory education laws ran up against parents who regarded them as a violation of their God-given right to employ their children as they wished. Political revenge might well await the enforcer—the truant officer, health officer, inspector of meat, dairies, or housing, or policeman. Political and often pecuniary rewards awaited those who would overlook matters of this type. There were other favors, tips on the location of a proposed public improvement or on the location of a road or a park relevant to real estate value. These were advantageous to the official and his friends to know and to control for their own personal profit. Real estate profit through advance notice or an actual share in the decision on a municipal improvement or purchase was one of the most lucrative perquisites of councilors or the "ring" members. A special instance of this was the desire of many members of Congress for seats on the low-status District of Columbia Committee so as to secure advance information as to what would be profitable real estate purchases in the District. In general, these examples came under the heading of "honest graft" in those days, as not necessarily costing the city treasury an undue amount. The term was invented by George W. Plunkett of Tammany as a rationalization.

## GRAFT FROM CONTRACTS AND FRANCHISES

Quite otherwise were the profits, direct and indirect, from lucrative city contracts. Probably in the majority of cities there was a tacit understanding that a favored contractor would "kick back" a substantial amount (10 per cent or more being quite usual) either to party campaign funds for which accounting was rare, as fees to a "political lawyer," with the ultimate distribution uncertain, or as out-and-out bribes to those with the power to make the decisions. There were always any number of devices to evade the intent of the law, even in situations where the law called for competitive bidding. Pittsburgh for years found that William Flinn, one of its two bosses, was always the lowest "responsible" bidder for contracts. In other instances, specifications were such that only the favored one could meet them. In New Orleans, around 1890, in spite of the protests of the property owners, almost all paving was with rosetta gravel (in which one man had a monopoly). In other cases, the lowest bid was accepted, but there would be advance assurance (private and arranged) that the inspectors would not insist that the contractor meet the specifications. Contractors in Portland (Oregon) in 1893 whose men voted "right" were laxly supervised. In still other instances, the bidders themselves formed rings, bid high, and arranged for distribution of the contracts among themselves. This practice seems to have been a particular bent among paving contractors. William Gabriel of Cleveland, high in Republican circles, will serve as an example. This was not incompatible with generous bribes to municipal officials or rings as well. Graft in contracts extended to the schools—to their construction and to the textbooks purchased. Things were probably not so flagrant in Cleveland, where campaign contributions and not bribes were the favored means of business.

Franchises and privileges for the railroads and the various utilities came to be special sources of demoralization, particularly for the councils that usually had the responsibility for granting them. Initially, a community welcomed the railroad and even subsidized its coming. With growing urbanization, it looked forward to waterworks, lighting (gas or electricity), street cars (horse or cable), and eventually electricity and the telephone. The earliest of the franchises were likely to be most liberal with respect to rate allowed, duration, and service rendered. The cities wanted the utilities and often urged their coming. Later, as the latter proved enormously profitable, the stakes grew high, and betrayal of the public interest probably took place in the majority of cases. Power to grant franchises greatly increased the desirability of membership on the council. Hazen Pingree, mayor of Detroit in the early 1890's wrote:

> My experiences in fighting monopolistic corporations as mayor of Detroit, and in endeavoring to save to the people some of their right as against their greed, have further convinced me that they, the corporations, are responsible for nearly all the thieving and boodling with which cities are made to suffer from their servants. They seek almost uniformly to secure what they want by means of bribes, and in this way they corrupt our councils and commissions.

Providence, in the 1890's allowed only property owners to vote. They elected businessmen to the city council. This council then awarded Nelson Aldrich, the state boss, a perpetual franchise, which he sold out at an enormous profit. He went to the Senate through wholesale bribery of rural voters, with money con- tributed by the sugar magnates for whom as congressman he had arranged a protective tariff. The city of Pawtucket, which sought to block a franchise, was overridden by the rurally dominated state legislature.

It was Lincoln Steffens who later dramatized beyond any forgetting the unholy link between the protected underworld, the city governments, and the portion of the business community in search of contracts and franchises—a link found in city after city. The story of his exposures belongs to the Progressive Era. At the time, these betrayals of the public interest were either not known or, if known, were enjoyed and shared, shrugged off and rationalized, or endured in futile fury.

Two or three further examples of documented franchise bribery might be cited. In 1884, in New York City, the Broadway Surface Railroad paid $25,000 to each of eighteen alderman and received the franchise. The rival company had offered the *city* $1 million. Another corporation set aside $100,000 to buy the council. The street-car companies of Indianapolis contributed to both political parties. So it went in city after city.

Some other examples of business corruption might be cited. Governor John P. Altgeld of Illinois sent a message (1895) to the state legislature, calling attention to the fantastically low rents paid by newspapers for school lands. In a most complex arrangement involving shipping companies, boarding-house keepers, "crimps" (recruiters of seamen), and the city authorities, the San Francisco waterfront instituted a reign of near-peonage, in which seamen were grossly overcharged for their lodging and shore "amenities," prevented from organized resistance, and virtually terrorized and blackmailed into signing on the ships again. In the early 1870's, local speculators of Dubuque, including two former mayors, bought up city bonds for a small amount and held out for redemption at par. Favored banks (that is, those contributing through appropriate channels to the city treasurer, the party, or the boss) received city deposits without having to pay interest thereon, or, as in Pittsburgh, paying the interest to the politicians. Finally, the employer power structure threw its weight and its funds in support of almost any administration that would protect strikebreakers, break up "radical" gatherings, and otherwise preserve the "American system" against alien ideas—this, without reference to the extent of the known corruption of the administration.

## THEFT, ASSESSMENT FAVORITISM, "KICKBACKS," "RAKE-OFFS"

As might be expected, there were a number of examples of actual theft, most frequently by a city treasurer. Judges would occasionally keep fines. A certain amount of this was to be expected in an age of ruthless money-making when business ethics condoned all kinds of sharp practices in the private sector. What was more discouraging was that many of these thieves remained unpunished, as the machine with its frequent control over the courts protected its own. City officials of Spokane even stole funds contributed for relief after its great fire (1889).

How widespread was political favoritism in tax assessment would be extraordinarily difficult to determine. The practice of underassessment across the board to avoid litigation was almost universal, and in some communities it had a statutory base. Certainly many corporations were favored, in part because they were deemed an asset to the community's economic life. What was more probable was the widespread fear that, if a person were to criticize the city administration, he would find his underassessment raised. This particular form of blackmail took place in blatant fashion at one time in Jersey City. It also occurred under Park Board administration in the Bronx in 1874. From time to time, there would be exposures in the local press of assessment anomalies, but the press was itself vulnerable to punitive retaliation of this type because of its frequent underassessment.

The practice of compensating certain employees by fees instead of fixed salaries lingered on, in spite of or often because of the large amounts of money involved. Such employees were usually expected, by virtue of their election or appointment, to "kick back" a substantial portion to the party organization. Such "kickbacks" from the receiver of taxes amounted in Philadelphia to $200,000 in one of the years after 1873—divided among the small number who constituted the gas-house ring. Other compensations by the fee system were abandoned in 1873, and the employees were put on salaries. Some nominations and appointments were sold, with the receipts going, it was hoped, to the party campaign funds, concerning the use of which there was rarely in these days any effective accounting. Political assessments of city employees probably ruled in the majority of the cities.

How much graft in fact found its way into the pockets of the city employees for their betrayal of trust or, for that matter, for services they should have rendered in any event, how much "rake-off" the ring or the boss took, will never be known. What was graft and what was "rake-off" shaded into a gray zone after a while. The amount must have been colossal in the cities—certainly enough, had it been dedicated to municipal administration, to have enhanced efficiency and service enormously, or to have cut the tax rate drastically. Utility rates would have tumbled and service improved....

## EXTORTION AND BLACKMAIL

Extortion and blackmail, if not standard practice, were frequent enough to call for comment. Once in a while, as in Fort Worth (1877), they were used in an intriguing and perhaps constructive fashion. It was proposed that the sale of intoxicants be forbidden at the theaters. The ordinance was tabled, with the notation that it would be passed unless one of the theater owners paid his taxes.

In Brooklyn during the Whitney administration, the head of the fire department blocked an electric franchise until he was given one-fifth of the company's stock and several other politicians had taken a cut.

The newspapers were particularly vulnerable to blackmail. A threat of loss of the city's advertising was a marvelous silencer. In Tacoma (1889), enough businessmen believed a particular gambling house was a community asset that the newspaper that had denounced its protected status as a result lost heavily in both advertising and circulation.

The gangs of Detroit seemed to be immune in the 1880's and able to bring about the promotion or dismissal of a policeman. Sailors, tugmen, longshoremen made up the bulk of their personnel. In the early 1880's in Indianapolis, citizens were arrested on trumped-up charges and fined by judges who at that time were paid by the fines.

## POLICE AND THE COURTS

... [D]ifficulties stemmed from the key role played by the police in the electoral process, the graft from the under-world, and the desire on the part of the allegedly more respectable for immunities. In Tacoma, the mayor reprimanded the chief of police for raiding a brothel in which a number of the city's influential men were found. All these factors meant that in city after city the police force was really regarded as an adjunct of the political party or machine. In some of the smaller cities, the patronage aspect was expressed in extreme form. For example, until 1891 each new mayor of Wilmington (Delaware) appointed a new set of policemen, usually of his own party.

Nor were the courts immune as adjuncts to corruption. The district attorney and the judges, especially the local ones, were usually elected, and by the same processes as the mayors and councils. The same network of political and corrupt immunities that pervaded the police and stemmed from the rings and other politicians was present in the courts. Four hazards to justice were thus in a sense vulnerable to pressure and purchase—the stages of arrest, prosecution, the verdicts (and delays) of the judge, and the possibilities of a packed or bribed jury. William Howard Taft commented at a later date as follows:

> [The] administration of criminal law is a disgrace to our civilization, and the prevalence of crime and fraud, which here is greatly in excess of that in European countries, is due largely to the failure of the law to bring criminals to justice.

Quite apart from overt corruption, there were numerous ways in which courts could reward the party faithful, such as by appointment as favored bondsmen, stenographers, or auctioneers.

It was not surprising that an exasperated and otherwise respectable public occasionally fought back by violent means. In Cincinnati (1884), so flagrant had been the court delays and acquittals that a mass meeting, held to protest the situation, evolved into a mob bent on direct action. They burned the courthouse and attempted to storm the jail. For days the mob ruled. Police and militia failed, and only federal troops finally restored order. There were over fifty deaths. In Dallas, in the early 1880's, the "respectable" element, despairing of action by the city government in closing some of the worst resorts, took to burning them. Acquittal of the murderers of the chief of police of New Orleans by a probably corrupted jury was followed by lynchings....

## SUMMARY SCENARIO

This in general was the scenario of most American cities about 1890: fitful reforms, usually not lasting; charters hopelessly tangled, with no agreement on remedies; civil service laws circumvented in the mad search for patronage opportunities; election frauds virtually normal; an underworld capitalizing on man's appetites and finding it easy to purchase allies in the police and the politician; countless opportunities for actual theft; business carrying over its disgraceful private ethics into subverting city government for its own ends, and city officials competing to obtain the opportunity to be lucratively subverted; citizens who might be expected to lead reforms generally indifferent, discouraged, frightened, and without the time necessary to give to the effort; a community with conflicting value systems into which the exploiter entered, albeit with an understanding and a sympathy denied to those from another class; ballots complicated; a nomination process seemingly built to invite control by the self-seeking; sinecures used to provide fulltime workers for the party machine; state governments ready to step in to aid in the corruption if local effort proved inadequate; confusion over the claims of party loyalty; a press often intimidated and frequently venal; countless opportunities to make decisions that would favor certain real estate over other locations; a burgeoning population rapidly urbanizing and dragging in its train innumerable problems of municipal services and aspirations.

For the unraveling of this tangled mess, the reformer and the career administrator had no acceptable philosophy.

# NO

## Jon C. Teaford

# TRUMPETED FAILURES AND UNHERALDED TRIUMPHS

In 1888 the British observer James Bryce proclaimed that "there is no denying that the government of cities is the one conspicuous failure of the United States." With this pronouncement he summed up the feelings of a host of Americans. In New York City, residents along mansion-lined Fifth Avenue, parishioners in the churches of then-sedate Brooklyn, even petty politicos at party headquarters in Tammany Hall, all perceived serious flaws in the structure of urban government. Some complained, for example, of the tyranny of upstate Republican legislators, others attacked the domination of ward bosses, and still others criticized the greed of public utility companies franchised by the municipality. Mugwump reformer Theodore Roosevelt decried government by Irish political machine hacks, the moralist Reverend Charles Henry Parkhurst lambasted the reign of rum sellers, and that pariah of good-government advocates, New York City ward boss George Washington Plunkitt, also found fault, attacking the evils of civil service. For each, the status quo in urban government was defective. For each, the structure of municipal rule needed some revision. By the close of the 1880s the litany of criticism was mounting, with one voice after another adding a shrill comment on the misrule of the cities.

During the following two decades urban reformers repeated Bryce's words with ritualistic regularity, and his observation proved one of the most-quoted lines in the history of American government. Time and again latter-day Jeremiahs damned American municipal rule of the late nineteenth century, denouncing it as a national blight, a disgrace that by its example threatened the survival of democracy throughout the world. In 1890 Andrew D. White, then-president of Cornell University, wrote that "without the slightest exaggeration... the city governments of the United States are the worst in Christendom—the most expensive, the most inefficient, and the most corrupt." Four years later the reform journalist Edwin Godkin claimed that "the present condition of city governments in the United States is bringing democratic institutions into contempt the world over, and imperiling some of the best things in our civilization." Such preachers as the Reverend Washington

From Jon C. Teaford, *The Unheralded Triumph: City Government in America, 1860–1900* (Johns Hopkins University Press, 1984). 

Gladden denounced the American city as the "smut of civilization," while his clerical colleague Reverend Parkhurst said of the nation's municipalities: "Virtue is at the bottom and knavery on top. The rascals are out of jail and standing guard over men who aim to be honorable and law-abiding." And in 1904 journalist Lincoln Steffens stamped American urban rule with an indelible badge of opprobrium in the corruption-sated pages of his popular muckraking exposé *The Shame of the Cities.* Books, magazines, and newspapers all recited the catalog of municipal sins.

Likewise, many twentieth-century scholars passing judgment on the development of American city government have handed down a guilty verdict and sentenced American urban rule to a place of shame in the annals of the nation. In 1933 a leading student of municipal home rule claimed that "the conduct of municipal business has almost universally been inept and inefficient" and "at its worst it has been unspeakable, almost incredible." That same year the distinguished historian Arthur Schlesinger, Sr., in his seminal study *The Rise of the City,* described the development of municipal services during the last decades of the nineteenth century and found the achievements "distinctly creditable to a generation... confronted with the phenomenon of a great population everywhere clotting into towns." Yet later in his study he returned to the more traditional position, recounting tales of corruption and describing municipal rule during the last two decades of the century as "the worst city government the country had ever known." Writing in the 1950s, Bessie Louise Pierce, author of the finest biography to date of an American city, a multivolume history of Chicago, described that city's long list of municipal achievements but closed with a ritual admission of urban shortcomings, citing her approval of Bryce's condemnation. Similarly, that lifelong student of American municipal history, Ernest Griffith, subtitled his volume on late-nineteenth-century urban rule "the conspicuous failure," though he questioned whether municipal government was a greater failure than state government.

Historians such as Schlesinger and Griffith were born in the late nineteenth century, were raised during the Progressive era, and early imbibed the ideas of such critics as Bryce and White. Younger historians of the second half of the twentieth century were further removed from the scene of the supposed municipal debacle and could evaluate it more dispassionately. By the 1960s and 1970s, negative summations such as "unspeakable" and "incredible" were no longer common in accounts of nineteenth-century city government, and historians professing to the objectivity of the social sciences often refused to pronounce judgment on the quality of past rule. Yet recent general histories of urban America have continued both to describe the "deterioration" of city government during the Gilded Age and to focus on political bosses and good-government reformers who were forced to struggle with a decentralized, fragmented municipal structure supposedly unsuited to fast-growing metropolises of the 1880s and 1890s. Some chronicles of the American city have recognized the material advantages in public services during the late nineteenth century, but a number speak of the failure of the municipality to adapt to changing realities and of the shortcomings of an outmoded and ineffectual municipal framework. Sam Bass Warner, Jr., one of the leading new urban historians of the 1960s, has characterized the pattern of urban rule as one of "weak, corrupt, unimaginative municipal government." Almost one hundred years after Bryce's original declaration, the story of American city government remains at best a tale of fragmentation and confusion and at worst one of weakness and corruption.

If modern scholars have not handed down such damning verdicts as the contemporary critics of the 1880s and 1890s, they have nevertheless issued evaluations critical of the American framework of urban rule. As yet, hindsight has not cast a golden glow over the municipal institutions of the late nineteenth century, and few historians or political scientists have written noble tributes to the achievements of American municipal government. Praise for the nation's municipal officials has been rare and grudging. Though many have recognized the elitist predilections of Bryce and his American informants, the influence of Bryce's words still persists, and the image of nineteenth-century city government remains tarnished. Historians have softened the harsh stereotype of the political boss, transforming him from a venal parasite into a necessary component of a makeshift, decentralized structure. Conversely, the boss's good-government foes have fallen somewhat from historical grace and are now typified as crusaders for the supremacy of an upper-middle-class business culture. But historians continue to aim their attention at these two elements of municipal rule, to the neglect of the formal, legal structure. They write more of the boss than of the mayor, more on the civic leagues than on the sober but significant city comptroller. Moreover they continue to stage the drama of bosses and reformers against a roughly sketched backdrop of municipal disarray. The white and black hats of the players may have shaded to gray, but the setting of the historian's pageant remains a ramshackle municipal structure.

Nevertheless, certain nagging realities stand in stark contrast to the traditional tableau of municipal rule. One need not look far to discover the monuments of nineteenth-century municipal achievement that still grace the nation's cities, surviving as concrete rebuttals to Bryce's words. In 1979 the architecture critic for the *New York Times* declared Central Park and the Brooklyn Bridge as "the two greatest works of architecture in New York... each... a magnificent object in its own right; each... the result of a brilliant synthesis of art and engineering after which the world was never quite the same." Each was also a product of municipal enterprise, the creation of a city government said to be the worst in Christendom. Moreover, can one visit San Francisco's Golden Gate Park or enter McKim, Mead, and White's palatial Boston Public Library and pronounce these landmarks evidence of weakness or failure? Indeed, can those city fathers be deemed "unimaginative" who hired the great landscape architect Frederick Law Olmsted to design the first public park systems in human history? And were the vast nineteenth-century water and drainage schemes that still serve the cities the handiwork of bumbling incompetents unable to cope with the demands of expanding industrial metropolises? The aqueducts of Rome were among the glories of ancient civilization; the grander water systems of nineteenth-century New York City are often overlooked by those preoccupied with the more lurid aspects of city rule.

A bright side of municipal endeavor did, then, exist. American city governments could claim grand achievements, and as Arthur Schlesinger, Sr., was willing to admit in 1933, urban leaders won some creditable victories in the struggle for improved services. Certainly there were manifold shortcomings: Crime and poverty persisted; fires raged and pavements buckled; garbage and street rubbish sometimes seemed insurmountable problems. Yet no government has ever claimed total success in coping with the problems of society; to some degree all have failed to service their populations adequately. If government ever actually succeeded, political scientists would have to retool and apply themselves to more intractable problems, and political philosophers would have to turn to less contemplative pursuits. Those with a negative propensity can always find ample evidence of "bad government," and late-nineteenth-century critics such as Bryce, White, and Godkin displayed that propensity. In their writings the good side of the municipal structure was as visible as the dark side of the moon.

Thus, observers of the late-nineteenth-century American municipality have usually focused microscopic attention on its failures while overlooking its achievements. Scoundrels have won much greater coverage than conscientious officials. Volumes have appeared, for example, on that champion among municipal thieves, New York City's political boss William M. Tweed, but not one book exists on the life and work of a perhaps more significant figure in nineteenth-century city government, Ellis Chesbrough the engineer who served both Boston and Chicago and who transformed the public works of the latter city. Only recently has an admirable group of studies begun to explore the work of such municipal technicians who were vital to the formulation and implementation of public policy. But prior to the 1970s accounts of dualistic conflicts between political bosses and good-government reformers predominated, obscuring the complexities of municipal rule and the diversity of elements actually vying for power and participating in city government. And such traditional accounts accepted as axiomatic the inadequacy of the formal municipal structure. Critics have trumpeted its failures, while its triumphs have gone unheralded.

If one recognizes some of the challenges that municipal leaders faced during the period 1870 to 1900, the magnitude of their achievements becomes clear. The leaders of the late nineteenth century inherited an urban scene of great tumult and stress and an urban population of increasing diversity and diversion.... The melting pot was coming to a boil, and yet throughout the 1870s, 1880s, and 1890s, waves of newcomers continued to enter the country, including more and more representatives of the alien cultures of southern and eastern Europe. To many in 1870, social and ethnic diversity seemed to endanger the very foundation of order and security in the nation, and municipal leaders faced the need to maintain a truce between Protestants and Catholics, old stock and new, the native business elite and immigrant workers.

The rush of migrants from both Europe and rural America combined with a high birth rate to produce another source of municipal problems, a soaring urban population.... During the last thirty years of the century, the nation's chief cities absorbed thousands of acres of new territory to accommodate this booming population, and once-compact cities sprawled outward from the urban core. This expansion sprawl produced demands for the extension of services and the construction of municipal facilities. The newly annexed peripheral wards needed sewer lines and water mains; they required fire and police protection; and residents of outlying districts expected the city to provide paved streets and lighting. Municipal governments could not simply maintain their services at existing levels; instead, they had to guarantee the extension of those services to thousands of new urban dwellers.

Improved and expanded municipal services, however, required funding, and revenue therefore posed another challenge for city rulers.... Inflation in the 1860s and economic depression in the 1870s exacerbated the financial problems of the city, leading to heightened cries for retrenchment. And throughout the 1880s and 1890s city governments faced the difficult problem of meeting rising expectations for services while at the same time satisfying demands for moderate taxes and fiscal conservatism. This was perhaps the toughest task confronting the late-nineteenth-century municipality.

During the last three decades of the century, American city government did, however, meet these challenges of diversity, growth, and financing with remarkable success. By century's close, American city dwellers enjoyed, on the average, as high a standard of public services as any urban residents in the world. Problems persisted, and there were ample grounds for complaint. But in America's cities, the supply of water was the most abundant, the street lights were the most brilliant, the parks the grandest, the libraries the largest, and the public transportation the fastest of any place in the world. American city fathers rapidly adapted to advances in technology, and New York City, Chicago, and Boston were usually in the forefront of efforts to apply new inventions and engineering breakthroughs to municipal problems. Moreover, America's cities achieved this level of modern service while remaining solvent and financially sound. No major American municipality defaulted on its debts payments during the 1890s, and by the end of the century all of the leading municipalities were able to sell their bonds at premium and pay record-low interest. Any wise financier would have testified that the bonds of those purported strongholds of inefficiency and speculation, the municipal corporations, were far safer investments than were the bonds of those quintessential products of American business ingenuity: the railroad corporations.

Not only did the city governments serve their residents without suffering financial collapse, but municipal leaders also achieved an uneasy balance of the conflicting forces within the city, accommodating each through a distribution of authority. Though commentators often claimed that the "better elements" of the urban populace had surrendered municipal administration to the hands of "low-bred" Irish saloonkeepers, such observations were misleading. Similarly incorrect is the claim that the business and professional elite abandoned city government during the late nineteenth century to decentralized lower-class ward leaders. The patrician, the plutocrat, the plebeian, and the professional bureaucrat all had their place in late-nineteenth-century municipal government; each staked an informal but definite claim to a particular domain within the municipal structure.

Upper-middle-class business figures presided over the executive branch and the independent park, library, and sinking-fund commissions. Throughout the last decades of the nineteenth century the mayor's office was generally in the hands of solid businessmen or professionals who were native-born Protestants. The leading executive officers were persons of citywide reputation and prestige, and during the period 1870 to 1900 their formal authority was increasing. Meanwhile, the legislative branch—the board of aldermen or city council—became the stronghold of small neighborhood retailers, often of immigrant background, who won their aldermanic seats because of their neighborhood reputation as good fellows willing to gain favors for their constituents. In some cities men of metropolitan standing virtually abandoned the city council, and in every major city this body was the chief forum for lower-middle-class and working-class ward politicians.

At the same time, an emerging body of trained experts was also securing a barony of power within city government. Even before the effective application of formal civil service laws, mayors and commissioners deferred to the judgment and expertise of professional engineers, landscape architects, educators, physicians, and fire chiefs, and a number of such figures served decade after decade in municipal posts, despite political upheavals in the executive and legislative branches. By the close of the century these professional civil servants were securing a place of permanent authority in city government. Their loyalty was not to downtown business interests nor to ward or ethnic particularism, but to their profession and their department. And they were gradually transforming those departments into strongholds of expertise.

The municipal professional, the downtown business leader, and the neighborhood shopkeeper and small-time politico each had differing concepts of city government and differing policy priorities. They thus represented potentially conflicting interests that could serve to divide the municipal polity and render it impotent. Yet, during the period 1870 to 1900, these elements remained in a state of peaceful, if contemptuous, coexistence. Hostilities broke out, especially if any element felt the boundaries of its domain were violated. But city governments could operate effectively if the truce between these elements was respected; in other words, if ward business remained the primary concern of ward alderman, citywide policy was in the hands of the business elite, and technical questions were decided by experts relatively undisturbed by party politics. This was the informal détente that was gradually developing amid the conflict and complaints.

Such extralegal participants as political parties and civic leagues also exerted their influence over municipal government, attempting to tip the uneasy balance of forces in their direction. The political party organization with its ward-based neighborhood bosses was one lever that the immigrants and less affluent could pull to affect the course of government. Civic organizations and reform leagues, in contrast, bolstered the so-called better element in government, the respected businessmen who usually dominated the leading executive offices and the independent commissions. Emerging professional groups such as engineering clubs and medical societies often lent their support to the rising ambitions and growing authority of the expert bureaucracy and permanent civil servants. And special-interest lobbyists like the fire insurance underwriters also urged professionalism in such municipal services as the fire department. Municipal government was no simple dualistic struggle between a citywide party boss with a diamond shirt stud and malodorous cigar and a good-government reformer with a Harvard degree and kid gloves. Various forces were pushing and pulling the municipal corporations, demanding a response to petitions and seeking a larger voice in the chambers of city government.

State legislatures provided the structural flexibility to respond to these demands. The state legislatures enjoyed the sovereign authority to bestow municipal powers and to determine the municipal structure, but when considering local measures, state lawmakers generally deferred to the judgment of the legislative delegation from the affected locality. If the local delegation favored a bill solely affecting its constituents, the legislature usually ratified the bill without opposition or debate. This rule of deference to the locality no longer applied, however, if the bill became a partisan issue, as it occasionally did. But in most cases authorization for new powers or for structural reforms depended on the city's representatives in the state legislature, and each session the state assemblies and senates rubber-stamped hundreds of local bills. Thus, indulgent legislator provided the vital elasticity that allowed urban governments to expand readily to meet new challenges and assume new responsibilities....

Even so, this process of perpetual adjustment resulted in a mechanism that succeeded in performing the job of city government. Municipal leaders adapted to the need for experts trained in the new technologies and hired such technicians. Moreover, downtown businessmen and ward politicos, the native-born and the immigrants, Protestants and Catholics, loosened the lid on the melting pot and reduced the boiling hostility of the mid-century to a simmer. The cities provided services; they backed off from the brink of bankruptcy; and the municipal structure guaranteed a voice to the various elements of society in both immigrant wards and elite downtown clubs.

Why, then, all the complaints? Why did so many critics of the 1880s and 1890s indulge in a rhetoric of failure, focusing on municipal shortcomings to the neglect of municipal successes? Why was municipal government so much abused? The answer lies in a fundamental irony: The late-nineteenth-century municipal structure accommodated everyone but satisfied no one. It was a system of compromise among parties discontented with compromise. It was a marriage of convenience, with the spouses providing a reasonably comfortable home for America's urban inhabitants. But it was not a happy home. The parties to the nuptials tolerated one another because they had to. Nevertheless, the businessman-mayors and plutocrat park commissioners disliked their dependence on ward politicians, whom they frequently regarded as petty grafters, and they frowned upon the power of the immigrant voters. Likewise, the emerging corps of civil servants was irked by interference from laypersons of both high and law status. And the plebeian party boss opposed efforts to extend the realm of the civil servants who had performed no partisan duties and thus merited no power. None liked their interdependence with persons they felt to be unworthy, incompetent, or hostile.

Enhancing this dissatisfaction was the cultural absolutism of the Victorian era. The late nineteenth century was an age when the business elite could refer to itself as the "best element" of society and take for granted its "God-given" superiority. It was an age when professional engineers, landscape architects, public health experts, librarians, educators, and fire fighters were first becoming aware of themselves as professionals, and with the zeal of converts they defended their newly exalted state of grace. It was also an age when most Protestants viewed Catholics as papal pawns and devotees of Italian idolatry, while most Catholics believed Protestants were little better than heathens and doomed to a quick trip to hell with no stops in purgatory. The late nineteenth century was not an age of cultural relativism but one of cultural absolutes, an age when people still definitely knew right from wrong, the correct from the erroneous. The American municipality, however, was a heterogeneous polyarchy, a network of accommodation and compromise in an era when accommodation and compromise smacked of unmanly dishonor and unprincipled pragmatism. Municipal government of the 1870s, 1880s, and 1890s rested on a system of broker politics, of bargaining and dealing....

Late-nineteenth-century urban government was a failure not of structure but of image. The system proved reasonably successful in providing services, but there was no prevailing ideology to validate its operation. In fact, the beliefs of the various participants were at odds with the structure of rule that governed them. The respectable elements believed in sobriety and government by persons of character. But the system of accommodation permitted whiskey taps to flow on the Sabbath for the Irish and for Germans, just as it allowed men in shiny suits with questionable reputations to occupy seats on the city council and in the municipal party conventions. The ward-based party devotees accepted the notions of Jacksonian democracy and believed quite literally in the maxim To the victor belong the spoils. But by the 1890s they faced a growing corps of civil servants more devoted to their profession than to any party. Although new professional bureaucrats preached a gospel of expertise, they still had to compromise with party-worshiping hacks and the supposedly diabolical forces of politics. Likewise, special-interest lobbyists such as the fire insurance underwriters were forced to cajole or coerce political leaders whom they deemed ignorant and unworthy of public office. Each of these groups worked together, but only from necessity and not because they believed in such a compromise of honor. There was no ideology of heterogeneous polyarchy, no system of beliefs to bolster the existing government structure. Thus late-nineteenth-century city government survived without moral support, and to many urban dwellers it seemed a bargain with the devil.

Twentieth-century historians also had reasons for focusing on urban failure rather than urban success. Some chroniclers in the early decades accepted rhetoric as reality and simply repeated the condemnations of critics such as Bryce, White, and Godkin. By the mid-century greater skepticism prevailed, but so did serious ills. In fact, the urban crisis of the 1960s provided the impetus for a great upsurge of interest in the history of the city, inspiring a search for the historical roots of urban breakdown and collapse. Urban problems were the scholars' preoccupation. Not until the much-ballyhooed "back-to-the-city" movement of the 1970s did the city become less an object of pity or contempt and more a treasured relic. By the late 1970s a new rhetoric was developing, in which sidewalks and streets assumed a nostalgic significance formerly reserved to babbling brooks and bucolic pastures.

The 1980s, then, seem an appropriate time to reevaluate the much-maligned municipality of the late nineteenth century. Back-to-the-city euphoria, however, should not distort one's judgment of the past. Instead, it is time to understand the system of city government from 1870 to 1900 complete with blemishes and beauty marks. One should not quickly dismiss the formal mechanisms of municipal rule as inadequate and outdated, requiring the unifying grasp of party bosses. Nor should one mindlessly laud municipal rule as a triumph of urban democracy. A serious appreciation of the municipal structure is necessary.

# POSTSCRIPT

## Was City Government in Late Nineteenth-Century America a "Conspicuous Failure"?

The opposing viewpoints expressed by Griffith and Teaford represent a long-standing scholarly debate about the consequences of boss politics in the United States. James Bryce, *The American Commonwealth,* 2 vols. (Macmillan, 1888); Moisei Ostrogorski, *Democracy and the Organization of Political Parties* (1902; Anchor Books, 1964); and Lincoln Steffens, *The Shame of the Cities* (Mc-Clure, Phillips, 1904), present a litany of misdeeds associated with those who controlled municipal government. Political bosses, these authors charge, were guilty of malfeasance in office and all forms of graft and corruption.

Efforts to rehabilitate the sullied reputations of the machine politicians can be dated to the comments of one of Boss Tweed's henchmen, George Washington Plunkitt, a New York City ward heeler whose turn-of-the-century observations included a subtle distinction between "honest" and "dishonest" graft. A more scholarly effort was presented by Robert K. Merton, a political scientist who identified numerous "latent functions" of the political machine. According to Merton, city bosses created effective political organizations that humanized the dispensation of assistance, offered valuable political privileges for businessmen, and created alternate routes of social mobility for citizens, many of them immigrants, who typically were excluded from conventional means of personal advancement.

There are several excellent urban history texts that devote space to the development of municipal government in the late nineteenth century. Among these are David R. Goldfield and Blaine A. Brownell, *Urban America: From Downtown to No Town* (Houghton Mifflin, 1979); Howard P. Chudacoff and Judith E. Smith, *The Evolution of American Urban Society,* 3d ed. (Prentice Hall, 1981); and Charles N. Glaab and A. Theodore Brown, *A History of Urban America,* 3d ed. (Macmillan, 1983). Various developments in the industrial period are discussed in Blake McKelvey, *The Urbanization of America, 1860–1915* (Rutgers University Press, 1963), and Raymond A. Mohl, *The New City: Urban America in the Industrial Age, 1860-1920* (Harlan Davidson, 1985). Boss politics is analyzed in William L. Riordon, *Plunkitt of Tammany Hall* (E. P. Dutton, 1963); Robert K. Merton, *Social Theory and Social Structure* (Free Press, 1957); and John M. Allswang, *Bosses, Machines, and Urban Voters: An American Symbiosis* (Kennikat Press, 1977). The most famous urban boss is analyzed in Alexander B. Callow, Jr., *The Tweed Ring* (Oxford University Press, 1966), and Leo Hershkowitz, *Tweed's New York: Another Look* (Anchor Press, 1977). Scott

Greer, ed., *Ethnics, Machines, and the American Future* (Harvard University Press, 1981), and Bruce M. Stave and Sondra Astor Stave, eds., *Urban Bosses, Machines, and Progressive Reformers*, 2d ed. (D. C. Heath, 1984), are excellent collections of essays on urban political machinery. Significant contributions to urban historiography are Sam Bass Warner, Jr., *Streetcar Suburbs: The Process of Growth in Boston, 1870–1900* (Harvard University Press, 1962); Stephan Thernstrom, *Poverty and Progress: Social Mobility in the Nineteenth-Century City* (Harvard University Press, 1964); Gunther Barth, *City People: The Rise of Modern City Culture in Nineteenth-Century America* (Oxford University Press, 1980); and Martin V. Melosi, *Garbage in the Cities: Refuse, Reform, and the Environment, 1880–1980* (Texas A & M University Press, 1982).

# ISSUE 7

## Did Booker T. Washington's Philosophy and Actions Betray the Interests of African Americans?

**YES: W. E. B. Du Bois,** from *The Souls of Black Folk* (1903)

**NO: Louis R. Harlan,** from "Booker T. Washington and the Politics of Accommodation," in John Hope Franklin and August Meier, eds., *Black Leaders of the Twentieth Century* (University of Illinois Press, 1982)

### ISSUE SUMMARY

**YES:** W. E. B. Du Bois, a founding member of the National Organization for the Advancement of Colored People, argues that Booker T. Washington became an apologist for racial injustice in America by failing to articulate the legitimate demands of African Americans for full civil and political rights.

**NO:** Professor of history Louis R. Harlan portrays Washington as a political realist who had the same long-range goals of progress toward equality as his black critics and whose policies and actions were designed to benefit black society as a whole.

In the late nineteenth and early twentieth centuries, most black Americans' lives were characterized by increased inequality and powerlessness. Although the Thirteenth Amendment had fueled a partial social revolution by emancipating approximately 4 million southern slaves, the efforts of the Fourteenth and Fifteenth Amendments to provide all African Americans with the protections and privileges of full citizenship had been undermined by the United States Supreme Court.

By 1910, seventy-five percent of all African Americans resided in rural areas. Ninety percent lived in the South, where they suffered from abuses associated with the sharecropping and crop-lien systems, political disfranchisement, and antagonistic race relations, which often boiled over into acts of violence, including race riots and lynchings. Black southerners who moved north in the decades preceding World War I to escape the ravages of racism instead discovered a society in which the color line was drawn more rigidly to limit black opportunities. Residential segregation led to the emergence of racial ghettos. Jim Crow also affected northern education, and competition for jobs produced frequent clashes between black and white workers. By the early twentieth century, then, most African Americans endured a second-class citizenship reinforced by segregation laws (both customary and legal) in the "age of Jim Crow."

Prior to 1895, the foremost spokesman for the nation's African American population was former slave and abolitionist Frederick Douglass, whose crusade for blacks emphasized the importance of civil rights, political power, and immediate integration. August Meier has called Douglass "the greatest living symbol of the protest tradition during the 1880s and 1890s." At the time of Douglass's death in 1895, however, this tradition was largely replaced by the emergence of Booker T. Washington. Born into slavery in Virginia in 1856, Washington became the most prominent black spokesman in the United States as a result of a speech delivered at the Cotton States Exposition in Atlanta, Georgia. Known as the "Atlanta Compromise," this address, with its conciliatory tone, found favor among whites and gave Washington, who was president of Tuskegee Institute in Alabama, a reputation as a "responsible" spokesman for black America.

What did Booker T. Washington really want for African Americans? Did his programs realistically address the difficulties confronted by blacks in a society where the doctrine of white supremacy was prominent? Is it fair to describe Washington simply as a conservative whose accommodationist philosophy betrayed his own people? Did the "Sage of Tuskegee" consistently adhere to his publicly stated philosophy of patience, self-help, and economic advancement?

One of the earliest and most outspoken critics of Washington's program was his contemporary, W. E. B. Du Bois. In a famous essay in *The Souls of Black Folk,* Du Bois levels an assault upon Washington's narrow educational philosophy for blacks and his apparent acceptance of segregation. By submitting to disfranchisement and segregation, Du Bois charges, Washington had become an apologist for racial injustice in the United States. He also claims that Washington's national prominence was bought at the expense of black interests throughout the nation.

Louis R. Harlan's appraisal of Washington, while not totally uncritical, illuminates the complexity of Washington's personality and philosophy. Washington, according to Harlan, understood the reality of southern race relations and knew what he was capable of accomplishing without endangering his leadership position, which was largely controlled by whites. He was, then, a consummate politician—master of the art of the possible in turn-of-the-century race relations.

# YES

## W. E. B. Du Bois

# OF MR. BOOKER T. WASHINGTON AND OTHERS

Easily the most striking thing in the history of the American Negro since 1876 is the ascendancy of Mr. Booker T. Washington. It began at the time when war memories and ideals were rapidly passing; a day of astonishing commercial development was dawning; a sense of doubt and hesitation overtook the freedmen's sons,—then it was that his leading began. Mr. Washington came, with a single definite programme, at the psychological moment when the nation was a little ashamed of having bestowed so much sentiment on Negroes, and was concentrating its energies on Dollars. His programme of industrial education, conciliation of the South, and submission and silence as to civil and political rights, was not wholly original;... But Mr. Washington first indisolubly linked these things; he put enthusiasm, unlimited energy, and perfect faith into this programme, and changed it from a by-path into a veritable Way of Life. And the tale of the methods by which he did this is a fascinating study of human life.

It startled the nation to hear a Negro advocating such a programme after many decades of bitter complaint; it startled and won the applause of the South, it interested and won the admiration of the North; and after a confused murmur of protest, it silenced if it did not convert the Negroes themselves.

To gain the sympathy and coöperation of the various elements comprising the white South was Mr. Washington's first task; and this, at the time Tuskegee was founded, seemed, for a black man, well-nigh impossible. And yet ten years later it was done in the word spoken at Atlanta: "In all things purely social we can be as separate as the five fingers, and yet one as the hand in all things essential to mutual progress." This "Atlanta Compromise" is by all odds the most notable thing in Mr. Washington's career. The South interpreted it in different ways: the radicals received it as a complete surrender of the demand for civil and political equality; the conservatives, as a generously conceived working basis for mutual understanding. So both approved it, and to-day its author is certainly the most distinguished Southerner since Jefferson Davis, and the one with the largest personal following.

From W. E. B. Du Bois, *The Souls of Black Folk* (1903). Reprint, Fawcett Publications, 1961.

Next to this achievement comes Mr. Washington's work in gaining place and consideration in the North. Others less shrewd and tactful had formerly essayed to sit on these two stools and had fallen between them; but as Mr. Washington knew the heart of the South from birth and training, so by singular insight he intuitively grasped the spirit of the age which was dominating the North. And so thoroughly did he learn the speech and thought of triumphant commercialism, and the ideals of material prosperity, that the picture of a lone black boy poring over a French grammar amid the weeds and dirt of a neglected home soon seemed to him the acme of absurdities. One wonders what Socrates and St. Francis of Assisi would say to this.

And yet this very singleness of vision and thorough oneness with his age is a mark of the successful man. It is as though Nature must needs make men narrow in order to give them force. So Mr. Washington's cult has gained unquestioning followers, his work has wonderfully prospered, his friends are legion, and his enemies are confounded. To-day he stands as the one recognized spokesman of his ten million fellows, and one of the most notable figures in a nation of seventy millions. One hesitates, therefore, to criticise a life which, beginning with so little, has done so much. And yet the time is come when one may speak in all sincerity and utter courtesy of the mistakes and shortcomings of Mr. Washington's career, as well as of his triumphs, without being thought captious or envious, and without forgetting that it is easier to do ill than well in the world.

The criticism that has hitherto met Mr. Washington has not always been of this broad character. In the South especially has he had to walk warily to avoid the harshest judgments,—and naturally so, for he is dealing with the one subject of deepest sensitiveness to that section. Twice—once when at the Chicago celebration of the Spanish-American War he alluded to the color-prejudice that is "eating away the vitals of the South," and once when he dined with President Roosevelt—has the resulting Southern criticism been violent enough to threaten seriously his popularity. In the North the feeling has several times forced itself into words, that Mr. Washington's counsels of submission overlooked certain elements of true manhood, and that his educational programme was unnecessarily narrow. Usually, however, such criticism has not found open expression, although, too, the spiritual sons of the Abolitionists have not been prepared to acknowledge that the schools founded before Tuskegee, by men of broad ideals and self-sacrificing spirit, were wholly failures or worthy of ridicule. While, then, criticism has not failed to follow Mr. Washington, yet the prevailing public opinion of the land has been but too willing to deliver the solution of a wearisome problem into his hands, and say, "If that is all you and your race ask, take it."

Among his own people, however, Mr. Washington has encountered the strongest and most lasting opposition, amounting at times to bitterness, and even to-day continuing strong and insistent even though largely silenced in outward expression by the public opinion of the nation. Some of this opposition is, of course, mere envy; the disappointment of displaced demagogues and the spite of narrow minds. But aside from this, there is among educated and thoughtful colored men in all parts of the land a feeling of deep regret, sorrow, and apprehension at the wide currency and ascendancy which some of Mr. Washington's theories have gained. These same men admire his sincerity of purpose, and are willing to forgive much to honest endeavor which is doing something worth the doing. They coöperate with Mr. Washington as far as they conscientiously can; and, indeed, it is no ordinary tribute to this man's tact and power that, steering as he must between so many diverse interests and opinions, he so largely retains the respect of all.

But the hushing of the criticism of honest opponents is a dangerous thing. It leads some of the best of the critics to unfortunate silence and paralysis of effort, and others to burst into speech so passionately and intemperately as to lose listeners. Honest and earnest criticism from those whose interests are most nearly touched,—criticism of writers by readers, of government by those governed, of leaders by those led,—this is the soul of democracy and the safeguard of modern society. If the best of the American Negroes receive by outer pressure a leader whom they had not recognized before, manifestly there is here a certain palpable gain. Yet there is also irreparable loss, —a loss of that peculiarly valuable education which a group receives when by search and criticism it finds and commissions its own leaders. The way in which this is done is at once the most elementary and the nicest problem of social growth. History is but the record of such group-leadership; and yet how infinitely changeful is its type and character! And of all types and kinds, what can be more instructive than the leadership of a group within a group?—that curious double movement where real progress may be negative and actual advance be relative retrogression. All this is the social student's inspiration and despair.

Now in the past the American Negro has had instructive experience in the choosing of group leaders, founding thus a peculiar dynasty which in the light of present conditions is worth while studying. When sticks and stones and beasts form the sole environment of a people, their attitude is largely one of determined opposition to and conquest of natural forces. But when to earth and brute is added an environment of men and ideas, then the attitude of the imprisoned group may take three main forms,—a feeling of revolt and revenge; an attempt to adjust all thought and action to the will of the greater group; or, finally, a determined effort at self-realization and self-development despite environing opinion. The influence of all of these attitudes at various times can be traced in the history of the American Negro, and in the evolution of his successive leaders....

Booker T. Washington arose as essentially the leader not of one race but of two,—a compromiser between the South, the North, and the Negro. Naturally the Negroes resented, at first bitterly, signs of compromise which surrendered their civil and political rights, even though this was to be exchanged for larger chances of economic development. The rich and dominating North, however, was not only weary of the race problem, but was investing largely in Southern enterprises, and welcomed any method of peaceful coöperation. Thus, by national opinion, the Negroes began to recognize Mr. Washington's leadership; and the voice of criticism was hushed.

Mr. Washington represents in Negro thought the old attitude of adjustment and submission; but adjustment at such a peculiar time as to make his programme unique. This is an age of unusual economic development, and Mr. Washington's programme naturally takes an economic cast, becoming a gospel of Work and Money to such an extent as apparently almost completely to overshadow the higher aims of life. Moreover, this is an age when the more advanced races are coming in closer contact with the less developed races, and the race-feeling is therefore intensified; and Mr. Washington's programme practically accepts the alleged inferiority of the Negro races. Again, in our own land, the reaction from the sentiment of war time has given impetus to race-prejudice against Negroes, and Mr. Washington withdraws many of the high demands of Negroes as men and American citizens. In other periods of intensified prejudice all the Negro's tendency to self-assertion has been called forth; at this period a policy of submission is advocated. In the history of nearly all other races and peoples the doctrine preached at such crises has been that manly self-respect is worth more than lands and houses, and that a people who voluntarily surrender such respect, or cease striving for it, are not worth civilizing.

In answer to this, it has been claimed that the Negro can survive only through submission. Mr. Washington distinctly asks that black people give up, at least for the present three things,—

First, political power,

Second, insistence on civil rights,

Third, higher education of Negro youth,—

and concentrate all their energies on industrial education, the accumulation of wealth, and the conciliation of the South. This policy has been courageously and insistently advocated for over fifteen years, and has been triumphant for perhaps ten years. As a result of this tender of the palm-branch, what has been the return? In these years there have occurred:

1. The disfranchisement of the Negro.
2. The legal creation of a distinct status of civil inferiority for the Negro.
3. The steady withdrawal of aid from institutions for the higher training of the Negro.

These movements are not, to be sure, direct results of Mr. Washington's teachings; but his propaganda has, without a shadow of doubt, helped their speedier accomplishment. The question then comes: Is it possible, and probable, that nine millions of men can make effective progress in economic lines if they are deprived of political rights, made a servile caste, and allowed only the most meagre chance for developing their exceptional men? If history and reason give any distinct answer to these questions, it is an emphatic *No.* And Mr. Washington thus faces the triple paradox of his career:

1. He is striving nobly to make Negro artisans business men and property-owners; but it is utterly impossible, under modern competitive methods, for workingmen and property-owners to defend their rights and exist without the right of suffrage.
2. He insists on thrift and self-respect, but at the same time counsels a silent submission to civic inferiority such as is bound to sap the manhood of any race in the long run.
3. He advocates common-school and industrial training, and depreciates institutions of higher learning; but neither the Negro common-schools, nor Tuskegee itself, could remain

open a day were it not for teachers trained in Negro colleges, or trained by their graduates.

This triple paradox in Mr. Washington's position is the object of criticism by two classes of colored Americans. One class is spiritually descended from Toussaint the Savior, through Gabriel, Vesey, and Turner, and they represent the attitude of revolt and revenge; they hate the white South blindly and distrust the white race generally, and so far as they agree on definite action, think that the Negro's only hope lies in emigration beyond the borders of the United States. And yet, by the irony of fate, nothing has more effectually made this programme seem hopeless than the recent course of the United States toward weaker and darker peoples in the West Indies, Hawaii, and the Philippines,—for where in the world may we go and be safe from lying and brute force?

The other class of Negroes who cannot agree with Mr. Washington has hitherto said little aloud. They deprecate the sight of scattered counsels, of internal disagreement; and especially they dislike making their just criticism of a useful and earnest man an excuse for a general discharge of venom from small-minded opponents. Nevertheless, the questions involved are so fundamental and serious that it is difficult to see how men like the Grimkes, Kelly Miller, J. W. E. Bowen, and other representatives of this group, can much longer be silent. Such men feel in conscience bound to ask of this nation three things:

1. The right to vote.
2. Civic equality.
3. The education of youth according to ability.

They acknowledge Mr. Washington's invaluable service in counselling patience an courtesy in such demands; they do not ask that ignorant black men vote when ignorant whites are debarred, or that any reasonable restrictions in the suffrage should not be applied; they know that the low social level of the mass of the race is responsible for much discrimination against it, but they also know, and the nation knows, that relentless color-prejudice is more often a cause than a result of the Negro's degradation; they seek the abatement of this relic of barbarism, and not its systematic encouragement and pampering by all agencies of social power from the Associated Press to the Church of Christ. They advocate, with Mr. Washington, a broad system of Negro common schools supplemented by thorough industrial training; but they are surprised that a man of Mr. Washington's insight cannot see that no such educational system ever has rested or can rest on any other basis than that of the well-equipped college and university, and they insist that there is a demand for a few such institutions throughout the South to train the best of the Negro youth as teachers, professional men, and leaders.

This group of men honor Mr. Washington for his attitude of conciliation toward the white South; they accept the "Atlanta Compromise" in its broadest interpretation; they recognize, with him, many signs of promise, many men of high purpose and fair judgment, in this section; they know that no easy task has been laid upon a region already tottering under heavy burdens. But, nevertheless, they insist that the way to truth and right lies in straightforward honesty, not in indiscriminate flattery; in praising those of the South who do well and criticising uncompromisingly those who do ill; in taking advantage of the opportunities at hand and urging their fellows to do the same, but at the same time remembering that only a firm adherence to their higher ideals and aspirations will ever keep those ideals within the realm of possibility. They do not expect that the free right vote, to enjoy civic rights, and to be educated, will come in a moment; they do not expect to see the bias and prejudices of years disappear at the blast of a trumpet; but they are absolutely certain that the way for a people to gain their reasonable rights is not by voluntarily throwing them away and insisting that they do not want them; that the way for a people to gain respect is not by continually belittling and ridiculing themselves; that, on the contrary, Negroes must insist continually, in season and out of season, that voting is necessary to modern manhood, that color discrimination is barbarism, and that black boys need education as well as white boys.

In failing thus to state plainly and unequivocally the legitimate demands of their people, even at the cost of opposing an honored leader, the thinking classes of American Negroes would shirk a heavy responsibility,—a responsibility to themselves, a responsibility to the struggling masses, a responsibility to the darker races of men whose future depends so largely on this American experiment, but especially a responsibility to this nation, —this common Fatherland. It is wrong to encourage a man or a people in evil-doing; it is wrong to aid and abet a national crime simply because it is unpopular not to do so. The growing spirit of kindliness and reconciliation between the North and South after the frightful difference of a generation ago ought to be a source of deep congratulation to all, and especially to those whose mistreatment caused the war; but if that reconciliation is to be marked by the industrial slavery and civic death of those same black men, with permanent legislation into a position of inferiority, then those black men, if they are really men, are called upon by every consideration of patriotism and loyalty to oppose such a course by all civilized methods, even though such opposition involves disagreement with Mr. Booker T. Washington. We have no right to sit silently by while the inevitable seeds are sown for a harvest of disaster to our children, black and white.

First, it is the duty of black men to judge the South discriminatingly. The present generation of Southerners are not responsible for the past, and they should not be blindly hated or blamed for it. Furthermore, to no class is the indiscriminate endorsement of the recent course of the South toward Negroes more nauseating than to the best thought of the South. The South is not "solid"; it is a land in the ferment of social change, wherein forces of all kinds are fighting for supremacy; and to praise the ill the South is to-day perpetrating is just as wrong as to condemn the good. Discriminating and broad-minded criticism is what the South needs,—needs it for the sake of her own white sons and daughters, and for the insurance of robust, healthy mental and moral development.

To-day even the attitude of the Southern whites toward the blacks is not, as so many assume, in all cases the same; the ignorant Southerner hates the Negro, the workingmen fear his competition, the money-makers wish to use him as a laborer, some of the educated see a menace in his upward development, while others—usually the sons of masters —wish to help him to rise. National opinion has enabled this last class to maintain the Negro common schools, and to protect the Negro partially in property, life, and limb. Through the pressure of the money-makers, the Negro is in danger of being reduced to semi-slavery, especially in the country districts; the workingmen, and those of the educated who fear the Negro, have united to disfranchise him, and some have urged his deportation; while the passions of the ignorant are easily aroused to lynch and abuse any black man. To praise this intricate whirl of thought and prejudice is nonsense; to inveigh indiscriminately against "the South" is unjust; but to use the same breath in praising Governor [Charles B.] Aycock, exposing Senator [John T.] Morgan, arguing with Mr. Thomas Nelson Page, and denouncing Senator Ben Tillman, is not only sane, but the imperative duty of thinking black men.

It would be unjust to Mr. Washington not to acknowledge that in several instances he has opposed movements in the South which were unjust to the Negro; he sent memorials to the Louisiana and Alabama constitutional conventions, he has spoken against lynching, and in other ways has openly or silently set his influence against sinister schemes and unfortunate happenings. Notwithstanding this, it is equally true to assert that on the whole the distinct impression left by Mr. Washington's propaganda is, first, that the South is justified in its present attitude toward the Negro because of the Negro's degradation; secondly, that the prime cause of the Negro's failure to rise more quickly is his wrong education in the past; and, thirdly, that his future rise depends primarily on his own efforts. Each of these propositions is a dangerous half-truth. The supplementary truths must never be lost sight of: first, slavery and race-prejudice are potent if not sufficient causes of the Negro's position; second, industrial and common-school training were necessarily slow in planting because they had to await the black teachers trained by higher institutions, —it being extremely doubtful if any essentially different development was possible, and certainly a Tuskegee was unthinkable before 1880; and, third, while it is a great truth to say that the Negro must strive and strive mightily to help himself, it is equally true that unless his striving be not simply seconded, but rather aroused and encouraged, by the initiative of the richer and wiser environing group, he cannot hope for great success.

In his failure to realize and impress this last point, Mr. Washington is especially to be criticised. His doctrine has tended to make the whites, North and South, shift the burden of the Negro problem to the Negro's shoulders and stand aside as critical and rather pessimistic spectators; when in fact the burden belongs to the nation, and the hands of none of us are clean if we bend not our energies to righting these great wrongs.

The South ought to be led, by candid and honest criticism, to assert her better self and do her full duty to the race she has cruelly wronged and is still wronging. The North—her co-partner in guilt—cannot salve her conscience by plastering it with gold. We cannot settle this problem by diplomacy and suaveness, by "policy" alone. If worse come to worst, can the moral fibre of this country survive the slow throttling and murder of nine millions of men?

The black men of America have a duty to perform, a duty stern and delicate,—a forward movement to oppose a part of the work of their greatest leader. So far as Mr. Washington preaches Thrift, Patience, and Industrial Training for the masses, we must hold up his hands and strive with him, rejoicing in his honors and glorying in the strength of this Joshua called of God and of man to lead the headless host. But so far as Mr. Washington apologizes for injustice, North or South, does not rightly value the privilege and duty of voting, belittles the emasculating effects of caste distinctions, and opposes the higher training and ambition of our brighter minds,—so far as he, the South, or the Nation, does this,—we must unceasingly and firmly oppose them. By every civilized and peaceful method we must strive for the rights which the world accords to men, clinging unwaveringly to those great words which the sons of the Fathers would fain forget: "We hold these truths to be self-evident: That all men are created equal; that they are endowed by their Creator with certain unalienable rights; that among these are life, liberty, and the pursuit of happiness."

# NO

Louis R. Harlan

## BOOKER T. WASHINGTON AND THE POLITICS OF ACCOMMODATION

It is ironic that Booker T. Washington, the most powerful black American of his time and perhaps of all time, should be the black leader whose claim to the title is most often dismissed by the lay public. Blacks often question his legitimacy because of the role that favor by whites played in Washington's assumption of power, and whites often remember him only as an educator or, confusing him with George Washington Carver, as "that great Negro scientist." This irony is something that Washington will have to live with in history, for he himself deliberately created the ambiguity about his role and purposes that has haunted his image. And yet, Washington was a genuine black leader, with a substantial black following and with virtually the same long-range goals for Afro-Americans as his rivals. This presentation is concerned with Washington's social philosophy, such as it was, but it also addresses his methods of leadership, both his Delphic public utterances that meant one thing to whites and another to blacks and his adroit private movements through the brier patch of American race relations. It does not try to solve the ultimate riddle of his character.

Washington's own view of himself was that he was the Negro of the hour, whose career and racial program epitomized what blacks needed to maintain themselves against white encroachments and to make progress toward equality in America. The facts of his life certainly fitted his self-image. He was the last of the major black leaders to be born in slavery, on a small farm in western Virginia in 1856. Growing up during the Reconstruction era in West Virginia, he believed that one of the lessons he learned was that the Reconstruction experiment in racial democracy failed because it began at the wrong end, emphasizing political means and civil rights acts rather than economic means and self-determination. Washington learned this lesson not so much through experiences as a child worker in the salt works and coal mines as by what he was taught as a houseboy for the leading family of Malden, West Virginia, and later as a student at Hampton Institute in Virginia. Hampton

From Louis R. Harlan, "Booker T. Washington and the Politics of Accommodation," in John Hope Franklin and August Meier, eds., *Black Leaders of the Twentieth Century* (University of Illinois Press, 1982). 

applied the missionary method to black education and made its peace with the white South.

After teaching school in his home town, Washington briefly studied in a Baptist seminary and in a lawyer's office. But he soon abandoned these alternative careers, perhaps sensing that disfranchisement and the secularization of society would weaken these occupations as bases for racial leadership. He returned to Hampton Institute as a teacher for two years and then founded Tuskegee Normal and Industrial Institute in Alabama in 1881. Over the next quarter of a century, using Hampton's methods but with greater emphasis on the skilled trades, Washington built up Tuskegee Institute to be an equal of Hampton.

Washington's bid for leadership went beyond education and institution-building, however. Symbolic of his fresh approach to black-white relations was a speech he gave in 1895 before a commercial exposition, known as the Atlanta Compromise Address, and his autobiography, *Up from Slavery* (1901). As Washington saw it, blacks were toiling upward from slavery by their own efforts into the American middle class and needed chiefly social peace to continue in this steady social evolution. Thus, in the Atlanta Compromise he sought to disarm the white South by declaring agitation of the social equality question "the merest folly" and proclaiming that in "purely social" matters "we can be as separate as the fingers, yet one as the hand in all things essential to mutual progress." These concessions came to haunt Washington as southerners used segregation as a means of systematizing discrimination, and northerners followed suit. And they did not stop at the "purely social."

Washington's concessions to the white South, however, were only half of a bargain. In return for downgrading civil and political rights in the black list of priorities, Washington asked whites to place no barriers to black economic advancement and even to become partners of their black neighbors "in all things essential to mutual progress." Washington saw his own role as the axis between the races, the only leader who could negotiate and keep the peace by holding extremists on both sides in check. He was always conscious that his unique influence could be destroyed in an instant of self-indulgent flamboyance.

Washington sought to influence whites, but he never forgot that it was the blacks that he undertook to lead. He offered blacks not the empty promises of the demagogue but a solid program of economic and educational progress through struggle. It was less important "just now," he said, for a black person to seek admission to an opera house than to have the money for the ticket. Mediating diplomacy with whites was only half of Washington's strategy; the other half was black solidarity, mutual aid, and institution-building. He thought outspoken complaint against injustice was necessary but insufficient, and he thought factional dissent among black leaders was self-defeating and should be suppressed.

Washington brought to his role as a black leader the talents and outlook of a machine boss. He made Tuskegee Institute the largest and best-supported black educational institution of his day, and it spawned a large network of other industrial schools. Tuskegee's educational function is an important and debatable subject, of course, but the central concern here is Washington's use of the school as the base of operations of what came to be

known as the Tuskegee Machine. It was an all-black school with an all-black faculty at a time when most black colleges were still run by white missionaries. Tuskegee taught self-determination. It also taught trades designed for economic independence in a region dominated by sharecrop agriculture. At the same time, by verbal juggling tricks, Washington convinced the southern whites that Tuskegee was not educating black youth away from the farms. Tuskegee also functioned as a model black community, not only by acquainting its students with a middle-class way of life, but by buying up the surrounding farmland and selling it at low rates of interest to create a community of small landowners and homeowners. The Institute became larger than the town.

Washington built a regional constituency of farmers, artisans, country teachers, and small businessmen; he expanded the Tuskegee Machine nationwide after the Atlanta Compromise seemed acceptable to blacks all over the country, even by many who later denounced it. His first northern black ally was T. Thomas Fortune, editor of the militant and influential New York *Age* and founder of the Afro-American Council, the leading forum of black thought at the time. Washington was not a member, but he usually spoke at the annual meetings, and his lieutenants so tightly controlled the council that it never passed an action or resolution not in Washington's interest. Seeking more direct allies, Washington founded in 1900 the National Negro Business League, of which he was president for life. The league was important not so much for what it did for black business, which was little, but because the local branch of the league was a stronghold of Washington men in every substantial black population center.

Other classes of influential blacks did not agree with Washington's stated philosophy but were beholden to him for the favors he did them or offered to do for them. He was not called the Wizard for nothing. White philanthropists who approved of him for their own reasons gave him the money to help black colleges by providing for a Carnegie library here, a dormitory there. Through Washington Andrew Carnegie alone gave buildings to twenty-nine black schools. Not only college administrators owed him for favors, but so did church leaders, YMCA directors and many others. Though never much of a joiner, he became a power in the Baptist church, and he schemed through lieutenants to control the secret black fraternal orders and make his friends the high potentates of the Pythians, Odd Fellows, and so on. Like any boss, he turned every favor into a bond of obligation.

It was in politics, however, that Washington built the most elaborate tentacle of the octopus-like Tuskegee Machine. In politics as in everything else, Washington cultivated ambiguity. He downgraded politics as a solution of black problems, did not recommend politics to the ambitious young black man, and never held office. But when Theodore Roosevelt became president in 1901 and asked for Washington's advice on black and southern appointments, Washington consented with alacrity. He became the chief black adviser of both Presidents Roosevelt and William Howard Taft. He failed in his efforts to liberalize Republican policy on voting rights, lynching, and racial discrimination, however, and relations between the Republican party and black voters reached a low ebb.

In patronage politics, however, Washington found his opportunity. For a man who minimized the importance of politics, Washington devoted an inordinate amount of his time and tremendous energy to securing federal jobs for his machine lieutenants. These men played a certain role in the politics of the period, but their first obligation was to the Tuskegean. Washington advised the presidents to replace the old venal officeholding class of blacks with men who had proven themselves in the independent world of business, but in practice it took only loyalty to Washington to cleanse miraculously an old-time political hack....

Washington's outright critics and enemies were called "radicals" because they challenged Washington's conservatism and bossism, though their tactics of verbal protest would seem moderate indeed to a later generation of activists. They were the college-educated blacks, engaged in professional pursuits, and proud of their membership in an elite class—what one of them called the Talented Tenth. The strongholds of the radicals were the northern cities and southern black colleges. They stood for full political and civil rights, liberal education, free expression, and aspiration. They dreamed of a better world and believed Booker T. Washington was a menace to its achievement....

Washington dismissed his black critics by questioning their motives, their claim to superior wisdom, and—the politician's ultimate argument—their numbers. Washington understood, if his critics did not, that his leadership of the black community largely depended on his recognition by whites as the black leader. If he did not meet some minimal standards of satisfactoriness to whites, another Washington would be created. He obviously could not lead the whites; he could not even divide the whites. He could only, in a limited way, exploit the class divisions that whites created among themselves. He could work in the cracks of their social structure, move like Brer Rabbit through the brier patch, and thus outwit the more numerous and powerful whites.

While Washington recognized the centrality of black-white relations in his efforts to lead blacks, he was severely restricted by the historical context of his leadership. It was an age of polarization of black and white. The overheated atmosphere of the South at the turn of the century resembled that of a crisis center on the eve of war. Lynching became a more than weekly occurrence; discrimination and humiliation of blacks were constant and pervasive and bred a whole literature and behavioral science of self-justification. Race riots terrorized blacks in many cities, and not only in the South. It would have required not courage but foolhardiness for Washington, standing with both feet in Alabama, to have challenged this raging white aggression openly and directly. Even unqualified verbal protest would have brought him little support from either southern blacks or white wellwishers. Du Bois took higher ground and perhaps a better vision of the future when he urged forthright protest against every white injustice, on the assumption that whites were rational beings and would respond dialectically to black protest. But few white racists of the early twentieth century cared anything for the facts. And when Du Bois in his Atlanta years undertook to implement his protest with action, he was driven to the negative means of refusing to pay his poll tax or refusing to ride segregated streetcars and elevators.

Instead of either confronting all of white America or admitting that his Faustian bargain for leadership had created a systemic weakness in his program, Washington simply met each day as it came, pragmatically, seeking what white allies he could against avowed white enemies. A serious fault of this policy was that Washington usually appealed for white support on a basis of a vaguely conceived mutual interest rather than on ideological agreement. For example, in both the South and the North Washington allied himself with the white upper class against the masses. In the South he joined with the planter class and when possible with the coal barons and railroad officials against the populists and other small white farmer groups who seemed to him to harbor the most virulent anti-black attitudes born of labor competition. Similarly, in the North, Washington admired and bargained with the big business class. The bigger the businessman, the more Washington admired him, as the avatar and arbiter of American society. At the pinnacle in his measure of men were the industrialists Carnegie, John D. Rockefeller, and Henry H. Rogers and the merchant princes Robert C. Ogden and Julius Rosenwald. To be fair to Washington, he appreciated their philanthropic generosity at least as much as he admired their worldly success, but his lips were sealed against criticism of even the more rapacious and ungenerous members of the business elite.

Washington made constructive use of his philanthropic allies to aid not only Tuskegee but black education and black society as a whole. He guided the generous impulse of a Quaker millionairess into the Anna T. Jeanes Foundation to improve the teaching in black public schools. He persuaded the Jewish philanthropist Julius Rosenwald to begin a program that lasted for decades for building more adequate black schoolhouses all over the South. Washington's influence on Carnegie, Rockefeller, Jacob Schiff, and other rich men also transcended immediate Tuskegee interests to endow other black institutions. In short, Washington did play a role in educational statesmanship. There were limits, however, to his power to advance black interests through philanthropy. When his northern benefactors became involved in the Southern Education Board to improve the southern public school systems, for example, he worked repeatedly but without success to get this board to redress the imbalance of public expenditures or even to halt the rapid increase of discrimination against black schools and black children. He had to shrug off his failure and get from these so-called philanthropists whatever they were willing to give.

Having committed himself to the business elite, Washington took a dim view of the leaders of the working class. Immigrants represented to him, as to many blacks, labor competitors; Jews were the exception here, as he held them up to ambitious blacks as models of the work-ethic and group solidarity. He claimed in his autobiography that his disillusionment with labor unions went back to his youthful membership in the Knights of Labor and stemmed from observation of their disruption of the natural laws of economics. In his heyday, however, which was also the age of Samuel Gompers, Washington's anti-union attitudes were explained by the widespread exclusion of blacks from membership in many unions and hence from employment in many trades. There is no evidence that Washington ever actively supported black strikebreaking, but his refusal to intervene in behalf of all-white unions is understandable. It was more often white employees rather than employers who excluded blacks, or so Washington believed. He worked hard to introduce black labor into the non-union, white-only cotton mills in the South, even to the extent of interesting northern capitalists in investing in black cotton mills and similar enterprises.

Washington was a conservative by just about any measure. Though he flourished in the Progressive era it was not he, but his opponents who were the men of good hope, full of reform proposals and faith in the common man. Washington's vision of the common man included the southern poor white full of rancor against blacks, the foreign-born anarchist ready to pull down the temple of American business, and the black sharecropper unqualified by education or economic freedom for the ballot. Though Washington opposed the grandfather clause and every other southern device to exclude the black man from voting solely on account of his color, Washington did not favor universal suffrage. He believed in literacy and property tests, fairly enforced. He was no democrat. And he did not believe in woman suffrage, either.

In his eagerness to establish common ground with whites, that is, with some whites, Washington overstepped his purpose in public speeches by telling chicken-thief, mule, and other dialect stories intended to appeal to white stereotypes of blacks, and he occasionally spoke of the Afro-American as "a child race." No doubt his intent was to disarm his listeners, and before mixed audiences he often alternately addressed the two groups, reassuring whites that blacks should cooperate with their white neighbors in all constructive efforts, but saying to blacks that in their cooperation there should be "no unmanly cowering or stooping." At the cost of some forcefulness of presentation, Washington did have a remarkable capacity to convince whites as well as blacks that he not only understood them but agreed with them. It is one of Washington's intangible qualities as a black leader that he could influence, if not lead, so many whites. The agreement that whites sensed in him was more in his manner than in his program or goals, which always included human rights as well as material advancement for blacks.

In his constant effort to influence public opinion, Washington relied on the uncertain instruments of the press and the public platform. A flood of books and articles appeared over his name, largely written by his private secretary and a stable of ghostwriters, because he was too busy to do much writing. His ghostwriters were able and faithful, but they could not put new words or new ideas out over his signature, so for the crucial twenty years after 1895, Washington's writings showed no fresh creativity or real response to events, only a steady flood of platitudes. Washington's speeches generally suffered from an opposite handicap, that he was the only one who could deliver them. But he was too busy making two or three speeches a day to write a new one for each occasion, so the audiences rather than the speeches changed. But everywhere he went, North, South, or West, he drew large crowds ready to hear or rehear his platitudes.

Washington did try to change his world by other means. Some forms of racial injustice, such as lynching, disfranchisement, and unequal facilities in education and transportation, Washington dealt with publicly and directly. Early in his career as a leader he tried to sidestep the lynching question by saying that, deplorable though it was, he was too busy working for the education of black youth to divide his energies by dealing with other public questions. Friends and critics alike sharply told him that if he proposed to be a leader of blacks, he was going to have to deal with this subject. So he began an annual letter on lynching that he sent to all the southern white dailies, and he made Tuskegee Institute the center of statistical and news information on lynching. He always took a moderate tone, deplored rape and crime by blacks, but always denied that the crime blacks committed was either the cause of or justification for the crime of lynching. He tried to make up for his moderation by persistence, factual accuracy, and persuasive logic. Disfranchisement of black voters swept through the South from Texas to Virginia during Washington's day. He publicly protested in letters to the constitutional conventions and legislatures in Alabama, Georgia, and Louisiana and aided similar efforts in several other states. He failed to stop lynching, to prevent the loss of voting rights, and to clean up the Jim Crow cars or bring about even minimal standards of fairness in the public schools. But he did try.

As for social segregation, Washington abided by southern customs while in the South but forthrightly declared it unreasonable for white southerners to dictate his behavior outside of the South. His celebrated dinner at the White House in 1901, therefore, though it caused consternation and protest among white southerners, was consistent with his lifetime practice. Tuskegee Institute underwent an elaborate ritual of segregation with every white visitor, but the man who came to dinner at the White House, had tea with the queen of England, and attended hundreds of banquets and private meals with whites outside the South certainly never internalized the attitudes of the segregators.

What Washington could not do publicly to achieve equal rights, he sought to accomplish secretly. He spent four years in cooperation with the Afro-American Council on a court case to test the constitutionality of the Louisiana grandfather clause, providing funds from his own pocket and from northern white liberal friends. In his own state of Alabama, Washington secretly directed the efforts of his personal lawyer to carry two grandfather-clause cases all the way to the U.S. Supreme Court, where they were lost on technicalities. He took the extra precaution of using code names in all the correspondence on the Alabama cases. Through private pressure on railroad officials and congressmen, Washington tried to bring about improvement in the Jim Crow cars and railroad waiting rooms. He had more success in the Dan Rogers case, which overturned a criminal verdict against a black man because blacks were excluded from the jury. He also secretly collaborated with two southern white attorneys to defend Alonzo Bailey, a farm laborer held in peonage for debt; the outcome here was also successful, for the Alabama peonage law was declared unconstitutional. These and other secret actions were certainly not enough to tear down the legal structure of white supremacy, but they show that Washington's role in Afro-American history was not always that of the accommodationist "heavy." He was working, at several levels and in imaginative ways, and always with vigor, toward goals similar to those of his critics. If his methods did not work, the same could be said of theirs. And he did not take these civil rights actions as a means of answering criticism, because he kept his part in the court cases a secret except to a handful of confidants, a secret not revealed until his papers were opened to historians in recent decades.

There was another, uglier side of Washington's secret behavior, however—his ruthless spying and sabotage against his leading black critics. Washington never articulated a justification for these actions, perhaps because, being secret, they did not require defense. And yet Washington and Emmett Scott left the evidence of his secret machinations undestroyed in his papers, apparently in the faith that history would vindicate him when all the facts were known. Then, too, Washington was not given to explaining himself....

The Booker T. Washington who emerges into the light of history from his private papers is a complex, Faustian character quite different from the paragon of self-uplift and Christian forbearance that Washington projected in his autobiography. On the other hand, there is little evidence for and much evidence against the charge of some of his contemporaries that he was simply an accommodationist who bargained away his race's birthright for a mess of pottage. Nor does he fit some historians' single-factor explanations of his career: that he offered "education for the new slavery," that he was a proto-black-nationalist, that he was or must have been psychologically crippled by the constraints and guilt feelings of his social role.

Washington's complexity should not be overstressed, however, for the more we know about anybody the more complex that person seems. And through the complexity of Washington's life, its busyness and its multiple levels, two main themes stand out, his true belief in his program for black progress and his great skill in and appetite for politics, broadly defined, serving both his goals and his personal power.

First, let us look closely at Washington's industrial education and small business program. It may have been anachronistic preparation for the age of mass production and corporate gigantism then coming into being, but it had considerable social realism for a black population which was, until long after Washington's death, predominantly rural and southern. Furthermore, it was well attuned to the growth and changing character of black business in his day. Increasingly, the nineteenth-century black businesses catering to white clients surrendered predominance to ghetto businesses such as banks, insurance companies, undertakers, and barbers catering to black customers. These new businessmen, with a vested interest in black solidarity, were the backbone of Washington's National Negro Business League. Washington clearly found congenial the prospect of an elite class of self-made businessmen as leaders and models for the struggling masses. There was also room for the Talented Tenth of professional men in the Tuskegee Machine, however. Washington welcomed every college-educated recruit he could secure. Directly or through agents, he was the largest employer in the country of black college graduates.

Second, let us consider Washington as a powerful politician. Though he warned

young men away from politics as a dead-end career, what distinguished Washington's career was not his rather conventional goals, which in public or private he shared with almost every other black spokesman, but his consummate political skill, his wheeling and dealing....

Washington's program was not consensus politics, for he always sought change, and there was always vocal opposition to him on both sides that he never tried to mollify. Denounced on the one hand by the Niagara Movement and the NAACP for not protesting enough, he was also distrusted and denounced by white supremacists for bringing the wooden horse within the walls of Troy. All of the racist demagogues of his time—Benjamin Tillman, James Vardaman, Theodore Bilbo, Thomas Dixon, and J. Thomas Heflin, to name a few—called Washington their insidious enemy. One descriptive label for Washington might be centrist coalition politics. The Tuskegee Machine had the middle and undecided majority of white and black people behind it. Washington was a rallying point for the southern moderates, the northern publicists and makers of opinion, and the thousands who read his autobiography or crowded into halls to hear him. Among blacks he had the businessmen solidly behind him, and even, as August Meier has shown, a majority of the Talented Tenth of professional men, so great was his power to reward and punish, to make or break careers. He had access to the wellsprings of philanthropy, political preferment, and other white sources of black opportunity. For blacks at the bottom of the ladder, Washington's program offered education, a self-help formula, and, importantly for a group demoralized by the white aggression of that period, a social philosophy that gave dignity and purpose to lives of daily toil.

It could be said with some justification that the Tuskegee Machine was a stationary machine, that it went nowhere. Because the machine was held together by the glue of self-interest, Washington was frequently disappointed by the inadequate response of his allies. The southern upper class did not effectively resist disfranchisement as he had hoped and never gave blacks the equal economic chance that he considered an integral part of the Atlanta Compromise. Washington's philanthropist-friends never stood up for equal opportunity in public education. Black businessmen frequently found their own vested interest in a captive market rather than a more open society. And Washington himself often took the view that whatever was good for Tuskegee and himself was good for the Negro.

To the charge that he accomplished nothing, it can only be imagined what Washington would have answered, since he did not have the years of hindsight and self-justification that some of his critics enjoyed. He would probably have stressed how much worse the southern racial reaction would have been without his coalition of moderates, his soothing syrup, and his practical message to blacks of self-improvement and progress along the lines of least resistance. Washington's power over his following, and hence his power to bring about change, have probably been exaggerated. It was the breadth rather than the depth of his coalition that was unique. Perhaps one Booker T. Washington was enough. But even today, in a very different society, Washington's autobiography is still in print. It still has some impalpable power to bridge the racial gap, to move new readers to take the first steps across the color line. Many of his ideas of self-help and racial solidarity still have currency in the black community. But he was an important leader because, like Frederick Douglass before him and Martin Luther King after him, he had the program and strategy and skill to influence the behavior of not only the Afro-American one-tenth, but the white nine-tenths of the American people. He was a political realist.

# POSTSCRIPT

## Did Booker T. Washington's Philosophy and Actions Betray the Interests of African Americans?

Discussions of race relations in the late nineteenth- and early twentieth-century United States invariably focus upon the ascendancy of Booker T. Washington, his apparent accommodation to existing patterns of racial segregation, and the conflicting traditions within black thought, epitomized by the clash between Washington and Du Bois. Seldom, however, is attention given to black nationalist thought in the "age of Booker T. Washington."

Black nationalism, centered on the concept of racial solidarity, has been a persistent theme in African American history and reached one of its most important stages of development between 1880 and 1920. In the late 1800s, Henry McNeal Turner and Edward Wilmot Blyden encouraged greater interest in the repatriation of black Americans to Africa, especially Liberia. This goal continued into the twentieth century and culminated in the "Back-to-Africa" program of Marcus Garvey and his Universal Negro Improvement Association. Interestingly, Booker T. Washington also exhibited nationalist sentiment by encouraging blacks to withdraw from white society, develop their own institutions and businesses, and engage in economic and moral uplift. Washington's nationalism concentrated on economic self-help and manifested itself in 1900 with the establishment of the National Negro Business League.

A thorough assessment of the protest and accommodationist views of black Americans is presented in August Meier, *Negro Thought in America, 1800–1915* (University of Michigan Press, 1963). Rayford Logan, *The Betrayal of the Negro: From Rutherford B. Hayes to Woodrow Wilson* (Macmillan, 1965), describes the last quarter of the nineteenth century as "the nadir" for black life. By far the best studies of Booker T. Washington are two volumes by Louis R. Harlan: *Booker T. Washington: The Making of a Black Leader, 1856–1901* (Oxford University Press, 1972) and *Booker T. Washington: The Wizard of Tuskegee, 1901–1915* (Oxford University Press, 1983). In addition, Harlan has edited the 13-volume *Booker T. Washington Papers* (University of Illinois Press, 1972–1984). For assessments of two of Booker T. Washington's harshest critics, see David Levering Lewis, *W. E. B. Du Bois: Biography of a Race, 1868–1919* (Henry Holt, 1993), the first of a projected two-volume study, and Stephen R. Fox, *The Guardian of Boston: William Monroe Trotter* (Atheneum, 1970). John H. Bracey, Jr., August Meier, and Elliott Rudwick, *Black Nationalism in America* (Bobbs-Merrill, 1970), provide an invaluable collection of documents pertaining to black nationalism. See also Edwin S. Redkey, *Black Exodus: Black Nationalist and Back-to-Africa Movements, 1890–1910* (Yale University Press, 1969), and Hollis R. Lynch, *Edward Wilmot Blyden: Pan-Negro Patriot, 1832–1912* (Oxford University Press, 1967). Diverse views of Marcus Garvey, who credited Booker T. Washington with inspiring him to seek a leadership role on behalf of African Americans, are found in Edmund David Cronon, *Black Moses: The Story of Marcus Garvey and the Universal Negro Improvement Association* (University of Wisconsin Press, 1955); Tony Martin, *Race First: The Ideological and Organizational Struggles of Marcus Garvey and the UNIA* (Greenwood Press, 1976); and Judith Stein, *The World of Marcus Garvey: Race and Class in Modern Society* (Louisiana State University Press, 1986).

# PART 3

# From Prosperity Through World War II

*The Progressive reformers ameliorated some of the worst problems of urban-industrial America in the early twentieth century but often created others by attempting to impose Anglo-Saxon Protestant standards on a diverse racial and immigrant population. America began to review its position in the world as a result of its new industrial power. In 1917 Woodrow Wilson invoked this expanded international role by leading the nation into a war "to make the world safe for democracy."*

*The 1920s are often portrayed as a hedonistic interlude for everyone between the Progressive and New Deal reform eras. Organizations like the Ku Klux Klan revealed a number of tensions between the values of the nation's rural past and the new social and moral values of modern America.*

*The onset of a more activist federal government accelerated with the Great Depression. With more than one-quarter of the workforce unemployed, Franklin D. Roosevelt was elected on a promise to give Americans a "new deal."*

*World War II short-circuited these plans but brought dramatic changes to the lives of American women, many of whom entered the labor force for the first time. In addition, the end of the war introduced people throughout the world to the anxious realities of the atomic age.*

# ISSUE 8

## Were the Progressives Imperialists?

**YES: William Appleman Williams,** from *The Tragedy of American Diplomacy,* 2d ed. (Dell Publishing, 1972)

**NO: Barton J. Bernstein and Franklin A. Leib,** from "Progressive Republican Senators and American Imperialism, 1898–1916: A Reappraisal," *Mid-America: An Historical Review* (July 1968)

### ISSUE SUMMARY

**YES:** Diplomatic historian William Appleman Williams argues that the demand for economic expansion through the development of markets abroad led Progressive politicians to support an imperialistic foreign policy that subverted the American commitment to the ideal of self-determination for the peoples of other nations.

**NO:** Historians Barton J. Bernstein and Franklin A. Leib conclude that Progressive Republicans in the U.S. Senate usually supported economic expansion overseas but were not, for the most part, committed to an aggressive imperialistic foreign policy.

Traditionally, the term *progressive* has been used by historians to describe the reform movement in the United States between 1901 and 1917. Operating at local, state, and national levels, largely as an urban, middle-class response to the effects of rapid industrialization and the rise of monopolistic capitalism, participants in progressive causes were responsible for a wide range of political, economic, and social reforms, many of which remain in effect today. For example, Progressives introduced city managers and planning commissions in hundreds of municipalities across the nation in order to attack the corruption and inefficiency that many believed to be the hallmarks of local government. Democracy was enhanced through changes in voting practices: the implementation of initiatives, referendums, and recalls; and the shift to popular election of U.S. senators. Some Progressives channeled their efforts into antitrust legislation, claiming that the trusts were undermining economic opportunities in the country. Other progressive reformers sought to protect American workers from the worst hazards associated with the factory system, and some sponsored conservation measures to protect the country's natural resources.

While Progressives devoted considerable attention to domestic reform, they also were concerned with the role of the United States in world affairs.

This was particularly true of the Progressives who held national office in the first two decades of the twentieth century. Theodore Roosevelt, for example, was deeply committed to expanding the country's influence throughout the world and even led an infamous charge against Spanish troops in Cuba as a colonel in the U.S. army during the short-lived but hard fought Spanish-American War in 1898. As president, in 1903, he supported a revolution in Panama to overthrow Colombian rule in order to gain access to the territory through which the already planned Panama Canal was to be built by the United States. The following year, he announced the Roosevelt Corollary to the Monroe Doctrine. Worried that European countries might intervene in the Dominican Republic to collect debts owed to European banks, Roosevelt declared that the United States should help "backward" countries to pay their bills. The Roosevelt Corollary stated that the United States had the authority to intervene directly on behalf of Latin American nations to preserve law and order.

Progressive leaders also hoped to extend U.S. economic influence around the world. This "dollar diplomacy" (which critics characterize as simply a nicer term for economic imperialism) encouraged the expansion of American business from Central America to China. In addition, the establishment of financial and business institutions beyond the boundaries of the United States occasionally required military intervention in order to protect those interests from anti-American uprisings in the host countries.

President Woodrow Wilson, another Progressive president, thought of foreign policy in moral terms, and during his two administrations, those governments that behaved improperly were likely to feel Wilson's wrath. Alleged insults to the honor of the United States by Mexico resulted in the Wilson-sponsored invasion of that nation by General John ("Black Jack") Pershing in 1913 and the landing of Marines at Vera Cruz in 1914. And, of course, Germany's refusal to abandon what Wilson believed to be the immoral tactic of submarine warfare ultimately resulted in the president's request for a declaration of war against Germany in April 1917.

Is it appropriate to characterize the Progressives as imperialists? For William Appleman Williams, who prior to his death was the most prominent of the so-called New Left historians, the answer is "Yes." Imperialistic practices grew out of a foreign policy at the turn of the century that emphasized the acquisition of new markets for American goods and intersected with a desire to reform underdeveloped societies by making them more like the United States. Hence, says Williams, the secular and religious ideologies associated with progressivism resulted in foreign interventions.

Historians Barton J. Bernstein and Franklin A. Leib challenge the assumption that links progressivism and imperialism. Their study of the policies of Progressive Republican senators in the period between the Spanish-American War and World War I concludes that most of these reformers opposed U.S. economic interests abroad and tried to avoid American military intervention.

# YES William Appleman Williams

## THE IMPERIALISM OF IDEALISM

Taken up by President Theodore Roosevelt and his successors, the philosophy and practice of the imperialism that was embodied in the Open Door Notes became the central feature of American foreign policy in the twentieth century. American economic power gushed into some underdeveloped areas within a decade and into many others within a generation. It also seeped, then trickled, and finally flooded into the more developed nations and their colonies until, by 1939, America's economic expansion encompassed the globe. And by that time the regions where America's position was not extensively developed were precisely the areas in which the United States manifested a determination to retain and expand its exploratory operations —or to enter in force for the first time.

Throughout those same years, the rise of a new crusading spirit in American diplomacy contributed to the outward thrust. Such righteous enthusiasm was both secular, emphasizing political and social ideology, and religious, stressing the virtues (and necessities) of Protestant Christianity. In essence, twentieth-century Manifest Destiny was identical with the earlier phenomenon of the same name....

Missionaries had always tended to operate on an assumption quite similar to the frontier thesis. "Missionaries are an absolute necessity," explained the Reverend Henry Van Dyke of Princeton in 1896, "not only for the conversion of the heathen, but also, and much more, for the preservation of the Church. Christianity is a religion that will not keep." Religious leaders began to link the missionary movement with economic expansion in what the Reverend Francis E. Clark of the Christian Endeavor organization called "the widening of our empire." The Board of Foreign Missions also welcomed such expansion as "an ally."

Then, beginning in the mid-1890s, the missionaries began to change their basic strategy in a way that greatly encouraged a liaison with secular expansionists. Shifting from an emphasis on the horrors of hell to a concern with practical reform as the lever of conversion, they increasingly stressed the need to remake the underdeveloped societies. Naturally enough, they were to be reformed in the image of the United States. Such changes would lead to regeneration identified with Christianity and witnesses for the Lord would accordingly increase.

Not only did this program mesh with the idea of American secular influence (how else were the reforms to be initiated?), but it was very similar to the argument that American expansion was justified because it created more progressive societies. Missionaries came to sound more and more like political leaders, who were themselves submerging their domestic ideological differences at the water's edge in a general agreement on expansion as a reform movement.

The domestic reformer La Follette offers an excellent example of this convergence of economic and ideological expansion that took place across political lines. He approved taking the Philippines because it would enable America "to conquer [its] rightful share of that great market now opening [in China] for the world's commerce." Expansion was also justified because the United States had a "bounden *duty* to establish and *maintain* stable government" in the islands. Pointing out that from the beginning "the policy of this government has been to expand," La Follette justified it on the grounds that "it has *made men free.*" Thus, he concluded, "we can legally and morally reserve unto ourselves perpetual commercial advantages of priceless value to our foreign trade for all time to come" by taking the Philippines.

Theodore Roosevelt's outlook reveals an even more significant aspect of this progressive integration of secular and ideological expansionism. His concern for economic expansion was complemented by an urge to extend Anglo-Saxon ideas, practices, and virtues throughout the world. Just as his Square Deal program centered on the idea of responsible leaders using the national government to regulate and moderate industrial society at home, so did his international outlook revolve around the idea of American supremacy being used to define and promote the interests of "collective civilization."

Thus it was necessary, he warned in his Presidential Message of December 1901, to exercise restraint in dealing with the large corporations. "Business concerns which have the largest means at their disposal... take the lead in the strife for commercial supremacy among the nations of the world. America has only just begun to assume the commanding position in the international business world which we believe will more and more be hers. It is of the utmost importance that this position be not jeopardized, especially at a time when the overflowing abundance of our own natural resources and the skill, business energy, and mechanical aptitude of our people make foreign markets essential."

Roosevelt integrated that kind of expansion with ideological considerations and imperatives to create an all-inclusive logic and set of responsibilities which made peace itself the consequence of empire. In his mind, at any rate, it was America's "duty toward the people living in barbarism to see that they are freed from their chains, and we can free them only by destroying barbarism itself." Thus, he concluded, peace cannot be had until the civilized nations have expanded in some shape over the barbarous nations."

The inherent requirements of economic expansion coincided with such religious, racist, and reformist drives to remake the world. The reason for this is not difficult to perceive. As they existed, the underdeveloped countries were poor, particularistic, and bound by traditions which handicapped business enterprise. They were not organized to mesh with modern industrial systems in a practical and efficient manner. It was economically necessary to change them *in certain ways and to a limited degree* if the fruits of expansion were to be harvested. As with the missionaries, therefore, the economic and political leaders of the country decided that what was good for Americans was also good for foreigners. Humanitarian concern was thus reinforced by hard-headed economic requirements.

The administrations of Theodore Roosevelt understood this relationship between economic expansion and overseas reform, and explicitly integrated it into the strategy of the Open Door Policy. It was often commented upon in dispatches and policy statements concerning China and Latin America. In his famous Corollary to the Monroe Doctrine, for example, Roosevelt (who thought of the Open Door Policy as the Monroe Doctrine for Asia) stressed the need for reforms and asserted the right and the obligation of the United States to see that they were made—and honored.

It was in connection with the Algeciras Conference of 1905–06, however, that the relationship was most fully (and even brilliantly) explained and formally made a part of the Open Door Policy. Growing out of the imperial rivalry in Africa between Britain, France, and Germany, the Algeciras (or Moroccan) Conference proceeded on two levels. The dramatic battle involved limiting German penetration to a minimum while giving it superficial concessions. In that skirmish the United States sided with England and France. But the conference also offered the United States a chance to renew and reinforce its old drive of the 1880s to secure equal commercial rights in Africa. Roosevelt and Secretary of State Elihu Root used the strategy of the open door to wage both campaigns. Their policy instructions on the specific problems of organizing an international Moroccan police force, and on instituting financial reforms, revealed their full understanding of the nature and the extent of the interrelationship between reform and economic expansion....

The broader aspects of the analysis and policy statement prepared by Roosevelt and Root are even more significant. That document establishes once and for all the connection between, and the convergence of, the drive for overseas economic expansion and the urge to reform other societies according to American and industrial standards. It likewise removes any doubt about whether or not American leaders were conscious of the relationship. And finally, it helps clarify the nature and the dimensions of the tragedy and the terror of American foreign policy that evolved out of the Open Door Policy.

On the one hand, of course, the positive features of the reforms, including the general concern to initiate a minimum of economic development, emerge very clearly. On the other hand, it becomes apparent that the United States was opening the door to serious and extensive unrest, as well as to potential economic development and political reform. Perhaps the failure to understand this, or a not unrelated kind of persistent wishful thinking that such unrest could somehow be avoided, provides the final, irreducible explanation of America's difficulties in foreign affairs during the twentieth century. For America's integrated reformist and economic expansion provoked trouble. And the reaction to the trouble ultimately took the form of terror.

First: it undertook to initiate and sustain drastic, fundamental changes in other societies. The process of wrenching Morocco, or China, or Nicaragua out of their neo-feudal, primarily agrarian condition into the industrial era involved harsh, painful alterations in an established way of life. Even under the best of circumstances, those consequences can only be mitigated. They cannot be entirely avoided.

Second: the United States identified itself as a primary cause of such changes. It thereby also defined itself as a principal source of the related pain and unhappiness. This is true, not only in connection with those groups in power which oppose the changes as they begin, but also for those who suffer from the consequences without means to oppose or moderate them, and even for others who generally approve of the new ways but despair of the costs and question the morality of outsiders interfering in such fundamental and extensive respects.

Third: the United States wanted to stop or stabilize such changes at a point favorable to American interests. This was at best naive. Even a modest familiarity with history reveals that such alterations have wide and continuing consequences. It was at worst a knowing effort to slap a lid on dynamic development. That attempt can only be described as a selfish violation of the idea and ideal of self-determination, and even as an evasion of the moral obligation to accept the consequences of one's own actions.

Fourth: the effort to control and limit changes according to American preferences served only to intensify opposition within the developing countries. The extent to which Algerian revolutionaries of the 1940s and 1950s revealed and illustrated all these points in their attitudes toward the United States offers a particularly relevant example of the tragic consequences of American reformist and economic expansion as it emerged during the Roosevelt administrations.

The integration of these elements was carried forward, and given classic expression in the rhetoric, style, and substance of the diplomacy of President Woodrow Wilson and Secretary of State Bryan. Both men were leaders of the American reform movement, and they brought to their conduct of foreign affairs a religious intensity and righteousness that was not apparent in earlier administrations and which may not have been matched since their time. As Protestants imbued with a strong sense of Anglo-Saxon self-consciousness, they personified the assertive idealism that complemented and reinforced the economic drive for markets.

Bryan was a Fundamentalist in religious matters. Typified by the famous "Cross of Gold" speech which climaxed his nomination for the presidency in 1896, his sense of calling and mission infused all his political actions with a kind of hell-fire enthusiasm and determination. Those characteristics could be misleading, and in the Crisis of the 1890s prompted a good many Americans to view Bryan as a threat to social order. But as revealed even in the "Cross of Gold" speech (where he defined everybody as a businessman), as well as in his actions, he was wholly a reform capitalist. Bryan himself joked about the misconception. Upon at least one occasion, when he visited the White House after his defeat in the election of 1904, he did so with considerable charm. President Roosevelt was one of those who had hurled all kinds of invective and wild charges at Bryan at one time or another during their political rivalry. As he arrived to make an invited call on the victor, Bryan revealed a kind of pleasant fatalism about such things. "Some people think I'm a terrible radical, but really I'm not so very dangerous after all."

As far as foreign affairs were concerned, Bryan's outlook was that of the Christian leader who concluded that his society needed overseas markets and was determined to find them. He fully intended, however, to do so in such a way that order and stability would be assured, a protestant peace secured and preserved, and the backward nations protected from rapacious foreigners while being led along the path of progress by the United States. Confident that Wilson was a man with the same goals, Bryan could without any reservations praise the President, in May 1914, as one who had "opened the doors of all the weaker countries to an invasion of American capital and American enterprise."

Candidly asserting America's "paramount influence in the Western Hemisphere," Bryan's objective was to "make absolutely sure our domination of the situation." Such moral and economic expansion, he explained in 1913, would "give our country such increased influence... that we could prevent revolutions, promote education, and advance stable and just government... we would in the end profit, negatively, by not having to incur expense in guarding our own and foreign interests there, and, positively, by the increase of trade."

While no less determined—his will won him more than one defeat—Wilson's idealism was that of the high church Presbyterian Calvinist who viewed himself and the United States as trustees of the world's welfare. The destiny of America was to be "the justest, the most progressive, the most honorable, the most enlightened Nation in the world." Small wonder, then, that Wilson led the country into World War I with the argument that "the world must be made safe for democracy." Or that he considered his own postwar program to be "the only possible" plan for peace which therefore "must prevail."

Wilson was both responsible and candid enough to admit that all was not perfect either in America or the rest of the world. But since he considered the philosophy of revolution to be "in fact radically evil and corrupting," he insisted that the only recourse was "a slow process of reform" led by trustees such as himself. At least, that is to say, *within* the United States. But America, just because it was the elect among the trustees of the world, had both a right and an obligation to use force "to do justice and assert the rights of mankind."

Wilson's imperialism of the spirit was well defined by his attitude toward the Philippines. The United States should grant independence to the Filipinos just as soon as American leadership had instructed them in the proper standards of national life, instilled in them the proper character, and established for them a stable and constitutional government. Such noble objectives justified—even demanded—the use of force. "When men take up arms to set other men free," he declared, "there is something sacred and holy in the warfare. I will not cry 'peace' as long as there is sin and wrong in the world."

But since Wilson's fundamental assumption about the nature of man was that he "lives not by what he does, but by what he thinks and hopes," this type of imperialism was, by the President's own standards, the most persuasive and extensive of any that could be devised.

For in effect—and in practice—it subverted Wilson's support for the principle of self-determination. He asserted that other peoples were at liberty, and had a right to be free; but he judged whether or not they chose freedom by his own standards. Or, as he put it during the Mexican crisis, he would approve and recognize none but "those who act in the interest of peace and honor, who protect private rights, and respect the restraints of constitutional provisions."

Both then and later, Wilson used American power to go behind the forms of government to see if the substance squared with his criteria and, if it did not, he deployed American power in an attempt to force reality into correspondence with his imagery and ideals. The policy was the broadest kind of imperialism. Thus his refusal to go along with American corporations that wanted to recognize and sustain the regime of Victoriano Huerta during the early phases of the Mexican Revolution is at most only half the story. Wilson was perfectly willing to intervene vigorously, even to the brink of war, in order to force the Mexicans to behave according to his standards. "I am going to teach the South American republics," he explained to a British diplomat, "to elect good men."

These features of Wilson's foreign policy have understandably led many historians, including some of his admirers, to characterize his diplomacy as "moral imperialism," "imperialism of the spirit," or "missionary diplomacy." While accurate as far as it goes, that approach is seriously misleading because it ignores or neglects the extensive degree to which Wilson advocated and supported overseas economic expansion. It also does Wilson an injustice. For he brought the two themes together in a manner that surpassed even the similar achievement of Roosevelt and Root.

The single most important insight into Wilson's propensity and ability to fuse those two traditions very probably lies in his Calvinistic *Weltanschauung.* Two of Calvin's central assumptions concerned the complementary nature of economics and morality, and the responsibility of the trustee for combining them to produce the welfare of the community. He emphasized these very clearly and forcefully in his writings, and tried to carry them out in actual practice. It is of course true that Wilson was not Calvin (though upon occasion the President's actions provoked some of his critics to remark that there seemed to be some confusion in his own mind on that issue). Nor was he a disciple in the rigid and narrow theological or clerical sense. But he did make sense out of reality from the basic vantage point offered by Calvinism, and his consolidation of economics and ideas stemmed from that conception of the world.

Granted this combination (contradictory as it may have been) of Calvinism and capitalism, the consideration most directly pertinent in comprehending Wilson's handling of foreign policy is his commitment to the frontier thesis of Frederick Jackson Turner. They enjoyed a close personal and intellectual friendship while Turner was developing his thesis about American expansion and its prosperity and democracy as an advanced student at Johns Hopkins University. Wilson accepted the argument as the central explanation of American history. "All I ever wrote on the subject," he later remarked of Turner, "came from him." That was true, even though it was an exaggeration. Wilson shaped and used the intellectual tool of interpreting American politics from the perspective of the British parliamentary system on his own (and it was a stimulating approach). Even so, the frontier thesis was a crucial element in his thinking about the past and the present.

Wilson put it very directly as early as 1896 in explaining the Crisis of the 1890s. "The days of glad expansion are gone, our life grows tense and difficult." He read George Washington's Farewell Address in the same light. Wilson argued that Washington "would seem to have meant, 'I want you to discipline yourselves and... be good boys until you... are big enough to stand the competition... until you are big enough to go abroad in the world.'" Wilson clearly thought that by 1901 the United States had become a big boy: expansion was a "natural and wholesome impulse." And in a speech on "The Ideals of America" of December 26, 1901, which was remarkable for its close following of the frontier thesis, he projected the process indefinitely: "Who shall say," he asked rhetorically, "where it will end?"

With the publication the next year of his five-volume *History of the American People,* it became apparent that Wilson saw overseas economic expansion as the frontier to replace the continent that had been occupied. A section in Volume V (which reads like a close paraphrase of some essays written by Brooks Adams) recommended increased efficiency in government so that the United States "might command the economic fortunes of the world." Referring a bit later to the Philippines as "new frontiers," he concluded his analysis by stressing the need for markets—markets "to which diplomacy, and if need be power, must make an open way." In a series of lectures at Columbia University in April 1907, he was even more forthright. "Since trade ignores national boundaries and the manufacturer insists on having the world as a market, the flag of his nation must follow him, and the doors of the nations which are closed must be battered down." "Concessions obtained by financiers must be safeguarded," he continued, "by ministers of state, even if the sovereignty of unwilling nations be outraged in the process. Colonies must be obtained or planted, in order that no useful corner of the world may be overlooked or left unused. Peace itself becomes a matter of conference and international combinations." It was something of an anti-climax to learn that Wilson expected "many sharp struggles for foreign trade."

His persistent repetition of that warning serves to symbolize the extent to which Wilson's campaign for the presidential nomination and election in 1912 stressed overseas economic expansion. During January and February he reviewed the importance of a merchant marine, and bewailed the weaknesses of the banking system which handicapped American financiers in overseas competition. By August, when he won the nomination, he was ready with a general interpretation. The United States was an "expanding" nation. "Our industries have expanded to such a point that they will burst their jackets if they cannot find a free outlet to the markets of the world.... Our domestic markets no longer suffice. We need foreign markets." And also, he added, a major effort to educate the general public on the problem and its solution. Wilson was even more specific about the reason behind his sense of urgency at a campaign dinner for his supporters among the working class. (Not many day laborers could afford the prices, but their leaders attended.) "We have reached, in short, a critical point in the process of our prosperity. It has now become a question with us," he warned, "whether it shall continue or shall not continue." "We need foreign markets," he reiterated, because "our domestic market is too small." And as McKinley and Root before him, Wilson in 1912 unequivocally pointed to Germany as the most dangerous rival of the United States in that economic struggle....

An understanding... of the... convergence of the reformist and economic drives for expansion, offers a key insight into America's entry into World War I. Most Americans shared Wilson's nationalistic outlook. None but a handful of citizens quarreled with his assertion that it was the destiny of the United States to become the "justest, the most progressive, the most honorable, the most enlightened Nation in the world." Indeed, a sizable plurality thought, if they did not assume, that the destiny was being realized in their own time. In the early months of the war, therefore, it was quite natural for them to feel, along with Wilson, that America had neither reason nor necessity to enter the conflict.

But, and again in agreement with Wilson, most Americans wanted the Allies to win, and they were willing to help bring about that result. Whatever the faults and sins of England and France, they were better than autocratic Germany. America could work with them toward a peaceful, prosperous, and moral world, whereas such would be impossible if Germany won. This attitude, and the actions which it prompted, led Wilson and America into a position where they had either to abandon their determination and destiny to lead the world or go to war.

The early economic decisions made by businessmen and the Wilson Administration committed the American economic system to the Allied war effort. That did not, in itself, make it inevitable that America's nonbelligerent alignment with the Allies would involve America in the war on their side; but it did make it extremely difficult for Wilson to achieve his objectives in any other way.

The American economy was in a depression when the war erupted. Financier J. Pierpont Morgan described the situation in an accurate and straightforward manner. "The war opened during a period of hard times that had continued in America for over a year. Business throughout the country was depressed, farm prices were deflated, unemployment was serious, the heavy industries were working far below capacity [and] bank clearings were off." [Frank A.] Vanderlip's comment was more elliptical: "The country was not in a prosperous situation."

The first economic shocks of the conflict subjected the system to even more difficulties. The stock market and the cotton exchange were closed on July 31, 1914, and did not reopen for public trading for many, many months. "We were looking after our own troubles," Vanderlip later explained, and "bankers in general were not considering technical matters of neutrality." Instead, Vanderlip went on, "we had the idea very much of keeping up our foreign trade throughout the world." In making that effort, it was not very surprising that American entrepreneurs concentrated on reopening their connections with the Allies, who together with their colonies had purchased 77 per cent of American exports in 1913—and with whom the majority of American bankers had their closest connections.

But in restoring America's foreign trade by tying it to England and France (and by expanding old connections with such nations as Russia), rather than by insisting upon economic neutrality, Wilson and American businessmen tied themselves to a prosperity based on the Allied war program. Wilson developed no other plan to end the depression, and hence this way of dealing with the problem exerted a subtle but persuasive influence on later decisions.

Economic ties to the Allies also reinforced the bias of Wilson's ideology and morality toward defining German naval warfare as the most important diplomatic issue of the war. Wilson denounced submarine warfare on moral and humanitarian grounds, whereas he opposed British trade restrictions on legal and historical precedents. And the fact that Wilson launched no crusade against the Allied food blockade of Germany, which had equally devastating moral and humanitarian consequences, dramatized this double standard.

This ability to make such fine moral discriminations forced Wilson into an extremely difficult situation. He hoped to remain a nonbelligerent until a stalemate developed and then step in as the arbiter of the settlement and as the architect of a world organization to establish and maintain peace. But by seeming to foreshadow the defeat of England and France, the success of submarine warfare also threatened his ability to lead the world to permanent peace. Wilson resolved his difficulties (and apparently eased his troubled conscience) by defining the situation as similar to the case of the Philippines. America was justified in using force "to do justice and assert the rights of mankind." To that end, war against Germany would be prosecuted until it established "a government we can trust."

By the time of World War I, therefore, the basic dilemma of American foreign policy was clearly defined. Its generous humanitarianism prompted it to improve the lot of less fortunate peoples, but that side of its diplomacy was undercut by two other aspects of its policy. On the one hand, it defined helping people in terms of making them more like Americans. This subverted its ideal of self-determination. On the other hand, it asserted and acted upon the necessity of overseas economic expansion for its own material prosperity. But by defining such expansion in terms of markets for American exports, and control of raw materials for American industry, the ability of other peoples to develop and act upon their own patterns of development was further undercut.

Those unfortunate aspects of American foreign policy were summarized rather well by an American reformer who at one time had shared the attitude of Roosevelt and Wilson. He even agreed that entry into World War I was necessary. But he broke with Roosevelt and Wilson over the very points which undercut the ideal, and the practice, of self-determination. Perhaps his judgment is too harsh, yet it offers an important insight into Wilson's failure and into America's difficulties at mid-century. For that reason, but not as a final verdict either on Wilson or the United States, it deserves consideration.

Looking back across the years, Raymond Robins reflected on the origins of the crisis in American diplomacy in these words: "Wilson was a great man but he had one basic fault. He was willing to do anything for people except get off their backs and let them live their own lives. He would never let go until they forced him to and then it was too late. He never seemed to understand there's a big difference between trying to save people and trying to help them. With luck you can help 'em—but they always save themselves."

One of the most helpful aspects of that estimate of Wilson and his diplomacy lies in the suggestion that it offers about American entry into the war and America's response to the revolutions which occurred during and at the end of that conflict. For given entry into the war on the grounds that "the world must be made safe for democracy," the crucial questions become those about the definition of democracy and the means to insure its security. Having answered those questions, it may then be possible to determine and understand the reasons why the effort did not succeed.

# NO

**Barton J. Bernstein and Franklin A. Leib**

## PROGRESSIVE REPUBLICAN SENATORS AND AMERICAN IMPERIALISM, 1898–1916: A REAPPRAISAL

Until recently historians generally concluded that there was a progressive consensus on foreign policy, but disagreed whether the progressives were interventionists or isolationists. Some historians accepted William Leuchtenburg's theory that the progressives ardently supported imperialism and a muscular foreign policy. Arthur Link, Eric Goldman and others, however, emphasized in their studies of World War I that the reformers usually considered intervention incompatible with domestic reform. As isolationists, according to this theory, they feared war, blamed it on the powerful economic interests, and wished to keep their nation safe and pure, thus protecting American civilization from European corruption. Concentrating on the issues leading to American intervention in World War I, Walter Trattner, Howard Allen and Warren Sutton recently dissented from these interpretations and concluded that there was no single progressive viewpoint on foreign policy toward Europe and that the reformers divided sharply on the war.

Because the controversy has come to focus primarily on whether the progressive reformers agreed about World War I, historians have generally neglected the central thesis of William Leuchtenburg's important essay—the intimate connection in liberal "ideology" between progressivism and imperialism. Surveying the years from 1898 to 1916, he concluded that the progressives enthusiastically supported vigorous expansion and that most of the reformers in Congress endorsed increased naval expenditures and imperialism in the Caribbean. Progressivism and imperialism, contended Leuchtenburg, who based his thesis heavily upon Theodore Roosevelt, Albert Beveridge, Herbert Croly, and the pronouncements of the short-lived Progressive party, sprang primarily from two common sources—faith in the mission of the United States to reform society and spread democracy at home and abroad, and confidence in pragmatism, which judged actions by their achievements and neglected their means. The progressives' ideology, argued

From Barton J. Bernstein and Franklin A. Leib, "Progressive Republican Senators and American Imperialism, 1898–1916: A Reappraisal," *Mid-America: An Historical Review,* vol. 50, no. 3 (July 1968), pp. 163–168, 173, 177–182, 186–188, 197–198, 201–205.  Notes omitted.

Leuchtenburg, was also shaped by racism, which made them more receptive to imperialism, and the Hamiltonian concept of positive government, which led them to stress vigorous central direction of the nation's destinies both at home and abroad and to regard with hostility crippling beliefs in limited government, states rights or isolationism.

His interpretation has raised many important questions about the "ideology" of progressivism, its varieties and its relationship to imperialism. A thorough examination of this important subject is necessarily well beyond the scope of an essay and would require an intensive study of a large and representative sample of the many types of progressives—from different reform movements, regions, parties, occupations, and even classes. Yet, despite the complexity of progressivism, it is possible and useful to explore even part of the problem by examining a selected group of reformers—the progressive Republican senators. Their ranks include such prominent reformers as Beveridge of Indiana, Robert La Follette of Wisconsin, William Borah of Idaho and George Norris of Nebraska; such lesser-known men as Albert Cummins of Iowa, Miles Poindexter of Washington, Joseph Bristow of Kansas, Jonathan Bourne of Oregon, and Joseph Dixon of Montana; such little-remembered men as Asle Gronna of North Dakota, John Works of California, William Kenyon of Iowa, Moses Clapp of Minnesota, and Coe Crawford of South Dakota; and such marginal reformers as Knute Nelson of Minnesota, Robert Gamble of South Dakota, Norris Brown and Elmer Burkett of Nebraska, and Jonathan Dolliver of Iowa.

By focusing upon them, the historian can study a group of progressives who, either by necessity or choice, often voted upon and sometimes discussed the more urgent and dramatic issues of foreign policy. While they were more likely than any other professionally-defined group of reformers to express their views or take positions on these matters, the investigation is not without inherent difficulties. Because these men were unusually busy and most were infrequently reflective, their comments on foreign affairs were usually unsystematic, often the quick responses to immediate issues. Seldom before the threat of war did they take the time to refine their thought or to generalize with care. More than occasionally, when swept by the passion of the issue or the vigor of their argument, they exaggerated their positions, thus moving carelessly beyond the immediate subject and becoming liable to contradictions with past or future statements. Yet, despite these difficulties, it is generally possible to describe the general patterns of their responses during these years to the shifting and often confused issues of imperialism, and in the case of the more important and prominent reformers to reconstruct and analyze their thought.

A study of the progressive Republican senators between 1898 and 1916 raises many doubts about the theory that progressivism and imperialism were clearly joined. On the basis of research largely in published materials, a new conclusion seems warranted. Though sharing the consensus on the need for overseas commercial expansion as a guarantee of domestic prosperity, they were not, with the notable exceptions of Beveridge and Poindexter, for the most part *committed* to aggressive, expansionist policies. During Roosevelt's seven years in the White House, while the future insurgents were moving toward progressivism, they usually remained loyal to the party and President, and with the exception of Beveridge, they tended merely to acquiesce in Roosevelt's adventurous foreign policy. During the Taft administration, however, as the President and the reformers split on domestic issues, a handful became critical of policies in Latin America, and Robert La Follette, the most prominent reformer in the Senate, began to assail Dollar Diplomacy and to condemn Caribbean adventurism. During the Wilson administration, as some Senate reformers deepened their understanding of imperialism, many, and particularly Borah and Norris, became more critical of an aggressive American foreign policy which sought to extend protectorates and financial control in Latin America. But the progressives were more troubled and often ambivalent about intervention which seemed neither aggressive nor self-serving—attempts to stop bloodshed or efforts to create order or democracy. Sometimes they couched their objections to intervention in a characteristic American rhetoric which emphasized the mission to maintain America's purity and concentrate upon domestic reform. But the concept of mission was also sufficiently loose to embrace their opponents' arguments for efforts abroad, and sometimes the reformers themselves uncomfortably invoked it to justify as humanitarian intervention conceived on behalf of order or democracy. Despite their wavering and their confusion, however, a few, most notably La Follette, Norris and Borah, generally resisted intervention on these grounds. Significantly, these three leading representatives of western progressivism were also the leaders in the Senate of anti-imperialism, and in the cases of La Follette and Norris, their growing opposition to Wilson's European policies was rooted in the same values and fears which shaped their anti-imperialism.

* * *

During the first part of this nineteen-year period, from about 1898 to about 1909, as a small group of Republicans moved toward progressivism, they joined other Republicans in supporting aggressive expansion. Their votes for imperialism should be understood, however, in the light of two related characteristics of the emerging reform movement—the slowly developing concern of reformers, first with local and state issues, and ultimately with national domestic matters, which then seemed unrelated to foreign policy, and their affection and admiration for Theodore Roosevelt, which enabled him to lead them and often safely to channel their energies while maintaining party unity....

The progressives' allegiance to Roosevelt reinforced party unity, which continued to be a powerful force during his Presidency. In the absence of any particular concern about the nation's foreign policy, they comfortably adhered to their party and President, supporting his adventurism with their votes, but seldom with their voices. When, for example, Roosevelt's maneuvers in "freeing" Panama and making a treaty for the canal were attacked by Senate Democrats, Beveridge and Clapp, as well as the marginal reformers, Nelson, Dolliver and Gamble, followed the party and endorsed the administration's action. Shortly after the battle on ratification, they again assisted their party and their administration by blocking a move to pay reparations to Colombia. Though these two votes supported interventionism, which Beveridge firmly endorsed, they should not be interpreted, automatically, as evidence of a commitment to imperialism by the others. On both issues Republican senators unanimously supported their President, while the Democrats split on the Panama treaty and maintained almost solid ranks in support of reparations. On such issues, a Republican vote against Roosevelt would have been considered disloyal to the party and might have been regarded as labeling the President's actions as immoral.

* * *

[T]he progressive Republicans during Taft's four years grew more independent of party direction. Led by La Follette, their revolt against the Payne-Aldrich Tariff in early 1909 widened the narrow breach. Brown, Burkett, Clapp, Cummins, Nelson, Bristow, Crawford, and Dolliver joined La Follette and Beveridge in opposing the Republican leadership of the Senate. In addition to these insurgents, among the Republican reformers in 1909 were Bourne, Dixon, Gamble, and Borah. And the elections of the next two years, though defeating Beveridge, added Works, Gronna and Poindexter, as well as Kenyon, elected to replace Dolliver who had died in 1910. Coupled with Democratic gains and losses among regular Republicans, the election placed the balance of power in the hands of the progressives. During these years, the reform-minded senators acted often in concert on domestic issues as they moved more directly into opposition against the Republican leadership in the Senate and began to spar with President Taft.

Though still largely indifferent to foreign policy, some of these progressives took the lead among the members of their party in the resistance to the Taft administration's program of naval expansion. Clapp, eager to stop the international naval race, again took up the cudgels in 1910. Too great a navy, "is a menace to the peace of the Republic," he explained, "for a nation such as the United States which won its freedom by arms develops a spirit a little bit along the line . . . into the shadowy but dangerous realm of the aggressive." The United States, he counseled, "ought to regard with some care and caution its own tendency perhaps to overreach and overawe other nations and other powers." Significantly, neither he nor his cohorts had ever criticized Roosevelt's foreign policy, and Clapp, perhaps in deftness or generosity, suggested that the danger lay in the future, not in the past or present. Despite the efforts of Clapp, who was joined in this massive defection of progressives by Bristow, Crawford, Cummins, Dixon, Dolliver, and La Follette, the administration secured the appropriation for two more battleships, receiving assistance from Beveridge, Borah, Brown, and Burkett. Significantly, while the regular Republicans overwhelmingly supported the larger naval program, the progressive Republicans voted heavily in opposition.

By early 1911, after nearly two years of discontent with Taft's domestic policies, many of the insurgents, together with prominent reformers outside Congress, formed the National Progressive League. Its "Declaration of Principles," drafted by La Follette who hoped that the organization would assist his quest for the Presidential nomination, expressed the reformers' dominant concern with domestic reform. Attacking the "special interests," which thwarted democracy and "baffled and defeated" attempts to reform business, the League announced its dedication to the promotion of popular government and progressive legislation, called for such direct democracy devices as initiative, referendum and recall, and urged some moderate welfare legislation. Apparently seeing no important connection with foreign policy, neither La Follette nor the other progressives chose to mention the subject.

Yet, within a month, La Follette moved to consider the subject he had virtually disregarded for nearly a decade. The leading reformer in the Senate and a potential Presidential candidate, he, unlike so many, held unimpeachable credentials as a progressive. Devoted to domestic reform, engaged in battling the trusts and extending democracy, he had directed all of his energies to that end. But in February of 1911—the first time for any progressive Republican in the upper house—he vigorously attacked a Republican administration's foreign policy. Believing that the State Department had traded American naval secrets to Argentina in return for her order of battleships from Bethlehem Steel, La Follette, supported by seven other progressives, demanded an investigation of what he later denounced as the reduction of the "State Department... into a trading outpost for Wall Street interests...."

The reasons for his conversion from indifference to anti-imperialism are unknown. Perhaps it was that Taft and his Secretary of State, Philander Knox, unlike their predecessors, had crudely emphasized that the administration's policies were designed to advance the interests of the major financiers and industrialists. Whatever the reasons, La Follette had come to believe that the powerful corporations that he was fighting at home, were benefiting from, and often controlling, the nation's foreign policy. The great trusts which frustrated democracy in the United States, according to his reasoning, also dominated the State Department and gained additional riches through their government-assisted ventures abroad. Significantly, La Follette emphasized the domestic perils of imperialism and only noted incidentally the injuries to foreign people and nations. It was a very subsidiary theme in his analyses at this time that Dollar Diplomacy also entailed the exploitation of other peoples.

Because of his primary concern with domestic America, his early anti-imperialism was limited. It stressed the advancement of his fellow citizens, even at the sacrifice of his fellow men. Despite his occasional strictures against racial discrimination in America, he was willing to countenance the exclusion of the Japanese, presumably in the interests of American labor. The United States, he complained, had surrendered its treaty right to exclude Japanese laborers. Suspecting that the administration had made a deal, he contended that "certain New York bankers" would receive the benefits—concessions for the construction of railroads in Manchuria. "The 'dollar diplomacy' is more interested in J. P. Morgan concessions... than in Japanese exclusion at home," he charged. "Is there anything," he asked, "which Mr. Knox and President Taft will not give to foreign nations in exchange for 'business' desired by their friends in Wall Street?"

Within a few weeks, La Follette again attacked the administration's foreign policy—this time Taft's policy in Mexico. In March of 1911, a few months after the Mexican Revolution against Díaz and while Congress was out of session, Taft ordered troops to the border and ships to the coast, ostensibly in order to protect American life and property. La Follette immediately protested. Charging that the President intended " 'to stamp out the Mexican insurrection,' against the dictatorship, and if necessary..., to 'intervene,'" he attacked Taft for moving toward war without Congressional authorization, and for throttling an insurrection against tyranny. "Since when," naively asked La Follette, forgetting about American policy in the Philippines, "has the government taken sides against an oppressed people struggling for liberty?"

Citing Cuba, where, he believed, the United States had "intervened to help a people struggling for their liberties," La Follette implied that Taft's action was the first "unwarranted and unaccountable use of the military establishment of our republic against a peaceful neighbor." Unable or unwilling to see the connection between the plan he suspiciously attributed to Taft and earlier American intervention designed to maintain order and stability and to protect American economic interests and opportunities, La Follette raised a series of sharp questions. Did the President move troops because his brother was director of the foreign corporation with the largest financial interest in Mexico? Or because J. P. Morgan & Co. or Kuhn, Loeb were the "fiscal agents for the bonds issued by the Díaz government and heavy holders of securities and concessions obtained from... Díaz?" "Is it possible that the army and navy are being used [to support] a gigantic Wall Street gamble?"...

Having broken with the Old Guard leadership of the Senate and having provoked Taft's hostility, the progressive Republican senators were no longer guided on foreign policy by party loyalty. Though they conferred frequently and often acted together on domestic issues, they lacked the interest even to seek to develop a unified position on foreign affairs. The progressives were never united on foreign policy, but some, and particularly Borah, now moved toward La Follette's position and became critical of Dollar Diplomacy. While the administration's Caribbean policy seldom led to formal international agreements requiring Senate ratification, a few issues did reach the upper chamber, and in the two most notable cases progressive Republicans contributed to the defeat of Dollar Diplomacy. The Senate would not approve treaties with Honduras and Nicaragua which guaranteed private American loans and allowed the United States to supervise the finances of these republics. Borah, by voting with the Democrats on the Senate Foreign Relations Committee, even prevented one of the treaties from reaching the Senate floor. "Among certain progressive Republicans," reported the *New York Times* in explaining opposition to the treaties, "there is a dislike for any plan that seems to involve favors to Wall Street bankers." Significantly, the *Outlook*, an eastern progressive magazine of which Roosevelt was a contributing editor, chided "those —especially the Progressives in the Senate—who objected to the treaties...." (Surveying the opposition, the *London Times* complained that "certain Radical Senators... cannot understand that international finance of this kind must always be the business of big [banking] houses.") Among the Republican senators, it is clear that a handful of progressives were the chief critics of Taft's Dollar Diplomacy, and La Follette and Borah were as vigorous in their opposition as the most strident anti-imperialists in the Democrats' ranks....

* * *

"President Taft, in defending his 'dollar diplomacy,'" wrote La Follette in December of 1912, "says the Administration is 'substituting dollars for bullets.' But does this business of assisting the banks to fat loans, secured by the government's army and navy, necessarily raise the alternative of dollars or bullets?" Emphasizing the injury to other peoples, the exploitation of the innocent, he asked rhetorically, "Isn't it rather a clash between Dollars and Humanity?" Looking forward to the end of Dollar Diplomacy, La Follette for the first time publicly criticized Roosevelt's imperialism. He cited Roosevelt's establishment of a "collecting agency in Santo Domingo for New York bankers," along with Taft's efforts in Nicaragua, Honduras, China, and Mexico on behalf of American capitalists, as examples of the "crude, sordid, blighting to international amity and accord." Dollar Diplomacy, he declared, "had no interest in the manner or form of government under which our neighbors to the southward live, so long as the wealth of those countries continue to flow." What he was condemning was intervention for exploitation, not intervention *per se.*

La Follette enthusiastically greeted the early statements of Woodrow Wilson and his Secretary of State, William Jennings Bryan, that the new administration was opening a new era in Latin American relations. Seven days after his inauguration, Wilson had explained that the United States only sought "the lasting interests of the peoples of the two continents, the security of governments intended for the people and for no special group or interest, and the development of personal and trade relationships... which shall redound to the profit and advantage of both [continents] and interfere with the rights and liberty of neither." Denying that "a gun-boat goes with each bond," Wilson and Bryan promised that their policies would contribute to even greater expansion of the nation's trade. "The President's policy," explained Bryan, "means extension, expansion, multiplication of American interests." "The effort to get a few dollars by the employment of unfair and offensive methods has prevented our industries from securing that large and lucrative business which could have come with a more liberal policy...."

Shortly after the inauguration, the implications of this policy became dimly visible when Bryan sought to establish a protectorate in Nicaragua and arrange a loan in return for an option on a canal route. Boldly moving beyond the Taft administration's milder but unsuccessful treaty which some progressive Republicans had resisted, Bryan had agreed to the protectorate at the behest of the president of Nicaragua, who had been rescued from revolution and was being kept in office by American marines. In effect, the protectorate would have confirmed by treaty the United States military domination of Nicaragua which Taft had initiated and the Wilson government intended to continue. By securing the canal route, Bryan believed that he was preventing foreign interests from gaining concessions in the hemisphere and thus he was protecting United States security. His larger goals were the maintenance of stability and the prevention of revolution, and he regarded this as a splendid opportunity to promote the new diplomacy.

"'Dollar diplomacy,' which was so strenuously denounced by Bryan," asserted recently-elected Senator George Norris, "looks like the proverbial 30 cents alongside of the proposed treaty with Nicaragua." Agreeing with this indictment, Borah immediately denounced the treaty as imperialism. This means, he warned, "the going up of the American flag all the way to the Panama Canal...." Because the Central American states were rich in resources and an "inviting field for exploitation," he foresaw that the extension of protectorates and the expansion of American capital would lead to continued intervention for the protection of American citizens and investments. Though the Central American Governments were inadequate by American standards, "nevertheless in their own way they are self-governing people," he contended, and they should not be taken over, subdued and ruled.

Borah's argument in some ways was similar to the anti-imperialist arguments against the annexation of the Philippines and the establishment of a protectorate in Cuba. Like those earlier opponents of American colonialism, he warned that America's traditional role was being dangerously altered and that her domination of foreign peoples was incompatible with professions of democracy. He, too, rejected the contention that America had a mission to uplift inferior peoples; unlike the earlier anti-imperialists, however, he also emphasized the mission at home—the reform of the nation. "I should rather turn our attention to the internal affairs of this Republic... and see if we cannot make our own people thoroughly satisfied with our own Government." Though he cast his argument partly in a conservative framework which stressed the need to protect cherished American values, his analysis also underscored the dangers of American investments in Latin America. A financial interest in such unstable countries, he feared, would compel frequent American intervention and increasing control of these peoples and nations....

* * *

While most progressive Republican senators remained generally unwilling to examine critically the past imperialist ventures of Roosevelt and McKinley, many vigorously opposed Wilson's adventurism in the Caribbean. Undoubtedly his leading critic within the band of reformers was Borah. He called for tolerance of any form of government in Latin America, asserting that the United States should not involve itself in the domestic affairs of a neighboring country unless its citizens, and not the rulers, called for assistance. He lamented that "we have an utter incapacity to attend to our business and to leave the internal concerns of other Governments" to their own citizens. Criticizing imperialism in the Caribbean, he opposed the extension of the Monroe Doctrine to justify intervention in the internal affairs of the southern republics.

Though he never objected to expanding trade with Latin America, he sought to block the loans and agreements which could lead to the establishment of protectorates and ultimately to domination of the hemisphere. He had stormed against Bryan's attempt to establish a protectorate in Nicaragua and repeatedly condemned the administration's foreign policy. When Bryan removed the provision for a protectorate and retreated to a milder treaty limited to the purchase of an interoceanic canal route, still the senator continued his bitter campaign. From 1914, when the treaty was renegotiated, until 1916, Borah savagely attacked. "We are not dealing with public officers whom the Nicaraguan people have set up or elected," he declared, "we are dealing with ourselves; we are dealing with the puppets we put in power."

Echoing these thoughts, Norris asserted, "We made a treaty with ourselves." Though other progressive Republicans did not discuss the agreement, they voted overwhelmingly against it, while the Senate approved it, 55–19. Of the progressives only Poindexter favored it. Clapp, Gronna, Kenyon, La Follette, Nelson, and Cummins, who had reversed himself, joined Norris and Borah to constitute almost half of the recorded opposition to American imperialism in Nicaragua....

* * *

Borah and La Follette, after Beveridge's defeat, were undoubtedly the two leading progressive Republicans in the Senate, and with Norris, they had also become the leading anti-imperialists. But as the issues of World War I began to dominate the dialogue on foreign policy and to push other matters to the periphery, La Follette and Norris began to differ sharply from Borah. Focusing on problems which they had often overlooked, their disagreement revealed important differences in their basic views of American foreign policy.

Borah, uneasily combining militant nationalism and hostility to intervention in Latin America, never doubted the need for overseas commercial expansion. Occasionally he linked investments abroad with the impulse for intervention, and he demonstrated how the expanding web of America's capital and her citizens in Latin American nations could compel military action to protect lives and property. Yet, his critique was sporadic and generally not broad enough to comprehend the issues raised by the war in Europe. Indeed, his nationalism was so great that he would not inhibit the exercise of American rights to travel or ship goods to Europe during the years before American entry into World War I. Nor could he countenance restrictions on trade which might have kept the United States out of the war at the price of serious injury to the American economy. With Poindexter and Nelson, he supported preparedness and opposed the efforts of men like Clapp, Works, Norris, Gronna, La Follette, and Beveridge to avoid policies which might lead to war.

Significantly, Beveridge, though still an ardent expansionist who criticized Wilson for his flabby Mexican policy, had moved closer to La Follette and Norris in his efforts to keep America out of the war. Like them, he opposed intervention on the Allied side—but partly because he looked forward to the destruction of the British Empire and America's seizure of British markets. As early as the turn of the century, Beveridge had emphasized the need for economic expansion abroad. He had stressed the economic benefits of colonialism and happily linked his argument to the American mission—to spread democracy and Christianity to the backward areas. The redemption of the world was America's unique obligation. For him, this faith justified the imperialism of nearly two decades of American policy, but he found that it did not justify the exercise of legal rights which could plunge the nation into war against a German civilization which he admired. Nor did he believe that war would ravage liberty in Europe or destroy important values, and therefore he never felt that America had a duty to intervene to rescue or redeem Europe. But he never rejected the idea of an American mission, only its application in this situation....

While neither Borah nor Beveridge interpreted the First World War within the framework of imperialism, some of the other progressive Republican senators understood it in that way. Believing that the war represented a clash between competing imperialist systems, La Follette and Norris also charged that the munitions-makers at home were trying to push America into the war. La Follette, the first progressive Republican senator to criticize Dollar Diplomacy, slowly developed a significant, though unoriginal, analysis of imperialism. Understanding the importance of foreign trade to the American economy, he counseled in 1915 that commerce should be directed away from war-covered Europe and to Latin America, where the United States could capture new markets. Unfortunately he was unsuccessful in altering the dependence of the American economy on Europe, and he could neither secure an embargo on the export of munitions nor prevent loans to the allies.

Coming under the influence of Frederic Howe's *Why War?*, La Follette moved closer to the Hobson-Lenin theories of imperialism. "Back of all modern war is practically one policy"—"FINANCIAL IMPERIALISM," he declared. "When capital has exploited its home country, when its profits have become so great as to depress interest rates," he explained, "then it goes abroad for investment into countries whose resources have not yet been exploited, where the demand for capital is strongest and interest rates are very high." Because these governments are generally unstable, capital, he argued, established the "new doctrine that the 'flag follows business,' and that the country must defend the financial interests of its citizens abroad." To this theory, he linked his original distaste for Dollar Diplomacy, his conviction that the munition-makers wanted war, and with Norris, his fears that American investors in Europe and an administration sympathetic to the need for foreign economic expansion would demand military intervention to extend and protect overseas opportunities and interests.

Norris, though less voluble in his opposition to imperialism, had also resisted the establishment of American protectorates. Unwilling to place stability or paternalism above self-determination, he had also objected to the doctrine that the "flag follows business." Like Borah and La Follette, he saw the contradiction between democratic principles at home and American domination abroad, and believed that a democratic nation should encourage independence and self-determination for other peoples. While these reformers hoped to see democracy flourish elsewhere, they came to value autonomy for other nations above adherence to American institutions. Though other peoples' independence might mean non-democratic institutions, these progressives were sufficiently tolerant to let nations choose their own form of government. It was possible for them to believe that Americans and their institutions were superior, and yet, by avoiding the imperialism of narrow idealism, to countenance departures from democratic norms.

Unlike La Follette and Norris, the other progressive Republican senators never seemed to develop such a clear view of American imperialism. Yet, aside from Poindexter and Beveridge, they had generally moved by the Wilson years to oppose the establishment of protectorates and the frequent use of troops and ships to maintain order and collect debts. Usually only when American blood was shed and treaty guarantees of protection unenforced or when countries were torn by bloody conflict would these reformers, acting as humanitarians and nationalists, consider endorsing intervention in the lands of the western hemisphere. And even then they were careful to limit American intervention, and they remained suspicious of United States financial interests abroad. While for many of these reformers the American mission could often mean more than giving advice and sometimes even entailed violations of a nation's sovereignty, it did not mean that the United States should be a policeman always on call and certainly not an avaricious guardian pursuing self-aggrandizement.

# POSTSCRIPT

## Were the Progressives Imperialists?

William Appleman Williams's view that the United States created an informal empire in Latin America, Asia, and even Europe through the penetration of American business interests has been carried forward by a number of his former students. For example, Walter LaFeber's *Inevitable Revolutions: The United States in Central America* (W. W. Norton, 1983) emphasizes the economic forces that shaped U.S. relations with its neighbors to the south. In particular, LaFeber applies the economic theory of "neodependency" to his discussion of U.S. involvement in the Caribbean basin. First outlined in the 1960s by a group of radical economists, this theory argues that the United States used its economic superiority to make Latin American nations dependent on the United States. A valuable critique of this interpretation (that predates LaFeber's study) can be found in David Ray, "The Dependency Model of Latin America Underdevelopment: Three Basic Fallacies," *Journal of Interamerican Studies and World Affairs* (February 1973).

The seminal article from which the preceding issue debate is drawn is William Leuchtenburg, "Progressivism and Imperialism: The Progressive Movement and American Foreign Policy, 1898–1916," *Mississippi Valley Historical Review* (December 1952). For discussions of Theodore Roosevelt's presidential foreign policy, see Howard K. Beale, *Theodore Roosevelt and the Rise of America to World Power* (Johns Hopkins University Press, 1956) and Frederick W. Marks III, *Velvet on Iron: The Diplomacy of Theodore Roosevelt* (University of Nebraska Press, 1988), as well as appropriate chapters of the following Roosevelt biographies: John Morton Blum, *The Republican Roosevelt* (Harvard University Press, 1954); William H. Harbaugh, *Power and Responsibility: The Life and Times of Theodore Roosevelt* (Farrar, Straus and Cudahy, 1961); and Lewis L. Gould, *The Presidency of Theodore Roosevelt* (University of Kansas Press, 1991). Walter and Marie Scholes, *The Foreign Policies of the Taft Administration* (University of Missouri Press, 1970) examines the diplomacy of Roosevelt's successor to the presidency. Woodrow Wilson's policies receive careful attention from Arthur Link in *Woodrow Wilson and the Progressive Era, 1910–1917* (Harper & Row, 1954) and *Wilson the Diplomatist: A Look at His Major Foreign Policies* (Johns Hopkins University Press, 1957). Wilson's difficulties in Mexico are the focus of Robert E. Quirk's *An Affair of Honor: Woodrow Wilson and the Occupation of Veracruz* (University of Kentucky Press, 1962).

# ISSUE 9

## Was Woodrow Wilson a Naive Idealist?

**YES: Henry Kissinger,** from *Diplomacy* (Simon & Schuster, 1994)

**NO: William G. Carleton,** from "A New Look at Woodrow Wilson," *The Virginia Quarterly Review* (Autumn 1962)

### ISSUE SUMMARY

**YES:** Former national security adviser and political scholar Henry Kissinger characterizes President Woodrow Wilson as a high-minded idealist. Kissinger argues that Wilson's emphasis on using morally elevated principles and his disdain for balance-of-power politics in the conduct of foreign affairs significantly shaped American foreign policy. However, according to Kissinger, Wilson's views have made it difficult for later presidents to develop a logical foreign policy based on national self-interest.

**NO:** William G. Carleton, a professor emeritus of history and political science, believes that Woodrow Wilson was the greatest president of the twentieth century and that Wilson understood better than his nationalistic opponents the new international role that America would play in world affairs.

Historians have dealt with Woodrow Wilson rather strangely. The presidential polls conducted by historian Arthur Schlesinger in 1948 and 1962, as well as the 1983 Murray-Blessing poll, ranked Wilson among the top 10 presidents. As you will see when you read the "No" selection, historian William G. Carleton considers him to be the greatest twentieth-century president, only two notches below Thomas Jefferson and Abraham Lincoln. Yet, among his biographers, Wilson, for the most part, has been treated ungenerously. They carp at him for being naive, overly idealistic, too inflexible, rigid, uncompromising, formal, stiff, unkind, disloyal to friends, overcompromising, oratorical, preachy, messianic, and moralistic. It appears that, like many of his contemporaries, Wilson's biographers respect the man but do not like the person.

Why has Wilson been treated with a nagging pettiness by historians? Perhaps the reasons have to do with Wilson's own introspective personality and his lack of formal political experience. He was, along with Jefferson, and to some extent Theodore Roosevelt, our most intellectual president. He spent nearly 20 years as a history and political science teacher and scholar at Bryn Mawr College, Wesleyan University, and Princeton University, his alma mater. While his multivolume *History of the United States* now appears dated as it gathers dust on musty library shelves, Wilson's Ph.D. dissertation on congressional government, which he wrote as a graduate student at Johns Hopkins University, remains a classic statement of the weakness of leadership in the American constitutional system.

In addition to working many years as a college professor, Wilson served a short stint as a lawyer and spent eight distinguished years as president of Princeton University, which he turned into one of the outstanding universities in the country. He introduced the preceptorial system, widely copied today, which supplemented course lectures with discussion conferences led by young instructors, and he took the lead in reorganizing the university's curriculum.

Historians agree that no president, with the exception of Franklin Roosevelt and perhaps Ronald Reagan, performed the ceremonial role of the presidency as well as Wilson. His speeches rang with oratorical brilliance and substance. No wonder he abandoned the practice of Jefferson and his successors by delivering the president's annual State of the Union Address to Congress in person rather than in writing.

During his first four years, Wilson also fashioned an ambitious legislative program. Wilson's "New Freedom" pulled together conservative and progressive, rural and urban, and southern and northern Democrats. This coalition passed such measures as the Underwood/Simmons Tariff Act, the first bill to significantly lower tariff rates since the Civil War, and the Owens/Keating Child Labor Act. It was through Wilson's adroit maneuvering that the Federal Reserve System was established. This banking measure, the most significant in U.S. history, established a major federal agency, which regulates the money supply in the country to this day. Finally, President Wilson revealed his flexibility when he abandoned his initial policy of rigid and indiscriminate trust-busting for one of regulating big business through the creation of the Federal Trade Commission.

It is in his roles as commander in chief and chief diplomat that Wilson has received his greatest criticisms. In the first selection, scholar-diplomat Henry Kissinger argues that because Woodrow Wilson believed that America was a morally superior nation, his intermingling of power and principle made it difficult for future presidents to develop a foreign policy based on a coherent outline of national interest. In the second selection, Professor William Carleton gives a spirited defense of Wilson's foreign policies. He believes that narrow-minded nationalists, like Senator Henry Cabot Lodge, destroyed the international peace of the postwar world by blocking America's entrance into the League of Nations.

# YES

## Henry Kissinger

# THE HINGE: THEODORE ROOSEVELT OR WOODROW WILSON

Until early in this century, the isolationist tendency prevailed in American foreign policy. Then, two factors projected America into world affairs: its rapidly expanding power, and the gradual collapse of the international system centered on Europe. Two watershed presidencies marked this progression: Theodore Roosevelt's and Woodrow Wilson's. These men held the reins of government when world affairs were drawing a reluctant nation into their vortex. Both recognized that America had a crucial role to play in world affairs though they justified its emergence from isolation with opposite philosophies.

Roosevelt was a sophisticated analyst of the balance of power. He insisted on an international role for America because its national interest demanded it, and because a global balance of power was inconceivable to him without American participation. For Wilson, the justification of America's international role was messianic: America had an obligation, not to the balance of power, but to spread its principles throughout the world. During the Wilson Administration, America emerged as a key player in world affairs, proclaiming principles which, while reflecting the truisms of American thought, nonetheless marked a revolutionary departure for Old World diplomats. These principles held that peace depends on the spread of democracy, that states should be judged by the same ethical criteria as individuals, and that the national interest consists of adhering to a universal system of law.

To hardened veterans of a European diplomacy based on the balance of power, Wilson's views about the ultimately moral foundations of foreign policy appeared strange, even hypocritical. Yet Wilsonianism has survived while history has bypassed the reservations of his contemporaries. Wilson was the originator of the vision of a universal world organization, the League of Nations, which would keep the peace through collective security rather than alliances. Though Wilson could not convince his own country of its merit, the idea lived on. It is above all to the drumbeat of Wilsonian idealism that American foreign policy has marched since his watershed presidency, and continues to march to this day.

America's singular approach to international affairs did not develop all at once, or as the consequence of a solitary inspiration. In the early years of the Republic, American foreign policy was in fact a sophisticated reflection of the American national interest, which was, simply, to fortify the new nation's independence. Since no European country was capable of posing an actual threat so long as it had to contend with rivals, the Founding Fathers showed themselves quite ready to manipulate the despised balance of power when it suited their needs; indeed, they could be extraordinarily skillful at maneuvering between France and Great Britain not only to preserve America's independence but to enlarge its frontiers. Because they really wanted neither side to win a decisive victory in the wars of the French Revolution, they declared neutrality. Jefferson defined the Napoleonic Wars as a contest between the tyrant on the land (France) and the tyrant of the ocean (England)—in other words, the parties in the European struggle were morally equivalent. Practicing an early form of nonalignment, the new nation discovered the benefit of neutrality as a bargaining tool, just as many an emerging nation has since.

At the same time, the United States did not carry its rejection of Old World ways to the point of forgoing territorial expansion. On the contrary, from the very beginning, the United States pursued expansion in the Americas with extraordinary singleness of purpose. After 1794, a series of treaties settled the borders with Canada and Florida in America's favor, opened the Mississippi River to American trade, and began to establish an American commercial interest in the British West Indies. This culminated in the Louisiana Purchase of 1803, which brought to the young country a huge, undefined territory west of the Mississippi River from France along with claims to Spanish territory in Florida and Texas—the foundation from which to develop into a great power....

Though in fact the British Royal Navy protected America from depredations by European powers, American leaders did not perceive Great Britain as their country's protector. Throughout the nineteenth century, Great Britain was considered the greatest challenge to American interests, and the Royal Navy the most serious strategic threat. No wonder that, when America began to flex its muscles, it sought to expel Great Britain's influence from the Western Hemisphere, invoking the Monroe Doctrine which Great Britain had been so instrumental in encouraging.

... By 1902, Great Britain had abandoned its claim to a major role in Central America.

Supreme in the Western Hemisphere, the United States began to enter the wider arena of international affairs. America had grown into a world power almost despite itself. Expanding across the continent, it had established its preeminence all around its shores while insisting that it had no wish to conduct the foreign policy of a Great Power. At the end of the process, America found itself commanding the sort of power which made it a major international factor, no matter what its preferences. America's leaders might continue to insist that its basic foreign policy was to serve as a "beacon" for the rest of mankind, but there could be no denying that some of them were also becoming aware that America's power entitled it to be heard on the issues of the day, and that it did not need to wait until all of mankind had become democratic to make itself a part of the international system.

No one articulated this reasoning more trenchantly than Theodore Roosevelt. He was the first president to insist that it was America's duty to make its influence felt globally, and to relate America to the world in terms of a concept of national interest. Like his predecessors, Roosevelt was convinced of America's beneficent role in the world. But unlike them, Roosevelt held that America had real foreign policy interests that went far beyond its interest in remaining unentangled. Roosevelt started from the premise that the United States was a power like any other, not a singular incarnation of virtue. If its interests collided with those of other countries, America had the obligation to draw on its strength to prevail....

For Roosevelt, muscular diplomacy in the Western Hemisphere was part of America's new global role. The two oceans were no longer wide enough to insulate America from the rest of the world. The United States had to become an actor on the international stage. Roosevelt said as much in a 1902 message to the Congress: "More and more, the increasing interdependence and complexity of international political and economic relations render it incumbent on all civilized and orderly powers to insist on the proper policing of the world."

Roosevelt commands a unique historical position in America's approach to international relations. No other president defined America's world role so completely in terms of national interest, or identified the national interest so comprehensively with the balance of power. Roosevelt shared the view of his countrymen, that America was the best hope for the world. But unlike most of them, he did not believe that it could preserve the peace or fulfill its destiny simply by practicing civic virtues. In his perception of the nature of world order, he was much closer to Palmerston or Disraeli than to Thomas Jefferson.

A great president must be an educator, bridging the gap between his people's future and its experience. Roosevelt taught an especially stern doctrine for a people brought up in the belief that peace is the normal condition among nations, that there is no difference between personal and public morality, and that America was safely insulated from the upheavals affecting the rest of the world. For Roosevelt rebutted each of these propositions. To him, international life meant struggle, and Darwin's theory of the survival of the fittest was a better guide to history than personal morality. In Roosevelt's view, the meek inherited the earth only if they were strong. To Roosevelt, America was not a cause but a great power—potentially the greatest. He hoped to be the president destined to usher his nation onto the world scene so that it might shape the twentieth century in the way Great Britain had dominated the nineteenth—as a country of vast strengths which had enlisted itself, with moderation and wisdom, to work on behalf of stability, peace, and progress.

... In a world regulated by power, Roosevelt believed that the natural order of things was reflected in the concept of "spheres of influence," which assigned preponderant influence over large regions to specific powers, for example, to the United States in the Western Hemisphere or to Great Britain on the Indian subcontinent. In 1908, Roosevelt acquiesced to the Japanese occupation of Korea because, to his way of thinking, Japanese-Korean relations had to be determined by the relative power of each country, not by the provisions of a treaty or by international law....

With Roosevelt holding such European-style views, it was not surprising that he approached the global balance of power with a sophistication matched by no other American president and approached only by Richard Nixon. Roosevelt at first saw no need to engage America in the specifics of the European balance of power because he considered it more or less self-regulating. But he left little doubt that, if such a judgment were to prove wrong, he would urge America to engage itself to re-establish the equilibrium. Roosevelt gradually came to see Germany as a threat to the European balance and began to identify America's national interest with those of Great Britain and France....

In one of history's ironies, America did in the end fulfill the leading role Roosevelt had envisioned for it, and within Roosevelt's lifetime, but it did so on behalf of principles Roosevelt derided, and under the guidance of a president whom Roosevelt despised. Woodrow Wilson was the embodiment of the tradition of American exceptionalism, and originated what would become the dominant intellectual school of American foreign policy—a school whose precepts Roosevelt considered at best irrelevant and at worst inimical to America's long-range interests....

Wilson's was an astonishing achievement. Rejecting power politics, he knew how to move the American people. An academic who arrived in politics relatively late, he was elected due to a split in the Republican Party between Taft and Roosevelt. Wilson grasped that America's instinctive isolationism could be overcome only by an appeal to its belief in the exceptional nature of its ideals. Step by step, he took an isolationist country into war, after he had first demonstrated his Administration's devotion to peace by a passionate advocacy of neutrality. And he did so while abjuring any selfish national interests, and by affirming that America sought no other benefit than vindication of its principles.

In Wilson's first State of the Union Address, on December 2, 1913, he laid down the outline of what later came to be known as Wilsonianism. Universal law and not equilibrium, national trustworthiness and not national self-assertion were, in Wilson's view, the foundations of international order. Recommending the ratification of several treaties of arbitration, Wilson argued that binding arbitration, not force, should become the method for resolving international disputes:

> There is only one possible standard by which to determine controversies between the United States and other nations, and that is compounded of these two elements: Our own honor and our obligations to the peace of the world. A test so compounded ought easily to be made to govern both the establishment of new treaty obligations and the interpretation of those already assumed....

America's influence, in Wilson's view, depended on its unselfishness; it had to preserve itself so that, in the end, it could step forward as a credible arbiter between the warring parties. Roosevelt had asserted that the war in Europe, and especially a German victory, would ultimately threaten American security. Wilson maintained that America was essentially disinterested, hence should emerge as mediator. Because of America's faith in values higher than the balance of power, the war in Europe now afforded it an extraordinary opportunity to proselytize for a new and better approach to international affairs.

Roosevelt ridiculed such ideas and accused Wilson of pandering to isolationist sentiments to help his re-election in 1916. In fact, the thrust of Wilson's policy was quite the opposite of isolationism. What Wilson was proclaiming was not America's withdrawal from the world but the universal applicability of its values and, in time, America's commitment to spreading them. Wilson restated what had become the conventional American wisdom since Jefferson, but put it in the service of a crusading ideology:

- America's special mission transcends day-to-day diplomacy and obliges it to serve as a beacon of liberty for the rest of mankind.
- The foreign policies of democracies are morally superior because the people are inherently peace-loving.
- Foreign policy should reflect the same moral standards as personal ethics.
- The state has no right to claim a separate morality for itself.

Wilson endowed these assertions of American moral exceptionalism with a universal dimension:

> Dread of the power of any other nation we are incapable of. We are not jealous of rivalry in the fields of commerce or of any other peaceful achievement. We mean to live our own lives as we will; but we mean also to let live. We are, indeed, a true friend to all the nations of the world, because we threaten none, covet the possessions of none, desire the overthrow of none.

No other nation has ever rested its claim to international leadership on its altruism. All other nations have sought to be judged by the compatibility of their national interests with those of other societies. Yet, from Woodrow Wilson through George Bush, American presidents have invoked their country's unselfishness as the crucial attribute of its leadership role. Neither Wilson nor his later disciples, through the present, have been willing to face the fact that, to foreign leaders imbued with less elevated maxims, America's claim to altruism evokes a certain aura of unpredictability; whereas the national interest can be calculated, altruism depends on the definition of its practitioner.

To Wilson, however, the altruistic nature of American society was proof of divine favor:

> It was as if in the Providence of God a continent had been kept unused and waiting for a peaceful people who loved liberty and the rights of men more than they loved anything else, to come and set up an unselfish commonwealth.

The claim that American goals represented providential dispensation implied a global role for America that would prove far more sweeping than any Roosevelt had ever imagined. For he had wanted no more than to improve the balance of power and to invest America's role in it with the importance commensurate with its growing strength. In Roosevelt's conception, America would have been one nation among many—more powerful than most and part of an elite group of great powers—but still subject to the historic ground rules of equilibrium.

Wilson moved America onto a plane entirely remote from such considerations.

Disdaining the balance of power, he insisted that America's role was "not to prove... our selfishness, but our greatness." If that was true, America had no right to hoard its values for itself. As early as 1915, Wilson put forward the unprecedented doctrine that the security of America was inseparable from the security of *all* the rest of mankind. This implied that it was henceforth America's duty to oppose aggression *everywhere:*

> ... because we demand unmolested development and the undisturbed government of our own lives upon our own principles of right and liberty, we resent, from whatever quarter it may come, the aggression we ourselves will not practice. We insist upon security in prosecuting our self-chosen lines of national development. We do more than that. We demand it also for others. We do not confine our enthusiasm for individual liberty and free national development to the incidents and movements of affairs which affect only ourselves. We feel it wherever there is a people that tries to walk in these difficult paths of independence and right.

Envisioning America as a beneficent global policeman, this foreshadowed the containment policy, which would be developed after the Second World War....

Germany's announcement of unrestricted submarine warfare and its sinking of the *Lusitania* became the proximate cause of America's declaration of war. But Wilson did not justify America's entry into the war on the grounds of specific grievances. National interests were irrelevant; Belgium's violation and the balance of power had nothing to do with it. Rather, the war had a moral foundation, whose primary objective was a new and more just international order. "It is a fearful thing," Wilson reflected in the speech asking for a declaration of war,

> to lead this great peaceful people into war, into the most terrible and disastrous of all wars, civilization itself seeming to be in the balance. But right is more precious than peace, and we shall fight for the things which we have always carried nearest our hearts, for democracy, for the right of those who submit to authority to have a voice in their own governments, for the rights and liberties of small nations, for a universal dominion of right by such a concert of free peoples as shall bring peace and safety to all nations and make the world itself at last free.

In a war on behalf of such principles, there could be no compromise. Total victory was the only valid goal. Roosevelt would almost certainly have expressed America's war aims in political and strategic terms; Wilson, flaunting American disinterest, defined America's war aims in entirely moral categories. In Wilson's view, the war was not the consequence of clashing national interests pursued without restraint, but of Germany's unprovoked assault on the international order. More specifically, the true culprit was not the German nation, but the German Emperor himself....

Wilson's historic achievement lies in his recognition that Americans cannot sustain major international engagements that are not justified by their moral faith. His downfall was in treating the tragedies of history as aberrations, or as due to the shortsightedness and the evil of individual leaders, and in his rejection of any objective basis for peace other than the force of public opinion and the worldwide spread of democratic institutions. In the process, he would ask the nations of Europe to undertake something for which they were neither philosophically nor historically prepared, and right after a war which had drained them of substance.

For 300 years, the European nations had based their world order on a balancing of national interests, and their foreign policies on a quest for security, treating every additional benefit as a bonus. Wilson asked the nations of Europe to base their foreign policy on moral convictions, leaving security to result incidentally, if at all. But Europe had no conceptual apparatus for such a disinterested policy, and it still remained to be seen whether America, having just emerged from a century of isolation, could sustain the permanent involvement in international affairs that Wilson's theories implied.

Wilson's appearance on the scene was a watershed for America, one of those rare examples of a leader who fundamentally alters the course of his country's history. Had Roosevelt or his ideas prevailed in 1912, the question of war aims would have been based on an inquiry into the nature of American national interest. Roosevelt would have rested America's entry into the war on the proposition—which he in fact advanced—that, unless America joined the Triple Entente, the Central Powers would win the war and, sooner or later, pose a threat to American security.

The American national interest, so defined, would, over time, have led America to adopt a global policy comparable to Great Britain's toward Continental Europe. For three centuries, British leaders had operated from the assumption that, if Europe's resources were marshaled by a single dominant power, that country would then have the resources to challenge Great Britain's command of the seas, and thus threaten its independence. Geopolitically, the United States, also an island off the shores of Eurasia, should, by the same reasoning, have felt obliged to resist the domination of Europe or Asia by any one power and, even more, the control of *both* continents by the *same* power. In these terms, it should have been the extent of Germany's geopolitical reach and not its moral transgressions that provided the principal *casus belli.*

However, such an Old World approach ran counter to the wellspring of American emotions being tapped by Wilson—as it does to this day. Not even Roosevelt could have managed the power politics he advocated, though he died convinced that he could have. At any rate, Roosevelt was no longer the president, and Wilson had made it clear, even before America entered the war, that he would resist any attempt to base the postwar order on established principles of international politics.

Wilson saw the causes of the war not only in the wickedness of the German leadership but in the European balance-of-power system as well. On January 22, 1917, he attacked the international order which had preceded the war as a system of "organized rivalries":

> The question upon which the whole future peace and policy of the world depends is this: Is the present war a struggle for a just and secure peace, or only for a new balance of power?... There must be, not a balance of power, but a community of power; not organized rivalries, but an organized common peace.

What Wilson meant by "community of power" was an entirely new concept that later became known as "collective security" (though William Gladstone in Great Britain had put forward a stillborn variation of it in the course of 1880). Convinced that all the nations of the world had an equal interest in peace and would therefore unite to punish those who disturbed it, Wilson proposed to defend the international order by the moral consensus of the peace-loving:

> ... this age is an age... which rejects the standards of national selfishness that once governed the counsels of nations and demands that they shall give way to a new order of things in which the only questions will be: "Is it right?" "Is it just?" "Is it in the interest of mankind?"

To institutionalize this consensus, Wilson put forward the League of Nations, a quintessentially American institution. Under the auspices of this world organization, power would yield to morality and the force of arms to the dictates of public opinion. Wilson kept emphasizing that, had the public been adequately informed, the war would never have occurred—ignoring the passionate demonstrations of joy and relief which had greeted the onset of war in *all* capitals, including those of democratic Great Britain and France. If the new theory was to work, in Wilson's view, at least two changes in international governance had to take place: first, the spread of democratic governments throughout the world, and, next, the elaboration of a "new and more wholesome diplomacy" based on "the same high code of honor that we demand of individuals."

In 1918, Wilson stated as a requirement of peace the hitherto unheard-of and breathtakingly ambitious goal of "the destruction of every arbitrary power anywhere that can separately, secretly and of its single choice disturb the peace of the world; or, if it cannot be presently destroyed, at the least its reduction to virtual impotence." A League of Nations so composed and animated by such attitudes would resolve crises without war, Wilson told the Peace Conference on February 14, 1919:

> ... throughout this instrument [the League Covenant] we are depending primarily and chiefly upon one great force, and that is the moral force of the public opinion of the world—the cleansing and clarifying and compelling influences of publicity... so that those things that are destroyed by the light may be properly destroyed by the overwhelming light of the universal expression of the condemnation of the world.

The preservation of peace would no longer spring from the traditional calculus of power but from worldwide consensus backed up by a policing mechanism. A universal grouping of largely democratic nations would act as the "trustee of peace," and replace the old balance-of-power and alliance systems.

Such exalted sentiments had never before been put forward by any nation, let alone been implemented. Nevertheless, in the hands of American idealism they were turned into the common currency of national thinking on foreign policy. Every American president since Wilson has advanced variations of Wilson's theme. Domestic debates have more often dealt with the failure to fulfill Wilson's ideals (soon so commonplace that they were no longer even identified with him) than with whether they were in fact lending adequate guidance in meeting the occasionally brutal challenges of a turbulent world. For three generations, critics have savaged Wilson's analysis and conclusions; and yet, in all this time, Wilson's principles have remained the bedrock of American foreign-policy thinking.

And yet Wilson's intermingling of power and principle also set the stage for decades of ambivalence as the American conscience tried to reconcile its principles with its necessities. The basic premise of collective security was that all nations would view every threat to security in the same way *and* be prepared to run the same risks in resisting it. Not only had nothing like it ever actually occurred, nothing like it was destined to occur in the entire history of both the League of Nations and the United Nations. Only when a threat is truly overwhelming and genuinely affects all, or most, societies is such a consensus possible—as it was during the two world wars and, on a regional basis, in the Cold War. But in the vast majority of cases—and in nearly all of the difficult ones—the nations of the world tend to disagree either about the nature of the threat or about the type of sacrifice they are prepared to make to meet it. This was the case from Italy's aggressions against Abyssinia in 1935 to the Bosnian crisis in 1992. And when it has been a matter of achieving positive objectives or remedying perceived injustices, global consensus has proved even more difficult to achieve. Ironically, in the post–Cold War world, which has no overwhelming ideological or military threat and which pays more lip service to democracy than has any previous era, these difficulties have only increased.

Wilsonianism also accentuated another latent split in American thought on international affairs. Did America have any security interests it needed to defend regardless of the methods by which they were challenged? Or should America resist only changes which could fairly be described as illegal? Was it the fact or the method of international transformation that concerned America? Did America reject the principles of geopolitics altogether? Or did they need to be reinterpreted through the filter of American values? And if these should clash, which would prevail?

The implication of Wilsonianism has been that America resisted, above all, the method of change, and that it had no strategic interests worth defending if they were threatened by apparently legal methods. As late as the Gulf War, President Bush insisted that he was not so much defending vital oil supplies as resisting the principle of aggression. And during the Cold War, some of the domestic American debate concerned the question whether America, with all its failings, had a moral right to organize resistance to the Moscow threat.

Theodore Roosevelt would have had no doubt as to the answer to these questions. To assume that nations would perceive threats identically or be prepared to react to them uniformly represented a denial of everything he had ever stood for. Nor could he envision any world organization to which victim and aggressor could comfortably belong at the same time. In November 1918, he wrote in a letter:

> I am for such a League provided we don't expect too much from it.... I am not willing to play the part which even Aesop held up to derision when he wrote of how the wolves and the sheep agreed to disarm, and how the sheep as a guarantee of good faith sent away the watchdogs, and were then forthwith eaten by the wolves.

The following month, he wrote this to Senator Knox of Pennsylvania:

> The League of Nations may do a little good, but the more pompous it is and the more it pretends to do, the less it will really accomplish. The talk about it has a grimly humorous suggestion of the talk about the Holy Alliance a hundred years ago, which had as its main purpose the perpetual maintenance of peace. The Czar Alexander by the way, was the President Wilson of this particular movement a century ago.

In Roosevelt's estimation, only mystics, dreamers, and intellectuals held the view that peace was man's natural condition and that it could be maintained by disinterested consensus. To him, peace was inherently fragile and could be preserved only by eternal vigilance, by the arms of the strong, and by alliances among the like-minded.

But Roosevelt lived either a century too late or a century too early. His approach to international affairs died with him in 1919; no significant school of American thought on foreign policy has invoked him since. On the other hand, it is surely the measure of Wilson's intellectual triumph that even Richard Nixon, whose foreign policy in fact embodied many of Roosevelt's precepts, considered himself above all a disciple of Wilson's internationalism, and hung a portrait of the wartime president in the Cabinet Room.

The League of Nations failed to take hold in America because the country was not yet ready for so global a role. Nevertheless, Wilson's intellectual victory proved more seminal than any political triumph could have been. For, whenever America has faced the task of constructing a new world order, it has returned in one way or another to Woodrow Wilson's precepts. At the end of World War II, it helped build the United Nations on the same principles as those of the League, hoping to found peace on a concord of the victors. When this hope died, America waged the Cold War not as a conflict between two superpowers but as a moral struggle for democracy. When communism collapsed, the Wilsonian idea that the road to peace lay in collective security, coupled with the worldwide spread of democratic institutions, was adopted by administrations of both major American political parties.

In Wilsonianism was incarnate the central drama of America on the world stage: America's ideology has, in a sense, been revolutionary while, domestically, Americans have considered themselves satisfied with the *status quo*. Tending to turn foreign-policy issues into a struggle between good and evil, Americans have generally felt ill at ease with compromise, as they have with partial or inconclusive outcomes. The fact that America has shied away from seeking vast geopolitical transformations has often associated it with defense of the territorial, and sometimes the political, *status quo*. Trusting in the rule of law, it has found it difficult to reconcile its faith in peaceful change with the historical fact that almost all significant changes in history have involved violence and upheaval.

America found that it would have to implement its ideals in a world less blessed than its own and in concert with states possessed of narrower margins of survival, more limited objectives, and far less self-confidence. And yet America has persevered. The postwar world became largely America's creation, so that, in the end, it did come to play the role Wilson had envisioned for it—as a beacon to follow, and a hope to attain.

# NO

William G. Carleton

# A NEW LOOK AT WOODROW WILSON

All high-placed statesmen crave historical immortality. Woodrow Wilson craved it more than most. Thus far the fates have not been kind to Wilson; there is a reluctance to admit him to as great a place in history as he will have.

Congress has just gotten around to planning a national memorial for Wilson, several years after it had done this for Theodore Roosevelt and Franklin D. Roosevelt. Wilson is gradually being accepted as one of the nation's five or six greatest Presidents. However, the heroic mold of the man on the large stage of world history is still generally unrecognized.

There is a uniquely carping, hypercritical approach to Wilson. Much more than other historical figures he is being judged by personality traits, many of them distorted or even fancied. Wilson is not being measured by the yardstick used for other famous characters of history. There is a double standard at work here.

What are the common errors and misrepresentations with respect to Wilson? In what ways is he being judged more rigorously? What are the reasons for this? Why will Wilson eventually achieve giant stature in world history?

* * *

There are two criticisms of Wilson that go to the heart of his fame and place in history. One is an alleged inflexibility and intransigence, an inability to compromise. The other is that he had no real understanding of world politics, that he was a naïve idealist. Neither is true.

If Wilson were indeed as stubborn and adamant as he is often portrayed he would have been a bungler at his work, for the practice and art of politics consist in a feeling for the possible, a sense of timing, a capacity for give-and-take compromise. In reality, Wilson's leadership of his party and the legislative accomplishments of his first term were magnificent. His performance was brilliantly characterized by the very qualities he is said to have lacked: flexibility, accommodation, a sense of timing, and a willingness to compromise. In the struggles to win the Federal Reserve Act, the Clayton Anti-Trust Law, the Federal Trade Commission, and other major measures of his domestic program, Wilson repeatedly mediated between the agrarian liberals and the conservatives of his party, moving now a little to the left, now to the right, now back to the left. He learned by experience, cast aside pride of opinion, accepted and maneuvered for regulatory commissions after having warned of their danger during the campaign of 1912, and constantly acted as a catalyst of the opposing factions of his party and of shifting opinion.

The cautious way Wilson led the country to military preparedness and to war demonstrated resiliency and a sense of timing of a high order. At the Paris Conference Wilson impressed thoughtful observers with his skill as a negotiator; many European diplomats were surprised that an "amateur" could do so well. Here the criticism is not that Wilson was without compromise but that he compromised too much.

Actually, the charge that Wilson was incapable of compromise must stand or fall on his conduct during the fight in the Senate over the ratification of the League of Nations, particularly his refusal to give the word to the Democratic Senators from the South to vote for the Treaty with the Lodge Reservations, which, it is claimed, would have assured ratification. Wilson, say the critics, murdered his own brain child. It is Wilson, and not Lodge, who has now become the villain of this high tragedy.

Now, would a Wilsonian call to the Southerners to change their position have resulted in ratification? Can we really be sure? In order to give Southerners time to readjust to a new position, the call from the White House would have had to have been made several weeks before the final vote. During that time what would have prevented Lodge from hobbling the League with still more reservations? Would the mild reservationists, all Republicans, have prevented this? The record shows, I think, that in the final analysis the mild reservationists could always be bamboozled by Lodge in the name of party loyalty. As the fight on the League had progressed, the reservations had become more numerous and more crippling. Wilson, it seems, had come to feel that there simply was no appeasing Lodge.

During the Peace Conference, in response to the Senatorial Round Robin engineered by Lodge, Wilson had reopened the whole League question and obtained the inclusion of American "safeguards" he felt would satisfy Lodge. This had been done at great cost, for it had forced Wilson to abandon his position as a negotiator above the battles for national advantages and to become a suppliant for national concessions. This had resulted in his having to yield points in other parts of the Treaty to national-minded delegations from other countries. When Wilson returned from Paris with the completed Treaty, Lodge had "raised the ante," the Lodge Reservations requiring the consent of other signatory nations were attached to the Treaty, and these had multiplied and become more restrictive in nature as the months went by. Would not then a "final" yielding by Wilson have resulted in even stiffer reservations being added? Was not Lodge using the Reservations to effect not ratification but rejection, knowing that there was a point beyond which Wilson could not yield?

Wilson seems honestly to have believed that the Lodge Reservations emasculated the League. Those who read them for the first time will be surprised, I think, to discover how nationally self-centered they were. If taken seriously, they surely must have impaired the functioning of the League. However, Wilson was never opposed to clarifying or interpretative reservations which would not require the consent of the other signatories. Indeed, he himself wrote the Hitchcock Reservations.

Even had the League with the Lodge Reservations been ratified, how certain can we really be that this would have meant American entrance into the League? Under the Lodge Reservations, every signatory nation had to accept them before the United States could become a member. Would all the signatories have accepted every one of the fifteen Lodge Reservations? The United States had no monopoly on chauvinism, and would not other nations have interposed reservations of their own as a condition to their acceptance of the Lodge Reservations?

At Paris, Wilson had personally experienced great difficulty getting his own mild "reservations" incorporated into the Covenant. Now, at this late date, would Britain have accepted the Lodge Reservation on Irish self-determination? In all probability. Would Japan have accepted the Reservation on Shantung? This is more doubtful. Would the Latin American states have accepted the stronger Reservation on the Monroe Doctrine? This is also doubtful. Chile had already shown concern, and little Costa Rica had the temerity to ask for a definition of the Doctrine. Would the British Dominions have accepted the Reservation calling for one vote for the British Empire or six votes for the United States? Even Lord Grey, who earlier had predicted that the signatories would accept the Lodge Reservations, found that he could not guarantee acceptance by the Dominions, and Canada's President of the Privy Council and Acting Secretary for External Affairs, Newton W. Rowell, declared that if this Reservation were accepted by the other powers Canada would withdraw from the League.

By the spring of 1920, Wilson seems to have believed that making the League of Nations the issue in the campaign of 1920 would afford a better opportunity for American participation in an effective League than would further concessions to Lodge. To Wilson, converting the Presidential election into a solemn referendum on the League was a reality. For months, because of his illness, he had lived secluded in the White House, and the memories of his highly emotional reception in New York on his return from Paris and of the enthusiasm of the Western audiences during his last speaking trip burned vividly bright. He still believed that the American people, if given the chance, would vote for the League without emasculating reservations. Does this, then, make Wilson naïve? It is well to remember that in the spring of 1920 not even the most sanguine Republican envisaged the Republican sweep that would develop in the fall of that year.

If the strategy of Wilson in the spring of 1920 was of debatable wisdom, the motives of Lodge can no longer be open to doubt. After the landslide of 1920, which gave the Republicans the Presidency and an overwhelming majority in a Senate dominated by Lodge in foreign policy, the Treaty was never resurrected. The Lodge Reservations, representing months of gruelling legislative labor, were cavalierly jettisoned, and a separate peace was made with Germany.

What, then, becomes of the stock charge that Wilson was intolerant of opposition and incapable of bending? If the truth of this accusation must rest on Wilson's attitude during the Treaty fight, and I think it must, for he showed remarkable adaptability in other phases of his Presidency, then it must fall. The situation surrounding the Treaty fight was intricately tangled, and there is certainly as much evidence on the side of Wilson's forbearance as on the side of his obstinacy.

A far more serious charge against Wilson is that he had no realistic understanding of world politics, that he was an impractical idealist whose policies intensified rather than alleviated international problems. Now what American statesman of the period understood world politics better than Wilson—or indeed in any way as well as he? Elihu Root, with his arid legalism? Philander Knox, with his dollar diplomacy? Theodore Roosevelt or Henry Cabot Lodge? Roosevelt and Lodge had some feel for power politics, and they understood the traditional balance of power, at least until their emotions for a dictated Allied victory got the better of their judgment: but was either of them aware of the implications for world politics of the technological revolution in war and the disintegration of the old balance of power? And were not both of them blind to a new force in world politics just then rising to a place of importance—the anti-imperialist revolutions, which even before World War I were getting under way with the Mexican Revolution and the Chinese Revolution of Sun Yat-sen?

Wilson is charged with having no understanding of the balance of power, but who among world statesmen of the twentieth century better stated the classic doctrine of the traditional balance of power than Wilson in his famous Peace Without Victory speech? And was it not Theodore Roosevelt who derided him for stating it? With perfectly straight faces Wilson critics, and a good many historians, tell us that TR, who wanted to march to Berlin and saddle Germany with a harsh peace, and FDR, who sponsored unconditional surrender, "understood" the balance of power, but that Wilson, who fought to salvage a power balance by preserving Germany from partition, was a simple-simon in world politics—an illustration of the double standard at work in evaluating Wilson's place in history.

Wilson not only understood the old, but with amazing clarity he saw the new, elements in world politics. He recognized the emergence of the anti-imperialist revolutions and the importance of social politics in the international relations of the future. He recognized, too, the implications for future world politics of the technological revolution in war, of total war, and of the disintegration of the old balance of power—for World War I had decisively weakened the effective brakes on Japan in Asia, disrupted the Turkish Empire in the Middle East and the Austro-Hungarian Empire in Europe, and removed Russia as a makeweight for the foreseeable future. Wilson believed that a truncated Germany and an attempted French hegemony would only add to the chaos, but he saw too that merely preserving Germany as a power unit would not restore the old balance of power. To Wilson, even in its prime the traditional balance of power had worked only indifferently and collective security would have been preferable, but in his mind the revolutionary changes in the world of 1919 made a collective-security system indispensable.

Just what is realism in world politics? Is it not the ability to use purposefully many factors, even theoretically contradictory ones, and to use them not singly and consecutively but interdependently and simultaneously, shifting the emphasis as conditions change? If so, was not Wilson a very great realist in world politics? He used the old balance-of-power factors, as evidenced by his fight to save Germany as a power unit and his sponsoring of a tripartite alliance of the United States, Britain, and France to guarantee France from any German aggression until such time as collective security would become effective. But he labored to introduce into international relations the new collective-security factors to supplement and gradually supersede in importance the older factors, now increasingly outmoded by historical developments. To label as doctrinaire idealist one who envisaged world politics in so broad and flexible a way is to pervert the meaning of words....

* * *

Ranking the Presidents has become a popular game, and even Presidents like to play it, notably Truman and Kennedy. In my own evaluation, I place Wilson along with Jefferson and Lincoln as the nation's three greatest Presidents, which makes Wilson our greatest twentieth-century President. If rated solely on the basis of long-range impact on international relations, Wilson is the most influential of all our Presidents.

What are the achievements which entitle Wilson to so high a place? Let us consider the major ones, although of course some of these are more important than others.

... [B]etter than any responsible statesman of his day, Wilson understood and sympathized with the anti-imperialist revolutions and their aspirations for basic internal reforms. He withdrew American support for the Bankers' Consortium in China, and the United States under Wilson was the first of the great powers to recognize the Revolution of Sun Yat-sen. Early in his term he had to wrestle with the Mexican Revolution. He saw the need for social reform; avoided the general war with Mexico that many American investors, Catholics, and professional patriots wanted; and by refusing to recognize the counter-revolution of Huerta and cutting Huerta off from trade and arms while allowing the flow of arms to Carranza, Villa, and Zapata, he made possible the overthrow of the counter-revolution and the triumph of the Revolution. What merciless criticism was heaped on Wilson for insisting that Latin Americans should be positively encouraged to institute reforms and develop democratic practices. Yet today Americans applaud their government's denial of Alliance-for-Progress funds to Latin American countries which refuse to undertake fundamental economic and social reforms and flout democracy.

... [C]onfronted with the stupendous and completely novel challenge of having to mobilize not only America's military strength but also its civilian resources and energies in America's first total war, the Wilson Administration set up a huge network of administrative agencies, exemplifying the highest imagination and creativity in the art of practical administration. FDR, in his New Deal and in his World War II agencies, was to borrow heavily from the Wilson innovations.

... Wilson's Fourteen Points and his other peace aims constituted war propaganda of perhaps unparalleled brilliance. They thrilled the world. They gave high purpose to the peoples of the Allied countries and stirred their war efforts. Directed over the heads of the governments to the enemy peoples themselves, they produced unrest, helped bring about the revolutions that overthrew the Sultan, the Hapsburgs, and the Hohenzollerns, and hastened the end of the war.

... [T]he Treaty of Versailles, of which Wilson was the chief architect, was a better peace than it would have been (considering, among other things, the imperialist secret treaties of the Allies) because of Wilson's labors for a just peace. The League of Nations was founded, and this was to be the forerunner of the United Nations. To the League was assigned the work of general disarmament. The mandate system of the League, designed to prepare colonial peoples for self-government and national independence, was a revolutionary step away from the old imperialism. The aspirations of many peoples in Europe for national independence were fulfilled. (If the disruption of the Austro-Hungarian Empire helped destroy the old balance of power, it must be said that in this particular situation Wilson's doctrine of national autonomy only exploited an existing fact in the interest of Allied victory, and even had there been no Wilsonian self-determination the nationalities of this area were already so well developed that they could not have been denied independence after the defeat of the Hapsburgs. Wilson's self-determination was to be a far more *creative* force among the colonial peoples than among the Europeans.) The Treaty restrained the chauvinism of the Italians, though not as much as Wilson would have liked. It prevented the truncating of Germany by preserving to her the Left Bank of the Rhine. The war-guilt clause and the enormous reparations saddled on Germany were mistakes, but Wilson succeeded in confining German responsibility to civilian damage and the expenses of Allied military pensions rather than the whole cost of the war; and had the United States ratified the Treaty and participated in postwar world affairs, as Wilson expected, the United States would have been in a position to join Britain in scaling down the actual reparations bill and in preventing any such adventure as the French seizure of the Ruhr in 1923, from which flowed Germany's disastrous inflation and the ugly forces of German nihilism. (There is poignancy in the broken Wilson's coming out of retirement momentarily in 1923 to denounce France for making "waste paper" of the Treaty of Versailles.) Finally, if Shantung was Wilson's Yalta, he paid the kind of price FDR paid and for precisely the same reason—the collapse of the balance of power in the immediate area involved.

... [T]he chief claim of Wilson to a superlative place in history—and it will not be denied him merely because he was turned down by the United States Senate—is that he, more than any other, formulated and articulated the ideology which was the polestar of the Western democracies in World War I, in World War II, and in the decades of Cold War against the Communists. Today, well past the middle of the twentieth century, the long-time program of America is still a Wilsonian program: international collective security, disarmament, the lowering of economic barriers between nations (as in America's support for the developing West European community today), anticolonialism, self-determination of nations, and democratic social politics as an alternative to Communism. And this was the program critics of Wilson called "anachronistic," a mere "throw-back" to nineteenth-century liberalism!

America today is still grappling with the same world problems Wilson grappled with in 1917, 1918, and 1919, and the programs and policies designed to meet them are still largely Wilsonian. But events since Wilson's time have made his solutions more and more prophetic and urgent. The sweep of the anti-imperialist revolutions propels us to wider self-determination and social politics. The elimination of space, the increasing interdependence of the world, the further disintegration of the balance of power in World War II, and the nuclear revolution in war compel us to more effective collective security and to arms control supervised by an agency of the United Nations.

There will be more unwillingness to identify Wilson with social politics abroad than with the other policies with which he is more clearly identified. Historians like to quote George L. Record's letter to Wilson in which he told Wilson that there was no longer any glory in merely standing for political democracy, that political democracy had arrived, that the great issues of the future would revolve around economic and social democracy. But Wilson stood in no need of advice on this score. Earlier than any other responsible statesman, Wilson had seen the significance of the Chinese Revolution of Sun Yat-sen and of the Mexican Revolution, and he had officially encouraged both. Wilson believed that economic and social reform was implicit in the doctrine of self-determination, especially when applied to the colonial peoples. He recognized, too, that the Bolshevist Revolution had given economic and social reform a new urgency in all parts of the world. He was also well aware that those who most opposed his program for a world settlement were the conservative and imperialist elements in Western Europe and Japan, that socialist and labor groups were his most effective supporters. He pondered deeply how closely and openly he could work with labor and socialist parties in Europe without cutting off necessary support at home. (This—how to use social democracy and the democratic left to counter Communism abroad and still carry American opinion—was to be a central problem for every discerning American statesman after 1945.) Months before he had received Record's letter, Wilson himself had expressed almost the same views as Record. In a long conversation with Professor Stockton Axson at the White House, Wilson acknowledged that his best support was coming from labor people, that they were in touch with world movements and were international-minded, that government ownership of some basic resources and industries was coming, even in the United States, and that it was by a program of social democracy that Communism could be defeated.

In 1918 two gigantic figures—Wilson and Lenin—faced each other and articulated the contesting ideologies which would shake the world during the century. Since then, the lesser leaders who have succeeded them have added little to the ideology of either side. We are now far enough into the century to see in what direction the world is headed, provided there is no third world war. It is not headed for Communist domination. It is not headed for an American hegemony. And it is not headed for a duality with half the world Communist and the other half capitalist. Instead, it is headed for a new pluralism. The emerging new national societies are adjusting their new industrialism to their own conditions and cultures; and their developing economies will be varying mixtures of privatism, collectivism, and welfarism. Even the Communist states differ from one another in conditions, cultures, stages of revolutionary development, and degrees of Marxist "orthodoxy" or "revisionism." And today, all national states, old and new, Communist and non-Communist, join the United Nations as a matter of course.

There will be "victory" for neither "side," but instead a world which has been historically affected by both. Lenin's international proletarian state failed to materialize, but the evolving economies of the underdeveloped peoples are being influenced by his collectivism. However, the facts that most of the emerging economies are mixed ones, that they are working themselves out within autonomous national frameworks, and that the multiplying national states are operating internationally through the United Nations all point to a world which will be closer to the vision of Wilson than to that of Lenin. For this reason Wilson is likely to become a world figure of heroic proportions, with an acknowledged impact on world history more direct and far-reaching than that of any other American.

# POSTSCRIPT

## Was Woodrow Wilson a Naive Idealist?

Henry Kissinger is particularly well suited to write a history of *Diplomacy* (Simon & Schuster, 1994). At Harvard he received a Ph.D. in political science and wrote a dissertation subsequently published as *A World Restored: Metternich, Castlereagh and the Problems of Peace, 1812–1822* (Houghton Mifflin, 1973). In it he admired how the major nations restored the balance of power in Europe once Napoleon was defeated. As President Nixon's chief assistant for national security affairs and later as Nixon's and then Ford's secretary of state in the 1970s, Kissinger became one of the nation's most active, visible, and controversial diplomats. He applied the "realistic" approach to American foreign policy that he had previously written about.

As an exponent of realism, Kissinger excoriates Wilson's handling of America's entrance into World War I and the subsequent negotiations of the peace treaty at Versailles. According to Kissinger, Wilson was reflective of an excessive moralism and naiveté, which Americans hold about the world even today. Rejecting the fact that the United States had a basic national interest in preserving the balance of power of Europe, Wilson told the American people that they were entering the war to "bring peace and safety to all nations and make the world itself at last free." Kissinger believes that Theodore Roosevelt, the realist, had a firmer handle on foreign policy than did Wilson, the idealist. But in the long run, Wilsonianism triumphed and has influenced every modern-day president's foreign policy.

Kissinger's critique of Wilson is similar to the realist critique of traditional American foreign policy put forth during the height of the cold war in the 1950s by journalist Walter Lippman and by political scientists Hans Morgenthau and Robert Endicott Osgood. Morgenthau and Osgood's study *Ideals and Self-Interest in America's Foreign Relations* (University of Chicago Press, 1953) established the realist/idealist dichotomy utilized by Kissinger. George F. Kennan, another "realistic" diplomat, advanced a similar criticism about what he called the "legalistic-moralistic" streak that could be found in American foreign policy; see *American Diplomacy, 1900–1950* (Mentor Books, 1951).

Scholars have criticized the realist approach to Wilson for a number of reasons. Some say that it is "unrealistic" to expect an American president to ask for a declaration of war to defend abstract principles such as the balance of power or our national interest. Presidents and other elected officials must have a moral reason if they expect the American public to support a foreign war in which American servicemen might be killed.

Many recent historians agree with David F. Trask that Wilson developed realistic and clearly articulated goals and coordinated his larger diplomatic aims with the use of force better than any other wartime U.S. president. See "Woodrow Wilson and the Reconciliation of Force and Diplomacy, 1917–1918," *Naval War College Review* (January/February 1975). Arthur S. Link, editor of *The Wilson Papers*, who has spent a lifetime writing about Wilson, follows a similar line of argument in his lectures delivered at Johns Hopkins University in 1956; see, for example, *Woodrow Wilson: Revolution, War, and Peace*, rev. ed. (Harlan Davidson, 1979). Finally, John Milton Cooper, Jr., in *The Warrior and the Priest: Woodrow Wilson and Theodore Roosevelt* (Harvard University Press, 1984), presents Wilson as the realist and Theodore Roosevelt as the idealist.

In the second selection William G. Carleton presents an impassioned defense of both Wilson's policies at Versailles as well as their implication for the future of American foreign policy. Carleton responds to the two main charges historians continue to level against Wilson: his inability to compromise and his naive idealism. Unlike Professor Thomas A. Bailey, who in *Woodrow Wilson and the Great Betrayal* (Macmillan, 1945) blames Wilson for failing to compromise with Senator Henry Cabot Lodge, Carleton excoriates the chairman of the Senate Foreign Relations Committee for adding "nationally self-centered" reservations that he knew would emasculate the League of Nations and most likely cause other nations to add reservations to the Treaty of Versailles. Wilson, says, Carleton, was a true realist when he rejected the Lodge reservations.

Nor was Wilson a naive idealist. "He recognized," says Carleton, "the emergence of the anti-imperialist revolutions ... the importance of social politics in the international relations of the future ... the implications for future world politics of the technological revolutions in war, of total war, and of the disintegration of the old balance of power." Carleton advanced many of the arguments that historians like Professors Trask and Link later used in defending Wilson's "higher realism."

Books continue to proliferate about Wilson. Critical from a realistic perspective are Jan Willem Schulte Nordholt, *Woodrow Wilson: A Life for World Peace* (University of California Press, 1991) and Lloyd E. Ambrosius, *Wilsonian Statecraft: Theory and Practice of Liberal Internationalism During World War I* (Scholarly Resources Books, 1991). Two older, mildly critical, well-written summaries are Daniel M. Smith's *The Great Departure: The United States and World War I, 1914–1920* (John Wiley, 1965) and Robert H. Ferrell, *Woodrow Wilson and World War I, 1917–1921* (Harper & Row, 1985).

Books sympathetic to Wilson include: Arthur Walworth, *Wilson and His Peacemakers: American Diplomacy at the Paris Peace Conference* (W. W. Norton, 1986) and Kendrick A. Clements, *The Presidency of Woodrow Wilson* (University Press of Kansas, 1992). See also the biography by August Heckscher, *Woodrow Wilson* (Scribners, 1991), and Thomas J. Knock, *To End All Wars: Woodrow Wilson and the Quest for a New World Order* (Oxford University Press, 1992).

# ISSUE 10

## Was the Ku Klux Klan of the 1920s an Extremist Movement?

**YES: David H. Bennett,** from *The Party of Fear: From Nativist Movements to the New Right in American History* (University of North Carolina Press, 1988)

**NO: Stanley Coben,** from *Rebellion Against Victorianism: The Impetus for Cultural Change in 1920s America* (Oxford University Press, 1991)

### ISSUE SUMMARY

**YES:** Professor of history David H. Bennett argues that the Ku Klux Klan of the 1920s was a traditional nativist organization supported mainly by fundamentalist Protestants who were opposed to the changing social and moral values associated with the Catholic and Jewish immigrants.

**NO:** Professor of history Stanley Coben believes that local Klansmen were not a fringe group of fundamentalists but were solid middle-class citizens who were concerned about the decline in moral standards in their communities.

There have been three Ku Klux Klans in American history: (1) the Reconstruction Klan, which arose in the South at the end of the Civil War and whose primary purpose was to prevent the newly emancipated blacks from voting and attaining social and economic equality with whites; (2) the 1920s Klan, which had national appeal and emerged out of disillusionment with the aftermath of U.S. intervention in World War I and the changing social and economic values that had transformed America as a result of the full-scale Industrial Revolution; and (3) the modern Klan, which arose after World War II in the rural areas of the Deep South and (like the Reconstruction Klan) came about to prevent blacks from attaining the political and legal rights guaranteed by the passage of the civil rights legislation in the 1950s and 1960s.

The Klan of the 1920s was founded in 1915 by William J. Simmons, a Methodist circuit preacher, and 15 of his followers. For five years the resurrected Klan consisted of only 4,000 or 5,000 members in scattered Klans throughout Georgia and Alabama. On June 7, 1920, Simmons signed a contract with two clever salespersons, Edward Clarke and Elizabeth Tyler, who pioneered some of the most remarkable organizing and mass marketing techniques of the pro-business decade of the 1920s. The campaign was an immediate success. Between June 1920 and October 1921, 85,000 men joined the Klan. Total membership figures are difficult to ascertain, but somewhere between 3 and 5 million people joined the Klan. This means that one of every four Protestant males in America was a member of the Klan.

The 1920s Klan differed greatly from its predecessors and successors because of its wide-ranging influence in politics across the nation. The Klan was not merely a southern movement but a national movement strongest in the Midwest and Southwest. Politically, Klan members dominated state legislatures in Oklahoma, Texas, and Indiana, and city councils in such far-western places as El Paso, Texas; Denver, Colorado; Anaheim, California; and Tillamook, Oregon. The Klan of the 1920s was the most powerful right-wing movement of the decade.

While the 1920s Klan disliked blacks, it focused its attacks upon the Catholic and Jewish immigrants who had been coming to America since the 1890s. Klansmen particularly disliked Catholics, who constituted 36 percent of the nation's population in 1920. Catholics were accused of placing loyalty to the pope ahead of loyalty to the nation. If Catholics gained political control, the Klan asserted, the separation of church and state would end, and freedoms of speech, press, and religious worship would also be abolished.

The Klan was also inspired by the xenophobic (fear of foreigners) atmosphere of the time. America's participation in World War I had ended in public disillusionment. The U.S. Senate reflected the country's dislike of all things foreign when it refused to ratify President Wilson's Treaty of Versailles. Antiforeign feelings were also reflected in the passage of the 1921 and 1924 reform laws, which severely curtailed immigration from southern and eastern Europe and completely excluded Japanese and other oriental groups.

Most explanations for the fall of the 1920s Klan seem unsatisfactory. Greed may have been one cause. Because there was so much money involved—it has been estimated that as much as $75 million in Klan initiation fees and wardrobes ended up in the pockets of various Klan leaders—everyone seemed to have their hand in the till. Moral hypocrisy also infiltrated the Klan. While many Klan members were afraid of the changing standards of morality and supported Klan politicians who preached law and order, the opposite was often the case. Third, the depression of the 1930s and World War II may have contributed to the Klan's fall by directing people's energies elsewhere.

Was the 1920s Ku Klux Klan an extremist organization? According to David H. Bennett, the Klan was a traditional nativist organization supported mainly by fundamentalist Protestants who were opposed to the changing social and moral values of the 1920s associated with the Catholic and Jewish immigrants. Stanley Coben recognizes that while the Klan was responsible for vigilante violence in both the North and South in the 1920s, most Klansmen were not traditional extremists. Instead, he argues, they were ordinary white middle-class Protestants who composed what he has described elsewhere as "the largest grassroots conservative (and sometimes reactionary) movement in American history."

**YES** **David H. Bennett**

# TRADITIONAL NATIVISM'S LAST STAND

## RESTATING THE THEMES OF NATIVISM

The Ku Klux Klan under Hiram Wesley Evans and associates offered a program reminiscent of its nativist progenitors, the Know Nothings and the APA. Klan papers and magazines, books and articles by Klan leaders, laid out the appeal of the new nativism.

One spokesman, Reverend E. H. Laugher, in *The Kall of the Klan in Kentucky,* explained that "the KKK is not a lodge or a society or a political party." Rather, it is a mass movement, "a crusade of American people who are beginning to realize that they have neglected their public and religious duty to stand up for Americanism." This meant remembering that America was discovered by Norsemen, colonized by Puritans, that the United States was "purely Anglo-Saxon and Nordic." It was essential to "preserve our racial purity," he insisted, to avoid "mongrelization." It was imperative to maintain separation of church and state because "the forces of Protestantism" were protectors of the "doctrine of Americanism." The Roman Catholic church, appealing to the polyglot peoples who threatened the good and pure society, must be blocked in its drive to dominate and destroy the great nation.

In *The Fiery Cross, The Kourier, The American Standard, Dawn, The Imperial Night-Hawk,* and other publications, Klan ideologists assaulted Catholics, Jews, and aliens. "Jesus was a Protestant," the faithful were told, he had "split with the priests" because he had truth and right on his side. The Roman Catholic church, laboring under "the growth of Popish despotism," was irreligious and un-American. In fact, the "Papacy's campaign against liberalism and freedom" made it a proper "ally of Mussolini's fascism," just as the church had been on the side of other autocracies since medieval times. In America, the "spirit of Bunker Hill and Valley Forge," that longing for democracy and individualism which informed the Revolution and the words of the Founding Fathers, was at odds with a "hierarchical Church, which, like an octopus, has stretched its tentacles into the very vitals of the body politic of the nation." The church's effort to undermine the public schools, to "reach out for the children of Protestantism," to "hit anywhere with any weapon" in an unscrupulous campaign to impose its will, meant that every Catholic in public life, from school board member to national politician, must be watched carefully. "Do you know," a Klan editorialist asked, "that eight states have Roman Catholic administrations, 690 public schools teach from the Roman Catholic catechism, sixty-two per-cent of all elected and appointed offices in the United States are now held by Catholics, who also are a majority of the teachers in many major city school systems?"

The threat of the church was everywhere. The "Romanized press" tried to propagandize a gullible public. Catholics evaded taxes as a matter of course, refusing to share the burdens of government, preferring to subsidize sinister schemes hatched by their prelates. The church used Jesuits to engage in "occult mental manipulations" and tried to "subjugate the Negro race through spiritual domination." The pope favored child labor, and because "20,000 ordained priests in America are vassals to this Imperial Monarch in Rome," the same could be expected of church leaders in the United States. Indeed, Catholics were in no sense trustworthy Americans; during the Great War, "German sentiment was the fruit of carefully prepared and skillfully disseminated Roman propaganda." But it would be wrong to conclude that the Klan was anti-Catholic, leaders insisted, because its arguments were "wholly and solely concentrated on being one hundred per cent American." In fact, one writer suggested, the Klan is "no more aimed at Roman Catholics than it would be aimed at Buddhists, Confucianists or Mohammedans, or anybody else who owes allegiance to any foreign person and/or religion."

Like the nineteenth-century nativists, Klan initiates were asked to protect America from the diabolical plans of Jesuits and other leaders of this un-American presence. From colonial days, anti-Catholicism had been a dominant theme in the history of these movements, a way of displacing fears and angers on alien intruders. In the 1920s, with Irish Catholics maintaining positions of prominence in urban and national politics, continuing to gain greater influence in a growing economy, Klan spokesmen returned to the old themes. The assault on the church was repeated in almost every Klan speech, article, and editorial. This modern Ku Klux Klan dressed its members in garb borrowed from the Reconstruction vigilante organization, but its real roots were in traditional nativism, stretching back much further in the American experience.

But to its attack on Catholicism, the modern Klan added an anti-Semitic element. The APA, emerging during the new immigration, had touched on this theme; Klan writers developed the argument. "Jews are everywhere a separate and distinct people, living apart from the great Gentile masses," said the author of *Klansmen: Guardians of Liberty*. But these people are not "home builders or tillers of the soil." Evans had made a similar argument in a speech at Dallas in December 1922: "The Jew produces nothing anywhere on the face of the earth. He does not till the soil. He does not create or manufacture anything for common use. He adds nothing to the sum of human welfare." Yet not only were Jews unproductive, Klan theoreticians insisted, they were un-American. They were not interested in integration: "No, not the Jew . . . he is different." These people, who "defied the melting pot for one thousand years," believed in their own superiority, in "Jewry Uber Alles."

They hatched secret plans to advance their interests, to "cause wars and to subjugate America." Certain conspiratorial Jews must be "absolutely and eternally" opposed when they plotted their "crimes and wrongs." They were nothing more than money-grubbing and immoral vultures, "moral lepers who gloat over human tragedy, rejoice in the downfall of the guileless and inexperienced." The unethical practices of Jewish businessmen —often seen as winners in the economic competition of the boom years—and the radical schemes of Jewish Marxists were considered equally repugnant, dangers to America. But so, too, was the cultural depravity of strategically placed "Semites" in the media. "Jew Movies Urge Sex and Vice," the Klan headline shouted like an echo from Ford's *Dearborn Independent;* "Jewish corruption in jazz" was a result of "their monopoly over popular songs." In the big cities, "ninety five per cent of bootleggers are Jews."

It was the Roaring Twenties, and as mores changed, as traditional social arrangements were overturned, as skirts went up and speakeasies flourished, as the movies and radio made their mark with Tin Pan Alley songs popularized by so many show business celebrities, the Klan found a way of identifying these disturbing developments in an antialien context, of standing up for America by assailing yet another band of un-Americans.

Still, the Jews were only one part of a larger alien problem in America. Again, like the Know Nothings and the patriotic fraternalists of the 1890s, these nativists were concerned with the threat they saw posed by all non-Anglo-Saxon immigrants and their descendants. Imperial Wizard Evans spoke of "the vast horde of immigrants who have reached our shores," these "Italian anarchists, Irish Catholic malcontents, Russian Jews, Finns, Letts, Lithuanians of the lowest class." Even after the Immigration Act of 1924, which Evans characterized as a "new era dawning for America" and took full credit for securing—"typifying the influence exerted by our organization"—he warned that undesirables "are still bootlegged into the nation," still try to "flaunt our immigration laws." This "polyglotism" was intolerable, for many of the most recent immigrants from southern and eastern Europe and from Asia still could not read and write English. They were unfamiliar with American history and tradition, "were unaware that America is fundamentally an Anglo-Saxon achievement." And because these alien peoples "congregate in our great centers, our cities are a menace to democracy," they are "modern Sodoms and Gomorrahs." Is "Petrograd in its ruin and desolation a picture of New York in the future"? There was only one possible response. "America for the Americans," Evans exhorted, for if "this state of affairs continues, the American race is doomed to cultural destruction." In words that might have been lifted from a Know Nothing broadside, he continued: "Illiteracy, disease, insanity, and mental deficiency are still pouring in among us."

The "foreigners" were responsible for a host of social problems. Evans lectured on "our alien crime-plague" and Klan papers reported on alien thugs, Italian mobsters and rum runners, even a "Newark alien hiding whiskey in U.S. flag." The aliens threatened female virtue: "Foreign women sell their bodies for gain." They threatened the safety of American womanhood: "Women Are Struck Down by Foreign Mob," screamed one headline, "Aliens Poison Hoosier Women," said another. Some aliens were radicals: "Russians Would Make America Red, Peril is a Very Real One." Others would destroy the nation through political sabotage: "Use the Ballot, the Italian Ambassador Recommends, to Advance the Interests of Italians' Native Land." And over all these perils loomed the threat of Irish Catholic party machine manipulators. Leaders of the church in America, most formidable of the foreign operatives, these "Irish Romanists in Tammany... lead the Jews, Poles, Italians, Germans, Czechs, Magyars"; it was a "vast army under command of the Irish Roman ward heelers." The only way to deal with the foreign devils, to safeguard our sacred institutions, was to re-Americanize the land. Evans announced: "Against us are all the forces of the mixed alliance composed of alienism, Romanism, hyphenism, Bolshevism and un-Americanism which aim to use this country as a dumping ground for the fermenting races of the Old World." But "we of the Klan are on the firing line... like the soldiers of the American Expeditionary Force in France, we stand up for America and take pride and joy in the wounds we receive... the Knights of the Ku Klux Klan have become the trustees under God for Protestant American nationalism."

The cause of the Klan, in the phrases of its spokesmen, could not have been more noble, more dangerous, or more urgent. But among those many American values that Klansmen were sworn to protect, one had particular urgency. This was the protection of "womanhood." In pursuing this goal, the Klan invoked memories of that long line of femininity's defenders who marched under the banners of nativism, back to the days of Maria Monk.

A Texas Klansman, author of *Religious and Patriotic Ideals of the Ku Klux Klan*, reminded initiates that they had sworn to "promote good works and thus protect the chastity of womanhood, the virtue of girlhood, the sanctity of the home." Spokesmen repeatedly used the term "chivalry" in describing the movement's principles. The role of women in the literature of the Klan was explicitly traditional. They were the moral arbiters of society, for "even in the midst of all the pressing duties of maternal care and home making, women have found time to keep the spiritual fire of the nation burning on the altar... women have been the conscience keepers of the race." But the role was not so traditional that women would be repressed, for it was "Rome Which Opposes the Advancement of Womanhood," said the headline, the Jesuits who favor policies pushing women into "semi-oriental seclusion." The Klan would preserve and protect women so they might aid in the shaping of American destiny; "the fate of the nation is in the hands of women." As one Klan newswriter put it, they can be "not only help meets but help mates." After all, the "very mentioning of the word 'woman' always arrests the attention of every true man. Whatever else the human heart may forget in the rough experiences of life, it cannot forget its mother."

The call to protect these fragile, sensitive, vulnerable women led to violence. Local Klans were accused of floggings, tar and featherings, and beatings in several states in the South, Southwest, and lower Midwest. The victims of the masked night riders often were alleged adulterers and wife-beaters, men said not to be supporting their families, men who had deserted their women. But the enemies of "pure womanhood" included sinners of both sexes. "Fallen women" were the targets in some rural bastions.

Young women accused of prostitution or adultery were stripped naked, tarred, left half-conscious with their hair shorn. The sexual frustrations of these bands of white-robed small-townsmen, envious of the freedom exercised by millions of more liberated urbanites in the jazz age, finding perverse pleasure in this part of their crusade for morality, reveling in the projection of their anger and the displacement of their resentments on these symbolic villains, recalled the nunnery craze of the early nineteenth century.

In fact, another generation of nativists meant another resurgence of convent tales. *Dawn* [a major Klan paper in Chicago] offered "Convent Cruelties: The True Story of Ex-Nun Helen Jackson," advertising offprints of this sadomasochistic piece for many months after initial publication. Other Klan journals featured, among several exposés, "Behind Convent Walls" and "Roman Priest Alienates Innocent Women's Love."

Women who knew their role and understood their place were offered membership in affiliate groups open to "patriotic ladies." Simmons's Kamelia had been disbanded, but Hiram Evans introduced the Women of the Ku Klux Klan, an organization which absorbed such local groups as Ladies of the Invisible Empire in Louisiana and the Order of American Women in Texas. This new national organization established its own Imperial Palace, a pillared mansion in Little Rock, Arkansas. It sent its own kleagles [officials in the Klan] into the field, calling on Klansmen to influence wives and sisters to join. By fall 1924, when the Ku Klux Klan said its membership numbered in the millions, the women's auxiliary claimed a following of two hundred thousand. The initiates were not, as one anti-Klan writer suggested, "nativist amazons." They were expected to perform customary housewifely chores; they prepared food for Klan outings, picnics, and klambakes. In fact, their order was little more than the instrument of one man's authority. James Comer, Evans's early ally and grand dragon of the Arkansas Klan, bankrolled the Women of the Ku Klux Klan and controlled its activities. He forced the resignation of its imperial commander to install Robbie Gill, an initiate friend who would soon be his wife, as new leader. It was Commander Gill who told the Second Imperial Klonvocation: "God gave Adam Woman to be his comrade and counselor... Eve's name meant life, society, company. Adam was lord and master." Like earlier nativists, Klansmen never questioned the assumption of male dominance. The American dream they sought to protect had no room for sexual equality. But the image of threatened womanhood was essential to their own search for masculine validation, even as it had been in the days of *The Awful Disclosures of Maria Monk.* That had been another age in which economic growth and status anxiety served as a setting for the resurgence of the antialien crusade.

The attacks on Catholics and foreigners and the vows to protect imperiled American women tied the Ku Klux Klan to a long history of similar movements. It was traditional nativism's last stand. Its emergence in the 1920s raised questions to which contemporary journalists and academics offered a variety of answers.

Reporter Robert L. Duffus, author of a series of anti-Klan articles in the *World's Work,* argued that many recruits came from "the back counties of the south and lower midwest," where men carry guns, women are objects of deference but also of exploitation, and the disappointed seek causes outside themselves. Professor Frank Tannenbaum, writing in 1924, agreed in part, seeing Klansmen as seekers after "artificial thrills" as a way of dealing with the boredom of small-town life, people ready to use coercion in defense of social status, people "losing their grip" in a world of change. But Tannenbaum also looked to recent events as a source of this mood of restlessness. The Great War aroused human passions, he suggested, the "hope of a new and beatific world after the defeat of the German devil." The Klan offered an explanation of why the war brought no "dawning of Utopia." It was the Catholic, the radical, the foreigner who was in league with the devil.

Later, scholars would embrace some of these views. Though not sharing pro-Klan journalist Stanley Frost's rosy vision of Klansmen as a knighthood of admirable reformers, they agreed that the Klan represented a response to the war, a zeal to cleanse and reform American society. The rise of fundamentalist fervor in the 1920s, which provided an additional setting for the Klan, was seen as another reaction to the war. Anti-Catholicism was in the air in many parts of the nation in these years. As with fundamentalism, the Klan's crusade for conformity to old values and old social arrangements was seen as a "characteristic response to a common disillusion."

The Ku Klux Klan, like the Red Scare, was given new life by the souring of the international crusade. Almost all students of the Klan have made this point. But the reason why the Klan grew in the 1920s had more to do with social and economic strains in a society experiencing almost unprecedented growth.

Those who joined were not, as Duffus suggested, only losers in the boom years. Along with poor farmers, blue-collar workers, mechanics, and day laborers some bankers, lawyers, doctors, ministers, and prosperous businessmen were recruited in different regions. There were communities in which political careers and professional success depended on membership. But the Klan appealed more to those who were not members of any elite. Imperial Wizard and Emperor Evans observed: "We are a movement of the plain people, very weak in the matter of culture, intellectual support and trained leadership.... We demand a return of power into the hands of the everyday, not highly cultured, not overly intellectualized but entirely unspoiled and not de-Americanized average citizens of the old stock." The Klan everywhere appealed to those who believed that their older vision of America was at risk. In the struggle to preserve enduring American values, the movement offered a sense of common purpose in service of a cause greater than self. It offered an idealism that had a magnetic pull for many. Its shrewd managers, interested in money, power, and influence for themselves, knew how to package the movement. But the popularity of the Klan, once it began to spread across the land, did not depend on the Clarkes and Tylers or their successors as marketing specialists and salesmen. Like the earlier nativist fraternities, it was rooted in a longing for order, in misty memories of some stable and happy past, in fears of what new perils modernity might bring, in the search for community in an age of flux.

The movement provided community. Local Klans sponsored Sunday dinners and square dances, basketball tournaments and rodeos, carnivals and circuses, fireworks displays featuring "electric fiery crosses," social events of all kinds. It was comforting to be in the Klan, and it could be fun. Klansmen also took care of each other. Businessmen placed ads for Klan Klothes Kleaned or Krippled Kars Kured, expecting fraternal ties would result in new customers. Other activities offered bonding through unified action to clean up the community: boycotts of businesses run by "immoral men," committees to ferret out bootleggers and bars.

The communal ties seemed at one with religious conviction. The movement that defended Protestantism won the tacit endorsement of many clergymen, some who joined the order. Most nationally prominent church leaders stayed away from the Klan, and some Methodist, Presbyterian, and Episcopalian notables and publications even attacked it, but these assaults from influential cosmopolitans only served to underscore Evans's claims that his movement was the instrument of the mass of common people. The Klan made inroads in many Protestant communities, particularly among Southern Baptists and others influenced by fundamentalist concerns. A major part of the Protestant press remained silent on the issue, but many local church papers endorsed the goals of an organization that appealed for support in the name of old-time values and that old-time religion.

The Klan's growth was meteoric. In 1924, Stanley Frost reported that "some say it has six million members." Frost himself claimed only some 4.5 million in the movement. Robert Duffus put the number at 2.5 million in 1923. Other guesses ranged upward of 5 million. It was impossible to be certain; the Klan left only fragmentary local records and no national archives. But one modern scholar, using available data, estimated it had over 2 million recruits in 1924; another, in a careful review of conflicting claims, put it at over 2 million initiates across the years, with some 1.5 million at any one time. What is certain is that it had become a true mass movement, one of the major developments in the history of the 1920s, a great monument to the antialien impulse in America.

## THE KLAN ACROSS AMERICA

But it did not prosper equally in all sections of the country. In the Deep South, where the Klan was born, it exerted considerable influence in some states. Still, its membership never exceeded a quarter of a million....

The Klan lasted longer in Indiana, home of its most powerful, most successful organization in the United States. The man who was instrumental in recruiting a quarter of a million knights statewide—almost forty thousand in Indianapolis—was Grand Dragon David C. Stephenson. Only thirty years old in 1921, Stephenson had been one of the four key state leaders helping Evans oust Simmons before the first national meeting in Atlanta. Rewarded with the organizing rights for twenty-three states in the North, this charismatic figure, who liked to compare himself to Napoleon, already was a successful coal dealer when he joined the Invisible Empire. But in the Klan, he would make a fortune in recruitment fees and build a reputation as a mesmerizing orator, the super salesman of the national Klan.

In Indiana, his order sponsored parades and athletic contests, field days and picnics. It offered community and festivity, but always in the name of protecting Protestant America from its enemies. In "Middletown," the Lynds found it had become a working-class movement and "tales against the Catholics ran like wild fire" through Muncie. Local Klansmen vowed they would unmask only "when and not until the Catholics take the prison walls down from their convents and nunneries." Anti-Catholic, anti-Semitic, antiblack rhetoric filled Stephenson's colorful speeches: the Klan stood for temperance and patriotism, the aliens were threatening traditional American values. This appeal was so successful that store owners soon put TWK [Trade with a Klansman] in their windows; the secrecy of the order could be violated with little fear of retaliation in a state in which hundreds of thousands were flocking to join the most popular movement in memory. In fact, so many initiates paid their klecktoken to Stephenson that it was estimated he made between $2 and $5 million in eighteen months. The grand dragon acquired a ninety-eight-foot yacht, which he kept on Lake Huron, a fleet of automobiles, a palatial suburban home, and elaborate offices in downtown Indianapolis. There, the mayor opposed "Steve" and his order until a Klansman named Edward Jackson won the Republican primary for governor in 1923. Now the Klan took control of the county party machinery. Jackson's subsequent election gave Stephenson and his movement state power unmatched by any other Klan.

A high point was reached with the fabled Konklave at Kokomo, when "200,000 men and women filled with love of country"—in the words of the *Fiery Cross* (Indiana State Edition)—gathered for the Klan's greatest single meeting. Tens of thousands of cars brought members from across Indiana and Ohio. Stephenson, attired in a sequined purple robe and escorted by his team of personal bodyguards, finally mounted the rostrum. He explained that he was late for the meeting because "the President of the United States kept me counselling upon matters of state." He proceeded to deliver a quintessentially nativist exhortation, filled with pleas for America and plans for vigilant opposition to the aliens. Always a riveting stump speaker, Stephenson was most respected for his organizational skills. But his Bonapartist complex and rumors of numerous sexual indiscretions and alcoholic binges soon led to conflicts with state and national Klan leaders. Evans turned against him, and he resigned as state grand dragon in September 1923. But D. C. Stephenson was not through. He marshaled support for a special state meeting the following May, in which his followers elected him once again their grand dragon, thus rejecting the authority of national headquarters. Stephenson continued to flout the hierarchical authority of the national Klan, staying in power during the election year of 1924, a time which marked the KKK's most significant impact in American politics. But by 1925, the Indiana chief was caught up in the scandal that ended in his prison sentence, a sordid affair that fatally wounded not only the Indiana Klan but the national movement as well....

Although the Klan had suffered setbacks in Oklahoma, Texas, Colorado, Oregon, Illinois, and other states by early 1925, it still seemed a formidable national movement in the year after the election. Then came the Stephenson scandal in Indiana. The grand dragon was implicated in the death of a statehouse employee named Madge Oberholtzer. Although it was widely reported that he had known many attractive women in Indianapolis, D. C. Stephenson chose to lavish particular attention on Oberholtzer. She later testified that he compelled her to drink with him, finally forcing her at gunpoint to a train. In the private compartment he attacked and "sexually mutilated" her. Oberholtzer took a fatal overdose of drugs after this incident, but she lingered for weeks before her death; she had time to dictate the entire story to the prosecuting attorney, one of the few officials Stephenson could not control in Marion County. The revelations devastated the entire movement. The desperate grand dragon, on trial for murder, was abandoned by his former henchman, Governor Ed Jackson. Panicky Klan papers now assailed their leader. The *Indian Kourier* headline declared: "D. C. Stephenson Not a Klansman," and called him an "enemy of the order," reporting that he had been "repudiated by all true Knights of the Empire." Stephenson responded by revealing the contents of his "little black box," which contained records implicating many highly placed, Klan-backed officials as corrupters, providing evidence of their malfeasance of office. The movement did not recover in Indiana. While Stephenson languished in jail (he would not be released until 1956), the Klan found its political influence evaporating, its membership deserting by the thousands. Hypocrisy, greed, and dishonesty by the leadership was bad enough, but Stephenson's violation of the symbolic crusade for purity, chastity, womanhood, and temperance was too much. As the greatest of the state Klans dissolved, the national empire of the Ku Klux Klan began to crumble everywhere.

By late in the decade, the Klan was a shell of the powerful movement of 1923–24. Although thousands of hooded men marched in the last great parade down the boulevards of Washington in the summer of 1925, many more were abandoning the order. Al Smith's presidential candidacy in 1928 was the occasion for one final, convulsive anti-Catholic effort by the Invisible Empire, but Herbert Hoover's victory owed little to the Klan. In the 1930s, the shriveled movement receded from public view, and its remaining publicists turned away from Catholicism to communism when seeking the alien menace within. Hiram Wesley Evans, before he lost what had become the all but meaningless title of imperial wizard in 1939, even accepted the invitation of church leaders to attend the dedication of the Roman Catholic Cathedral, ironically built on the site of the old Imperial Headquarters in Atlanta. The old order was no more. By 1944, with the federal government pressing for the payment of back taxes on Klan profits from the prosperous 1920s, remaining national officers officially disbanded the Ku Klux Klan.

Although small state and local organizations calling themselves Ku Klux Klan, using the terminology of the earlier movement, and dressing members in similar regalia would reemerge in the late 1940s to play occasional roles in antiblack and anti–civil rights violence up through the 1980s, the great Klan of the 1920s was long dead. It had faltered so quickly after the spectacular growth early in the decade for many reasons. It lacked a clear legislative agenda. It experienced heavy weather in the political struggles in several states, where adroit enemies could use its weaknesses to build support for their own interests. It was led, in many areas, by people who were the embodiment of precisely those qualities that Klan ideology asked initiates to oppose: heavy drinkers and swindlers, sexual exploiters and dishonest manipulators of the theme of patriotism. In the end, the movement that offered fraternity to men in tumultuous times, that provided a nativist response to the crisis of values troubling so many in the Roaring Twenties, could not endure the revelations of scandal, the lack of constancy, the confused policies of the leadership. Like its antialien progenitors, the Ku Klux Klan was a movement that symbolized a longing for order, a desire to displace anger and anxiety. With no programmatic reason for being, men would desert it if it ceased to fulfill its symbolic function. As major newspapers turned against it, as articulate figures in the ministry and education, as well as in public life, pointed to its hypocrisy and treated it with scathing contempt, the mass of members simply drifted away. As with the Red Scare, the patriotic activity of the 1890s, and the antialien excitement of the pre–Civil War years, nativism's last stand had a relatively short run.

# NO

## Stanley Coben

# THE GUARDIANS

The early twentieth-century assaults on Victorianism provoked a strong organized defense by fundamentalists, Prohibitionists, and various conservative and patriotic organizations. However, the huge nationwide Ku Klux Klan, with at least three million members, emerged as the most visible and powerful guardian of Victorianism during the 1920s.

Unlike the vigilante groups which had used the name Ku Klux Klan after the Civil War and during the mid-twentieth-century battles against integration, the Klan of the 1920s did not focus on protecting white supremacy in the South. At the height of the Klan's power in 1924, Southerners formed only 16 percent of its total membership. Over 40 percent of early twentieth-century Klan members lived in the three midwestern states of Indiana, Ohio, and Illinois. The Klan enrolled more members in Connecticut than in Mississippi, more in Oregon than in Louisiana, and more in New Jersey than in Alabama. Klan membership in Indianapolis was almost twice that in South Carolina and Mississippi combined.

Also, Klan members in the mid-1920s were not any more violent than other native, white, middle-class Protestant males. After the Klan organized nationally for maximum profit and political action in 1921, the organization expelled members and whole chapters charged with having taken part in vigilante activities. However, inconclusive newspaper and government investigations into the activities of a small minority of early Klansmen during 1921 gave the organization a violent image. The name Ku Klux Klan (adopted mainly because of the Klan's role in the immensely popular film, *The Birth of a Nation*), the Klan's secrecy, and the order's refusal to admit anyone except native white Protestant males contributed to this image, especially among blacks, Catholics, Jews, and champions of civil liberties.

The image of the Klan held by critics of the organization during the 1920s was affected too by the Klan's rhetoric. That rhetoric reflected still widely accepted Victorian ideas about a racial hierarchy and about the dangers to American society posed by Catholics, blacks, Jews, and Asians. These popular beliefs had assisted the passage of immigration-restriction acts and had helped to defeat the presidential bid of Al Smith. They already had led to nationwide segregation and to disenfranchisement of southern blacks.

Therefore, almost nowhere that Klan-backed politicians won power did Klan racist rhetoric need to be transformed into legislation. Nowhere did Klansmen running for office need to advocate violence under any circumstance, even against blacks in the South.

The near absence of Klan violence against southern blacks was explained, in part, by a perceptive editorial in the Savannah, Georgia, *Tribune*, a black-owned newspaper which strongly supported Marcus Garvey's black nationalist Universal Negro Improvement Association and was outspoken about civil-rights violations. The *Tribune*'s editorial (whose conclusions were corroborated by other evidence), published July 13, 1922, stated:

> The evidence is that in the South the Ku Klux are not bothering with the Negroes. The naked truth is that when a band of lynchers sets out to kill a Negro they do not take the trouble to mask. They do not think it necessary to join a secret society, pay initiation fees and buy regalia when Negroes are the quarry.

A Georgia mob did not find it necessary to don masks before lynching Leo Frank in 1915, the year that the early twentieth-century Klan met to organize outside Atlanta.

* * *

The Klan's primary objectives consisted of guarding the major Victorian concepts and the interests these protected. The ideas of character, largely reserved for white Protestants, the home and family in which character was formed, and distinctly separate gender roles stood foremost among these concepts. A series of articles entitled "The Klansman's Criterion of Character," published weekly from March 1 to March 29, 1924, in the Klan's national newspaper *Searchlight*, illustrated what the Klan expected of its leaders as well as of its ordinary members.

Jesus provided the chief model for *Searchlight*'s definition of character: "He never compromised when dealing with the leaders of the Jews. He would not lie in order to save his own life." Jesus "was the unflinching, accomplishing, achieving Christ, because he was the purposeful, steadfast, determined Christ." Furthermore, Jesus accomplished his great mission on earth without the advantages enjoyed by members of the privileged business elites and the intelligentsia: "He controlled no centers of influence; He commanded neither learning nor wealth."

*Searchlight* implied that Klan members had undertaken the task of guarding, in the United States, Jesus' accomplishments:

> The Klan is engaged in a holy crusade against that which is corrupting and destroying the best in American life. The Klan is devoted to the holy mission of developing that which is right and clean and beneficent in our country. The Klan is active in its ministry of helpfulness and service.... Such enthusiastic devotion to right principles and the holy cause must characterize true Klansmen, if they are to be like Him whom they have accepted as their "Criterion of Character."

The "Kloran" of the "Knights of the Ku Klux Klan," the order's ritual book used to conduct all meetings and initiations, declared on its cover the order's dedication to "Karacter, Honor, Duty."

Every recent study that has examined the characteristics of klan members—in urban and rural communities of California, Colorado, Georgia, Indiana, Ohio, Oregon, Tennessee, Texas, and Utah—has found that Klansmen constituted a cross section of the local native white Protestant male population, except for the very top and bottom socioeconomic levels of that population. Virtually every Klan candidate for state and local office appealed to this constituency—Klan and non-Klan—with promises to reduce or eliminate those results of character defects which threatened the home and family: violations of Prohibition especially, but also drug abuse, prostitution, gambling, political corruption, traffic violations, and Sunday blue-law offenses.

As local Klan chapters, or Klaverns, prepared to sweep almost every political office in rural Fremont County, Colorado, the county's Klan leaders invited a national Klan lecturer, "Colonel" McKeever, to help bring out the Klan vote. Speaking to an overflow audience in the Canon City armory (1920 population of 4,551), the county's largest community, McKeever proclaimed a typical Klan message:

> The Klan stands for law enforcement; money and politics must cease to play a role [particularly in Prohibition enforcement] in our courts. The Klan stands for the American home; there is no sanctuary like a mother's heart, no altar like a mother's knee. The Klan stands for good men in office.

The Klan attempted to combat all "forces of evil which attack the American home." Threatening the "purity of women," claimed an editorial in the *Fiery Cross*, Indiana's Klan newspaper, were businessmen who employed female secretaries: "Everyone knows of instances where businessmen insist on dating secretaries and imply that should they refuse, their jobs are in danger."...

* * *

Klan membership held a strong attraction for large numbers of men who already belonged to secret white Protestant fraternal organizations.... The Klan offered a more blatant racism, anti-Catholicism, and anti-Semitism, as well as direct participation in politics to members of such societies as the Masons, Odd Fellows, and Knights of Pythias. Moreover, the basic objectives of these other orders resembled those of the Klan in respects more important than ritual and fraternity. The most recent and discerning historian of the Freemasons, Lynn Dumenil, summarized the fundamental Masonic aims: "Not only would America become homogenous again, but the perpetuation of the values of native, Protestant Americans would be assured."

Kleagles received instructions to contact local ministers, fraternal lodge members, and potentially favorable newspaper editors upon entering a community. They were to ascertain the strongest needs of local white Protestants with the aid of these contacts and to begin enrolling members....

The most thorough statistical analyses of Klan membership during the 1920s have been written by Christopher Cocoltchos, Leonard Moore, and Robert Goldberg. A clear pattern emerges from Cocoltchos's information about Orange County, California, Moore's study of Indiana, and Goldberg's analysis of the Colorado Klan. Other recent books and articles support their conclusions.

These studies of members' characteristics found that Klansmen represented a near cross section of the white Protestant male population in their communities. Everywhere, the Klan fought to overcome the power of business and professional elites, except in some small towns. Outside those towns, few members of these elites joined the Klan, and those who did tended to be the younger members who evidently believed that their ambitions could be best furthered by the Klan.

In these communities as a whole, Catholics, blacks, Jews, and recent immigrants formed a very small part of the population. The few exceptions were the black population of Indianapolis, which almost equaled the proportion of blacks in the country; the German Catholic population of Anaheim, California, which led the anti-Klan elite there; and the Mexican-American Catholic population of Orange County, which was thoroughly segregated when the Klan was organized and which the Klan consequently ignored altogether. The percentages of those minorities in these communities were insignificant compared with the proportions of these same minorities in major cities like New York, Chicago, Cleveland, and St. Louis, where native white Protestants constituted a minority of the residents (in some cases, less than one-quarter).

Klansmen were concentrated in middle white-collar positions and among small businessmen. Those who were blue-collar workers were overwhelmingly in skilled positions. Members belonged to all major Protestant denominations, but the Klan included very few members of fundamentalist sects. They attended services in Northern Methodist and Disciples of Christ churches especially. Klansmen generally had lived in their communities longer than nonmembers, usually at least ten years before they joined the order, yet they tended to be younger. Well over three-quarters of them were married. They belonged to more civic and fraternal organizations, particularly to the Masons. They possessed greater wealth, more property, and registered to vote in 1924 in much larger proportions than did nonmembers in their communities. Klansmen in the mid-1920s decidedly were not a fringe group of vigilantes; they were solid middle-class citizens and individuals of high Victorian character.

Indiana served as the focal point of Klan power in America. The Indiana Klan enrolled more members and a much larger proportion of the state population than did the Klaverns of any other state. The state capital, Indianapolis, was referred to by a leading historian of the Klan as the "Center of Klandom."

Information about Klan members' characteristics in three Indiana communities, representative of the states' large and small cities and of its rural towns, illustrates the Klan's composition in Indiana. The three communities are Indianapolis, a major industrial and commercial city whose population in 1920 was 314,000; Richmond, an industrial city with a population of 27,000 in 1920; and Crown Point, a commercial township of 4,312, which served the surrounding farming area.

Individuals in high white-collar occupations among Indianapolis's Klan members equalled almost exactly the proportion of men with that status in the city as a whole. However, the Indianapolis Klan contained none of the high executives of the city's largest corporations—such as Van Camp, one of the largest food canning companies in the nation; Eli Lilly, a major pharmaceutical manufacturer; and the Stutz and Dusenburg motor-car companies. Disciples of Christ, Lutheran, and United Brethren ranked highest among the church affiliations of Indianapolis's Klansmen.

About 75 percent of Richmond's Klan members occupied white-collar or skilled-worker positions compared to 64 percent of non-Klansmen in such positions. However, non-Klansmen filled the city's highest white-collar jobs in considerably larger proportions than did Klansmen. The greatest differences between the Protestant church affiliations of Richmond's Klan members and those of Richmond's citizens as a whole lay in the much higher proportion of Klansmen who belonged to Presbyterian, United Brethren, Disciples of Christ, and Episcopal congregations.

The occupational profile of Crown Point's Klan members resembled that of Indianapolis and Richmond Knights. Moore found that "Crown Point's wealthiest citizens did not appear to play any role in the Klan." Sixty-one percent of Crown Point's church-member Knights belonged to Methodist, Lutheran, Presbyterian, or Disciples of Christ congregations.

In each of these three Indiana communities, Kleagles and local Klan organizers used vocal and written criticism of American Catholics, blacks, Jews, and recent immigrants as part of their recruiting rhetoric. However, Moore concluded that the Indiana Klan "did not employ violence as a strategy, and only a tiny fraction of the hooded order's membership ever engaged in violent or threatening acts."

The characteristics of Orange County Klansmen differed little from those of the Indiana members. For fast growing Anaheim, the county seat, Cocoltchos derived statistical information for Klan, non-Klan, and active anti-Klan residents. The latter included those who had joined the club devoted to defeating the Klan politically and also those who had signed both of the petitions opposing the Anaheim Klan.

A much higher proportion of Anaheim Klansmen held professional and administrative jobs than did non-Klansmen, but twice as high a percentage of active anti-Klansmen—who included the city's established business, professional and farming elite—occupied such positions as Klan members. Klansmen worked in trade, service, and skilled positions in greater proportions than did either of the other groups.

Over half the Anaheim Klansmen with a specific church affiliation belonged to Disciples of Christ and Northern Methodist congregations. Catholic was the largest single church affiliation among those actively opposed to the Klan —over 25 percent.

Cocoltchos also collected statistics for Anaheim Klan leaders and the anti-Klan elite, which led activities in the city directed against the Klan. His data proved very informative for an understanding of the Klan's conflicts with the Anaheim business and professional elite.

The anti-Klan elite of three hundred individuals overlapped to a very large extent Anaheim's traditional elite. The median age of the elite in 1924 was fifty-four years compared to forty-two-and-a-half years for Klan leaders. The median years of prior residence in Anaheim was thirty-and-a-half years for the elite and fifteen years for Klan leaders in 1924. Ninety percent of elite members belonged to civic clubs, while 72 percent of Klan leaders did.

Forty-five percent of the elite occupied professional and administrative positions compared to 27 percent of the Klan leaders. Half of the latter worked in the retail and wholesale trades. The median wealth of Klan leaders amounted to

$7,460 compared to $36,534 for members of the anti-Klan elite. Seventy-two percent of Klansmen had already run for or held public office in 1924 compared to 55 percent of the elite. The Klan leaders, despite their role as prosperous community activists, faced a near united front of Anaheim's wealthy, well-entrenched business, professional, and large farmer elite.

In the smaller city of Fullerton, California, Klansmen differed from the non-Klan population largely in their much larger proportion of members working in service and skilled jobs. Klan members owned more property and acknowledged much greater median wealth. A significantly higher proportion of them were married, belonged to civic clubs, and voted in 1924. Klansmen belonged predominantly to Disciples of Christ, Northern Methodist, Episcopalian, and Northern Baptist churches.

Half of the Ku Klux Klan's members in Colorado lived in the capital and largest city, Denver. A much higher percentage of Denver's Klansmen worked in both high and middle white-collar occupations than did members of the male population as a whole. However, Goldberg found that "Denver's elite clubs listed only a handful of Klansmen among their members," and none belonged to the most prestigious social clubs, such as the Denver Club, the Denver Country Club, and the University Club. Only one Klan member was listed in Denver's Social Register. A much lower proportion of Klansmen than male citizens of Denver worked in skilled, semi-skilled, and unskilled labor jobs. Goldberg was unable to collect information about individual church membership, but over 70 percent of Denver's Disciples of Christ churches, 33 percent of its Methodist churches, and 25 percent of its Baptist churches actively supported the Klan.

A Kleagle did not arrive in Canon City, Colorado (with a population of 4,551 in 1920) and surrounding rural Fremont County until 1923. Of the Klan's members between 1924 and 1928, 40 percent occupied high or middle white-collar positions. Only 1.5 percent worked at unskilled jobs. One-quarter of Canon City's Klansmen belonged to the Masons as well. Klan-member ministers guided the town's Methodist and Baptist churches and the fundamentalist Church of Christ congregation.

These statistics bear out Leonard Moore's conclusions about the meaning of the latest books and articles about the Klan:

> Together, these recent works make it nearly impossible to interpret the 1920's Klan as an aberrant fringe group.... In-depth analysis of state and community Klans from different regions of the country make it clear... that the Klan was composed primarily of average citizens representing nearly all parts of America's white Protestant society....

* * *

Leonard Moore summarized what he called the Klan's "basic message":

> The average white Protestant was under attack: his values and traditions were being undermined; his vision of America's national purpose and social order appeared threatened; and his ability to shape the course of public affairs seemed to have been diminished.

Basing its political activity upon this message and the failure of state and local elites to address it satisfactorily, the Klan won a high degree of political power and influence in the states of Alabama,

California, Colorado, Georgia, Indiana, Kansas, Louisiana, Oklahoma, Oregon, and Texas. It took political control of hundreds of American cities and towns, including Akron, Atlanta, Birmingham, Dallas, Denver, El Paso, Evansville, Gary, Indianapolis, Little Rock, Oklahoma City, Portland, Oregon, Terre Haute, and Youngstown.

However, the powerful business elite of Richmond, Indiana, thwarted the Klan's political efforts. Richmond's major employers were International Harvester and the Pennsylvania Railroad. The successful anti-Klan forces were led by members of the Rotary Club, limited to representatives of the city's industrial corporations, top executives of its other businesses, and its most successful retail merchants. The Rotary received aid from the Kiwanis Club, dominated by small businessmen and city officials.

Explaining the Klan's near-total triumph in Indiana, Moore concluded that the state and local elites "stood nearly alone as a white Protestant social group unwilling to support the Klan." That group, he declared, surpassed Indiana's Catholics, blacks, and Jews as the order's chief opponents. When Indiana's Klan chapters sought political power, Moore found "their most powerful rivals were ... the Rotary Club and the Chamber of Commerce, not the powerless or nonexistent ethnic minorities." When the Klan swept the state election of 1924, "the real victims were not the state's Catholics but the Republican ... political establishment, which, almost overnight, found itself removed from power."

In Indianapolis, businessmen organized in the Chamber of Commerce and the Indiana Taxpayers' Association formed an important component of the Old Guard Republican establishment. School issues symbolized the conflict between the Old Guard and the Klan. Voters, led by the Klan, approved a series of school bond issues, meant to renovate dilapidated schools and to alleviate overcrowding in the city's elementary and high schools. The Chamber of Commerce and the Taxpayers' Association organized a Citizen's League to hide their own opposition to all spending for schools, except for a segregated high school to educate the city's black children. The school board refused to appropriate funds for any other construction. In the school-board election of 1925, the Klan elected all five of its candidates to replace the five Citizens' League incumbents. A school construction program started soon afterward. Aided by voter mobilization for the school-board election, the Klan won virtually every city political office in 1925.

In Lake County, where Crown Point served as county seat, Moore concluded: "Prohibition enforcement and public corruption had a ... preponderant influence on Klan political victories." Exports of liquor by Chicago criminal organizations had left Lake County soaked in alcohol and full of corruption. In the November 1924 elections, every Lake County candidate endorsed by the Klan— including those in Crown Point—won election....

* * *

Starting in the mid-1920s, the Ku Klux Klan ebbed in numbers and in influence. The three chief reasons for this decline were the inability of the order to achieve its promises, the demoralization of members because of scandals involving Klan leaders and spokesmen (whom members expected to appear and act more honestly than their opponents), and counterattacks by the ethnic and religious groups and business elites which held political control of the nation's major cities.

After an initial burst of enthusiasm for the Klan, when it gained control of city, county, and state governments, inexperienced Klan elected officials found their programs rendered ineffective by professional politicians. Therefore voters—including Klan members—who had supported the Klan were disappointed by the order's accomplishments.

For example, in Indiana, where the Klan elected its candidate for governor and won large majorities in both houses of the legislature in 1925, Klansmen enacted only one of their proposals into law. That measure, obliging all public schools to teach their students about the United States Constitution, obtained bipartisan support.

Other bills introduced by Klan legislators—such as legislation mandating daily Bible reading in Indiana's schools, forcing parochial schools to use the same textbooks as public schools, and compelling public schools to hire only public-school graduates as teachers—failed to pass. Legislators, especially in the state senate, and the Klan governor killed such measures rather than face the controversy that such blatant attacks on religious liberty would cause. The near certainty of adverse judicial decisions increased the reluctance of these politicians (particularly those who hoped to seek national office) to risk their careers.

Indiana Grand Dragon David C. Stephenson's crimes damaged the Klan most. Stephenson collected over a million dollars from Klansmen between 1922 and 1924. Most of this was used to support a most un-Klansmanlike life-style. He bought luxurious automobiles, an imposing suburban home, and a yacht on which he entertained numerous women. He also purchased a large liquor supply. Several times, his drinking binges brought him close to arrest by police.

In April 1925, Stephenson took one of his female companions, twenty-eight-year-old Madge Oberholtzer of Indianapolis, on an overnight train ride to Hammond, Indiana. During this trip, Stephenson repeatedly raped Oberholtzer. When they arrived in Hammond, she bought and swallowed a deadly poison. It took effect during the return trip to Indianapolis, but Stephenson refused to let the suffering woman see a physician until they reached Indianapolis. By then it was too late.

Before Oberholtzer died, she gave police a full statement. The State of Indiana charged Stephenson with causing her suicide because he had forced her to lose "that which she held dearer than life—her chastity." Stephenson was indicted and convicted of kidnapping, rape, and second-degree murder. He received a sentence of life imprisonment.

Stephenson confidently expected a pardon from Indiana's Governor Ed Jackson, a Klansman. When Jackson refused his request, Stephenson offered to testify about the corruption of Jackson and other state and local Klan officials. As a result, Mayor John Duvall of Indianapolis went to prison for violating the Corrupt Practices Act—so did the county sheriff, its congressman, the city purchasing agent, and a large number of less important Klan officeholders. Based on Stephenson's testimony, a grand jury indicted Governor Jackson for bribery, but he escaped prison because the statute of limitations on his offenses had expired. Soon after these revelations Klan membership in Indiana began shrinking. Fewer than seven thousand members remained by 1928.

Stephenson's trial, well publicized by newspapers and magazines, distressed Klansmen throughout America. Their outrage increased when they learned about the crimes of Dr. John Galen Locke, Colorado's Grand Dragon and Denver's Exalted Cyclops. In January 1925, Locke arranged the kidnapping of Klan member Keith Boehm, a high-school student. Taken to Locke's office and threatened with castration unless he married his pregnant girlfriend, Boehm agreed to the marriage. Locke explained to the Denver *Post* that "When I learned of what happened... I meant to see to it that young Boehm, as a Klansman, should do the manly thing." The district attorney brought kidnapping and conspiracy charges against Locke. Luckily for Locke, Klan opponent Judge Ben B. Lindsay of the juvenile court disqualified himself from the case. Locke's attorney engineered changes of venue until the case landed before a Klansman judge who found technical reasons to dismiss it.

Then federal Treasury officials charged Locke with failing to report any income or to pay income taxes despite the fees he earned as a physician and from Klan initiation fees and commissions on the sale of Klan robes. Locke went to prison until Colorado's governor, who had been chosen by the Grand Dragon, established a fund to pay Locke's back taxes. Other Klansmen paid Locke's fine. Mass defections from Colorado's Klan began. Imperial Wizard Hiram Evans requested Locke's resignation, and Locke immediately complied.

In Anaheim, the politically defeated Chamber of Commerce and Rotary Club collected sufficient signatures on petitions late in 1924 to force recently elected Klan city council members into a recall election. Minor scandals and a failure to appreciably diminish Prohibition violations already had cost the Klan some support. Anaheim's Klan leader, Reverend Mr. Meyers, sought to renew Klan members' enthusiasm by bringing Protestant evangelist E. E. Bulgin to the city in January 1925 to conduct revival meetings. Bulgin arrived on January 11, set up his tent, and began the services.

A group of Anaheim's ministers sent Bulgin and local newspapers a letter inquiring whether he had been brought to Anaheim "for the express purpose of assisting in the re-election of the members of the city council whose removal is being sought because of their Klan affiliations." Bulgin proclaimed his neutrality concerning the election. At the following evening's revival meeting, however, Bulgin told his assembled flock that "the way to vote right and never make a mistake is to find out what side the ex-saloonkeepers, the bootleggers and the harlots are on and get on the other side." Bulgin's nightly meetings attracted large and enthusiastic audiences.

Representatives of the Chamber of Commerce and of the Rotary and the Lion's clubs of Anaheim contacted the Knights of Columbus and the Catholic Truth Society in many parts of the West, asking for information about Bulgin. An Okmulgee, Oklahoma, attorney replied that Bulgin's real specialty was selling stock in fictitious or worthless mining companies. In return, he had taken deeds to some citizens' homes. Telegrams from Eastland, Texas, and Lewiston, Idaho, stated that Bulgin had been chased out of those cities after being charged with fraud in numerous lawsuits. Two of Anaheim's newspapers printed these replies.

On February 3, 1925, almost 77 percent of Anaheim's voters—a larger proportion than the record turnout less than six months before that had elected the Klan councilmen—went to the polls. Every Klan-endorsed council member was recalled by a substantial margin.

The Ku Klux Klan paid dearly for its obvious role in reinvigorating Victorian racism and religious bigotry. Kenneth Jackson pointed out that "Relatively few reports of Klan-related violence between 1915 and 1924 are contained in the files of United States Department of Justice." However, in September 1923, the *Literary Digest*, a Klan opponent, published an article entitled "The Klan as a Victim of Mob Violence." The Indiana state *Fiery Cross* complained in 1924 that "The list of the outrages against Klansmen is so long that it would take weeks to compile even an incomplete list."

In dozens of cities—such as Fort Worth; San Antonio; Terre Haute; and Portland, Maine—Klan headquarters and meeting places were bombed and burned. After numerous warnings, the shop believed to be the publication headquarters of the Chicago Klan's journal, *Dawn*, was gutted by a bomb. An editorial in the *Fiery Cross* asked plaintively: Why does not anyone "ever read about halls of the Knights of Columbus being destroyed mysteriously?"

Catholics and blacks had threatened the Klan with violence. The editor of the *Catholic World*, published by the Paulist Fathers, warned early in 1923 that because of the Klan, Catholics "may be driven to self-defense, even to the extent of bloodshed." The equally staid *Bulletin* of the National Catholic Welfare Council declared:

> In this struggle for the supremacy of law and order over lawlessness and despotism, no quarter should be given those self-appointed patriots who distort and disgrace our Americanism and whose weapons are darkness, the mask, violence, intimidation and mob rule.

The Harlem-based radical black nationalist African Black Brotherhood proclaimed in its journal that "The nation-wide mobilization under the Christian cross and the Stars and Stripes of cracker America is plainly an act of war . . . , war of the cracker element of the white race against the whole Negro race." The Chicago *Defender*, the most widely read black newspaper in the United States, urged its readers in a front-page editorial to prepare to fight "against sons who now try to win by signs and robes what their fathers lost by fire and sword."

When the Klan began organizing in and around the nation's largest cities, members of the order soon discovered that white Protestant authority no longer prevailed throughout the land. In these cities Catholics, blacks, Jews, and recent immigrants formed a majority of the population—sometimes a very large majority.

Soon after Kleagles ventured into New York City, Irish Catholic Mayor John F. Hylan told his police commissioner in 1922: "I desire you to treat this group of racial and religious haters as you would the Reds and bomb throwers. Drive them out of our city." Two New York City grand juries commenced investigations of the Klan, and the New York City Council quickly passed legislation forcing associations not incorporated in New York to file membership lists. Klan members in New York and suburban Westchester County during the 1920s totalled about 16,000, less than Klan membership in Akron or Youngstown, Ohio.

Chicago's large Klan chapter did nothing to help enforce Prohibition laws.

However, the West Suburban Ministers and Citizens Association organized to help enforce those laws in and around Chicago. Soon afterward, the association's leader, a minister, was found shot to death a block from Al Capone's headquarters in suburban Cicero. This warning ended private attempts to fight Prohibition offenses in Chicago.

The Chicago City Council appointed a five-man committee in December 1922 to investigate the Klan and then report back to the council. The five members were identified as Ald. Robert J. Mulcahy, Irish; Ald. Louis B. Henderson, black; Ald. U. S. Schwartz, Jewish; Ald. S. S. Walkowiak, Polish; and Ald. Oscar H. Olsen, Norwegian. Largely as a result of the committee's unanimous report, the city council resolved by a vote of fifty-six to two to rid Chicago's municipal payroll of Klansmen. The Illinois legislature also received the report and consequently passed a bill prohibiting the wearing of masks in public. The measure cleared the Illinois House of Representatives by a vote of 100 to 2, and the Illinois State Senate by 26 to 1. Illinois's Klansmen were thus forced to hold most of their parades, picnics, and other gatherings in Indiana and Ohio.

Boston's Mayor James Michael Curley barred Klan meetings in Boston, and the city council approved his order. He gave speeches before burning crosses and in an emotion-choked voice always proclaimed: "There it burns, the cross of hatred upon which Our Lord, Jesus Christ, was crucified—the cross of human avarice, and not the cross of love and charity. . . ." Homes and stores of suspected Klansmen in Boston were bombarded with bricks and stones.

On the outskirts of major cities, where the Klan sometimes dared to march or meet, the Knights received even worse treatment. Ten thousand Klansmen gathered near Carnegie, just outside Pittsburgh, on August 25, 1923, to witness an initiation featuring an address by Imperial Wizard Hiram Evans. When they tried to march back to the heavily Catholic, immigrant, and black town, however, a mob stood in their path. The Klansmen continued marching through a hail of rocks and bottles. Then a volley of shots rang out. One Klansman lay dead, a dozen others fell seriously wounded, and about a hundred more suffered minor injuries. The other Klan members turned and ran.

Commenting on the Carnegie massacre, the Washington *Star* declared that "Parades of the Klan, with its masked and hooded members, tend to create disorder and rioting." An editorial in the Washington *Post* stated that the paper agreed with the *New York Times* that "The Klan is merely reaping as it has sown."

Other Klan meetings were broken up by lethal shotgun blasts. In New York's suburban county of Queens, police ended a Memorial Day parade of 4,000 Klansmen by waving waiting cars through the whole parade line.

Hiram Evans summarized the Klan's plight when he stated in March 1926 that "The Nordic American today is a stranger in large parts of the land his fathers gave him. Moreover, he is a most unwelcome stranger, and one most spat upon."

Evans described accurately the result of the Klan's defense of Victorianism's essence. The most important social trends and the great social reform movements of the nineteenth and twentieth centuries had indeed left Klansmen strangers in most of the land their ancestors had settled.

# POSTSCRIPT

## Was the Ku Klux Klan of the 1920s an Extremist Movement?

Bennett places the 1920s Ku Klux Klan within the nativist tradition of American right-wing political movements. He argues that Klan ideology reasserted its hostility toward the Catholic and Jewish immigrants from southern and eastern Europe who had poured into America since the 1890s. He points out that Irish Catholics were associated with the saloons and the political bosses who controlled the machines in the large cities. In Bennett's view, the Klan was made up of Protestant fundamentalists who wished to reassert the traditional values of an earlier America.

Coben argues that many Klansmen were attracted to the Klan because they were legitimately concerned with the breakdown of traditional standards of morality and the increases in alcohol consumption and crime that they believed were occurring in their communities. Coben also argues that Klansmen were more often middle-class businessmen, small shopkeepers, and skilled workers who were fighting the well-to-do businessmen, the large farmers, and their allied Catholic, Jewish, and black ethnic groups for political control.

Recent scholarship on the 1920s Klan has focused on its grass-roots participation in local and state politics. Klansmen are viewed less as extremists and more as political pressure groups whose aims were to gain control of various local and state governmental offices. The best overview of this perspective is Shawn Lay, ed., *The Invisible Empire in the West: Toward a New Historical Appraisal of the Ku Klux Klan of the 1920s* (University of Illinois Press, 1992).

Indiana was at the heart of the second Klan and is the focus of much recent research. A good starting point is William E. Wilson's "That Long Hot Summer in Indiana," *American Heritage* (August 1965). M. William Lutholtz gives a well-researched but old-fashioned interpretative journalistic study of the amoral, opportunistic *Grand Dragon: D.C. Stephenson and the Ku Klux Klan in Indiana* (Purdue University Press, 1991), while Leonard J. Moore, in *Citizen Klansmen: The Ku Klux Klan in Indiana, 1921–1928* (University of North Carolina Press, 1991), sees the Indiana group as concerned, middle-class citizens who are challenging the local elites to clean up the political and immoral corruption in the state in order to reinforce traditional family values. Nancy MacLean, in *Behind the Mask of Chivalry: The Making of the Second Ku Klux Klan* (Oxford University Press, 1994), argues that the second Klan's lower middle class subverted traditional Republican values into a "reactionary populism" that bore a "family resemblance" to the movement Hitler rode to power in the 1930s.

# ISSUE 11

## Was the New Deal an Effective Answer to the Great Depression?

**YES: William E. Leuchtenburg,** from "The Achievement of the New Deal," in Harvard Sitkoff, ed., *Fifty Years Later: The New Deal Evaluated* (Alfred A. Knopf, 1985)

**NO: Gary Dean Best,** from *Pride, Prejudice, and Politics: Roosevelt Versus Recovery, 1933–1938* (Praeger, 1991)

### ISSUE SUMMARY

**YES:** Professor of history William E. Leuchtenburg contends that the New Deal extended the power of the national government in order to humanize the worst features of American capitalism.

**NO:** Professor of history Gary Dean Best argues that Roosevelt established an antibusiness environment with the creation of the New Deal regulatory programs, which retarded the nation's economic recovery from the Great Depression until World War II.

The catastrophe triggered by the 1929 Wall Street debacle crippled the American economy, deflated the optimistic future most Americans assumed to be their birthright, and ripped apart the values by which the country's businesses, farms, and governments were run. In the 1920s the whirlwind of a boom economy had sucked people into its vortex. During the next decade, the inertia of the Great Depression stifled their attempts to make ends meet.

The world depression of the 1930s began in the United States, which is where some of the most serious effects were felt. The United States had suffered periodic economic setbacks—in 1873, 1893, 1907, and 1920—but those slumps had been limited and temporary. The omnipotence of American productivity, the ebullient American spirit, and the self-deluding thought "it can't happen here" blocked out any consideration of an economic collapse that might devastate the capitalist economy and threaten U.S. democratic government.

All aspects of American society trembled from successive jolts; there were 4 million unemployed people in 1930 and 9 million more by 1932. Those who had not lost their jobs took pay cuts or worked for scrip. Charitable organizations attempted to provide for millions of homeless and hungry people, but their resources were not adequate. There was no security for those whose savings were lost forever when banks failed or stocks declined.

Manufacturing halted, industry shut down, and farmers destroyed wheat, corn, and milk rather than sell them at a loss. Worse, there were millions of homeless Americans—refugees from the cities roaming the nation on freight trains, victims of the drought of the Dust Bowl seeking a new life farther west, and hobo children estranged from their parents. Physicians reported increased cases of malnutrition. Some people plundered grocery stores rather than starve.

Business and government leaders alike seemed immobilized by the economic giant that had fallen to its knees. "In other periods of depression there has always been hope, but as I look about, I now see nothing to give ground for hope—nothing of man," said former president Calvin Coolidge on New Year's Day 1933. Herbert Hoover, the incumbent president at the start of the Great Depression, attempted some relief programs. However, they were ineffective considering the magnitude of the unemployment, hunger, and distress. Nor did Hoover's initiatives recognize the need for serious changes in the relationship between the federal government and society or for any modification of its relationship with individual Americans.

As governor of New York, Franklin D. Roosevelt (who was elected president in 1932) had introduced some relief measures, such as industrial welfare and a comprehensive system of unemployment remedies, to alleviate the social and economic problems facing the citizens of the state. Yet his campaign did little to reassure his critics that he was more than a "Little Lord Fauntleroy" rich boy who wanted to be the president. In light of later developments, Roosevelt may have been the only presidential candidate to deliver more programs than he actually promised.

In the following selections, William E. Leuchtenburg claims that Roosevelt's New Deal revolutionized American politics, reorganized the government to increase the powers of the presidency, and assumed responsibility for managing the economy. But conservative historian Gary Dean Best is highly critical of Roosevelt's pragmatic approach to solving the depression. Roosevelt established an antibusiness environment, maintains Best, when he created a host of New Deal regulatory programs whose long-range effect was to retard the nation's economic recovery until World War II.

# YES William E. Leuchtenburg

## THE ACHIEVEMENT OF THE NEW DEAL

The fiftieth anniversary of the New Deal, launched on March 4, 1933, comes at a time when it has been going altogether out of fashion. Writers on the left, convinced that the Roosevelt experiment was either worthless or pernicious, have assigned it to the dustbin of history. Commentators on the right, though far less conspicuous, see in the New Deal the origins of the centralized state they seek to dismantle. Indeed, the half-century of the age of Roosevelt is being commemorated in the presidency of Ronald Reagan, who, while never tiring of quoting FDR, insists that the New Deal derived from Italian fascism....

During the 1960s historians not only dressed up these objections as though they were new revelations but carried their disappointment with contemporary liberalism to the point of arguing either that the New Deal was not just inadequate but actually malign or that the New Deal was so negligible as to constitute a meaningless episode. This estimate derived in large part from disaffection with the welfare state, which Herbert Marcuse in *One-Dimensional Man* characterized as "a state of unfreedom," and which, as one critic noted, some considered "the ultimate form of repressive superego." The New Deal was now perceived to be elitist, since it had neglected to consult the poor about what legislation they wanted, or to encourage the participation of ghetto-dwellers in decision-making. Roosevelt's policies, historians maintained, redounded to the benefit of those who already had advantages—wealthier staple farmers, organized workers, business corporations, the "deserving poor"—while displacing sharecroppers and neglecting the powerless. An "antirevolutionary response to a situation that had revolutionary potentialities," the New Deal, it was said, missed opportunities to nationalize the banks and restructure the social order. Even "providing assistance to the needy and... rescuing them from starvation" served conservative ends, historians complained, for these efforts "sapped organized radicalism of its waning strength and of its potential constituency among the unorganized and discontented." The Roosevelt Administration, it has been asserted, failed to achieve more than it did not as a result of the strength of conservative opposition but because of the intellectual deficiencies of the

New Dealers and because Roosevelt deliberately sought to save "large-scale corporate capitalism." In *Towards a New Past,* the New Left historian Barton Bernstein summed up this point of view: "The New Deal failed to solve the problem of depression, it failed to raise the impoverished, it failed to redistribute income, it failed to extend equality and generally countenanced racial discrimination and segregation."

Although the characterization of Bernstein as "New Left" suggests that he represents a deviant persuasion, the New Left perspective has, in fact, all but become the new orthodoxy, even though there is not yet any New Left survey of the domestic history of the United States in the 1930s. This emphasis has so permeated writing on the New Deal in the past generation that an instructor who wishes to assign the latest thought on the age of Roosevelt has a wide choice of articles and anthologies that document the errors of the New Deal but no assessment of recent vintage that explores its accomplishments.

The fiftieth anniversary of the New Deal provides the occasion for a modest proposal—that we reintroduce some tension into the argument over the interpretation of the Roosevelt years. If historians are to develop a credible synthesis, it is important to regain a sense of the achievement of the New Deal. As it now stands, we have a dialectic that is all antithesis with no thesis. The so-called "debate" about the New Deal is not truly a debate, for even some of the historians who dispute the New Left assertions agree that one can only take a melancholy view of the period. The single question asked is whether the failure of the New Deal was the fault of the Roosevelt Administration or the result of the strength of conservative forces beyond the government's control; the fact of failure is taken as the basic postulate. As a first step toward a more considered evaluation, one has to remind one's self not only of what the New Deal did not do, but of what it achieved.

## NEW DEAL CHANGES

Above all, one needs to recognize how markedly the New Deal altered the character of the State in America. Indeed, though for decades past European theorists had been talking about *der Staat,* there can hardly be said to have been a State in America in the full meaning of the term before the New Deal. If you had walked into an American town in 1932, you would have had a hard time detecting any sign of a federal presence, save perhaps for the post office and even many of today's post offices date from the 1930s. Washington rarely affected people's lives directly. There was no national old-age pension system, no federal unemployment compensation, no aid to dependent children, no federal housing, no regulation of the stock market, no withholding tax, no federal school lunch, no farm subsidy, no national minimum wage law, no welfare state. As late as Herbert Hoover's presidency, it was regarded as axiomatic that government activity should be minimal. In the pre-Roosevelt era, even organized labor and the National Conference of Social Workers opposed federal action on behalf of the unemployed. The New Deal sharply challenged these shibboleths. From 1933 to 1938, the government intervened in a myriad of ways from energizing the economy to fostering unionization....

This vast expansion of government led inevitably to the concentration of much greater power in the presidency, whose authority was greatly augmented under FDR. Rexford Tugwell has written of Roosevelt: "No monarch,... unless it may have been Elizabeth or her magnificent Tudor father, or maybe Alexander or Augustus Caesar, can have given quite that sense of serene presiding, of gathering up into himself, of really representing, a whole people." The President became, in Sidney Hyman's words, "the chief economic engineer," to whom Congress naturally turned for the setting of economic policy. Roosevelt stimulated interest in public affairs by his fireside chats and freewheeling press conferences, shifted the balance between the White House and Capitol Hill by assuming the role of Chief Legislator, and eluded the routinized traditional departments by creating emergency agencies. In 1939 he established the Executive Office of the President, giving the Chief Executive a central staff office for the first time. "The verdict of history," wrote Clinton Rossiter, "will surely be that he left the Presidency a more splendid instrument of democracy than he found it."

To staff the national agencies, Roosevelt turned to a new class of people: the university-trained experts. Before FDR, professors had not had an important role in the national government, save briefly in World War I, but when Roosevelt ran for president in 1932, he recruited advisers, most of them from Columbia University, who supplied him with ideas and helped write his speeches. During the First Hundred Days, large numbers of professors, encouraged by FDR's reliance on the Brain Trust, flocked to Washington to draft New Deal legislation and to administer New Deal agencies. The radical literary critic Edmund Wilson wrote, "Everywhere in the streets and offices you run into old acquaintances: the editors and writers of the liberal press, the 'progressive' young instructors from the colleges, the intelligent foundation workers, the practical idealists of settlement houses." He added: "The bright boys of the Eastern universities, instead of being obliged to choose, as they were twenty years ago, between business, the bond-selling game and the field of foreign missions, can come on and get jobs in Washington."...

This corps of administrators made it possible for Roosevelt to carry out a major change in the role of the federal government. Although the New Deal always operated within a capitalist matrix and the government sought to enhance profitmaking, Roosevelt and his lieutenants rejected the traditional view that government was the handmaiden of business or that government and business were coequal sovereigns. As a consequence, they adopted measures to discipline corporations, to require a sharing of authority with government and unions, and to hold businessmen accountable....

Through a series of edicts and statutes, the administration invaded the realm of the banker by establishing control over the nation's money supply. The government clamped an embargo on gold, took the United States off the gold standard, and nullified the requirement for the payment of gold in private contracts. In 1935 a resentful Supreme Court sustained this authority, although a dissenting justice said that this was Nero at his worst. The Glass-Steagall Banking Act (1933) stripped commercial banks of the privilege of engaging in investment banking, and established federal insurance of bank deposits, an innovation which the leading monetary historians have called "the structural change most conducive to monetary stability since bank notes were taxed out of existence immediately after the Civil War." The Banking Act of 1935 gave the United States what other industrial nations had long had, but America lacked —central banking. This series of changes transformed the relationship between the government and the financial community from what it had been when Grover Cleveland had gone, hat in hand, to beseech J. P. Morgan for help. As Charles Beard observed: "Having lost their gold coins and bullion to the Federal Government and having filled their vaults with federal bonds and other paper, bankers have become in a large measure mere agents of the Government in Washington. No longer do these powerful interests stand, so to speak, 'outside the Government' and in a position to control or dictate to it."

A number of other enactments helped transfer authority from Wall Street to Washington. The Securities Act of 1933 established government supervision of the issue of securities, and made company directors civilly and criminally liable for misinformation on the statements they were required to file with each new issue. The Securities and Exchange Act of 1934 initiated federal supervision of the stock exchanges, which to this day operate under the lens of the Securities and Exchange Commission (SEC). The Holding Company Act of 1935 levelled some of the utility pyramids, dissolving all utility holding companies that were more than twice removed from their operating companies, and increased the regulatory powers of the SEC over public utilities. Robert Sobel has concluded that the 1934 law marked "a shift of economic power from the lower part of Manhattan, where it had been for over a century, to Washington." To be sure, financiers continued to make important policy choices, but they never again operated in the uninhibited universe of the Great Bull Market. By the spring of 1934, one writer was already reporting:

> Financial news no longer originates in Wall Street.... News of a financial nature in Wall Street now is merely an echo of events which take place in Washington.... The pace of the ticker is determined now in Washington not in company boardrooms or in brokerage offices.... In Wall Street it is no longer asked what some big trader is doing, what some important banker thinks, what opinion some eminent lawyer holds about some pressing question of the day. The query in Wall Street has become: "What's the news from Washington?"

The age of Roosevelt focused attention on Washington, too, by initiatives in fields that had been regarded as exclusively within the private orbit, notably in housing. The Home Owners' Loan Corporation, created in 1933, saved tens of thousands of homes from foreclosure by refinancing mortgages. In 1934 the Federal Housing Administration (FHA) began its program of insuring loans for the construction and renovation of private homes, and over the next generation more than 10 million FHA-financed units were built. Before the New Deal, the national government had never engaged in public housing, except for the World War I emergency, but agencies like the Public Works Administration now broke precedent. The Tennessee Valley Authority laid out the model town of Norris, the Federal Emergency Relief Administration (FERA) experimented with subsistence homesteads, and the Resettlement Administration created greenbelt communities, entirely new towns girdled by green countryside. When in 1937 the Wagner-Steagall Act created the U.S. Housing Authority, it assured public housing a permanent place in American life.

## A NEW DEAL FOR THE COMMON MAN

The New Deal profoundly altered industrial relations by throwing the weight of the government behind efforts to unionize workers. At the outset of the Great Depression, the American labor movement was "an anachronism in the world," for only a tiny minority of factory workers were unionized. Employers hired and fired and imposed punishments at will, used thugs as strikebreakers and private police, stockpiled industrial munitions, and ran company towns as feudal fiefs. In an astonishingly short period in the Roosevelt years a very different pattern emerged. Under the umbrella of Section 7(a) of the National Industrial Recovery Act of 1933 and of the far-reaching Wagner Act of 1935, union organizers gained millions of recruits in such open-shop strongholds as steel, automobiles, and textiles. Employees won wage rises, reductions in hours, greater job security, freedom from the tyranny of company guards, and protection against arbitrary punishment. Thanks to the National Recovery Administration and the Guffey acts, coal miners achieved the outlawing of compulsory company houses and stores. Steel workers, who in 1920 labored twelve-hour shifts seven days a week at the blast furnaces, were to become so powerful that in the postwar era they would win not merely paid vacations but sabbatical leaves. A British analyst has concluded: "From one of the most restrictive among industrially advanced nations, the labour code of the United States (insofar as it could be said to exist before 1933) was rapidly transformed into one of the most liberal," and these reforms, he adds, "were not the harvest of long-sustained agitation by trade unions, but were forced upon a partly skeptical labor movement by a government which led or carried it into maturity."

Years later, when David E. Lilienthal, the director of the Tennessee Valley Authority, was being driven to the airport to fly to Roosevelt's funeral, the TVA driver said to him:

> I won't forget what he did for me.... I spent the best years of my life working at the Appalachian Mills... and they didn't even treat us like humans. If you didn't do like they said, they always told you there was someone else to take your job. I had my mother and my sister to take care of. Sixteen cents an hour was what we got; a fellow can't live on that, and you had to get production even to get that, this Bedaux system; some fellows only got twelve cents. If you asked to get off on a Sunday, the foreman would say, "All right you stay away Sunday, but when you come back Monday someone else will have your job." No, sir, I won't forget what he done for us.

Helen Lynd has observed that the history of the United States is that of England fifty years later, and a half century after the welfare state had come to Western Europe, the New Deal brought it to America. The NRA wiped out sweatshops, and removed some 150,000 child laborers from factories. The Walsh-Healey Act of 1936 and the Fair Labor Standards Act of 1938 established the principle of a federally imposed minimal level of working conditions, and added further sanctions against child labor. If the New Deal did not do enough for the "one-third of a nation" to whom Roosevelt called attention, it at least made a beginning, through agencies like the Farm Security Administration, toward helping sharecroppers, tenant farmers, and migrants like John Steinbeck's Joads. Most important, it originated a new system of social rights to replace the dependence on private charity. The Social Security Act of 1935 created America's first national system of old-age pensions and initiated a federal-state program of unemployment insurance. It also authorized grants for the blind, for the incapacitated, and for dependent children, a feature that would have unimaginable long-range consequences....

Roosevelt himself affirmed the newly assumed attitudes in Washington in his annual message to Congress in 1938 when he declared: "Government has a final responsibility for the well-being of its citizenship. If private co-operative endeavor fails to provide work for willing hands and relief for the unfortunate, those suffering hardship from no fault of their own have a right to call upon the Government for aid; and a government worthy of its name must make fitting response."

## A NEW DEAL FOR THE UNEMPLOYED

Nothing revealed this approach so well as the New Deal's attention to the plight of the millions of unemployed. During the ten years between 1929 and 1939, one scholar has written, "more progress was made in public welfare and relief than in the three hundred years after this country was first settled." A series of alphabet agencies—the FERA, the CWA, the WPA —provided government work for the jobless, while the National Youth Administration (NYA) employed college students in museums, libraries, and laboratories, enabled high school students to remain in school, and set up a program of apprentice training. In Texas, the twenty-seven-year-old NYA director Lyndon Johnson put penniless young men like John Connally to work building roadside parks, and in North Carolina, the NYA employed, at 35 cents an hour, a Duke University law student, Richard Nixon.

In an address in Los Angeles in 1936, the head of FDR's relief operations, Harry Hopkins, conveyed the attitude of the New Deal toward those who were down and out:

> I am getting sick and tired of these people on the W.P.A. and local relief rolls being called chiselers and cheats.... These people... are just like the rest of us. They don't drink any more than us, they don't lie any more, they're no lazier than the rest of us—they're pretty much a cross section of the American people.... I have never believed that with our capitalistic system people have to be poor. I think it is an outrage that we should permit hundreds and hundreds of thousands of people to be ill clad, to live in miserable homes, not to have enough to eat; not to be able to send their children to school for the only reason that they are poor. I don't believe ever again in America we are going to permit the things to happen that have happened in the past to people. We are never going back... to the days of putting the old people in the alms houses, when a decent dignified pension at home will keep them there. We are coming to the day when we are going to have decent houses for the poor, when there is genuine and real security for everybody. I have gone

> all over the moral hurdles that people are poor because they are bad. I don't believe it. A system of government on that basis is fallacious.

Under the leadership of men like Hopkins, "Santa Claus incomparable and privy-builder without peer," projects of relief agencies and of the Public Works Administration (PWA) changed the face of the land. The PWA built thoroughfares like the Skyline Drive in Virginia and the Overseas Highway from Miami to Key West, constructed the Medical Center in Jersey City, burrowed Chicago's new subway, and gave Natchez, Mississippi, a new bridge, and Denver a modern water-supply system. Few New Yorkers today realize the long reach of the New Deal. If they cross the Triborough Bridge, they are driving on a bridge the PWA built. If they fly into La Guardia Airport, they are landing at an airfield laid out by the WPA. If they get caught in a traffic jam on the FDR Drive, they are using yet another artery built by the WPA. Even the animal cages in Central Park Zoo were reconstructed by WPA workers. In New York City, the WPA built or renovated hundreds of school buildings; gave Orchard Beach a bathhouse, a mall, and a lagoon; landscaped Bryant Park and the campus of Hunter College in the Bronx; conducted examinations for venereal disease, filled teeth, operated pollen count stations, and performed puppet shows for disturbed children; it built dioramas for the Brooklyn Museum; ran street dances in Harlem and an open-air night club in Central Park; and, by combining neglected archives, turned up forgotten documents like the court proceedings in the Aaron Burr libel case and the marriage license issued to Captain Kidd. In New York City alone the WPA employed more people than the entire War Department....

The New Deal showed unusual sensitivity toward jobless white-collar workers, notably those in aesthetic fields. The Public Works of Art Project gave an opportunity to muralists eager for a chance to work in the style of Rivera, Orozco, and Siqueiros. The Federal Art Project fostered the careers of painters like Stuart Davis, Raphael Soyer, Yasuo Kuniyoshi, and Jackson Pollock. Out of the same project came a network of community art centers and the notable *Index of American Design*....

The Federal Writers' Project provided support for scores of talented novelists and poets, editors and literary critics, men like Ralph Ellison and Nelson Algren, John Cheever and Saul Bellow. These writers turned out an exceptional set of state guides, with such features as Conrad Aiken's carefully delineated portrayal of Deerfield, Massachusetts, and special volumes like *These Are Our Lives,* a graphic portfolio of life histories in North Carolina, and *Panorama,* in which Vincent McHugh depicts "the infinite pueblo of the Bronx." Project workers transcribed chain-gang blues songs, recovered folklore that would otherwise have been lost, and collected the narratives of elderly former slaves, an invaluable archive later published in *Lay My Burden Down*....

Some thought it an ill omen that the Federal Theatre Project's first production was Shakespeare's *Comedy of Errors,* but that agency not only gave employment to actors and stage technicians but offered many communities their first glimpse of live drama....

Roosevelt, it has been said, had a "proprietary interest in the nation's estate," and this helps account for the fact that the 1930s accomplished for soil conservation and river valley development what the era of Theodore Roosevelt had done for the forests. The Tennessee Valley Authority, which drew admirers from all over the world, put the national government in the business of generating electric power, controlled floods, terraced hillsides, and gave new hope to the people of the valley. In the Pacific Northwest the PWA constructed mammoth dams, Grand Coulee and Bonneville. Roosevelt's "tree army," the Civilian Conservation Corps, planted millions of trees, cleared forest trails, laid out picnic sites and campgrounds, and aided the Forest Service in the vast undertaking of establishing a shelterbelt —a windbreak of trees and shrubs: green ash and Chinese elm, apricot and blackberry, buffalo berry and Osage orange from the Canadian border to the Texas panhandle. Government agencies came to the aid of drought-stricken farmers in the Dust Bowl, and the Soil Conservation Service, another New Deal creation, instructed growers in methods of cultivation to save the land. As Alistair Cooke later said, the favorite of the New Dealers was the farmer with the will to "take up contour plowing late in life."

These services to farmers represented only a small part of the government's program, for in the New Deal years, the business of agriculture was revolutionized. Roosevelt came to power at a time of mounting desperation for the American farmers. Each month in 1932 another 20,000 farmers had lost their land because of inability to meet their debts in a period of collapsing prices. On a single day in May 1932, one-fourth of the state of Mississippi went under the sheriff's hammer. The Farm Credit Administration of 1933 came to the aid of the beleaguered farmer, and within eighteen months, it had refinanced one-fifth of all farm mortgages in the United States. In the Roosevelt years, too, the Rural Electrification Administration literally brought rural America out of darkness. At the beginning of the Roosevelt era, only one farm in nine had electricity; at the end, only one in nine did not have it. But more important than any of these developments was the progression of enactments starting with the first AAA (the Agricultural Adjustment Act) of 1933, which began the process of granting large-scale subsidies to growers. As William Faulkner later said, "Our economy is not agricultural any longer. Our economy is the federal government. We no longer farm in Mississippi cotton fields. We farm now in Washington corridors and Congressional committee rooms."

## GOVERNMENT OF AND FOR MORE OF THE PEOPLE

At the same time that its realm was being expanded under the New Deal, the national government changed the composition of its personnel and of its beneficiaries. Before 1933, the government had paid heed primarily to a single group—white Anglo-Saxon Protestant males. The Roosevelt Administration, however, recruited from a more ethnically diverse group, and the prominence of Catholics and Jews among the President's advisers is suggested by the scintillating team of the Second Hundred Days, Corcoran and Cohen. The Federal Writers' Project turned out books on Italians and Albanians, and the Federal Theatre staged productions in Yiddish and wrote a history of the Chinese stage in Los Angeles. In the 1930s women played a more prominent role in government than they ever had before, as the result of such appointments as that of Frances Perkins as the first female cabinet member, while the influence of Eleanor Roosevelt was pervasive....

Although in some respects the New Deal's performance with regard to blacks added to the sorry record of racial discrimination in America, important gains were also registered in the 1930s. Blacks, who had often been excluded from relief in the past, now received a share of WPA jobs considerably greater than their proportion of the population. Blacks moved into federal housing projects; federal funds went to schools and hospitals in black neighborhoods; and New Deal agencies like the Farm Security Administration (FSA) enabled 50,000 Negro tenant farmers and sharecroppers to become proprietors. "Indeed," one historian has written, "there is a high correlation between the location of extensive FSA operations in the 1930s and the rapidity of political modernization in black communities in the South in the 1960s." Roosevelt appointed a number of blacks, including William Hastie, Mary McLeod Bethune, and Robert Weaver, to high posts in the government. Negroes in the South who were disfranchised in white primaries voted in AAA crop referenda and in National Labor Relations Board plant elections, and a step was taken toward restoring their constitutional rights when Attorney General Frank Murphy set up a Civil Liberties Unit in the Department of Justice. The reign of Jim Crow in Washington offices, which had begun under Roosevelt's Democratic predecessor, Woodrow Wilson, was terminated by Secretary of the Interior Harold Ickes who desegregated cafeterias in his department. Ickes also had a role in the most dramatic episode of the times, for when the Daughters of the American Revolution (DAR) denied the use of their concert hall to the black contralto Marian Anderson, he made it possible for her to sing before thousands from the steps of Lincoln Memorial; and Mrs. Roosevelt joined in the rebuke to the DAR. Anderson's concert on Easter Sunday 1939 was heard by thousands at the Memorial, and three networks carried her voice to millions more. Blacks delivered their own verdict on the New Deal at the polling places. Committed to the party of Lincoln as late as 1932, when they voted overwhelmingly for Hoover, they shifted in large numbers to the party of FDR during Roosevelt's first term. This was a change of allegiance that many whites were also making in those years.

## THE DURABLE LEGACY OF THE NEW DEAL

The Great Depression and the New Deal brought about a significant political realignment of the sort that occurs only rarely in America. The Depression wrenched many lifelong Republican voters from their moorings. In 1928, one couple christened their newborn son "Herbert Hoover Jones." Four years later they petitioned the court, "desiring to relieve the young man from the chagrin and mortification which he is suffering and will suffer," and asked that his name be changed to Franklin D. Roosevelt Jones. In 1932 FDR became the first Democrat to enter the White House with as much as 50 percent of the popular vote in eighty years—since Franklin K. Pierce in 1852. Roosevelt took advantage of this opportunity to mold "the FDR coalition," an alliance centered in the low-income districts of the great cities and, as recently as the 1980 election, the contours of the New Deal coalition could still be discerned.

Indeed, over the past half-century, the once overpowering Republicans have won control of Congress only twice, for a total of four years. No less important was the shift in the character of the Democratic party from the conservative organization of John W. Davis and John J. Raskob to the country's main political instrumentality for reform. "One political result of the Roosevelt years," Robert Burke has observed, "was a basic change in the nature of the typical Congressional liberal." He was no longer a maverick, who made a fetish of orneriness, no longer one of the men Senator Moses called "the sons of the wild jackass," but "a party Democrat, labor-oriented, urban, and internationalist-minded."

Furthermore, the New Deal drastically altered the agenda of American politics. When Arthur Krock of the *New York Times* listed the main programmatic questions before the 1932 Democratic convention, he wrote: "What would be said about the repeal of prohibition that had split the Republicans? What would be said about tariffs?" By 1936, these concerns seemed altogether old fashioned, as campaigners discussed the Tennessee Valley Authority and industrial relations, slum clearance and aid to the jobless. That year, a Little Rock newspaper commented: "Such matters as tax and tariff laws have given way to universally human things, the living problems and opportunities of the average man and the average family."

The Roosevelt years changed the conception of the role of government not just in Washington but in the states, where a series of "Little New Deals"—under governors like Herbert Lehman in New York—added a thick sheaf of social legislation, and in the cities. In Boston, Charles Trout has observed, city council members in 1929 "devoted endless hours to street paving." After the coming of the New Deal, they were absorbed with NRA campaigns, public housing, and WPA allotments. "A year after the crash the council thought 5,000 dollars an excessive appropriation for the municipal employment bureau," but during the 1930s "the unemployed drained Boston's treasury of not less than 100,000,000 dollars in direct benefits, and the federal government spent even more."

In a cluster of pathbreaking decisions in 1937, the Supreme Court legitimized this vast exercise of authority by government at all levels. As late as 1936, the Supreme Court still denied the power of the United States government to regulate agriculture, even though crops were sold in a world market, or coal mining, a vital component of a national economy, and struck down a minimum wage law as beyond the authority of the state of New York. Roosevelt responded with a plan to "pack" the Court with as many as six additional Justices, and in short order the Court, in what has been called "the Constitutional Revolution of 1937," sounded retreat. Before 1937 the Supreme Court stood as a formidable barrier to social reform. Since 1937 not one piece of significant social legislation has been invalidated, and the Court has shifted its docket instead to civil rights and civil liberties....

The New Deal accomplished all of this at a critical time, when many were insisting that fascism was the wave of the future and denying that democracy could be effective....

In these "dark and leaden thirties," Professor Berlin [wrote], "the only light in the darkness that was left was the administration of Mr. Roosevelt and the

New Deal in the United States. At a time of weakness and mounting despair in the democratic world Mr. Roosevelt radiated confidence and strength.... Even to-day, upon him alone, of all the statesmen of the thirties, no cloud rested neither on him nor on the New Deal, which to European eyes still looks a bright chapter in the history of mankind."

For the past generation, America has lived off the legacy of the New Deal. Successive administrations extended the provisions of statutes like the Social Security Act, adopted New Deal attitudes toward intervention in the economy to cope with recessions, and put New Deal ideas to modern purposes, as when the Civilian Conservation Corps served as the basis for both the Peace Corps and the VISTA program of the War on Poverty. Harry Truman performed under the shadow of FDR, Lyndon Johnson consciously patterned his administration on Roosevelt's, Jimmy Carter launched his first presidential campaign at Warm Springs, and Ronald Reagan has manifested an almost obsessive need to summon FDR to his side. Carl Degler has observed:

> Conventionally the end of the New Deal is dated with the enactment of the Wages and Hours Act of 1938. But in a fundamental sense the New Deal did not end then at all. Americans still live in the era of the New Deal, for its achievements are now the base mark below which no conservative government may go and from which all new reform now starts.... The reform efforts of the Democratic Truman, Kennedy, and Johnson administrations have been little more than fulfillments of the New Deal....

By restoring to the debate over the significance of the New Deal acknowledgment of its achievements, we may hope to produce a more judicious estimate of where it succeeded and where it failed. For it unquestionably did fail in a number of respects. There were experiments of the 1930s which miscarried, opportunities that were fumbled, groups who were neglected, and power that was arrogantly used. Over the whole performance lies the dark cloud of the persistence of hard times. The shortcomings of the New Deal are formidable, and they must be recognized. But I am not persuaded that the New Deal experience was negligible. Indeed, it is hard to think of another period in the whole history of the republic that was so fruitful or of a crisis that was met with as much imagination.

# NO

## Gary Dean Best

# PRIDE, PREJUDICE AND POLITICS: ROOSEVELT VERSUS RECOVERY, 1933–1938

This book had its genesis in the fact that I have for a long time felt uncomfortable with the standard works written about Franklin Delano Roosevelt and the New Deal, and with the influence those works have exerted on others writing about and teaching U.S. history. Although I approach the subject from a very different perspective, Paul K. Conkin's preface to the second edition of *The New Deal* (1975) expressed many of my own misgivings about writings on the subject. Conkin wrote that "pervading even the most scholarly revelations was a monotonous, often almost reflexive, and in my estimation a very smug or superficial valuative perspective—approval, even glowing approval, of most enduring New Deal policies, or at least of the underlying goals that a sympathetic observer could always find behind policies and programs."

Studies of the New Deal such as Conkin described seemed to me to be examples of a genre relatively rare in U.S. historiography—that of "court histories."...

But, like most historians teaching courses dealing with the Roosevelt period, I was captive to the published works unless I was willing and able to devote the time to pursue extensive research in the period myself. After some years that became possible, and this book is the result.

My principal problem with Roosevelt and the New Deal was not over his specific reforms or his social programs, but with the failure of the United States to recover from the depression during the eight peacetime years that he and his policies governed the nation. I consider that failure tragic, not only for the 14.6 percent of the labor force that remained unemployed as late as 1940, and for the millions of others who subsisted on government welfare because of the prolonged depression, but also because of the image that the depression-plagued United States projected to the world at a crucial time in international affairs. In the late 1930s and early 1940s, when U.S. economic strength might have given pause to potential aggressors in the world, our economic weakness furnished encouragement to them instead.

From the standpoint, then, not only of our domestic history, but also of the tragic events and results of World War II, it has seemed to me that Roosevelt's failure to generate economic recovery during this critical period deserved more attention than historians have given it.

Most historians of the New Deal period leave the impression that the failure of the United States to recover during those eight years resulted from Roosevelt's unwillingness to embrace Keynesian spending. According to this thesis, recovery came during World War II because the war at last forced Roosevelt to spend at the level required all along for recovery. This, however, seemed to me more an advocacy of Keynes' theories by the historians involved than an explanation for the U.S. failure to recover during those years. Great Britain, for example, managed to recover by the late 1930s without recourse to deficit spending. By that time the United States was, by contrast, near the bottom of the list of industrial nations as measured in progress toward recovery, with most others having reached the predepression levels and many having exceeded them. The recovered countries represented a variety of economic systems, from state ownership to private enterprise. The common denominator in their success was not a reliance on deficit spending, but rather the stimulus they furnished to industrial enterprise.

What went wrong in the United States? Simplistic answers such as the reference to Keynesianism seemed to me only a means of avoiding a real answer to the question. A wise president, entering the White House in the midst of a crippling depression, should do everything possible to stimulate enterprise. In a free economy, economic recovery means *business* recovery. It follows, therefore, that a wise chief executive should do everything possible to create the conditions and psychology most conducive to business recovery —to encourage business to expand production, and lenders and investors to furnish the financing and capital that are required. An administration seeking economic recovery will do as little as possible that might inhibit recovery, will weigh all its actions with the necessity for economic recovery in mind, and will consult with competent business and financial leaders, as well as economists, to determine the best policies to follow. Such a president will seek to promote cooperation between the federal government and business, rather than conflict, and will seek to introduce as much consistency and stability as possible into government economic policies so that businessmen and investors can plan ahead. While obviously the destitute must be cared for, ultimately the most humane contribution a liberal government can make to the victims of a depression is the restoration of prosperity and the reemployment of the idle in genuine jobs.

In measuring the Roosevelt policies and programs during the New Deal years against such standards, I was struck by the air of unreality that hung over Washington in general and the White House in particular during this period. Business and financial leaders who questioned the wisdom of New Deal policies were disregarded and deprecated because of their "greed" and "self-interest," while economists and business academicians who persisted in calling attention to the collision between New Deal policies and simple economic realities were dismissed for their "orthodoxy." As one "orthodox" economist pointed out early in the New Deal years,

> economic realism . . . insists that policies aiming to promote recovery will, in fact, retard recovery if and where they fail to take into account correctly of stubborn facts in the existing economic situation and of the arithmetic of business as it must be carried out in the economic situation we are trying to revive. The antithesis of this economic realism is the vaguely hopeful or optimistic idealism in the field of economic policy, as such, which feels that good intentions, enough cleverness, and the right appeal to the emotions of the people ought to insure good results in spite of inconvenient facts.

Those "inconvenient facts" dogged the New Deal throughout these years, only to be stubbornly resisted by a president whose pride, prejudices, and politics would rarely permit an accommodation with them.

Most studies of the New Deal years approach the period largely from the perspective of the New Dealers themselves. Critics and opponents of Roosevelt's policies and programs are given scant attention in such works except to point up the "reactionary" and "unenlightened" opposition with which Roosevelt was forced to contend in seeking to provide Americans with "a more abundant life." The few studies that have concentrated on critics and opponents of the New Deal in the business community have been by unsympathetic historians who have tended to distort the opposition to fit the caricature drawn by the New Dealers, so that they offer little to explain the impact of Roosevelt's policies in delaying recovery from the depression.

The issue of *why* businessmen and bankers were so critical of the New Deal has been for too long swept under the rug, together with the question of *how* Roosevelt and his advisers could possibly expect to produce an economic recovery while a state of war existed between his administration and the employers and investors who, alone, could produce such a recovery. Even a Keynesian response to economic depression is ultimately dependent on the positive reactions of businessmen and investors for its success, as Keynes well knew, and those reactions were not likely to be as widespread as necessary under such a state of warfare between government and business. Businessmen, bankers, and investors may have been "greedy" and "self-interested." They may have been guilty of wrong perceptions and unfounded fears. But they are also the ones, in a free economy, upon whose decisions and actions economic recovery must depend. To understand their opposition to the New Deal requires an immersion in the public and private comments of critics of Roosevelt's policies. The degree and nature of business, banking, and investor concern about the direction and consequences of New Deal policies can be gleaned from the hundreds of banking and business periodicals representative of every branch of U.S. business and finance in the 1930s, and from the letters and diaries of the New Deal's business and other critics during the decade.

* * *

Statistics are useful in understanding the history of any period, but particularly periods of economic growth or depression. Statistics for the Roosevelt years may easily be found in *Historical Statistics of the United States* published by the Bureau of the Census, U.S. Department of Commerce (1975). Some of the trauma of the depression years may be inferred from the fact that the population of the United States grew by over 17 million between 1920 and 1930, but by only about half of that (8.9 million) between 1930 and 1940.

*Historical Statistics* gives the figures... for unemployment, 1929–1940. These figures are, however, only estimates. The federal government did not monitor the number of unemployed during those years. Even so, these figures are shocking, indicating as they do that even after the war had begun in Europe, with the increased orders that it provided for U.S. mines, factories, and farms, unemployment remained at 14.6 percent.

One characteristic of the depression, to which attention was frequently called during the Roosevelt years, was the contrast between its effects on the durable goods and consumer goods industries. Between 1929 and 1933, expenditures on personal durable goods dropped by nearly 50 percent, and in 1938 they were still nearly 25 percent below the 1929 figures. Producers' durable goods suffered even more, failing by nearly two-thirds between 1929 and 1933, and remaining more than 50 percent below the 1929 figure in 1938. At the same time, expenditures on nondurable, or consumer, goods showed much less effect. Between 1929 and 1933 they fell only about 14.5 percent, and by 1938 they exceeded the 1929 level. These figures indicate that the worst effects of the depression, and resultant unemployment, were being felt in the durable goods industries. Roosevelt's policies, however, served mainly to stimulate the consumer goods industries where the depression and unemployment were far less seriously felt.

One consequence of Roosevelt's policies can be seen in the U.S. balance of trade during the New Deal years. By a variety of devices, Roosevelt drove up the prices of U.S. industrial and agricultural products, making it difficult for these goods to compete in the world market, and opening U.S. markets to cheaper foreign products.... With the exception of a $41 million deficit in 1888, these were the only deficits in U.S. trade for a century, from the 1870s to the 1970s.

... [W]hile suicides during the Roosevelt years remained about the same as during the Hoover years, the death rate by "accidental falls" increased significantly. In fact, according to *Historical Statistics*, the death rate by "accidental falls" was higher in the period 1934–1938 than at any other time between 1910 and 1970 (the years for which figures are given).

Interestingly, the number of persons arrested grew steadily during the depression years. In 1938 nearly twice as many (554,000) were arrested as in 1932 (278,000), and the number continued to increase until 1941. And, while the number of telephones declined after 1930 and did not regain the 1930 level until 1939, the number of households with radios increased steadily during the depression years. And Americans continued to travel. Even in the lowest year, 1933, 300,000 Americans visited foreign countries (down from 517,000 in 1929), while the number visiting national parks, monuments, and such, steadily increased during the depression—in 1938 nearly five times as many (16,331,000) did so as in 1929 (3,248,000).

Comparisons of the recovery of the United States with that of other nations may be found in the volumes of the League of Nations' *World Economic Survey* for the depression years. [A] table (from the volume of 1938/39) shows comparisons of unemployment rates. From this

it can be seen that in 1929 the United States had the lowest unemployment rate of the countries listed; by 1932 the United States was midway on the list, with seven nations reporting higher unemployment rates and seven reporting lower unemployment. By mid-1938, however, after over five years of the New Deal, only three nations had higher unemployment rates, while twelve had lower unemployment. The United States, then, had lost ground in comparison with the other nations between 1932 and 1938.

The *World Economic Survey* for 1937/38 compared the levels of industrial production for 23 nations in 1937, expressed as a percentage of their industrial production in 1929.... It must be remembered that the figures for the United States reflect the level of industrial production reached just before the collapse of the economy later that year. Of the 22 other nations listed, 19 showed a higher rate of recovery in industrial production than the United States, while only 3 lagged behind. One of these, France, had followed policies similar to those of the New Deal in the United States. As the *World Economic Survey* put it, both the Roosevelt administration and the Blum government in France had "adopted far-reaching social and economic policies which combined recovery measures with measures of social reform." It added: "The consequent doubt regarding the prospects of profit and the uneasy relations between business-men and the Government have in the opinion of many, been an important factor in delaying recovery," and the two countries had, "unlike the United Kingdom and Germany," failed to "regain the 1929 level of employment and production." The *World Economic Survey* the following year (1939) pointed out that industrial production in the United States had fallen from the 92.2 to 65 by June 1938, and hovered between 77 and 85 throughout 1939. Thus, by the end of 1938 the U.S. record was even sorrier than revealed by the [data].

* * *

Every survey of American historians consistently finds Franklin Delano Roosevelt ranked as one of this nation's greatest presidents. Certainly, exposure to even a sampling of the literature on Roosevelt and the New Deal can lead one to no other conclusion. Conventional wisdom has it that Roosevelt was an opportune choice to lead the United States through the midst of the Great Depression, that his cheerful and buoyant disposition uplifted the American spirit in the midst of despair and perhaps even forestalled a radical change in the direction of American politics toward the right or the left. Roosevelt's landslide reelection victory in 1936, and the congressional successes in 1934, are cited as evidence of the popularity of both the president and the New Deal among the American people. Polls by both Gallup and the Democratic National Committee early in the 1936 campaign, however, give a very different picture, and suggest that the electoral victories can be as accurately accounted for in terms of the vast outpourings of federal money in 1934 and 1936, and the inability or unwillingness of Landon to offer a genuine alternative to the New Deal in the latter year. To this must be added the fact that after early 1936 two of the most unpopular New Deal programs—the NRA and the AAA—had been removed as issues by the Supreme Court.

Conventional wisdom, in fact, suffers many setbacks when the Roosevelt years are examined from any other perspective than through a pro-New Deal Prism

—from the banking crisis of 1933 and the first inaugural address, through the reasons for the renewed downturn in 1937, to the end of the New Deal in 1937–1938. The American present has been ill-served by the inaccurate picture that has too often been presented of this chapter in the American past by biographers and historians. Roosevelt's achievements in alleviating the hardship of the depression are deservedly well known, his responsibility for prolonging the hardship is not. His role in providing long-overdue and sorely needed social and economic legislation is in every high school American history textbook, but the costs for the United States of his eight-year-long war against business recovery are mentioned in none.

Such textbooks (and those in college, too) frequently contain a chapter on the Great Depression, followed by one on the New Deal, the implication being that somewhere early in the second of the chapters the depression was ended by Roosevelt's policies. Only careful reading reveals that despite Roosevelt's immense labors to feed the unemployed, only modest recovery from the lowest depths of the depression was attained before the outbreak of World War II. Roosevelt, readers are told, was too old-fashioned, too conservative, to embrace the massive compensatory spending and unbalanced budgets that might have produced a Keynesian recovery sooner. But World War II, the books tell us, made such spending necessary and the recovery that might have occurred earlier was at last achieved.

Generations of Americans have been brought up on this version of the New Deal years. Other presidential administrations have been reevaluated over the years, and have risen or fallen in grace as a result, but not the Roosevelt administration. The conventional wisdom concerning the Roosevelt administration remains the product of the "court historians," assessments of the New Deal period that could not have been better written by the New Dealers themselves. The facts, however, are considerably at variance with this conventional wisdom concerning the course of the depression, the reasons for the delay of recovery, and the causes of the recovery when it came, finally, during World War II.

From the uncertainty among businessmen and investors about the new president-elect that aborted a promising upturn in the fall of 1932, to the panic over the prospect of inflationary policies that was a major factor in the banking crisis that virtually paralyzed the nation's economy by the date of his inauguration, Roosevelt's entry into the White House was not an auspicious beginning toward recovery. The prejudices that were to guide the policies and programs of the New Deal for the next six years were revealed in Roosevelt's inaugural address, although the message was largely overlooked until it had become more apparent in the actions of the administration later. It was an attitude of hostility toward business and finance, of contempt for the profit motive of capitalism, and of willingness to foment class antagonism for political benefit. This was not an attitude that was conducive to business recovery, and the programs and policies that would flow from those prejudices would prove, in fact, to be destructive of the possibility of recovery.

There followed the "hundred days," when Roosevelt rammed through Congress a variety of legislation that only depressed business confidence more. The new laws were served up on attractive platters, with tempting descriptions —truth in securities, aid for the farmer, industrial self-regulation—but when the covers were removed the contents were neither attractive nor did they match the labels. By broad grants of power to the executive branch of the government, the legislation passed regulation of the U.S. economy into the hands of New Dealers whose aim was not to promote recovery but to carry out their own agendas for radical change of the economic system even at the expense of delaying recovery. Thus, truth in securities turned to paralysis of the securities markets, aid for the farmer became a war against profits by processors of agricultural goods, and industrial self-regulation became government control and labor-management strife. International economic cooperation as a device for ending the depression was abandoned for an isolationist approach, and throughout 1933 the threat of inflation added further uncertainty for businessmen and investors.

The grant of such unprecedented peacetime authority to an American president aroused concern, but these after all were only "emergency" powers, to be given up once recovery was on its way. Or were they? Gradually the evidence accumulated that the Tugwells and the Brandeisians intended to institutionalize the "emergency" powers as permanent features of American economic life. By the end of 1933, opposition to the New Deal was already sizable. Business alternated between the paralysis of uncertainty and a modest "recovery" born of purchases and production inspired by fear of higher costs owing to inflation and the effects of the AAA and NRA. The implementation of the latter two agencies in the fall of 1933 brought a renewed downturn that improved only slightly during the winter and spring. A renewed legislative onslaught by the New Deal in the 1934 congress, combined with labor strife encouraged by the provisions of the NIRA, brought a new collapse of the economy in the fall of 1934, which lowered economic indices once again to near the lowest levels they had reached in the depression.

The pattern had been established. The war against business and finance was under way, and there would be neither retreat nor cessation. Roosevelt's pride and prejudices, and the perceived political advantages to be gained from the war, dictated that his administration must ever be on the offensive and never in retreat. But the administration suffered defeats, nevertheless, and embarrassment. The Supreme Court proved a formidable foe, striking down both the NRA and the AAA. Dire predictions from the administration about the implications for the economy of the loss of the NRA proved embarrassing when the economy began to show gradual improvement after its departure. But defeat did not mean retreat. Under the goading of Felix Frankfurter and his disciples, Roosevelt became even more extreme in his verbal and legislative assault against business. Their attempts to cooperate with the Roosevelt administration having been spurned, businessmen and bankers awakened to the existence of the war being waged upon them and moved into opposition. Roosevelt gloried in their opposition and escalated the war against them in the 1936 reelection campaign.

Reelected in 1936 on a tidal wave of government spending, and against a lackluster Republican campaigner who offered no alternative to the New Deal, Roosevelt appeared at the apogee of his power and prestige. His triumph was, however, to be short-lived, despite an enhanced Democratic majority in Congress. A combination of factors was about to bring the New Deal war against business to a stalemate and eventual retreat. One of these was his ill-advised attempt to pack the Supreme Court with subservient justices, which aroused so much opposition even in his own party that he lost control of the Democrat-controlled Congress. More important, perhaps, was the growing economic crisis that the Roosevelt administration faced in 1937, largely as a result of its own past policies. The massive spending of 1936, including the payment of the veterans' bonus, had generated a speculative recovery during that year from concern about inflationary consequences. Fears of a "boom" were increased as a result of the millions of dollars in dividends, bonuses, and pay raises dispensed by businesses late in 1936 as a result of the undistributed profits tax. The pay raises, especially, were passed on in the form of higher prices, as were the social security taxes that were imposed on businesses beginning with 1937. Labor disturbances, encouraged by the Wagner Labor Act and the Roosevelt alliance with John L. Lewis' Congress of Industrial Organizations in the 1936 campaign, added further to the wage-price spiral that threatened as 1937 unfolded. Massive liquidations of low-interest government bonds, and sagging prices of the bonds, fueled concern among bankers and economists, and within the Treasury, that a "boom" would imperil the credit of the federal government and the solvency of the nation's banks whose portfolios consisted mainly of low-interest government bonds.

In considering the two principal options for cooling the "boom"—raising interest rates or cutting federal spending—the Roosevelt administration chose to move toward a balanced budget. It was a cruel dilemma that the New Dealers faced. All knew that the economy had not yet recovered from the depression, yet they were faced with the necessity to apply brakes to an economy that was becoming overheated as a consequence of their policies. Moreover, the reduction in consumer purchasing power caused by the cuts in federal spending was occurring at the same time that purchasing power was already being eroded as a result of the higher prices that worried the administration. Private industry, it should have been obvious, could not "take up the slack," since the Roosevelt administration had done nothing to prepare for the transition from government to private spending that John Maynard Keynes and others had warned them was necessary. The New Dealers had been far too busy waging war against business to allow it the opportunity to prepare for any such transition.

In fact, far from confronting the emergency of 1937 by making long-overdue attempts to cooperate with business in generating recovery, Roosevelt was busy pressing a new legislative assault against them. Denied passage of his legislative package by Congress during its regular 1937 session, Roosevelt called a special session for November despite evidence that the economy had begun a new downturn. Even the collapse of the stockmarket, within days after his announcement of the special session, and the growing unemployment that soon followed, did not deter Roosevelt from his determination to drive the legislative assault through it. With the nation in the grips of a full-blown economic collapse, Roosevelt offered nothing to the special session but the package of antibusiness legislation it had turned down in the regular session. Once again he was rebuffed by Congress. The nation drifted, its economic indices falling, with its president unwilling to admit the severity of the situation or unable to come to grips with what it said about the bankruptcy of the New Deal policies and programs.

By early 1938, Roosevelt was faced with problems similar to those he had faced when he first entered the White House five years earlier, but without the political capital he had possessed earlier. In 1933 the Hoover administration could be blamed for the depression. In 1938 the American people blamed the Roosevelt administration for retarding recovery. Five years of failure could not be brushed aside. Five years of warfare against business and disregard of criticism and offers of cooperation had converted supporters of 1933 into cynics or opponents by 1938. Even now, however, pride, prejudice, and politics dominated Roosevelt, making it impossible for him to extend the needed olive branch to business. The best that he could offer in 1938 was a renewal of federal spending and more of the same New Deal that had brought the nation renewed misery. In the 1938 congressional session he continued to press for passage of the antibusiness legislation that had been rejected by both sessions of 1937.

But Congress was no longer the pliant body it had been in 1933, and in the 1938 congressional elections the people's reaction was registered when the Republicans gained 81 new seats in the House and 8 in the Senate—far more than even the most optimistic Republican had predicted. If the message was lost on Roosevelt, it was obvious to some in his administration, notably his new Secretary of Commerce Harry Hopkins and his Secretary of the Treasury Henry Morgenthau. Two of the earliest business-baiters in the circle of Roosevelt advisers, they now recognized the bankruptcy of that course and the necessity for the administration to at last strive for recovery by removing the obstacles to normal and profitable business operation that the New Deal had erected. This was not what Roosevelt wanted to hear, nor was it what his Frankfurter disciples wanted him to hear. These latter knew, as Hopkins and Morgenthau had learned earlier, just which Rooseveltian buttons could be pushed to trigger his antibusiness prejudices and spite. A battle raged within the New Deal between the Frankfurter radicals and the "new conservatives," Hopkins and Morgenthau, amid growing public suspicion that the former were not interested in economic recovery.

It was not a fair battle. Hopkins and Morgenthau knew how to play the game, including use of the press, and had too many allies. They did not hesitate to talk bluntly to Roosevelt, perhaps the bluntest talk he had heard since the death of Louis McHenry Howe. Moreover, Roosevelt could afford the loss of a Corcoran and/or a Cohen, against whom there was already a great deal of congressional opposition, but a break with both Hopkins and Morgenthau would have been devastating for an administration already on the defensive. Gradually the Frankfurter radicals moved into eclipse, along with their policies, to be replaced increasingly by recovery and preparedness advocates, including many from the business and financial world.

Conventional wisdom has it that the massive government spending of World War II finally brought a Keynesian recovery from the depression. Of more significance, in comparisons of the prewar and wartime economic policies of the Roosevelt administration, is the fact that the war against business that characterized the former was abandoned in the latter. Both the attitude and policies of the Roosevelt administration toward business during the New Deal years were reversed when the president found new, foreign enemies to engage his attention and energies. Antibusiness advisers were replaced by businessmen, pro-labor policies became pro-business policies, cooperation replaced confrontation in relations between the federal government and business, and even the increased spending of the war years "trickled down" rather than "bubbling up." Probably no American president since, perhaps, Thomas Jefferson ever so thoroughly repudiated the early policies of his administration as Roosevelt did between 1939 and 1942. This, and not the emphasis on spending alone, is the lesson that needs to be learned from Roosevelt's experience with the depression, and of the legacy of the New Deal economic policies.

The judgment of historians concerning Roosevelt's presidential stature is curiously at odds with that of contemporary observers. One wonders how scholars of the Roosevelt presidency are able so blithely to ignore the negative assessments of journalists, for example, of the stature of Raymond Clapper, Walter Lippmann, Dorothy Thompson, and Arthur Krock, to name only a few. Can their observations concerning Roosevelt's pettiness and spitefulness, their criticism of the obstacles to recovery created by his anticapitalist bias, and their genuine concern over his apparent grasp for dictatorial power be dismissed so cavalierly? Is there any other example in U.S. history of an incumbent president running for reelection against the open opposition of the two previous nominees of his own party? Will a public opinion poll ever again find 45 percent of its respondents foreseeing the likelihood of dictatorship arising from a president's policies? Will a future president ever act in such a fashion that the question will again even suggest itself to a pollster? One certainly hopes not.

Perhaps the positive assessment of Roosevelt by American historians rests upon a perceived liberalism of his administration. If so, one must wonder at their definition of liberalism. Surely a president who would pit class against class for political purposes, who was fundamentally hostile to the very basis of a free economy, who believed that his ends could justify very illiberal means, who was intolerant of criticism and critics, and who grasped for dictatorial power does not merit description as a liberal. Nor are the results of the Gallup poll mentioned above consistent with the actions of a liberal president. If the perception is based on Roosevelt's support for the less fortunate "one-third" of the nation, and his program of social legislation, then historians need to be reminded that such actions do not, in themselves, add up to liberalism, they having been used by an assortment of political realists and demagogues—of the left and the right—to gain and hold power.

There were certainly positive contributions under the New Deal, but they may not have outweighed the negative aspects of the period. The weight of the negative aspects would, moreover, have been much heavier except for the existence of a free and alert press, and for the actions of the Supreme Court and Congress in nullifying, modifying, and rejecting many of the New Deal measures. When one examines the full range of New Deal proposals and considers the implications of their passage in the original form, the outline emerges of a form of government alien to any definition of liberalism except that of the New Dealers themselves. Historians need to weigh more thoroughly and objectively the implications for the United States if Roosevelt's programs had been fully implemented. They need also to assess the costs in human misery of the delay in recovery, and of reduced U.S. influence abroad at a critical time in world affairs owing to its economic prostration. We can only speculate concerning the possible alteration of events from 1937 onward had the United States faced the world with the economic strength and military potential it might have displayed had wiser economic policies prevailed from 1933 to 1938. There is, in short, much about Roosevelt and the New Deal that historians need to reevaluate.

# POSTSCRIPT

## Was the New Deal an Effective Answer to the Great Depression?

Both Leuchtenburg and Best agree that the New Deal concentrated a tremendous amount of power in the executive branch of the government. They also acknowledge that it was World War II—not the New Deal's reform programs—that pulled the United States out of the depression.

But the two writers disagree with each other in their assumptions and assessments of the New Deal. Leuchtenburg grew up during the depression and sympathizes with the social and economic changes brought about by Roosevelt. Elsewhere he has called the New Deal a "halfway revolution; it swelled the ranks of the bourgeoisie but left many Americans—share croppers, slum dwellers, most Negroes—outside of the new equilibrium." In the essay presented here, Leuchtenburg chides left-wing critics of the New Deal who blame Roosevelt for not ending racial segregation or hard-core poverty. Leuchtenburg reminds us of what the New Deal accomplished, not what it failed to do.

Leuchtenburg feels that Roosevelt saved capitalism in 1933 with his "hundred days" reforms. James MacGregor Burns, however, author of one of the best political biographies of Roosevelt, *Roosevelt: The Lion and the Fox* (Harcourt, Brace, 1956), believes that Roosevelt retarded the recovery and created a recession in 1937 when he attempted to balance the budget.

Best assesses the New Deal from a conservative perspective. While he acknowledges Roosevelt's "role in providing long-overdue and sorely needed social and economic legislation," he accuses Roosevelt of prolonging the depression because of his hostility toward big business. In Best's view, Roosevelt should have sought a "business recovery," which would have encouraged businesses to expand production with financing by lenders and investors and with as little government interference as possible.

Best's major failing is his inability to view the human side of the New Deal. By concentrating on the strengths and weaknesses of a business recovery, he seems to forget that the New Deal was much more than the sum total of a number of economic statistics. Since that time, people have come to expect the national government to manage the economy responsibly.

There is voluminous literature on the Great Depression and the New Deal. Comprehensive and up-to-date syntheses and bibliographies can be found in Robert S. McElvaine, *The Great Depression: America, 1929–1941* (Times Books, 1984) and Anthony J. Badger, *The New Deal: The Depression Years, 1933–1940* (Farrar, Straus & Giroux, 1989). For a convenient reproduction of approximately 150 of "the most important" articles on all aspects of this topic, see

*The Great Depression and the New Deal* (Garland Publishing, 1990), edited by Melvyn Dubofsky and Stephen Burnwood.

A knowledge of economic history is essential to understanding the depression. John Kenneth Galbraith, in *The Great Crash, 1929* (Houghton Mifflin, 1955), discusses the events that caused the depression, aiming daggers at Presidents Coolidge and Hoover and the members of the economic establishment. Conservative economists Milton Friedman and Ann Jacobson Schwartz disagree with Galbraith and emphasize the failure of the changing monetary policies of the Federal Reserve Board in *The Great Contraction, 1929–1933* (Princeton University Press, 1965). Studs Terkel presents interviews with hundreds of people who suffered through the economic dislocation in *Hard Times* (Pantheon Books, 1970). Robert S. McElvaine edited a sample of the 15 million letters in the Franklin D. Roosevelt library that were sent to federal agencies in *Down and Out in the Great Depression: Letters from the Forgotten Man* (University of North Carolina Press, 1983).

Radical criticisms of the New Deal and its legacy became common in the 1960s. A good starting point is Howard Zinn, ed., *New Deal Thought* (Bobbs-Merrill, 1966). Two of the most sophisticated New Left criticisms are Barton J. Bernstein, *The New Deal: The Conservative Achievements of Liberal Reform* (Pantheon Books, 1967) and Paul K. Conklin, *The New Deal,* 2d ed. (Harlan Davidson, 1975). Steve Fraser and Gary Gerstle edited a series of social and economic essays, which they present in *The Rise and Fall of the New Deal Order, 1930–1980* (Princeton University Press, 1989).

Contemporary left-wing critics are dissected in Arthur M. Schlesinger, Jr.'s *The Politics of Upheaval, vol. 3* (Houghton Mifflin, 1960), but the standard work is now Alan Brinkley's overview *Voices of Protest: Huey Long, Father Coughlin and the Great Depression* (Alfred A. Knopf, 1982).

The standard conservative critique of the New Deal is Edgar E. Robinson's scathing *The Roosevelt Leadership, 1933–1945* (Lippincott, 1955). The most recent collection of neoconservative essays can be found in *The New Deal and Its Legacy: Critique and Reappraisal* (Greenwood Press, 1989), edited by Robert Eden.

The celebration of Roosevelt's 100th birthday in 1982 and the 50th anniversary of the New Deal in 1983 inspired a number of conferences and the subsequent publication of the papers. Among the most important are: Harvard Sitkoff, ed., *Fifty Years Later: The New Deal Evaluated* (Alfred A. Knopf, 1985); Wilbur J. Cohen, ed., *The Roosevelt New Deal: A Program Assessment Fifty Years After* (Lyndon B. Johnson School of Public Affairs, 1986); and Herbert D. Rosenbaum and Elizabeth Barteline, eds., *Franklin D. Roosevelt: The Man, the Myth, the Era, 1882–1945* (Greenwood Press, 1987). Many of the essays in these collections deal with the new interest in African Americans, women, and other aspects of social history, as well as more traditional subjects.

# ISSUE 12

## Did World War II Liberate American Women?

**YES: Sherna Berger Gluck,** from *Rosie the Riveter Revisited: Women, the War, and Social Change* (Twayne, 1987)

**NO: Elaine Tyler May,** from *Homeward Bound: American Families in the Cold War Era* (Basic Books, 1988)

### ISSUE SUMMARY

**YES:** Sherna Berger Gluck, a lecturer in oral history, recognizes that although most women lost their industrial jobs after World War II, their wartime experiences transformed their concept of themselves as women and produced rising expectations that fueled the new women's consciousness movement.

**NO:** Professor of American studies Elaine Tyler May insists that World War II underscored women's tasks as homemakers, consumers, and mothers and reinforced sex segregation in the American workforce.

In studying the past, historians often attempt to identify certain "watershed" events—those critical episodes or periods during which significant changes occurred in the life of a nation or the world as a whole and produced an environment markedly different from that which had existed previously. In American history, scholars often describe the American Revolution, the Civil War, and the Great Depression and Franklin Roosevelt's New Deal as watersheds. The same is true for the Second World War.

Most students probably think of World War II in military terms. Precipitated by the rise of the Fascist movement in Italy and the National Socialist (Nazi) party in Germany, and exacerbated by Adolf Hitler's totalitarian aggression, the fighting of World War II (1939–1945) resulted in widespread devastation in Europe and Asia and horrifying casualty rates for all of the nations involved. The United States, although initially separated from the conflict by geography and a policy of neutrality, found itself on the verge of military intervention even before Japanese planes appeared over the horizon at Pearl Harbor on December 7, 1941. As had been the case in World War I, American political leaders explained U.S. involvement not only as a response to direct attacks on a peace-loving nation but also as a mission to guarantee freedom around the globe.

As the United States became a major participant in the war, American society experienced a number of dramatic changes. The creation of new executive agencies expanded the federal bureaucracy well beyond its New Deal levels and increased presidential power. Military spending stimulated economic production and placed the final nail in the coffin of the Great Depression. Economic growth combined with labor shortages generated by military enlistments and the draft paved the way for the employment of many Americans who were previously excluded from the full range of job opportunities. African Americans and members of other minority groups were beneficiaries of these momentous changes. So, too, were women, who came to play a vital role in production on the home front.

During the 1930s, with unemployment rates near 25 percent, most American women restricted their work to traditional domestic labor in the home. Few opportunities for women existed in industry or manufacturing when so many American men were out of work. By 1940, however, the expansion of production to meet wartime demands opened many doors that were previously closed to female workers. After Pearl Harbor, in fact, employers openly encouraged women to join the industrial labor pool. "Rosie the Riveter" became a national symbol of women's efforts to do their part to defeat the forces of evil in Europe and Asia. By 1944, 37 percent of all adult women in the United States (19,370,000) were in the work force. Married women represented over 70 percent of the increase in female employees, a significant shift away from traditional patterns in which the vast majority of working women had been young and single.

The following selections explore the impact of the changes wrought by World War II on the socioeconomic status of American women. What types of employment opportunities were made available to women? Did these experiences permanently transform women's status, or were the changes merely fleeting and temporary? In the first selection, Sherna Berger Gluck insists that the issue of changing status must be examined over an extended period of time. Her study, based on oral interviews with female aircraft workers in Los Angeles, California, indicates that even though most of these women lost their industrial jobs at the end of the war, their experiences played a vital role in the process by which they redefined themselves. Their employment fostered a consciousness-raising among them that was handed down to their daughters. Hence, the resulting changes were psychologically permanent and liberating. Elaine Tyler May, however, argues that women's employment during the Second World War was a product of temporary extensions of patriotism and a sense of domestic responsibility resulting from the wartime emergency. Not only did the popular media continue to emphasize the familial image of women, but these attitudes also reinforced gender segregation within the labor force. Consequently, at the end of the war, women lost nearly all of the "men's jobs" to returning male veterans.

# YES

## Sherna Berger Gluck

# WHAT DID IT ALL MEAN?

*Well, men, it looks like Hitler, Hirohito and Company at last are in for a peck of trouble. They've got the women of this country all riled up. And as anybody knows, when the gals play marbles, it's really for keeps.*

—Douglas Airview, February 1942

The writer of these condescending lines announcing the entry of women into production jobs at Douglas Aircraft probably had little comprehension of the magnitude of that event. Yet, within a few months of the U.S. declaration of war, these early entrants to the aircraft industry in Los Angeles represented over half of the women aircraft workers in the country. By mid-1943, at the peak of women's employment in aircraft, the Los Angeles women aircraft workers continued to make up over one-third of the nationwide total.

Women's entry into defense jobs signaled a major breakthrough in their employment patterns. Those jobs, concentrated in heavy industry, were both better paying and laden with symbolic value—they were men's jobs. Moreover, many women were drawn into employment who normally would not have been. The debate among historians about the significance of the wartime experience for women partially revolves around the question of how permanent the wartime employment changes were. William Chafe has argued that the war represents a watershed in women's history, whereas Karen Anderson, D'Ann Campbell, and Susan Hartmann have suggested that continuity rather than change characterized women's lives after the war.

... Rather than debating the *degree* of change resulting from the wartime experiences, the life stories of ... former aircraft workers encourage, instead, a study of the *process* of change.

A criticism often leveled against the use of oral history to interpret events is that oral history narrators are "special" people. Obviously, they are the survivors in a society. But more than that, they are usually the "winners," not the "losers"—the people who, according to conventional standards, succeeded. As a result, they think enough of themselves to allow their stories to be recorded. Although this kind of bias is not as apparent in other forms of historical documentation, they have other shortcomings. Aggregate statistical data can measure overall behavior or characteristics and can also be used to compare these at two different points in time. But since little is known about the individuals who comprise the aggregate, it is not possible to explore the variations among them. Furthermore, to study the *process* of change, it is necessary to follow individuals through time, not merely to look at them at a beginning point and an end point. Oral history allows for this longitudinal approach.

When I first began trying to make sense of the total body of forty-five oral histories we had recorded, I thought I saw a distinct pattern emerging. The wartime work experience had meant different things to women, depending on how old they were and at what stage they were in their life cycle. For the longtime workers, the jobs had been important in a basic material sense; and for many of the full-time homemakers they had dramatically affected their self-esteem. In that first reading, however, I dismissed the experience as being a relatively unimportant interlude for the young single workers: I didn't look much beyond the fact that the young single workers had usually rejected the alternative, more lucrative jobs in the aircraft industry in favor of traditional women's roles. In other words, I depended too heavily on an assessment of change that was based on women's participation in the labor force. But that is only one indicator of change. A careful reading of the oral histories points to less tangible effects and also reveals the private face of change.

## THE WORLD OF WORK

In his "National Defense blues," Huddy Ledbetter ("Leadbelly") gloated over the fate that had befallen the women who had gotten too big for their britches:

> I had a little woman
>
> Working on that National Defense
>
> That woman got to the place, alas
>
> She did not have no sense....
>
> Every payday come, her check was big as mine....
>
> Now the defense is gone
>
> Listen to my song
>
> Since that defense is gone
>
> That woman done lose her home.

It is true that most women working in national defense did lose their jobs. For instance, in Los Angeles, only 14 percent of the women wartime aircraft workers still held their jobs in June of 1946—just slightly over one-fourth the number who had earlier indicated a desire to continue their aircraft employment. Instead, most of them were either working at other jobs or had left the labor force. Leadbelly was only partially right, however. As Tina Hill's and Marye Stumph's stories show, many women were able to buy their first homes—and hold onto them.

Even if they were generally unable to retain their jobs in aircraft in the immediate postwar years, women workers did maintain some of the inroads they had made into heavy industry. These advances were by no means spectacular and were further diminished by the new sexual division of labor that had emerged, wherein women were assigned to different jobs than men—and paid less. Yet women did receive better wages in these durable manufacturing jobs than in traditional women's work, and the work they performed challenged prevailing definitions of womanhood.

Perhaps because they started from an even lower position, black women were able to benefit more. Before the war, the majority of black working women were relegated to the white woman's kitchen. In Los Angeles, for instance, in 1940, two-thirds of employed black women worked as domestics. By 1950, this proportion dropped to 40 percent and was accompanied by an increase of black women in durable manufacturing.

The labor force statistics give us the bare bones—a hint that there was at least a modicum of change in the opportunities for working-class women.[1] The oral histories give us insight into women's attitudes and feelings about work, the personal "whys" and "why nots" of changed employment patterns.

The most obvious employment gains were often made by women who were fighters or by those who were ready to make changes, like Tina Hill and Bea Morales Clifton. Tina did not have to fight on her own, however. The black community had mobilized during the war and, with the help of the United Auto Workers union, had been able to maintain a foothold for both men and women. Bea, even if she was ready to do so, didn't have to fight. Instead, she was able to take advantage of the later industrial expansion stimulated by the Korean conflict.

Unfortunately, not all the women who wished to stay were fighters nor were there organizations to help working-class women fight, except for the unions, most of which have blemished records on this score. As a result, the majority of women aircraft workers who remained in the work force left their aircraft jobs and returned to traditional women's work.

Registered in these statistics are both women who were forced out and others who made the choice voluntarily. There were those like Marye Stumph, who would have liked to have kept their aircraft jobs—and even had a fair amount of seniority—but were not willing to challenge the cultural expectation that women were there only for the duration. They accepted the layoff and sought other work. On the other hand, others had little desire to stay, feeling that the jobs were not "women's work." Like Margie Salazar McSweyn, they were pleased to prove that they could temporarily do the work, but preferred traditional women's occupations.

Not all women, however, who went into service and clerical occupations did so because they were governed by ideas of what was "men's work" and what was "women's work." There were often no other viable alternatives. A single mother of a young child, like Juanita Loveless, could not find many jobs besides waitressing that provided the flexibility in scheduling she needed. Perhaps the lives of women like Juanita would have been different had services established during the war, like child care, been institutionalized. Certainly without support for working mothers, many women were forced to make choices within a very limited range.

Even if most women were not yet ready to challenge the status quo, the benefits reaped by those who were should not be discounted. It is, after all, through the steps made by path breakers that opportunities are expanded. Others waited, expressing themselves more quietly, in the private arena. Today, in the contemporary climate of expanded roles for women, they can more openly express their support for these changes—as evidenced by the overwhelming support for women's rights among most of the forty-five women whose oral histories were recorded.

## THE BOUNDARIES OF WOMEN'S SOCIAL WORLD

The social world of most working-class women has been more circumscribed, historically, than men's. Women's lives were played out in their own relatively homogeneous communities. Even wage-earning women had only limited contact with other races. Except for black women, who worked *for* white women, there were few jobs where the races worked together.

As the racial barriers in the defense industries were forced down, black women in particular eagerly sought jobs. In Los Angeles, the racial composition of the different aircraft plants varied, depending on company policy, on the strength of the union's antidiscrimination position, and on the geographic location of the plant. North American Aircraft, for instance, was located at the edge of the black community and was represented by a CIO union with a strong antidiscrimination clause. It had the highest proportion of black workers among the aircraft plants —8 percent. On the other hand, Lockheed Aircraft, whose main plant was located in the white community of Burbank, was represented by an AFL union with a white-only membership clause. Thus, despite an active recruitment policy by management, slightly less than 5 percent of all Lockheed employees were black. In contrast, at Lockheed's downtown subassembly plant, over half of the workers were people of color. Although no separate records were kept on workers of Mexican ancestry, there is some evidence that they, too, were concentrated in certain plants, particularly in the subassembly plants closer to the east-side Mexican communities. For instance, both Margie McSweyn and Bea Clifton worked at the downtown subassembly plant.

There is ample evidence in the files of the Fair Employment Practices Commission and in the oral histories presented here, that black women were often assigned different and more difficult jobs. It is also clear that old prejudices and stereotypes continued to rear their head, as when Juanita Loveless, a white Texan, refused to train black workers because they were "slow." The women's counselors, like Susan Laughlin, were often called upon to deal with these problems.

Nevertheless, in many of the accounts, there are signs of relatively open interaction among Afro-American, Anglo, and Mexican workers (Asian and Native American workers were a rarity). Mexican and Anglo women went to lunch together, as Bea Clifton recounted; and Margie McSweyn talked about going to a party thrown by an Anglo co-worker. It was also the first time that both Margie and Bea related to Anglo men. The relationships between black and white women were usually restricted to the plant, and Charlcia Neuman and her co-workers were unusual in their attempt to include a black crew member in a party.

Despite the limited nature of the social contacts between the races, a significant breakthrough had been made. The social worlds of these working-class women had been expanded, and many of the women acknowledged the significance of this intangible by-product of their wartime work experience.

For the younger women, the boundaries of social propriety were extended as well. The war plants served as the hub of social life for the young workers. Each of the large Los Angeles aircraft plants had recreation clubs and many had recreation centers. Activities like horseback riding, bowling, and swimming were regularly scheduled, even after the midnight shift. At North American, the Special Recreation Office offered a dating service. The plants also arranged for their women workers to entertain servicemen. That is how Marie Baker resumed her social life after her divorce.

Even if young women did not directly participate in these scheduled activities, the atmosphere created by them and the freer interaction promoted between men and women expanded the boundaries of their worlds. Despite the eight-year age difference between Margie McSweyn and Betty Boggs, both had been relatively sheltered. But within the context of unity and trust engendered by patriotism, it became easier for women like them to spread their wings. From Juanita Loveless's account it is obvious that the developing youth culture touched more than just those working in the war plants, but for many, like Betty Boggs, it was clearly their point of contact.

The war hastened the process whereby the United States became a more complex and less homogeneous society. By being pulled into war industries, women were active participants in that process.

## THE PRIVATE WORLD OF WOMEN'S CONSCIOUSNESS

Men suspected that women would be changed by their wartime work experience, and their reactions ranged from cautious welcomes to vituperative attacks. Feminists of the period often exhorted women to change, warning that otherwise they would become subjugated like the women of Nazi Germany. Even as moderate and "feminine" a publication as *Woman's Home Companion* sounded the trumpets for change:

> In free nations, I can, with man, help build a better world, Or I can shirk the responsibility and assume again the status of an inferior creature. The one way is hard and burdensome for I must think and act in my own right. The other way is easy. I have known it for centuries.

Working-class women who took war jobs might not have read the middle-class magazine where these words were printed, but in their own ways, and by their own actions, it is clear that they subscribed to these ideas. One of the striking themes in the oral histories is the desire of the women to test themselves, stretch themselves, prove themselves. This note was most commonly struck by women new to the work force, but it was not just a matter of being introduced to the world of work. Someone like Margie McSweyn, for example, who had eagerly abandoned production work wanted first to prove to herself she could do it. That done, she and many wage-earning women were often ready to return to "women's work."

Many women with whom we spoke proudly proclaimed how they had "held their own with men." In retrospect, this is probably what laid the groundwork for the transformation of someone like Bea Morales Clifton from a woman who timidly defined herself as "just a mother of four" to a self-confident participant in the wider world. Even Betty Boggs, who was forced to abandon her dream of becoming an aeronautical engineer, was still bolstered by the idea of women being able to do something different. Most of the women were profoundly affected by the chance to prove their competence in the male world—except for Tina Hill,

Marye Stumph, and Juanita Loveless who were primarily concerned about improving their material conditions.

In fact, recurrent in the responses of the majority of the two hundred women with whom we talked was this message: the unintended effect of their wartime work experience was a transformation in their concept of themselves as women. This change was not translated into a direct challenge of the status quo. At the time, it was probably not even recognized by most of the women, but it did affect their status in their own eyes—and in their homes.

For the first time, many of these former war workers spoke up and challenged the male prerogative to make the big decisions. The money they had earned and saved lent them moral authority, but it was the confidence they had developed that enabled them to exert that authority. Studies of changing power relationships in the family in the 1950s have suggested that working-class wives who had worked in the past participated more in these kinds of decisions. D'Ann Campbell has surmised that this expanded role was derived more from women's increased exposure to the wider world outside the home than from their work experience. It is hard to separate these issues or to assess their relative weight, but the oral histories do reveal that the work process itself engendered feelings and attitudes in the women that had a lasting effect.

Sometimes the experience was translated directly to the next generation. Charlcia Neuman, for instance, fully accepted the traditional definition of the wife's role. She would never have taken a job had the war not temporarily legitimized a woman like herself going to work for the duration. That brief experience, by her own account, caused her to think about better preparing her daughter for the world of work.

The effect on their daughters of the mothers' changed consciousness is also hard to assess. Eight of the forty-three production workers whose full life histories were recorded had daughters who were between the ages of five and thirteen during the war years. All these mothers had high expectations of their daughters and tried to guide them into getting an education and toward being more independent. This was unusual for working-class mothers in the 1940s, when working-class men, spurred on by the GI bill, were only just beginning to aspire to a college education.

Despite their mothers' aspirations for them, the daughters often married young and initially did not have goals that broke with tradition. Subsequently, many of them did carve out an independent course for themselves—at just about the time when women of their generation were supposed to be in the grips of the feminine mystique. From what can be learned about the daughters in their mothers' interviews, they seem to have broken with tradition more frequently than did the women who were already young adults during the war years.

Margie McSweyn, Juanita Loveless, and Betty Boggs were a part of that young adult cohort: single women aged seventeen to twenty-five during the war. Like the older, married women, many of these younger women were also pleased with their ability to hold their own with men, but the work experience itself seems to have been less important to them. Rather than representing a discontinuity in their lives, it was taken in stride as a natural part of their development.

Most of this cohort married by war's end or shortly after and took up full-time homemaking, at least temporarily. Just as it had been for their mothers, their family role was of primary importance; but unlike their mothers' generation, their relationships with their husbands were relatively more egalitarian. Furthermore, the majority of them expanded the definition of their family role to include participation in the public world of wage-earning work outside the home. (Among the two hundred women interviewed by phone, sixty were single and between the ages of seventeen and twenty-five when they took their war jobs. Among those in this group who later married, over half ultimately combined their domestic role with wage-earning work.)

In their different ways, Betty Boggs and Margie McSweyn are typical of this transitional generation: a generation that differed from the previous one and that charted a course that was adopted with even greater regularity by the next one. The wartime job had left an imprint on young women like Boggs and McSweyn, but they were essentially in step with the rest of their generation and were probably affected more by general social currents than by their specific wartime experience.

Of what broader significance, then, was the changed consciousness of women that resulted from their wartime experience? For one thing, it contributed to the tide of rising expectations of women. That tide, ultimately, led to the birth and growth of a social movement for women in the 1960s, just as the rising tide of expectations among blacks fueled the civil rights movement. Furthermore, we must remember that the generation of older, married women who were so deeply affected was that of the mothers of those who built the current women's movement. Even if the mothers' experience had little *direct* effect on their own daughters, it may have helped foster the development of a working-class feminist consciousness among young women.

## SOCIAL CHANGE AND THE "FEMININE MYSTIQUE"

After four years of war, which had followed on the heels of the Great Depression, the country started gearing up for a return to "normalcy." Articles about accommodating the needs of the returning servicemen were common, and the women's magazines filled their pages with advertising and stories that promoted a renewed domesticity. In this idealization of family life, male and female roles were once again polarized. D'Ann Campbell has argued that this need to return to normalcy helps explain why the wartime potential for change in women's lives was unrealized.

The magazine prescriptions for domestic bliss continued well into the 1950s and 1960s. By then, television was also delivering its own brand of the same message. "Father Knows Best" became the postwar counterpart of "One Man's Family." Suburban home ownership, coupled with a soaring birthrate seemed to lend credence to the reality of this image of stability and a happy return to the status quo. Then, in the early 1960s, with *The Feminine Mystique,* Betty Friedan exposed the myth.

Friedan did nothing to dispel the idea that women were firmly held in the grip of these cultural ideals. In fact, her argument was just the opposite. She took the messages of the popular media to be not only prescriptions for but also reflections of women's behavior. After all, educated middle-class women like herself were suffering from "the problem that had no name" because they had bought into these ideals. Students of women's history understand that the prescriptive messages of popular culture do not necessarily measure behavior. Yet we are still seduced into using these messages as a clue to actual behavior. Furthermore, in a variation of the trickle-down theory, these white middle-class ideals are assumed to be equally valid in describing the behavior of the working class and of all women of color.

The cultural ideals projected in the mass media and other forms of prescriptive literature are important to our understanding of society, but I think we can learn more by viewing them as possible *reactions* to behavior rather than *reflections* of it. If people were behaving according to the cultural ideals, why was it necessary to continue to promote them so stridently? On the other hand, if behavior was running counter to the ideals, then the unrelenting harangues might be viewed as last-ditch efforts to make women fall into line. In other words, perhaps the postwar messages can better be understood as a measure of the amount of change that was occurring in the society—as an attempt to stem the tide of that change.

Indeed, despite the consistency with which the message of the feminine mystique was initially delivered, by the mid-1950s popular magazines were beginning to catch up with reality. In 1956, special issues of both *Look* and *Life* were devoted to the changing American woman. In an editorial introduction, *Look* went so far as to suggest that women were groping their way "toward a new true center: neither Victorian nor rampantly feminist." In an ironic twist that highlights the changing values, Lucille Ball, the brassy, dippy housewife of "I Love Lucy," fought a public battle to continue to work while she was pregnant.

Many of these media acknowledgments of change were a direct result of the increased number and proportion of women in the work force, especially married women. But changes in values and behavior do not occur rapidly and are not easily attributed to an immediate cause. The increased proportion of married women in the work force was the result of a gradual process. It was already in evidence before the war, was accelerated as a result of the war, and was further fueled in the 1950s by the desire to maintain improved standards of living in the face of inflation. That is what brought mothers like Margie McSweyn back into the work force.

The ideology of the feminine mystique was promulgated, certainly, and many white middle-class college-educated women subscribed to it, at least temporarily. But there were also women who had changed and were in the process of changing in the postwar years, including both the former war workers and their daughters. By using the concept of the feminine mystique to describe women's lives in the period between the war and the rebirth of feminism in the 1960s, we see only stasis. We are blinded to the slow incremental process of change, and, as a result, we underestimate the role that women's war-time experience played in that process.

Social change is difficult to measure. Two points in time are examined and a judgment of continuity or change is made based on the similarity or difference between these points. When we look at women's lives in the immediate postwar decade, we can see many ways in which they were remarkably similar to what they had been like in the years immediately preceding the war. The majority of women continued to define themselves primarily as wives and mothers. If they were wage earners, they were usually still restricted to lower paying feminized occupations. Yet these oral histories have revealed the often private and subtle ways in which individual women were changed by their wartime experience.

These individual changes were not merely ephemeral. For it is the changes that individuals experience that both push for and support social transformation. The connection is not always immediate or clear. There is usually a lag, with ideas preceding practice. For example, despite a growing belief in egalitarian marriage over the past forty years, household responsibilities only now are beginning to be equalized.

The potential for social transformation was created by the wartime need for women workers. For a brief period, images of women were revised, employment opportunities were expanded, and public policy was enacted that created new services for women. These were necessary, but not sufficient conditions. Social values also had to change, including women's definitions of themselves. Women's wartime experience played a vital role in that process of redefinition —the reverberations of which are still being felt today.

## NOTES

1. Some of the changes, like the increased proportion of married women in the work force, represented an acceleration of trends that were obvious even before the war. Others, like the entry of women into nontraditional jobs, might either have not otherwise happened or have happened only much later.

# NO

## Elaine Tyler May

# WAR AND PEACE: FANNING THE HOME FIRES

Reminiscing about life in the United States after World War II, Joseph Adelson aptly described the "spirit of the times" as profoundly domestic. The utopian vision included "replenished" families with male providers "secure in stable careers" and female housewives "in comfortable homes" who would "raise perfect children." It was a dream that Americans had carried with them since the depression. Like the depression, World War II brought new challenges and new disruptions to families. For many who looked forward to building stable and secure homes after the depression, the war put their hopes on hold. When thousands of men were called to war, their unquestionably manly responsibilities as soldiers took precedence over their roles as breadwinners. While the men vanished to foreign shores to fend off the enemy, the women were left to fend for themselves.

The war emergency required the society to restructure itself and opened the way for the emancipation of women on an unprecedented scale. The potential for gender equality, thwarted during the 1930s, now had a chance to reach fruition. The depression ended abruptly: the unemployment rate fell from 14 percent to nearly zero. In response to the needs of an expanding wartime economy, public policy shifted dramatically from barring women from jobs to recruiting them. Married women were not only tolerated in the paid labor force, they were actively encouraged to take "men's jobs" as a patriotic duty to keep the war economy booming while the men went off to fight. Public opinion followed suit. During the depression, 80 percent of Americans objected to wives working outside the home; by 1942, only 13 percent still objected.

As a result of the combined incentives of patriotism and good wages, women began streaming into jobs. By 1945, the number of employed women had leapt 60 percent. Three-quarters of these new workers were married, and a third had children under age 14. War-production needs might have led to a restructuring of the labor force along gender-neutral lines, ending sex segregation in the workplace and bringing about a realignment of domestic roles. The dislocation of wartime might have led to the postponement of

From Elaine Tyler May, *Homeward Bound: American Families in the Cold War Era* (Basic Books, 1988).

marriage and child rearing, continuing the demographic trends of the thirties toward later marriage, a lower marriage rate, and fewer children. But nothing of the kind took place. The potential for significant alterations in gender arrangements was, once again, thwarted. In spite of the tremendous changes brought about by the war, the emergency situation ultimately encouraged women to keep their sights set on the home, and men to reclaim their status as the primary breadwinners and heads of households.

Instead of deterring Americans from embarking on family life, the war may have sped up the process. Women entered war production, but they did not give up on reproduction. The war brought a dramatic reversal to the declining marriage rate of the 1930s. Over one million more families were formed between 1940 and 1943 than would have been expected during normal times, and as soon as the United States entered the war, fertility increased. Between 1940 and 1945, the birthrate climbed from 19.4 to 24.5 per one thousand population. The marriage age dropped and the marriage rate accelerated, spurred, in part, by the possibility of draft deferments for married men in the early war years and by the imminence of the men's departure for foreign shores. Thus, a curious phenomenon marked the war years: a widespread disruption of domestic life accompanied by a rush into marriage and parenthood....

The popular culture reflected widespread admiration for the many thousands of female war workers, but affirmed the primacy of domesticity for women. Wartime films presented these contradictory messages to their female viewers, who constituted two-thirds of the movie audience. Numerous popular movies portrayed tough heroines who took on previously male responsibilities and survived on their own or with the support of other women. Whether in military situations, as in *Here Come the Waves* or *So Proudly We Hail*, or as war workers, in films such as *Swing Shift Maisie* or *Government Girl*, women displayed courage and independence. Major stars of the decade, such as Katharine Hepburn, were noted for their dignity and strength, both on and off the screen.

Other popular media also emphasized women's capabilities, most notably the popular "Wonder Woman," who made her comic-strip debut in 1941. But the independent heroine did not replace the familial image of women. Often the spunky career woman married her ardent suitor in the end, as did the nurse in *This Is The Army*. In popular magazine fiction, women remained devoted to their homes and families rather than to careers. One study found that although female characters were more likely to hold jobs in the 1940s than in the 1930s or the 1950s, the stories of the war decade represented "the strongest assault on feminine careerism." Heroines who gave up a career for marriage were portrayed favorably, while those who combined a career and family were condemned as poor wives and mothers. As in the depression, wartime gave rise to two different popular images of women: one independent, the other domestic.

The emancipated heroine did not survive in peacetime, however. After the war, independent heroines were replaced by less positive images of women in films. In these movies, female sexuality was portrayed as a positive force only if it led to an exciting marriage; otherwise, it was dangerous. The popular and aesthetically compelling *film noir* genre, which evolved during and after the war, explored themes of personal anxiety and alienation. Films in this genre often portrayed female sexuality as both powerful and dangerous. Barbara Stanwyck played an evil wife who plotted to kill her husband in *Double Indemnity* (1944), and Rita Hayworth's sexy character destroyed her man in the 1947 film, *The Lady from Shanghai.* Perhaps the most telling saga of the transformation of female sexuality in the popular culture is the career of Marilyn Monroe. Monroe first achieved notice when *Yank* magazine published a picture of her working in a war production plant, and she became popular as one of the noted "pin-up girls" of wartime. Like the other famous pin-ups, including Betty Grable and Rita Hayworth, she served, presumably, as an inspiration to the fighting men. After the war, she appeared in *film noir* movies that portrayed her sexuality as a destructive force.

In the popular media, women's sexuality became increasingly central to their identity. The promising as well as the troublesome potential of female eroticism found expression in the plots and genres of the decade. From the late forties to the fifties, subordination made the difference between good or bad female sexuality. Sexy women who became devoted sweethearts or wives would contribute to the goodness of life; those who used their sexuality for power or greed would destroy men, families, and even society. Marilyn Monroe's films demonstrate this dichotomy. In *Niagara,* made in 1953, Monroe portrayed a woman whose aggressive sexuality ultimately leads to the deaths of her husband, her lover, and herself. *Niagara* was one of the last films to portray Monroe's sexuality as dangerous; in most of her films in the 1950s, she portrayed a harmless "sex kitten" whose childlike innocence and sexual allure contribute to men's power and enjoyment, without threatening them.

In their off-screen lives, female film stars began to portray a new model of womanhood. During the war, they were suddenly featured in popular magazines chiefly as wives and mothers. Joan Crawford, for example, evolved from the embodiment of female independence and overt sexuality to become a paragon of domesticity. The shift began even before the United States officially entered the war; 1940 marked a change from the dominant themes of the depression. A typical 1940 *Photoplay* feature focused on film star Claudette Colbert. In a stance different from that of the 1930s, in which women were criticized for submerging their identities in marriage, the magazine stated approvingly, "Step over this charming threshold and meet—not a star and her husband—but a doctor and his wife." . . .

Overall, then, Hollywood's professed advocacy of gender equality evaporated during the forties. Two positive images of women had shared the limelight during wartime: the independent heroine and the devoted sweetheart and wife. After the war, as subservient homemakers moved into center stage, emancipated heroines gave way to predatory female villains. Even Wonder Woman lost some of her feminist characteristics and became more dependent on men. The dramatic shift in the popular culture raises a fundamental question, Why did the emphasis on domesticity emerge in the era of Rosie the Riveter? Clues to this apparent irony are found in what some historians consider to be the most substantial change of the 1940s: the entry of an unprecedented number of women into the paid labor force. In examining who these women were and what they did—particularly their long-term opportunities—one can see that the possibilities for employed women were much more limited than they seemed.

Women entered jobs at the beginning of the 1940s with tremendous disadvantages. In 1939, the median annual income of women was $568—and $246 for black women—compared to $962 for men. By 1940, only 9.4 percent of union members were women, although women were 25 percent of the operatives. Women had few bargaining levers with which to improve their working conditions. Considering the strong sentiment against female employment that had prevailed in the 1930s, it is not surprising to find that even feminist organizations stressed women's need to work over their right to employment—a strategy that underscored women's responsibilities to their families.

Moreover, young married women, those most likely to have children at home, made the smallest gains in employment over the decade—less than prewar predictions would have indicated. Since single women had been the largest proportion of paid female workers before the war, the demands of production during the 1940s quickly exhausted the supply. Few young single women were available, for with the war came a rapid drop in the marriage age and a rise in the birthrate. Thus, young women who might have been expected to spend a few years holding a job were now marrying and having children; once they had small children, they were encouraged to stay home.

Although some day care centers were established for the children of employed mothers, they were generally considered harmful to a child's development. Public funds were not allocated for day care centers until 1943, and even then, the centers provided care for only 10 percent of the children who needed it. Americans were reluctant to send their children out of the home for care. Most no doubt shared the sentiments of the public official who proclaimed that "the best service a mother can do is to rear her children in the home."

The decline in the number of employable young women led to the employment of numerous older married women. These women were the fastest growing group among the employed, a trend that would continue after the war. During the war, the proportion of all women who were employed rose from 28 percent to 37 percent, and women were 36 percent of the civilian labor force. Three-fourths of these new female employees were married. By the end of the war, fully 25 percent of all married women were employed—a huge gain from 15 percent at the end of the 1930s. Because most of these workers had spent their early adult years as homemakers, they were unlikely to enter careers that required training and experience and that had a significant potential for good pay, advancement, or job security. As a result, their large number contributed to the increasing segregation of women into low-level "female" jobs.

Rosie the Riveter was the notable exception, but the women she represented were a temporary phenomenon. Nearly all the "men's jobs" filled by women went back to men when the war ended. Even during the war, both the popular literature and the politicians exhorted married women to return to their domestic duties and single women to relinquish their jobs and find husbands when the hostilities ceased. This advice reflected not only the affirmation of home and family, but the prevailing suspicion of women—especially unmarried women—who entered the world of men.

During the war, single women were often seen as potential threats to stable family life and to the moral fiber of the nation. A typical wartime pamphlet warned, "The war in general has given women new status, new recognition.... Yet it is essential that women avoid arrogance and retain their femininity in the face of their own new status.... In her new independence she must not lose her humanness as a woman. She may be the woman of the moment, but she must watch her moments." This theme echoed through the prescriptive literature written during the war. One textbook explained why women had to watch their moments so carefully: "The greater social freedom of women has more or less inevitably led to a greater degree of sexual laxity, a freedom which strikes at the heart of family stability.... When women work, earn, and spend as much as men do, they are going to ask for equal rights with men. But the right to behave like a man [means] also the right to misbehave as he does. The decay of established moralities [comes] about as a by-product." In this remarkable passage, the authors state as if it were a scientific formula their opinion that social freedom and employment for women would cause sexual laxity, moral decay, and the destruction of the family. Such assumptions were widely shared. Many professionals and observers agreed with the sociologist Willard Waller that women had "gotten out of hand" during the war....

The employment of women during the war, then, created a great deal of ambivalence. While encouraged to enter the paid labor force, women's public presence gave rise to concerns about the long-term effects of the changes that were taking place while the men were overseas. These concerns were eased by viewing women's jobs as temporary extensions of patriotism and domestic responsibilities that resulted from the emergency situation. Above all, women were expected to remain "feminine"—a term that implied submissiveness and allure along with sexual chastity—and to embrace domesticity after the war.

Nowhere was this ambivalence more obvious than in the military. For the first time, women were encouraged to join the armed forces and to enter every part of the military service except combat. As Oveta Culp Hobby, director of the Women's Army Auxiliary Corps, proclaimed, women "are carrying on the glorious tradition of American womanhood. They are making history!... This is a war which recognizes no distinctions between men and women." To the female Americans she hoped to recruit, she said, "This is YOUR war." Women of "excellent character" who could pass an intelligence test could join the WAACS, provided they had no children under age 14; and unmarried, healthy women with no dependents under age 18 could enlist in the WAVES. A WAVE who married might remain in the service, as long as she had finished basic training and her husband was not in the service. The birth of a child brought an "honorable discharge."

At first glance, it appears that the armed forces offered dramatic new opportunities for women, but, on closer examination, it is clear that these wartime endeavors were temporary. It was impossible to combine jobs in the service with family life. Moreover, to dispel prevailing notions that military work would make women "masculine" or ruin their moral character, the armed services portrayed female recruits as "feminine" and domestically inclined. For example, the caption to a photograph of a young WAVE in a guidebook for women in the armed services and war industries described her as "pretty as her picture... in the trim uniform that enlisted U.S. Navy Waves will wear in winter... smartly-styled, comfortable uniforms... with a soft rolled-brim hat." Women in the military were needed for their "delicate hands" and "precision work at which women are so adept" and in hospitals where "there is a need in a man for comfort and attention that only a woman can fill." Women's corps leaders did little to challenge prevailing notions about female domesticity; they assured the public that after the war, enlisted women would be "as likely as other women to make marriage their profession."

These publicity measures met with only partial success amid public sentiment that was suspicious of women in nontraditional roles. In fact, rumors about the supposedly promiscuous sexual behavior and scandalous drunkenness of female recruits were so widespread that the armed forces had to refute the charges publicly. One result was the institutionalization of the double standard in the military: men were routinely supplied with contraceptives and encouraged to use them to prevent the spread of venereal disease, but women were denied access to birth control devices. In the rare cases in which sexual transgressions were discovered, women were punished more severely than were men.

Wartime also revived a long-dormant concern about lesbianism. The mobilization encouraged female camaraderie in military as well as civilian life, which raised suspicions that were translated into public policy. Although enlisted women could be dismissed for lesbianism, few were. The armed services were reluctant to enforce such policies because they did not want to acknowledge that military life fostered the development of lesbian relationships and communities. Calling attention to this fact would be more detrimental, they believed, than looking the other way, especially since they were making such strenuous efforts to portray the women's military corps *as* the training ground for future wives and mothers. Yet the repressive measures established during the war carried over into the postwar years, when the marital-heterosexual imperative became even more intense, contributing to increasing persecution of homosexual men and women.

Women who took wartime jobs in the industrial sector, like those in the armed forces, were assured that their domestic skills would suit them well in industrial production. Women war workers "have special capacities for work requiring 'feel,' that is minute assembly work and adjustments. Women are especially capable in grinding where fine tolerances are necessary." Automation had reduced the amount of physical strength needed for most jobs, and women's "nimble fingers" were well suited to the tasks at hand. Propaganda efforts launched by the War Manpower Commission and the Office of War Information to draw women into the labor force presented war work as glamorous and exciting, but its main appeal was to patriotism. Patriotism, along with altruism and self-sacrifice, were less threatening motives for women to take jobs because they implied impermanence. Although women had many other reasons for taking war production work—not the least of which was good pay—government propaganda during the war laid the groundwork for the massive layoffs of female employees after the war.

Women's tasks in the home were also given a patriotic purpose. Millions of women were involved in volunteer work during the war in such tasks as canning, knitting, saving fats, and making household goods last longer. Just as women's homemaking skills were critical for the survival of their families during the depression, so their domestic work made important contributions to the war effort.

Wartime elevated another female task to a patriotic level: purchasing. Purchasing power has been rooted in patriotic ideals since the days of the Revolution, when Americans joined ranks to boycott English goods and wear homespuns. During World War II, the management of personal finances became a problem of national concern. Bank deposits were at a record high, but spending was frustrated by shortages and rationing. The 6.5 million women who entered the labor force during the war acquired $8 billion more to spend. Since women usually did most of the purchasing for their families, much of the literature on the need for cautious consumerism was directed toward them. One typical example was a 1942 public affairs pamphlet, *How To Win on the Home Front*. The pamphlet addressed the problem of "more money to spend, less to buy." In a section entitled "Mrs. America Enlists," the author encouraged frugality: "In 1942 alone... the cost of the war to the consumers of the country is estimated at 3,500,000 automobiles, 2,800,000 refrigerators, 11,300,000 radios, 1,650,000 vacuum cleaners, and 1,170,000 washing machines.... The government is taking from the people what is needed to win the war. Consumers... must get along with what is left." Housewives were called on to be "militant consumers.... Their weapons are intelligent buying, conservation, and cooperation.... Their budget is their battle plan."

More important than resourceful homemaking and careful consuming was parenting during wartime. Working mothers were warned "to see that their physical absence from home does not carry over into a mental absence after working hours." War should not undermine women's primary task: "If they carry out their pregnancies successfully, this is the most important patriotic job they can do." If these priorities shifted, "the whole structure of civilization may become undermined." No public official was more adamant on this issue than J. Edgar Hoover, Director of the Federal Bureau of Investigation. In a 1944 article entitled "Mothers... Our Only Hope," he pointed to "parental incompetence and neglect" as the causes for "perversion" and "crime." War jobs were not appropriate for mothers, Hoover claimed. "She already has her war job. Her patriotism consists in not letting quite understandable desires to escape for a few months from a household routine or to get a little money of her own tempt her to quit it. *There must be no absenteeism among mothers....* Her patriotic duty is not on the factory front. It is on the home front!"

Mothers were praised for doing their jobs well, but if they were not attentive enough or were too attentive, they became the decade's villains. It was in 1942 that Philip Wylie coined the term "Momism" in his best-selling book, *Generation of Vipers*. "Momism," according to Wylie and his many followers, was the result of frustrated women who smothered their children with overprotection and overaffection, making their sons in particular weak and passive. As a fervent patriot during the war and a virulent anticommunist after the war, Wylie argued that the debilitating effects of Momism would seriously weaken the nation and make it vulnerable to an enemy takeover.

The vast changes in gender arrangements that some feared and others hoped for never fully materialized. Actually, the war underscored women's tasks as homemakers, consumers, and mothers just as powerfully as it expanded their paid jobs. For all the publicity surrounding Rosie the Riveter, few women took jobs that were previously held exclusively by men, and those who did earned less than men. Developments in the female labor force foreshadowed a pattern that continued after the war: the numerical expansion of opportunities flowing into an increasingly limited range of occupations. Although women demonstrated their eagerness for nontraditional work and proved themselves competent, few were able to retain those jobs after the war. As a result, wartime ultimately reinforced the sex-segregation of the labor force.

After the war, nearly all the Rosies who had riveted had to find something else to do. They did not simply go home, as the government propaganda urged them to do. Even if the potential for a restructured work force withered when the men reclaimed their old jobs, the promise of altered domestic roles still remained alive. Three out of four employed women hoped to keep working after the war, including 69 percent of the working wives. Somehow, home life would have to respond to the increasing number of married women who would be employed. Presumably, family routines as well as power relations would shift if women became breadwinners along with men. But the policies of the government, private sector employers, and even unions made it difficult for women to avoid economic dependence, even if they continued to hold jobs. Although it was still possible for most women who wanted a job to find one, the economic status of employed women deteriorated significantly after the war. Women's average weekly pay declined from $50 to $37—a drop of 26 percent, compared to a national postwar decrease of only 4 percent. Three-fourths of the women who had been employed in war industries were still employed in 1946, but 90 percent of them were earning less than they had earned during the war.

The range of jobs for women in the military also shrank considerably after the war, owing in part to negative public opinion that would no longer tolerate "unfeminine" military occupations for women in peacetime. As a result, women left the armed services. Fewer than half, however, were able to find jobs that made use of the skills they had learned in the military. To make matters worse, these female veterans were considered dependents rather than providers in their homes, and therefore were ineligible for many of the important veterans benefits that were available to their male counterparts.

All female employees found it increasingly difficult to combine the responsibilities of a family with employment. The few child care facilities that had been established by the federal government during the war closed, and mothers of small children faced even more intense pressures to stay home. Two million women left their jobs after the war. The number of employed women aged 20 to 34 dropped to one million below the prewar predictions. The retreat of these women made room for more older women to enter the paid labor force in the expanding pink-collar sector. Therefore, the actual number of women in gainful employment continued to rise after the war, even though the range of employment available to them narrowed. Black women were hit especially hard by the restructuring of the female labor force. Although they experienced a slight overall gain, their income was still less than half that of white women at the end of the decade....

In the wake of World War II, then, the short-lived affirmation of women's independence gave way to a pervasive endorsement of female subordination and domesticity. Ironically, the sudden emancipation of women during wartime gave rise to a suspicion surrounding autonomous women that had not been present during the depression. In the 1930s, while single women carved out a respected niche in the public arena, joined by married women who had to seek employment as a result of economic misfortune, the sex-segregation of the paid labor force was never violated. Moreover, although gender roles were unavoidably reversed in many homes, such reversals were often experienced as negative results of the disaster. During the war, however, even though the paid labor force remained predominantly sex segregated, women began to fill many jobs previously defined as "male." Not only were these female war workers accorded widespread publicity, they were praised for their skills and patriotism. Their war work, however, also appeared threatening because it demonstrated that women could do "men's work" and survive without men. The sexual independence of women was also feared; many believed it would weaken the nation during wartime and threaten the family later.

In addition to the ambivalence surrounding new roles for women, postwar life in general seemed to offer mixed blessings. Americans had postponed and pent up their desires to create something new and liberating, but unleashing those desires could lead to chaos as well as security. During the war, savings reached an all-time high as people banked one-fourth of their disposable income—more than triple the proportion saved during decades before and since. People looked forward to spending their money when the war ended, in much the same way as they looked forward to delayed gratifications in other areas of life. While Rosie riveted, men far from home hung pictures of sweethearts and sexy film stars on their walls and looked ahead to going home to sexually charged relationships. But according to widely expressed concerns, too much money, strong women, and too much sex might destroy the dream of the good life unless they were channeled in appropriate and healthy ways. Many hoped that women would be emancipated from their jobs and into the home, which would be enhanced by sex as well as consumer goods. But if all went awry, happiness and security would remain out of reach. The nightmare side of the postwar dream included "domineering" women and economic insecurity, all waiting to overwhelm the returning veterans hoping to get their jobs and their "girls" back.

And so the potential for a new model family, with two equal partners who shared breadwinning and homemaking tasks, never gained widespread support. In the long run, neither policymakers nor the creators of the popular culture encouraged that potential. Instead, they pointed to traditional gender roles as the best means for Americans to achieve the happiness and security they desired. Public policies and economic realities during the depression and the war limited the options of both women and men and reinforced traditional arrangements in the home. Even during the war, Americans were heading homeward toward gender-specific domestic roles.

# POSTSCRIPT

## Did World War II Liberate American Women?

Both of the essays in this issue are products of the historiographical debate sparked by William Chafe's *The American Woman: Her Changing Social, Economic, and Political Roles, 1920–1970* (Oxford University Press, 1972). In this first scholarly study of women's roles in the years after suffrage, Chafe emphasizes the remarkable changes produced in women's economic lives by the outbreak of World War II. Whereas most working women prior to the war had been young and single, Chafe notes, between 1940 and 1944 married women outnumbered single women in the female work force. Women whose husbands were in the military were twice as likely to be employed outside the home as other women. By 1945 half of all female employees were over the age of 35. In addition, American women benefited from a shift in emphasis from domestic service to manufacturing occupations, especially in defense industries, and the disparity in wages between men and women narrowed.

A number of feminist scholars have challenged Chafe's conclusions by insisting that women's wartime experiences represented continuity with, rather than change from, the past. While admitting that economic opportunities opened for women during the conflict, these historians focus upon the temporary nature of the experiences. For example, Karen Anderson's *Wartime Women: Sex Roles, Family Relations, and the Status of Women During World War II* (Greenwood Press, 1981) and Susan M. Hartmann's *The Home Front and Beyond: American Women in the 1940s* (Twayne, 1982) make the argument (consistent with that presented in May's essay) that women entered the labor force out of a sense of patriotic obligation rather than from personal ambition. Moreover, a number of institutional barriers, such as insufficient government support for adequate day-care facilities, limited the potential for progress in the economic lives of American women. Other studies that support these views are D' Ann Campbell, *Women at War With America: Private Lives in a Patriotic Era* (Harvard University Press, 1984); Maureen Honey, *Creating Rosie the Riveter: Class, Gender, and Propaganda During World War II* (University of Massachusetts Press, 1984); and Ruth Milkman, *Gender at Work: The Dynamics of Job Discrimination by Sex During World War II* (University of Illinois Press, 1987).

The literature on the United States during World War II is extensive. The best discussions of home front activities are found in Richard Polenberg, *War and Society: The United States, 1941–1945* (J. B. Lippincott, 1972); John Morton Blum, *V Was for Victory: Politics and American Culture During World War II* (Harcourt Brace Jovanovich, 1976); and Allan M. Winkler, *Home Front U.S.A.: America During World War II* (Harlan Davidson, 1986).

# ISSUE 13

## Was It Necessary to Drop the Atomic Bomb to End World War II?

**YES: McGeorge Bundy,** from *Danger and Survival* (Random House, 1988)

**NO: Martin J. Sherwin,** from *A World Destroyed: Hiroshima and the Origins of the Arms Race* (Vintage Press, 1987)

**ISSUE SUMMARY**

**YES:** Professor of history McGeorge Bundy maintains that President Truman wisely dropped the atomic bomb in order to end the war as quickly as possible.

**NO:** Professor of history Martin J. Sherwin argues that American policymakers ruled out all other options and dropped the atomic bomb, an understandable but unnecessary act.

America's development of the atomic bomb began in 1939 when a small group of scientists led by well-known physicist Albert Einstein called President Franklin D. Roosevelt's attention to the enormous potential uses of atomic energy for military purposes. In his letter, Einstein warned Roosevelt that Nazi Germany was already experimenting in this area. The program to develop the bomb, which began very modestly in October 1939, soon expanded into the $2 billion Manhattan Project, which combined the talents and energies of scientists (many of whom were Jewish refugees from Hitler's Nazi Germany) from universities and research laboratories across the country. The Manhattan Project was the beginning of the famed military-industrial-university complex that we take for granted today.

Part of the difficulty in reconstructing the decision to drop the atomic bomb lies in the rapidity with which events moved in the spring of 1945. On May 7, 1945, Germany surrendered. Almost a month earlier the world was stunned by the death of FDR, who was succeeded by Harry Truman, a former U.S. senator who was chosen as a compromise vice-presidential candidate in 1944. The man from Missouri had never been a confidant of Roosevelt. Truman did not even learn of the existence of the Manhattan Project until 12 days after he became president, at which time Secretary of War Henry L. Stimson advised him of a "highly secret matter" that would have a "decisive" effect upon America's postwar foreign policy.

Because Truman was unsure of his options for using the bomb, he approved Stimson's suggestion that a special committee of high-level political, military, and scientific policymakers be appointed to consider the major issues. The committee recommended unanimously that "the bomb should be used against Japan as soon as possible . . . against a military target surrounded by other buildings . . . without prior warning of the nature of the weapon."

A number of scientists disagreed with this report. They recommended that the weapon be tested on a desert island before representatives of the United Nations and that an ultimatum be sent to Japan warning of the destructive power of the bomb. Should the Japanese reject the warning, these young scientists suggested that the bomb be used only "if sanction of the United Nations (and of public opinion at home) were obtained."

A second scientific committee created by Stimson rejected both the test demonstration and warning alternatives. This panel felt that if the bomb failed to work during the demonstration, there would be political repercussions both at home and abroad.

Thus, by the middle of June 1945, the civilian leaders were unanimous that the atomic bomb should be used. During the Potsdam Conference in July, Truman learned that the bomb had been successfully tested in New Mexico. The big three—Truman, Atlee, and Stalin—issued a warning to Japan to surrender or suffer prompt and utter destruction. When the Japanese equivocated in their response, the Americans replied by dropping an atomic bomb on Hiroshima on August 6, which killed 100,000 people, and a second bomb on August 9, which leveled the city of Nagasaki. During this time the emperor pleaded with the Japanese military to end the war. On August 14 the Japanese accepted the terms of surrender with the condition that the emperor not be treated as a war criminal.

Was it necessary to drop the atomic bomb on Japan in order to end the war? In the following selections, McGeorge Bundy, a former high-level governmental official who helped Stimson write his memoirs in the late 1940s, advances a modified traditional view of the events. American policymakers, he argues, were guided by short-run considerations and dropped the bomb for military reasons. The successful explosion at Hiroshima also shortened the war because it led to the Russian declaration of war on Japan a week ahead of schedule and forced the Japanese militarists to adhere to the emperor's wishes and surrender less than a week later. Martin J. Sherwin takes issue with Bundy's analysis and advances a modified revisionist thesis. The atomic bomb was dropped, he says, because policymakers preferred it over alternative options such as a modification of unconditional surrender, the continuation of a naval blockade and conventional air bombardment, or the awaiting of a Russian declaration of war against Japan and its invasion of Manchuria.

# YES McGeorge Bundy

## DANGER AND SURVIVAL

In the decades since Hiroshima a number of writers have asserted a quite different connection between the American thinking on the bomb and the Soviet Union—namely that a desire to impress the Russians with the power of the bomb was a major factor in the decision to use it. This assertion is false, and the evidence to support it rests on inferences so stretched as to be a discredit both to the judgment of those who have argued in this fashion and the credulity of those who have accepted such arguments. There is literally no evidence whatever that the timetable for the attack was ever affected by anything except technical and military considerations; there is no evidence that anyone in the direct chain of command from [President Harry S.] Truman to [Secretary of War Henry L.] Stimson to [Secretary of State George C.] Marshall to [Brigadier General Leslie R.] Groves ever heard of or made any suggestion that either the decision itself or the timing of its execution should be governed by any consideration of its effect on the Soviet Union.

What is true—and important—is that these same decision makers were full of hope that the bomb would put new strength into the American power position. As we shall see, they were in some confusion as to how this "master card" (Stimson's term) should be played, but they would have been most unusual men if they had thought it irrelevant. It is also true that Byrnes [James F. Byrnes, who headed the office of War Mobilization] in particular was eager to get the war in Japan over before the Russians came in, thinking quite wrongly that their moves on the mainland might thus be forestalled. In May he also argued with Leo Szilard [a physicist who predicted the problem of uncontrolled nuclear weapons proliferation] on the question whether the use of the bomb in Japan would make the Soviet Union harder or easier to deal with—but this was merely an argument with a scientist who was presenting a contrary view, not a statement of basic reasons for the decision. That decision belonged, by all the accepted practices of wartime Washington, in the hands of the commander in chief and the Pentagon; Byrnes supported it, but he did not originate it or modify it in any way. At the most the opinions of Byrnes deprived Truman of the different advice that he might have heard from a different secretary of state. But the name of a man who would have been ready and able to sway Truman from the course so powerfully supported by Stimson and Marshall, and so deeply consonant with the wartime attitudes of the American people and with his own, does not leap to mind. Ending the war in complete victory just as fast as possible was a totally dominant motive in its own right. This preemptive purpose, along with the compulsive secrecy of the whole business, certainly made men slow to attend to other considerations, one of which could well have been a more thoughtful look at the real effect the use of the bomb would have on Moscow. But this is a totally different point well made by later and more careful critics.

Each of the realities that produced the Japanese surrender was purposely concealed from Japan, and each of these concealments was governed on the American side by the conviction that for use against Japan the bomb was indeed *a military weapon like any other,* if more so. Keep the value of surprise and do not give warning; use it to bring your enemy to the very brink of surrender *before* you make a concession on the emperor that might otherwise seem weak or embarrass you at home, and use it right on schedule if its use can help to minimize the role of an increasingly troubling ally.

What you do not think of separately, you seldom think of all at once, so it is not surprising that no one fully examined the possibilities of a triple demarche: warning of the bomb, warning of Soviet entry, and assurances on the emperor. Obviously Potsdam was no place for such thoughts [the Potsdam Conference was held between Truman, Soviet premier Joseph Stalin, and British prime minister Winston Churchill to discuss possible action against Japan]; by then the basic decisions had been made, and no senior American at Potsdam was in a mood for reversing them. A more interesting question is what might have happened in May and June, in Washington, if there had been a group charged with the duty of considering the bomb, the emperor, and the Soviet pledge, all together, in the context of achieving early surrender, and if that group had been charged to consider also the possible advantages of *not* having to use the bomb. Or better yet, what might have happened if the same questions had been examined even earlier, by Roosevelt and a few advisers?

There are several tantalizing hints that Franklin Roosevelt was troubled about the basic question of using the weapon against Japan in a way that his successor never was. In a most secret private memorandum that no other senior American saw until after he was dead, Roosevelt agreed with Churchill, at Hyde Park on September 18 or 19, 1944, that "when a 'bomb' is finally available, it might perhaps, after mature consideration, be used against the Japanese...." Four days later he asked [Office of Scientific Research and Development director Vannevar] Bush, in a long and general exchange, whether the bomb should actually be used against the Japanese or tested and held as a threat. The two men agreed that the question should be carefully discussed, but Roosevelt also accepted Bush's argument that it could be "postponed for quite a time" in view of the fact that "certainly it would be inadvisable to make a threat unless we were distinctly in a position to follow it up if necessary." So twice in less than a week Roosevelt thought about *whether* and *how* to use the bomb.

Six weeks later, in a fireside chat on the eve of the election, he made his one public reference to the bomb. It was cryptic and not much noticed at the time, but its meaning is plain enough now. Speaking of the need to put a lasting end to "the agony of war," he warned of terrible new weapons:

> Another war would be bound to bring even more devilish and powerful instruments of destruction to wipe out civilian populations. No coastal defenses, however strong, could prevent these silent missiles of death, fired perhaps from planes or ships at sea, from crashing deep within the United States itself.

The records at Hyde Park show that this extraordinary forecast was the product of the president's own changes in the speechwriter's draft, and it takes no great leap of imagination to suppose that a man facing a decision on the use of just such a "devilish" device would have thought about it pretty hard. Yet in the same speech Roosevelt called it an all-important goal to win the war "at the earliest moment." In 1944 he said to his secretary Grace Tully, without telling her what the Manhattan Project was about [Manhattan Project refers to the coordinated efforts to develop the atomic bomb], that "if it works, and pray God it does, it will save many American lives." He also told his son James in January 1945 that there was a new weapon coming along that would make an invasion of Japan unnecessary. It would therefore be wrong to conclude that Roosevelt would not have used the bomb *in some fashion.* Nevertheless the joint memorandum with Churchill and the conversation with Bush do give the impression that the question of actually dropping an atomic bomb on a Japanese target was for Roosevelt a real question as it was not for Truman, or indeed for Stimson and Byrnes. The men at the top when the time came had the rapid ending of the war as their wholly dominant purpose.

Sometime in December Roosevelt heard a recommendation for an international demonstration from Alexander Sachs, the friend who had brought him Einstein's letter back at the beginning. But he did not follow up on this conversation with anyone else; indeed he never again pressed his September question to Bush. Here, as on still larger questions of long-run atomic policy, he kept his counsel. In his last few months a posture that had been established by the combined force of his passionate concern for secrecy and his desire not to be crowded by advice was reinforced by the dreadful weight of his own growing fatigue. If something did not have to be done now, he would not do it. In the winter of 1944–45 both the first nuclear test and the final climax of the war on Japan still seemed far away. Given the orders for secrecy that he had given so explicitly in October 1941 and reinforced so strongly ever since, his own delay meant delay by everyone.

But what was too far away in the winter was also too near in the spring. Consider the case of [Undersecretary of the Navy] Ralph Bard: In early May he joins a committee whose first business is to plan the actions required by an expected use of the bomb. He is exposed to the problems and possibilities of warning and demonstration only on May 31; both the soldiers and the physicists, well ahead of him in both exposure and expertise, argue that sudden surprise use is more likely to work. Nowhere in this meeting or in a second discussion on June 18 is he asked to relate this problem to that of the emperor, or to that of Russian entry. Is it surprising that it takes him until June 27 to work out those connections for himself, probably helped by talks with [Assistant Secretary of War John J.] McCloy? But by then it is really too late; his committee has long since been recorded the other way, and in any case Bard has no standing on two of the three questions he has correctly pulled together; even his second thoughts on explicit warning about the bomb have an air of indecisiveness.

Or consider the effort of McCloy. He gets his one big chance on June 18 almost by accident. He is present and prepared because Stimson, feeling unwell, has not initially intended to come. But when he does speak, at the president's direction, one part of his proposal, for an explicit warning on the bomb, is not supported by his own secretary or indeed by the president. They have already decided the matter the other way two weeks earlier. His proposal on the emperor is referred to the unenthusiastic Byrnes. McCloy impressed the president; on August 14 Truman called him up and ordered him over to the White House to attend the announcement of the Japanese surrender. After the ceremony, the president told the assistant secretary that he had given more help than anyone else. But what Truman clearly meant was help in ending the war before an invasion, not in ending it before using the bomb. Helping Harry Truman to be ready to "let 'em keep the emperor" was not trivial, but it was not the same as a full study of the fateful choices on the use of the bomb, and no one knew that better than McCloy himself. Like Bard, but with the advantage of a direct order to speak his mind, he did what he could. Through no fault of his, it was too little and too late.

It is hard to avoid the conclusion that the real opportunities had been missed earlier. Let us suppose Roosevelt himself had established a council not unlike the Interim Committee, but with an earlier start and a wider charge. Might not all these possible ways to peace have been examined, at least, and possibly tried? The use of Alamogordo [an air base in New Mexico where the first atomic bomb was successfully detonated] for demonstration and warning could have been imagined more easily before its imminence made men tense. The role of the emperor, which divided the government so sharply when stated in terms of its effect on the Japanese political future, might not have been so divisive if considered in the context of trying to start the atomic age the right way. I find it relevant that two of those most wary of the emperor, [Assistant Secretaries of State Dean] Acheson and [Archibald] MacLeish, later showed themselves intensely aware of the magnitude of the issues presented by nuclear weapons. In July 1945 they were not authorized parties to the secret.

In earlier months, with Soviet participation still clearly desired, it might not have been impossible to think through a pattern of combined action that was at least worth consideration—and quite possibly action. The inclusion of the Soviets is difficult; it inevitably engages wider questions about the bomb in relation to the Soviet Union that we have yet to consider. Yet American decisions to give assurances on the emperor and to demonstrate the bomb, if announced in time to Moscow, might in themselves have produced prompt Soviet action of a sort that would help bring surrender from Tokyo. Moreover the later fear of an unwanted Russian role in the main islands of Japan was not a fear of what the Soviets could insist on, but rather of what the Americans themselves might unwisely concede. The forces occupying these islands would always be those allowed ashore by the United States Navy, and in any case a Russian claim to an occupation zone in the main islands would have failed by the precedents already established in Europe. Certainly the Russians wanted such a zone, but there was no good reason, still less any need, to let them have it.

All these possible means of ending the war without using the bomb are open to question; they remain possibilities, not certainties. It remains remarkable that nothing remotely like them was ever even considered, by any senior body, or by any single individual except Ralph Bard. After the war Colonel Stimson, with the fervor of a great advocate and with me as his scribe, wrote an article intended to demonstrate that the bomb was not used without a searching consideration of alternatives. That some effort was made, and that Stimson was its linchpin, is clear. That it was as long or wide or deep as the subject deserved now seems to me most doubtful. Franklin Roosevelt, the great man who himself had the earliest recorded doubts of use without warning, was probably also the principal obstacle to such consideration.

Yet if Stimson claimed too much for the process of consideration, his basic defense remains strong, within his own assumption that in the context of the war against Japan the bomb was a weapon like any other. Its use did surely help to end the war. The attack on Hiroshima, by the persuasive evidence of the Japanese best placed to know, provided a shock of just the sort the peace party and the emperor needed to force the issue. It also served to accelerate the Soviet entry (a point that Stimson and I, among other defenders of the decision, later failed to emphasize). Stalin at Potsdam had said he would be ready by August 15, but after Hiroshima, on August 6, he decided on an earlier date and thus provided a second and nearly simultaneous shock. When the Soviet Union broadcast its declaration of war, before dawn on August 9, three Soviet armies were already invading Manchuria. The Japanese decision for surrender came less than twenty-four hours later. Efforts to measure the two shocks against each other are futile; both were powerful, and different Japanese advisers weighed them differently. The two together brought a Japanese response that led in turn to the American assurance on the emperor. So in the event the use of the bomb did catalyze the rapid convergence of the three actions that both forced and permitted surrender.

Even today we cannot know *by how much* this extraordinary set of events shortened the war—whether by days, weeks, or months. None of the retrospective estimates, long or short, is entitled to high credibility; in particular one should be skeptical of the estimates of officers who thought their own preferred weapons had almost finished the job. No such guesswork, in advance, could be a basis for action or inaction at the time. I have argued my own present belief that there were things that might have been done to increase the chance of early surrender, but I have also had to recognize how hard it was to decide to do those things as matters actually stood in May, June, and July.

And if perhaps, or even probably, there were better courses, we must also recognize that we are measuring a real decision against might-have-beens. The bomb did not win the war, but it surely was responsible for its ending when it did. To those who cheered at the time —and they were the vast majority— that was what mattered most. The bomb did shorten the war; to those in charge of its development that had been its increasingly manifest destiny for years.

## MORAL QUESTIONS

There remain two questions of morality, one specific and one general: Even if Hiroshima was necessary, or at least defensible, what of Nagasaki? Long before Alamogordo and Potsdam it was agreed to seek authority for more than one attack in a single decision, and Truman accepted that arrangement. This decision was defended later on the ground that it was not one bomb or even two, but the prospect of many, that was decisive.

But Hiroshima alone was enough to bring the Russians in; these two events together brought the crucial imperial decision for surrender, just *before* the second bomb was dropped. The news of Nagasaki arrived during a meeting that had been called by Prime Minister Suzuki Kantarō after the emperor had told him expressly that he wanted prompt surrender on whatever terms were necessary. There can be little doubt that the news of a second terrible attack strengthened the peace party and further shook the diehards, but the degree of this effect cannot be gauged. It is hard to see that much could have been lost if there had been more time between the two bombs. If the matter had not been settled long since, in a time when victory seemed much less close than it did on August 7, or if the authority to order the second attack had simply been retained in Washington, one guesses that the attack on Nagasaki would have been delayed for some days; the bomb in actual use was a shock in Washington too. Such a delay would have been relatively easy, and I think right.

More broadly, what if the notion of dropping the bomb on a city was simply wrong—not just hasty because there should have been warning, or gratuitous because assurance on the emperor could have done the job, or excessive because a smaller target could have been used just as well, or even dangerous because of its impact on the Russians (an argument we have yet to consider)—but just plain wrong? This fundamental question has been addressed most powerfully by Michael Walzer [editor of *Dissent*], and his argument deserves respectful attention, although—or perhaps because —*no one* put it forward before Hiroshima.

All of the alternatives to surprise attack on a city that were proposed or considered by anyone who knew about the bomb, in 1944–45, were put forward in terms that allowed for such possible use if other alternatives failed. Roosevelt asked Bush about a demonstration and a threat, but he recognized in the same conversation that you do not make a threat you are not able to carry out if necessary. The Franck committee [consisting of Szilard, physicist James Franck, and others who understood the destructive potential of nuclear weapons] proposed a demonstration, and George Marshall at one point considered a uniquely military installation (as distinct from a city full of such installations), but both recognized that it might be necessary to go on to urban targets. Bard, with all his desire for a complex diplomatic demarche, never argued against using the bomb if the demarche failed, nor did McCloy. No one ever went beyond the argument that we should use up other forms of action—warnings, demonstrations, or diplomacy—before an urban attack. Szilard came closest; in a petition Truman almost surely never saw—he was already at Potsdam when it was signed on July 17—Szilard and sixty-seven colleagues asked Truman not to decide on use "without seriously considering the moral responsibilities which are involved." Yet even this petition conceded that "the war has to be brought to a successful conclusion and attacks by atomic bombs may very well be an effective method of warfare." No one ever said simply, do not use it on a city *at all.*

That is what Walzer says, and he says it powerfully. To underline the strength of his conviction he accepts in its strongest form the contention that the bomb was less terrible than the kinds of warfare it helped to end. His reply is that the attack on Hiroshima was still wrong, because it violated a fundamental rule of war—that the rights of noncombatants must be respected. The citizens of Hiroshima had done nothing that justified the terrible fate that overtook them on August 6; to kill them by tens of thousands merely in order to shock their government into surrender was a violation of the great tradition of civilized warfare under which "the destruction of the innocent, whatever its purposes, is a kind of blasphemy against our deepest moral commitments." Walzer grants an exception for "supreme emergency"—for the British, perhaps, when they were embattled alone against Hitler. But where, he asks, was the supreme emergency for the United States in August 1945? Even if Hiroshima was less murderous than continued firebombings and blockade, it was wrong, and all that the comparison can demonstrate is the equal wickedness of the existing "conventional" unlimited war. You might justify any one of these kinds of war against civilians if it was all that stood between you and a Hitler: If we don't do X to him, *he* will do Y (much worse) to us. But it is quite another matter to say, "If we don't do X, *we* will do Y."

Walzer's is a powerful argument, but it runs as forcefully against incendiaries as against nuclear bombs. His moral argument against the use of the bomb requires an equal moral opposition to the whole long, brutal tendency of modern war makers to accept, and sometimes even to seek, the suffering of civilians in the search for victory. He may well be deeply right, but we have seen already the enormous distance between this view of war making and what Americans actually thought in 1945. To reject the climactic acts as immoral Walzer must reject so very much else that his judgment becomes historically irrelevant. The change in strategy and tactics required by his argument is one that no political leader could then have imposed. By requiring too much he proves too little.

The war against Japan that had such momentum by the summer of 1945 may well have involved much immorality and in more ways than Walzer had space to catalogue. But that was the war that needed ending, and so much the weapon did. To those who were caught up in that war on both sides, it was no small service. I should declare a personal interest: If the war had gone on to a campaign in the main Japanese islands, the infantry regiment of which I was then a member would have been an early participant, and I do not to this day see how that campaign could have been readily avoided if there had been no urban bombing and no threat of an atomic bomb. If as a company commander I had ventured to take Walzer's view, with officers or men, I think I would have been alone, and even to reach the question of taking such a lonely view I would have had to have more understanding than I did.

There remains a final question: Was not the nuclear weapon, in and of itself, morally or politically different from firebombs and blockades, and in ways that should have required that it not be used? Cannot Walzer's argument be amended and strengthened, by remarking that even these "primitive" nuclear weapons were so terrible, not only in their explosive and incendiary effect but also in their radiation, that it was morally wrong to be the first to use them? And especially because the American effort had uncovered, as early as 1942, the still more terrible prospect of thermonuclear weapons, was there not also a political imperative to set an example of restraint? Although none of them ever presented such an argument in categorical terms, thoughts like these were strong among men like Franck, Szilard, and Bard. But since they all agreed that the bomb might be used on an inhabited target if all else failed to bring surrender, they accepted the terms of debate that in fact were followed. When their proposals were judged unlikely to end the war as quickly as direct military use, they could not fall back on a claim that here was a moral or political imperative against killing civilians in this new and terrible way. Even the doubters were in some measure prisoners of the overriding objective of early victory.

Yet it is right for us all to ponder these more absolute questions. I do not myself find Hiroshima more *immoral* than Tokyo or Dresden, but I find the *political* question more difficult. The nuclear world as we now know it is grimly dangerous; might it be less dangerous if Hiroshima and Nagasaki had never happened? If so, a stretchout of the anguish of war might have been a small price to pay. No one can make such an assessment with certainty: as we move on to later events we shall encounter evidence that weighs on both sides. All that we can say here is that the Americans who took part in the decisions of 1945 were overwhelmingly governed by the immediate and not the distant prospect. This dominance of clear present purpose over uncertain future consequences is a phenomenon we shall meet again.

Historically almost predestined, by the manner of its birth and its development, made doubly dramatic by the fateful coincidence that it was ready just when it might be decisive, and not headed off by any carefully designed alternative—of threat, assurance, demonstration, or all of them together—the bomb dropped on Hiroshima surely helped to end a fearful war. It was also the fierce announcement of the age of nuclear weapons. To the men who made and used it, or at least to many of them much of the time, this double meaning of what they were doing was evident.... In the summer of 1945 their overriding present purpose was to shorten the war, and in that they succeeded.

Given this overriding purpose it was natural for most of them to accept the argument for using the new weapons by surprise just as soon and just as impressively as possible. The president with doubts never acted on them or set others free to work them through. The president without such doubts never looked behind the assumptions of April, the recommendations of June, or the final approvals of July, nor did anyone close to him ever press him to do so. Whether broader and more extended deliberation would have yielded a less destructive result we shall never know. Yet one must regret that no such effort was made.

# NO

## Martin J. Sherwin

# A WORLD DESTROYED

On July, 16, 1945, dawn broke twice over the Alamagordo desert in New Mexico. At 5:30 A.M., thirty minutes before the sun rose, science preempted nature with "a lighting effect... equal to several suns at midday." Just five and a half years after the discovery of nuclear fission, Manhattan Project scientists had constructed and successfully tested an atomic bomb. By raising the consequences of war to the level of Armageddon, the atomic bomb elevated the stakes of peace beyond historical experience. In physicist I. I. Rabi's cryptic phrase: "Suddenly the day of judgment was the next day and has been ever since."...

## HIROSHIMA AS MORAL HISTORY

More than four decades after the destruction of Hiroshima and Nagasaki, the relevance of the fate of those cities has not diminished, nor have the debates they ignited. No one who looks closely at those debates will fail to recognize that there are issues at stake that go beyond military history. There are questions of morality, national character, and this nation's responsibility for the shape of the postwar world. Hiroshima not only introduced the nuclear age, it also served as the symbolic coronation of U.S. global power. The atomic bomb, as more than one contemporary cartoonist depicted it, was our scepter, and its use contributed to the image of our international authority.

But military power was not the only foundation for authority. "The position of the United States as a great humanitarian nation" was also important, Under Secretary of the Navy Ralph Bard wrote to the Secretary of War on June 27, 1945. Urging that the Japanese be warned several days prior to the attack, Bard sought to modify the decision taken on May 31 that "we could not give the Japanese any warning; that we could not concentrate on a civilian area; but that we should seek to make a profound psychological impression on as many of the inhabitants as possible." "At the suggestion of Dr. [James B.] Conant the Secretary [of War Henry L. Stimson] agreed," the minutes of the Interim Committee continued: *"the most desirable target would be a vital war plant employing a larger number of workers and closely surrounded by workers' houses*" (emphasis added).

Bard's advice went unheeded, however, and an early irony of Hiroshima was that the very act symbolizing our wartime victory was quickly turned against our peacetime purposes. At the 1946–1948 Tokyo War Crimes Trials, which, like the Nuremberg trials, were a symbolic expression of our moral authority, Justice Radhabinod Pal of India cited Hiroshima and Nagasaki as evidence against our claim to rule by right of superior virtue. The atomic bombings, he wrote in a dissenting opinion, were "the only near approach [in the Pacific War] to the directive... of the Nazi leaders during the Second World War."

President Truman's earliest public explanations for the bombings of Hiroshima and Nagasaki addressed the issues of just cause and morality that Pal later raised. "We have used [the atomic bomb]," he stated, "in order to shorten the agony of war, in order to save the lives of thousands and thousands of young Americans." But several days later he added less lofty reasons. Responding to a telegram criticizing the atomic bombings, the President wrote:

> Nobody is more disturbed over the use of Atomic bombs than I am but I was greatly disturbed over the unwarranted attack by the Japanese on Pearl Harbor and their murder of our prisoners of war. The only language they seem to understand is the one we have been using to bombard them.
>
> When you have to deal with a beast you have to treat him as a beast. It is most regrettable but nevertheless true.

But in the aftermath of Hiroshima, many thoughtful commentators began to view the bomb itself as the "beast." "For all we know," H. V. Kaltenborn, the dean of radio news commentators, observed on August 7, "we have created a Frankenstein! We must assume that with the passage of only a little time, an improved form of the new weapon we use today can be turned against us."

At some level, this thought has been the enduring nightmare of the nuclear age, a vision of an inevitable holocaust imbedded deep within our culture. "How does the universe end?" Billy Pilgrim, the protagonist in Kurt Vonnegut's *Slaughterhouse Five*, asks his omniscient Trafalmadorian captors. The novel continues:

> "We blow it up, experimenting with new fuels for our flying saucers. A Trafalmadorian test pilot presses a starter button, and the whole Universe disappears."
>
> "If you know this," said Billy, "isn't there some way you can prevent it? Can't you keep the pilot from pressing the button?"
>
> "He has always pressed it, and he always will. We always let him and we always will let him. The moment is structured that way."

The structure of the nuclear age—deterrence and the inexorable accumulation of the weapons designed to promote its purposes—has encouraged a deadening sense that there are forces at work beyond political control. The American public's feeling of powerlessness before those forces may be the single most important reason behind the belief that a massive arsenal of nuclear weapons is needed to guarantee our national security. Even here, the moral dimension of the debate over the atomic bombings of Hiroshima and Nagasaki is relevant, for it is of paramount importance to those who wish to rely upon nuclear weapons that they are not tarnished with a sense of guilt that could inhibit their use as an instrument of diplomacy.

This concern about the practical effects of "Hiroshima guilt" was discussed soon after the war by the Manhattan Project's chief science administrator, James Conant, who had returned full time to his post as president of Harvard University. Raising the issue in a letter to former Secretary of War Henry L. Stimson, he wrote of his concern about the "spreading accusation that it was entirely unnecessary to use the atomic bomb at all," particularly among those he described as "verbal minded citizens not so generally influential as they were influential among the coming generations of whom they might be teachers or educators." To combat that view, he urged Stimson to write an article on "the decision to use the bomb," which subsequently appeared in the February 1947 issue of *Harper's* magazine.

If "the propaganda against the use of the atomic bomb had been allowed to grow unchecked," Conant wrote to Stimson after reading a prepublication version of the article, "the strength of our military position by virtue of having the bomb would have been correspondingly weakened," and the chances for international control undermined. "Humanitarian considerations" that led citizens to oppose the strengthening of the U.S. atomic arsenal, in Conant's opinion, were likely to subvert the common effort to achieve an international atomic energy agreement. "I am firmly convinced," he told Stimson, "that the Russians will eventually agree to the American proposals for the establishment of an atomic energy authority of world-wide scope, *provided they are convinced that we would have the bomb in quantity and would use it without hesitation in another war.*"

Stimson's article responded to Conant's practical concerns. Explaining the steps in the decision strictly in the context of the Pacific War and the objective of "avoiding the enormous losses of human life which otherwise confronted us," he left no room for the suggestion that considerations beyond the war could have been factors, or that in future similar circumstances the government would not be compelled to take similar actions. The war had not ended when the bomb became available; the decision flowed inexorably out of those circumstances: "In light of the alternatives which, on a fair estimate, were open to us I believe that no man, in our position and subject to our responsibilities," Stimson wrote, "holding in his hands a weapon of such possibilities, could have failed to use it and afterwards looked his countrymen in the face."

The primary argument for the "necessity" of using the atomic bomb was saving American lives. President Truman wrote in his memoirs that half a million U.S. soldiers would have been killed had the planned invasions been launched. Winston Churchill claimed that the figure was closer to a million. Could any responsible Commander-in-Chief send so many young men to die on foreign shores when an alternative like the atomic bomb was readily at hand?

As stated, the question answers itself. As stated, it also distorts the nature of the historical problem. Before the decision to use atomic bombs can be properly understood, many other questions need to be considered. They range from the expected impact of the use of the bomb on the Japanese during the war to the influence such a demonstration might have on the Soviet behavior afterward. They include questions related to bureaucratic momentum and political expediency; to the instinct for revenge as well as the pressure for results; to scientific pride and economic investments; to Roosevelt's legacy and Truman's insecurity.

In the original edition of *A World Destroyed* I sought to analyze these questions within their historical context, limiting the discussion to what was said and done before the bombs were dropped. My narrative tacitly accepted the published casualty estimates as a compelling influence limiting decision makers' choices. But recently discovered estimates of invasion casualties dramatically contradict the figures released by Truman, Churchill, and Stimson. These require some comments on the information that has shaped the postwar debate.

Historians have known for decades that several alternatives to atomic bombing or an invasion of Japan were considered during May and June 1945. The first was to modify unconditional surrender. Having broken the Japanese diplomatic code, the Department of State's Far Eastern specialists were sanguine that the peace advocates in the Imperial Cabinet could win capitulation if the United States assured Japan that it would maintain the Emperor and the Imperial Dynasty. The second alternative was to delay the atomic bombings until after August 8, the final day on which Stalin could live up to his agreement to enter the war against Japan within three months of Germany's surrender. [On August 8 the Soviet Union declared war on Japan.] The third alternative, Admiral William D. Leahy wrote to the Joint Chiefs of Staff on June 14, 1945, was "to defeat Japan by isolation, blockade, and bombardment by sea and air forces."

All of these suggestions were viable alternatives, but none of them was without its particular disadvantages.

The first option, modifying unconditional surrender, was politically risky. Introduced by Roosevelt and accepted by the Allies, the unconditional surrender had become the basis upon which the public expected the war to be concluded. From the point of view of Truman and his advisers, tampering with this doctrine appeared fraught with unattractive political dangers. [Nevertheless, *after* the Soviets declared war on Japan and *after* both available bombs had been dropped, unconditional surrender was modified according to the terms stated above.]

Second, a Japanese surrender (precipitous or otherwise) following the entry of the Soviet Union into the Pacific War would have facilitated the expansion of Soviet power in the Far East. By summer of 1945 such an option was anathema to Truman and his advisers.

Finally, continuing the blockade and bombardment promised no immediate results and might, as the Joint War Plans Committee wrote to the President, "have an adverse effect upon the U.S. position vis-à-vis other nations who will, in the meantime, be rebuilding their peacetime economy."

In the summer of 1945 it was therefore not the lack of an alternative that might induce Japan's surrender that led to the use of atomic bombs. It was the undesirability of relying on the available alternatives *given the nuclear option.* The nuclear option was preferred because it promised dividends—not just the possibility that it would end the war but the hope that it would eliminate the need to rely on one of the other alternatives.

The question of how policymakers came to understand their choices is probed throughout *A World Destroyed.* It is a question we should keep before us as the recent discovery of the actual invasion casualty estimates should make clear. The casualty estimates announced by Truman in the aftermath of Hiroshima were grossly exaggerated.... For example, on June 15, 1945, the Joint War Plans Committee (JWPC) estimated that about 40,000 Americans would be killed and 150,000 wounded if *both* southern Kyushu and the Tokyo plain had to be invaded (on November 1, 1945, and March 1, 1946, respectively). General George C. Marshall, Army Chief of Staff, who Truman cited in his memoirs as the source of the estimate that an invasion would cost "half a million American lives," endorsed an estimate on June 7 that was similar to the one produced a week later by the Joint War Plans Committee. On June 18, General Douglas MacArthur, the commander of U.S. Pacific forces, concurred with the range of JWPC's estimates. On July 9 a memorandum to the Joint Staff Planners entitled "Note by the Secretaries" included a revised casualty estimate of 31,000 killed, wounded, and missing for the first 30 days of the planned operation against Kyushu. [During the first 30 days of the Normandy invasion, the killed/wounded/missing count for U.S. troops was 42,000.]

In the end the most destructive conventional war of the century was concluded with the first nuclear warfare in history. Many who advocated that alternative hoped it would contribute to a postwar settlement that would banish those weapons—others hoped it would establish their value. But whatever they believed, those who felt called upon to defend the bombing of Hiroshima and Nagasaki came to recognize more clearly in retrospect what a few had warned in prospect: that nuclear war was beyond the reach of conventional moral categories.

Though no American President could be expected to have chosen an invasion of Japan if a plausible alternative was available, the fact that several available alternatives had been rejected increased the moral burden of justifying the extraordinary consequences of Hiroshima and Nagasaki. Americans had self-consciously fought World War II to preserve the values of their civilization. Is it surprising that in its aftermath those who had directed the war conspired to explain its terrible conclusion as unavoidable and consistent with those values?

Reflecting on the choices the administration had faced in the summer of 1945, former Secretary of War Stimson felt compelled to admit the possibility that refusing to modify unconditional surrender might have been a mistake—a mistake that could have *delayed* the end of the war. Composing his memoirs several years after the war, he wrote "that history might find that the United States, by its delay in stating its position [on the conditions of surrender], had prolonged the war."

Despite Stimson's singular remark, and the general availability of information about the other options, the invasion has remained *the* alternative to the atomic bombings in public discussions. Perhaps this is because the invasion remains the least ambiguous of the options. Or perhaps it is because it lends to the bombings an implicit moral legitimacy. According to the figures released, the magnitude of the projected slaughter of invading Americans was even greater than the actual slaughter of Japanese civilians. As reports, images, and tales of death, dying, and suffering from nuclear warfare filtered into the American press, the alternatives to the invasion were filtered out.

The manipulation of the estimated casualty figures, and thereby the history of the decision-making process that led to the atomic bombings of Hiroshima and Nagasaki, has masked an important lesson. The choice in the summer of 1945 was not between a conventional invasion or a nuclear war. It was a choice between various forms of diplomacy and warfare. While the decision that Truman made is understandable, it was not inevitable. It was even avoidable. In the end, that is the most important legacy of Hiroshima for the nuclear age.

## LOS ALAMOS AND HIROSHIMA

The confluence of the invention of weapons that could destroy the world and a foreign policy of global proportions removed the physical and psychological barriers that had protected the United States from the full force of international affairs before World War II. In the context of the cold war, politics no longer stopped at the water's edge. On the contrary, politics often began there. No group of Americans was more alert to this change than the scientists of the Manhattan Project, who had brought it about. To Robert Oppenheimer, the new alignment of science and power threatened "the life of science [and] the life of the world." The change in scale and stakes involved scientists more, he said, "than any other group in the world." The existence of the atomic bomb linked science to national security and made scientists into military assets. The twin "evils of secrecy and control strike at the very roots of what science is and what it is for," Oppenheimer warned his former colleagues at Los Alamos in November 1945.

The question of the meaning and uses of science raised by Oppenheimer took on a new sense of immediacy for all scientists after the war. With the advent of the atomic age, the answer to the question of science and the state inevitably became tied to the political and national defense issues generated by the cold war. As a result, the boundary between science and politics blurred, and the public's attitude toward science was increasingly defined by political criteria. In such an environment Bernard Baruch could suggest that "science should be free but only when the world has been freed from the menaces which hang over us."

The scientists disagreed. Fearing that science would become the first political victim of their success, Percy W. Bridgman, the president of the American Physical Society, responded to the threat of external control of science with the declaration that "society is the servant of science.... Any control which society exerts over science and invention must be subject to this condition."

With Bridgman, the scientist's, view at one pole and the converse approach expressed by Baruch at the other, it is not too much to suggest that there arose a split between "two cultures." But it was not, as C. P. Snow argued, a division having to do with a nonscientist's knowledge of the second law of thermodynamics or a scientist's ability to quote Shakespeare. It touched upon a deeper issue—the nature of freedom and power in a democratic society.

Oppenheimer spoke of this issue from a scientific perspective in answering the question he raised. "If you are a scientist," he said, "you believe that it is good to find out how the world works...

that it is good to turn over to mankind at large the greatest possible power to control the world and to deal with it according to its lights and its values." It was not for the scientist to judge, he implied, whether those lights and values were adequate to control new understandings. Nor was it for society to judge, he added explicitly, what the scientist should and should not seek to discover. Any such external control "is based on a philosophy incompatible with that by which we live, and have learned to live in the past." If society was not the servant of science, it certainly was a collaborator. To politicize science was to destroy it. A free state could only be well served by science if scientists were free to publish and discuss their research. A state was not free, he implied, if the life of science was not open and free of political control.

To keep politics out of science, scientists responded politically. Some counseled the Administration privately against policies that would lead to military control, while others led a successful campaign against military domination of the Atomic Energy Commission. However, in the ensuing cold war, civilian control of atomic energy proved to be illusory. Military requirements held sway, loyalty and security programs were vigorously enforced, and government support led to far more control than anticipated. Though scientists gained greater opportunities to participate in policy formulation, their advice was expected to support basic policies decided by others. This was the clear message communicated by the removal of Oppenheimer's security clearance in 1954.

After the war, the scientific community itself appeared to divide "culturally." Scientists such as Oppenheimer, Vannevar Bush, James Conant, Ernest Lawrence, and Karl and Arthur Compton worked closely with the government. In contrast, Leo Szilard, Eugene Rabinowitch, and other leaders of the Federation of American (Atomic) Scientists became vocal critics of the Truman Administration's policies. The division among scientists was fundamentally political, yet both groups shared an abiding faith in science. The scientific community was united by an unstated assumption that what was good for science was good for world peace. But how was peace best attained?

All scientists agreed that avoiding an atomic arms race with the Soviet Union was the most important issue of the day. The revolution in weapons technology, they maintained, could lead either to a peaceful diplomatic revolution or a nuclear-armed world. If an arms-control plan was not adopted, an arms race would harness science to military requirements. To avoid this catastrophe the veterans of the Manhattan Project lobbied vigorously to scuttle the military's attempt to capture the atom.

The outlines of that debate emerged during the war and became established soon afterward. Though only 13 atomic bombs existed in 1947, by 1948 the number had escalated to 50. In 1949, when the Soviet Union exploded its first atomic bomb, President Truman faced conflicting recommendations. One group of scientists and politicians urged him to opt for a program to develop a hydrogen bomb, a proposal that represented a "quantum leap" into the realm of megaton weapons. On the other side of the argument were the scientists of the Atomic Energy Commission's General Advisory Committee (GAC), who recommended against such an escalation, proposing instead that the

President adhere to the principle of sufficiency. "To the argument that the Russians may succeed in developing [the hydrogen bomb]," the members of GAC wrote in October 1949 to the President, "we would reply that our undertaking it will not prove a deterrent to them. Should they use the weapon against us, reprisals by our large stock of atomic bombs would be comparably effective to the use of a super [H]bomb." The moral consequences of technology were also at issue. "We base our recommendation," the committee members also wrote, "on our belief that the extreme dangers to mankind inherent to the proposal [for a super] wholly outweigh any military advantage that could come from this development."

But in January 1950 Truman opted for the hydrogen bomb. The principle of the nuclear containment of the Soviet Union —an idea that was first developed during the war in the context of the decision to use the atomic bomb against Japan—was now firmly set in place.

On October 16, 1945, his last day as director of the Los Alamos Scientific Laboratory, Robert Oppenheimer, who would write the GAC's report opposing the "super," accepted a certificate of appreciation from the Secretary of War on behalf of the laboratory with these words:

> It is our hope that in years to come we may look at this scroll, and all that it signifies with pride.
>
> Today that pride must be tempered with a profound concern. If atomic bombs are to be added as new weapons to the arsenals of a warring world, or to the arsenals of nations preparing for war, then the time will come when mankind will curse the names of Los Alamos and Hiroshima.

In the context of a nuclear-armed world, "how well they meant" and "how well we mean" cannot be the central points.

# POSTSCRIPT

## Was It Necessary to Drop the Atomic Bomb to End World War II?

Although he was appalled by the use of the atomic bomb, Bundy argues that the alternatives of a test demonstration and specific warning were rejected because Truman, along with everybody else, wanted the war to end as quickly as possible. The achievement of this goal is substantiated by an important work by Robert J. C. Butow, *Japan's Decision to Surrender* (Stanford University Press, 1954), whose thorough examination of Japanese sources demonstrates the importance of the bomb on the emperor's decision to pressure the Japanese military to surrender.

Since Sherwin's book was first published in 1975, new documents have come to light that seriously question the 300,000 to 500,000 American casualties that were estimated to result from the alternative plan of invading Japan. According to a document issued by the Joint War Plans Committee (JWPC) on June 15, 1945, approximately 40,000 U.S. soldiers would be killed and 15,000 wounded if both southern Krushu and the Tokyo plain were invaded in late 1945 and early 1946. Other analyses by Generals Marshall and MacArthur agree with the JWPC estimates. Sherwin's 1987 edition of *A World Destroyed* contains these documents, and a full discussion of whether or not a landed invasion should have been considered is in Barton Bernstein's "A Postwar Myth: 500,000 U.S. Lives Saved," *Bulletin of Atomic Scientists* (June/July 1986).

Two other issues deserve consideration: FDR's untimely death and the use of a second bomb at Nagasaki. Bundy shows that in 1944 FDR questioned whether or not the bomb should be "used against Japan or tested and held as a threat." He became ill in 1945 and died before the bomb was dropped, which allows us to speculate whether or not Roosevelt would have chosen a different alternative than his successor, Truman.

Both writers agree that military considerations were paramount. Sherwin, though, argues that U.S. officials viewed the bomb as a political/diplomatic weapon, which is why Roosevelt refused to share information about the Manhattan Project with Stalin as he did with Churchill. It also explains why Truman was not willing to wait for a Russian invasion of Manchuria, which may have given Russia the claim to an occupation zone in postwar Japan.

J. Samuel Walker has written the most recent and important article on the use of the bomb, entitled "The Decision to Use the Bomb: A Historiographical Update," *Diplomatic History* (Winter 1990).

There are three major additions to the continuing A-bomb controversy. James Hershberg has written a magisterial biography of the Harvard president and chairman of the National Defense Research Committee, *James Conant and the Birth of the Nuclear Age: From Harvard to Hiroshima* (Alfred A. Knopf, 1993). David Holloway uses the newly opened Soviet archives to write about *Stalin and the Bomb: The Soviet Union and Atomic Energy, 1939–1956* (Yale University Press, 1994) and concludes that nothing the United States did could have stopped the arms race. "Leave them in peace," Stalin said about the physicists working on the bomb. "We can always shoot them later." Finally, public historians clashed with interest groups once again in "The new battle of Hiroshima," *Newsweek* (August 29, 1994), when the Smithsonian Institute, under pressure from the American Legion and other veterans groups, modified its exhibit on the 50th anniversary of the dropping of the atomic bomb to include the traditional military reasons for the use of the bomb against the Japanese.

# PART 4

# The Cold War and Beyond

*The United States emerged from World War II in a position of global responsibility and power, but the struggle between the United States and the Soviet Union, which began near the end of the war, dominated U.S. foreign policy for more than 40 years. Since the war, many events have brought about numerous changes, both in the United States and in the world. These include: the resumption of domestic reform, which culminated in the Great Society and debate over the efficacy of government efforts at social engineering; the war in Vietnam, the outcome of which still influences U.S. policymakers today; and the civil rights movement, which resulted in many positive political and economic changes for middle-class blacks. This section concludes with an issue on President Nixon, who played a major role in the political life of the country and whose legacy continues to be debated.*

# ISSUE 14

## Did the Great Society Fail?

**YES: Charles Murray,** from "The Legacy of the 60's," *Commentary* (July 1992)

**NO: Joseph A. Califano, Jr.,** from "How Great Was the Great Society?" in Barbara C. Jordan and Elspeth D. Rostow, eds., *The Great Society: A Twenty Year Critique* (LBJ Library and LBJ School of Public Affairs, 1986)

### ISSUE SUMMARY

**YES:** Conservative social critic Charles Murray argues that not only did the Great Society's retraining, anticrime, and welfare programs not work, but they actually contributed to the worsening plight of U.S. inner cities.

**NO:** Joseph A. Califano, Jr., a former aide to President Lyndon Johnson, maintains that the Great Society programs brought about positive revolutionary changes in the areas of civil rights, education, health care, the environment, and consumer protection.

As we come to the end of the twentieth century, historians can look back at the era's three major political reform movements: Progressivism (1900–1917); the New Deal (1933–1938); and the Great Society (1963–1965). There were a number of similarities among the three movements. They were all led by activist, Democratic presidents—Woodrow Wilson, Franklin Delano Roosevelt, and Lyndon Baines Johnson. Top-heavy Democratic congressional majorities were created, which allowed the reform-minded presidents to break through the gridlock normally posed by an unwieldy Congress and pass an unusual amount of legislation in a short time span. Finally, all three reform currents came to a sudden stop when America's entrance into war diverted the nation's physical and emotional resources away from reform efforts at home.

Progressivism, the New Deal, and the Great Society also had to grapple with the social and economic problems of a nation where the majority of people lived in cities with populations of 100,000 or more and worked for large corporations. In order to solve these problems, government could no longer be a passive observer of the Industrial Revolution. Reformers believed that government would have to intervene in order to make capitalism operate fairly. Two approaches were used: (1) regulating the economy from the top down and (2) solving social problems from the bottom up.

World War II, the subsequent cold war, a world economy that was dominated by the United States until the late 1960s, and a general prosperity that prevailed in the economic cycle kept reform efforts at a minimum during the Truman (1945–1953) and Eisenhower (1953–1961) presidencies.

In 1960, when Democrat John F. Kennedy defeated Republican Richard Nixon, there were two major social and economic problems that remained unresolved by the New Deal: (1) the failure to integrate blacks into the mainstream of American society and (2) the failure to provide a decent standard of living for the hard-core poor, the aged, the tenant farmers, the migrant workers, the unemployed coal miners and mill workers, and the single mother of the inner city. Early in Kennedy's administration, Congress passed the Area Redevelopment Act of 1961, which provided close to $400 million in federal loans and grants for help to 675 "distressed areas" of high unemployment and low economic development. The president had plans for a more comprehensive attack on poverty, but his assassination on November 22, 1963, prevented implementation.

Kennedy's successor, Lyndon Johnson, took advantage of the somber mood of the country after Kennedy's assassination and of his landslide election victory in 1964, which created top-heavy Democratic congressional majorities of 295 to 140 in the House of Representatives and 68 to 32 in the Senate. Johnson believed that the Great Society and its programs were to be the completion of the New Deal. The Civil Rights Act of 1964 and the Voting Rights Act of 1965 introduced blacks into the mainstream of American society. Medicare and Medicaid tied health care for the elderly and poor people to the society security system. And the Elementary Secondary Education and the Higher Education Acts of 1965 provided funds for low-income local school districts and scholarships and subsidized low-interest loans for needy college students.

In January 1964 Johnson called for an "unconditional war on poverty." Later that year the Economic Opportunity Act was passed. This created an Office of Economic Opportunity (OEO), which set up a variety of community action programs for the purpose of expanding the educational, health care, housing, and employment opportunities in poor neighborhoods. Between 1965 and 1970 the OEO operated on the cheap, establishing such Community Action Programs (CAPs) as the Job Corps, which trained lower-class teenagers and young adults for employment, and Head Start, whose purpose was to give underprivileged preschool children skills that they could use when they attended regular elementary schools.

In the first selection, Charles Murray argues that the liberal Great Society retraining, anticrime, and welfare programs not only did not work but contributed to the worsening plight of U.S. inner cities. In the second selection, Joseph A. Califano, Jr., argues that the Great Society programs brought about positive revolutionary changes in the areas of civil rights, education, health care, the environment, and consumer protection.

# YES

## Charles Murray

# THE LEGACY OF THE 60's

"Is President Bush hinting that the Peace Corps destroyed the moral fiber of poor people?" asked Albert Shanker, the president of the American Federation of Teachers, responding to the claim by the White House spokesman, Marlin Fitzwater, that the failed social programs of the 1960's were responsible for the Los Angeles riot. For Senator Daniel Patrick Moynihan, Attorney General William Barr's assertion that the Great Society caused the breakdown of family structure was "one of the most depraved statements I have ever heard from an American official." Even Republican campaign strategists were having none of the administration line, the New York *Times* reported. "Next," one of them was quoted as saying, "Marlin [Fitzwater] will blame the savings-and-loan crisis on Woodrow Wilson."

Speaking of blame, I must take a share of it for the ridicule heaped on the administration, for in 1984 I published a book called *Losing Ground* which concluded that the reforms of social policy in the 60's directly made things worse for the American poor. And, ineptly as the administration went about pressing its point, I agree with Fitzwater's more ambitious thesis. The conditions in South-Central Los Angeles in 1992 that produced the riot *are* importantly a product of those reforms of a quarter-century ago....

The post-L.A. received wisdom seems to have three components. First, since the Republicans have been in power for twelve years, current social policy is their social policy. Second, the plight of black America got worse in the 80's. Third, we know by this time that some programs worked, with Head Start and Job Corps heading the list, so it is time to hitch up our pants and start doing the things that we know how to do.

All three of these contentions are wrong—with qualifications, of course, but still wrong.

* * *

For most of affluent America, the social policies of the 60's are over and done with. Most of these people have long since sent their children to private

From Charles Murray, "The Legacy of the 60's," *Commentary* (July 1992).  Notes omitted.

schools or moved to suburbs where the public schools are run as the parents wish. Most live in communities where the cops roust suspicious people, the Supreme Court be damned, and crime is low; or they live in urban enclaves where (within the enclave) crime is low. As for the rules about welfare and food stamps and social services, these never affected the affluent.

Within the inner city, however, especially among the poor, and most especially among the black poor, the 60's remain in full flower. An adolescent on the streets of an inner city as of 1992 lives in a governmental and policy environment only marginally different from the one that had evolved by the early 70's.

The schools work much as they did then. The reforms of the 60's saw an elaborate social agenda laid on the schools, the imposition of restrictions on how schools could deal with problem students (and, indirectly, how effectively they could educate gifted students), and layers of bureaucracy and books of rules that went along with vastly expanded federal assistance.

Suburban schools jettisoned much of this nonsense in the 80's. But the reforms of the 60's dove-tailed nicely with the propensity of big-city school bureaucracies to become ever more immobile, for the teachers' unions to hedge their responsibilities ever more restrictively, and for big-city pressure groups to use the schools as a political football. A few cities such as Chicago are making desperate attempts to break out of this bind, but with little success. Whatever was wrong with the training and the social signals being given by the educational system to an inner-city adolescent in the early 70's is still wrong today, and the reforms of the 60's still bear important responsibility for that.

Welfare remains more generous than it was during the heyday of the 60's reforms. I know this conflicts with the endlessly repeated claim that the purchasing power of welfare benefits has fallen so much that we are back to the levels of the 50's. But this argument is always expressed in terms of the purchasing power of the Aid to Families with Dependent Children (AFDC) benefits. If instead one includes all the major elements in the welfare package—adding in food stamps, Medicaid, and housing subsidies—then benefits increased rapidly during the decade from 1965 to 1974, retreated modestly in real value throughout the rest of the 70's, and rose during the 80's.

Being more precise involves getting into the question of how Medicaid and housing benefits are to be valued. But throughout the range of the accepted methods, it remains true that the value of the welfare package in 1992 is higher than it was when Ronald Reagan took office, and that it is at the level of the early 70's, just below the peak. Furthermore, these statements are based on calculations that do not include Women, Infants, and Children (WIC) benefits, school-lunch programs, and the many special funds and services for welfare recipients that are part of the package in most major cities.

In short, the assertion that the situation facing a potential welfare mother in 1992 is significantly different from the situation that has faced her ever since the end of the 60's reforms is simply wrong. The key point about welfare is this: in 1960, it was so meager that only a small set of young women at the very bottom layer of society could think it was "enough" to enable a women to keep a baby without a husband. By 1970, it was "enough," both in the resources it provided and in the easier terms under which it could be obtained, to enable a broad stratum of low-income women to keep a baby without a husband. That remains true today.

The changes during the Reagan years consisted of the amendments to the Omnibus Budget Reconciliation Act (OBRA) in 1981, which tightened the eligibility rules for receiving AFDC payments, and the welfare reform bill of 1988. The OBRA amendments represented a significant change, moving away from the assumptions of the 60's, and it produced a reduction in the welfare rolls. Had there been another half-dozen reforms with the same weight and vector, the Reagan administration could properly claim to have had its own welfare policy. But the OBRA amendments were an isolated exception, and their effects were limited to potential recipients who possessed substantial independent income—not the heart of the welfare problem.

The only other significant change in the welfare system, in 1988, went in the opposite direction. The rhetoric was new, reflecting the principle that society expects welfare recipients to work. But the work and training aspects of the bill were deferred and indefinite. The immediate effect was to expand benefits by granting AFDC women a year of Medicaid coverage and child-care benefits after leaving the rolls. As in the reforms of the 60's, the intent was to give women on welfare an incentive to get jobs, but, again as in the reforms of the 60's, the legislation ignored the effects on women who were not on welfare.

Since 1988, the AFDC rolls have broken out of the narrow range within which they had been moving for a decade and have been climbing steadily. Some blame it on the recession, even though welfare rolls have not previously tracked with unemployment. It seems more likely that we are observing the replay of an old phenomenon: whenever Congress has legislated a new incentive for women to leave welfare, the unintended downward pull into the welfare system has outweighed the intended upward push out.

* * *

With regard to crime, the situation in the 90's compared to the 60's is mixed. The 60's gave the nation a fundamentally new stance toward law enforcement and punishment. The number of prisoners dropped during the 60's—not just prisoners in proportion to arrests, but the raw number. Meanwhile, the Supreme Court was handing down the decisions—*Miranda, Mapp,* and the rest of the usual suspects—that are notorious for restricting the police. The administration of justice during the 60's became more haphazard, with wider use of plea bargains, longer delays between arrest and trial, trial and sentencing, sentencing and execution of judgment, along with other changes that reduced the swiftness and certainty of punishment for crime. It also happened that crime increased by an astonishing amount during the 60's.

What is different today? Yes, everyone now favors law and order, including the Supreme Court. But the major decisions of the 60's have been narrowed only at the margins, not reversed. The rules of the game remain essentially the same as they were at the end of the reform period. If you get picked up today for a felony in a big city, chances are you will be back on the street tomorrow, even if you have a prior record. If your case is pursued at all (many are not), chances are you will be able to plea-bargain it down to a much lesser charge. Unless you have a long prior record, chances are you will do no jail time. All of these procedures will probably take months to transpire.

In one respect, policy has unquestionably changed. The prison population more than doubled during the 80's, indicating that the risks of going to prison if caught were raised. To that extent, those who say that the Republicans established their own policy and are accountable for it have a point. There are, however, three bottom lines in the crime game. The first is your chance of being punished if you get caught, and that has indeed gone up. But the second is the chance of getting caught at all, and that has either remained steady since the end of the reform period or dropped. The third is opportunities to make money from crime, and this has remained at least constant and, in the drug trade, expanded.

It is unclear how these conflicting trends might balance out in the eyes of an adolescent standing on a streetcorner contemplating whether to get involved in a hustle. It is certainly a mistake to think that the law-and-order years of the Republicans have made a major difference in that adolescent's perception of how the criminal-justice system works. The system of 1992 is still essentially the system that was shaped by the reform period.

None of this discussion is intended to imply that we could return to the pre-reform levels of crime or illegitimacy if we repealed a few laws and reversed a few Supreme Court decisions. On the contrary, the social dynamics of the inner city have taken on a life of their own, and I think it is unlikely that anything short of radical changes will produce much of an effect on the behaviors associated with the underclass. But if the question is how the social policy of the 60's can be responsible for the problems of the 90's, the answer is straightforward: the reform period set those dynamics in motion and, with minor exceptions, the policies it produced are still in effect.

* * *

The next question is whether the 80's saw blacks lose ground, thereby producing the "rage and frustration" that are said to have caused the Los Angeles riot. Unquestionably, some things did get worse, principally antagonism between the races. But racial hostility is one thing; the facts regarding black progress and regression during the 80's are another. (All the [relevant] data... may be found in the basic statistical compendia of the Bureau of the Census, the National Center for Health Statistics, and the Departments of Labor and Education.)...

* * *

What is one to make of [the] heterogeneous set of indicators and results? Partisans of both sides will seize upon the indicators that suit them, but the pattern is probably susceptible to a few generalizations. One is that black status improved in both the 70's and 80's on things that primarily reflect external conditions or behaviors by the black middle class. Infant mortality drops as medical technology improves; black enrollment in college expands with financial help and affirmative action; white-collar employment grows among blacks who have taken advantage of educational opportunities.

The second general comment is that the deterioration in black status is concentrated in the mainsprings of the underclass: dropout from the labor force among young males and births to single young women, both of which continued to grow in the 80's, though more slowly than in the 70's. As long as these behaviors continue, the plight of the black inner city will deepen.

The final general comment is that the 80's come out of the comparison much better than the day-to-day media accounts would lead one to expect. People who want to indict the 80's as a decade of neglect must find other data. I am unaware of any major surprises that lurk in such other measures, but perhaps they exist. If anyone finds them, I suggest only that the presenter follow [this] procedure...: show the figures for 1960 and 1970 along with those for 1980 and 1990, and focus on indicators that represent how people's lives have changed, not how government spending has changed.

* * *

So far as government spending goes, there is now almost a mantra: "We know Head Start works. We know Job Corps works." Other programs sometimes make the list, but these are the stars. Commentary on the problems of the black inner city also has recently begun to assume that certain solutions will work, if only we do the obvious thing and try them.

Thus one often reads op-ed columns in which it is assumed that of course black teenage girls would have fewer babies if only they had access to better sex education, or that of course the unemployment rate among teenage black males would go down if only jobs were made available. This self-assurance is invincibly ignorant of history. The effects of such programs have been assessed, we have a rich and reasonably consistent body of results, and those results are not encouraging.

Head Start is a striking example. Let me begin by saying that I think a good preschool is generally a good thing for the same reason that kindergarten is a good thing, and I am in favor of providing good preschools for disadvantaged children. Head Start, however, is not being discussed just as a nice thing to do for children, but as an example of how we can make progress in the inner city.

The reality is that no program of the 60's has been more often evaluated, more thoroughly, than Head Start—a synthesis published in 1983 annotated 1,500 studies. This work has produced a few broad conclusions. One is that Head Start programs, properly implemented, can enhance some aspects of social development and school performance. But these effects are spotty, and when they occur they fade, disappearing altogether after about three years. All in all, Head Start is not exactly a failure (it is still a nice thing to do for kids), but neither is there any reason to believe that anything will change in the inner city if only Congress fully funds Head Start.

But surely we know that Head Start reduces delinquency and unemployment and pregnancies in later life? No. We have a handful of experimental programs that have made such claims with varying degrees of evidence to back them up, but none of them bears much resemblance to Head Start.

By far the best known of these is the Perry Preschool Program from Ypsilanti, Michigan, which had 58 youngsters and a control group of 65. (Let us pause for a moment and consider what would happen to someone who tried to claim that an intervention strategy did *not* work on the basis of one program with 58 youngsters.) Perry Preschool had four teachers each year, and in any one year these four teachers together were dealing with no more than a total of 24 children —a 1:6 ratio. The teachers were handpicked, highly trained and motivated. They received further extensive training in the special curriculum adopted for the program. In addition to the daily preschool time, the program included an hour-and-a-half home visit to each mother each week.

The first salient point is thus that Perry Preschool was a handcrafted little jewel that the federal government cannot conceivably replicate nationwide—not because there is not enough money (though that is part of it), but because of the nature of large programs. Bureaucracies give you Head Starts, not Perry Preschools.

The other salient point has to do with outcomes. Perry Preschool is the chief source of the claim that preschool intervention can reduce high-school dropout, unemployment, delinquency, and pregnancies. Yet when the program's 58 children were assessed at age nineteen, 33 percent had dropped out of high school, 41 percent were unemployed, 31 percent had been arrested, and the 25 girls had experienced 17 pregnancies. All of these numbers were evidence of success because the rates for the control group were even worse, but it is not the sort of success that the advocates of Head Start can afford to describe explicitly.

* * *

Like Head Start, the Job Corps has been evaluated many times over the years. When the results have been aggregated over all centers, they have usually shown modest gains in average earnings—a matter of a few hundred dollars per year. When evaluators examine individual centers, anecdotal evidence indicates that some are more effective than others. The best ones have a demanding work load, strict rules of behavior, and strict enforcement (which means that many of the entrants never finish the course).

In other words, the Job Corps works for young people who are able to get up every morning, stick with a task, accept a subordinate relationship, and work hard. These people also tend to do well without the Job Corps. Not even the best of the Job Corps centers has a good track record with young people who cannot make themselves get up every morning, who get discouraged easily, get mad when someone tells them what to do, and take a nap when no one is watching. But the latter are among the characteristics of the chronically unemployed.

We have a great deal of experience with job programs that try to deal with the chronically unemployed and the inner-city youth who has never held a job. After twelve years in which social programs have been unpopular, it is easy to forget how massive those job programs were. At their height in the late 70's, the programs under the Comprehensive Employment and Training Act (CETA) had nearly four million first-time entrants in a single year and an annual budget equivalent to $19 billion in 1990 dollars. The evaluations of CETA came in, and the consensus conclusion was that it had some positive impact on women, but not on men. This is consistent with findings from other, small-scale demonstration projects such as those conducted by the Manpower Demonstration Research Corporation and early results from the evaluation of the Job Training Partnership Act.

Unfortunately, the failure to affect males is decisive, for a core problem in the inner city is that males are not assuming their role in the community as husbands, fathers, and providers. If job programs are to be the answer for the 90's, what is it that we propose to do differently this time around?

More generally, attempts to solve the problems of the inner city have a consistent record. The failures vastly outnumber the successes. The claimed successes tend to evaporate when an independent evaluator assesses them. The handful of successes that survive scrutiny are local, small-scale, initiated and run by dedicated people, and operated idiosyncratically and pragmatically—all the things that large-scale federal programs inherently cannot be. Nor, as the government has found after many attempts, can the successes be franchised like a McDonald's, for the idiosyncratic capabilities of the founders turn out to be crucial to the success of the original.

Ever since the conclusion that "nothing works" was advanced in the 80's, the advocates of new programs have tried to show why it is an exaggeration. They have been able to do so, insofar as some problems (such as poverty among the elderly) can be cured by writing enough checks, a task at which the federal government excels. But when it comes to programs that will change the behavior of adolescents and young adults, the record of federal social programs (and most state and municipal social programs) remains dismal. The resurgence of optimism about social programs represents a mismatch between the actual nature of the underclass and the way people want it to be, and a mismatch between the actual way that large-scale programs are implemented and the way each new generation of reformers thinks it can implement them.

* * *

These observations are out of season. It is a time for lighting candles. But there is a case to be made for cursing the darkness. South-Central Los Angeles and inner cities throughout America did not need to evolve the way they have done. Until the last few decades, poor communities throughout American history had been able to function as communities, despite objective deprivation and oppression far greater than any community faces in 1992. Then, in the space of a few years, just as we were finally lifting the objective elements of deprivation and oppression, we inadvertently undercut the pilings on which communities rest.

It turns out that communities survive by socializing their young to certain norms of behavior. They achieve that socialization with the help of realities to which parents can point—you have to work, or you won't eat; if you don't have a husband, you won't be able to take care of your children; if you commit crimes, you will go to jail. From this raw material, communities fashion the gentler rewards and penalties of social life that constrain unwanted behaviors and foster desired ones. Outside the inner city, we are busily reconstructing the damage done to the social fabric during the reform period of the 60's, with considerable success. Inside the inner city, that fabric has become so tattered that it is difficult to see any external means of restoration.

I will therefore refrain from concluding with my own ten-point plan. All we can be sure of is that authentic solutions will be radical ones. There are essentially two alternatives. One is authoritarian, treating the inner city as occupied territory and its citizens as wards to be tutored and manipulated by the wise hand of the state. The other, and in my view the only choice that American democracy can live with, is to take seriously the old aphorism that the only way to make a man trustworthy is to trust him. The only way that inner-city communities will again begin to function as communities is if the individuals within them are again permitted and required to engage in that most Jeffersonian of enterprises, self-governance.

# NO

## Joseph A. Califano, Jr.

# HOW GREAT WAS THE GREAT SOCIETY?

Historians should make no mistake in judging the Johnson administration. What Lyndon Johnson and the Great Society were about twenty years ago was revolution.

President Johnson came to office in an America where the economy had been stagnant for several years; an America where movie theaters and restaurants within a short walk of our nation's Capitol were still segregated, for whites only; an America of unparalleled abundance and prosperity in which more than 20 percent of the people lived in poverty.

It was also an America feeling the birth pains of urbanization and the world's first postindustrial society, a nation becoming a lonely crowd, troubled by the organization men in gray flannel suits, the beat generation, and everything getting bigger than life.

The modern age that had brought America unprecedented material riches had also brought an assault on the individuality of the human spirit. The loneliness of the large city was replacing the friendliness of the rural hamlet. Chain stores with anonymous clerks and thousands of products were turning the neighborhood grocer, haberdasher, and druggist into Norman Rockwell antiques. Computers were replacing people as bill collectors. The mass production of automobiles exceeded our ability to construct and repair roads. Real estate was owned and being traded by people who never saw it. Products were sold and money lent by distant corporations, far away from buyers and borrowers across America. Television was nationalizing culture and taste, reshaping politics and entertainment, and bringing bad news into living rooms every night.

The task of preserving personal identity and human dignity was difficult enough for the affluent middle class of America; it was impossible for the poor who struggled in a supersociety that threatened to engulf the individual with its supermarketplace, superuniversities, overcrowded urban schools and courts, big unions, big corporations, big governments.

Against this backdrop, it's not surprising that Lyndon Johnson's historic University of Michigan commencement speech described the Great Society which he aspired to create as "a place where men are more concerned with the quality of their goals than the quantity of their goods . . . a challenge constantly renewed, beckoning us toward a destiny where the meaning of our lives matches the marvelous products of our labor." President Johnson voiced the hope that in the future men would look back and say: "It was then, after a long and weary way, that man turned the exploits of his genius to the full enrichment of his life."

How much of Johnson's hope did the Great Society realize? Was it good or bad for America?

The cornerstone of the Great Society was a robust economy. With that, the overwhelming majority of the people could get their fair share of America's prosperity. A growing economic pie also allowed the affluent to take bigger pieces, even as we committed a larger portion to the public sector.

Despite a growing economy, some citizens needed special help. There were those who needed the sort of support most of us got from our mothers and fathers: a decent place to live, clothing, health care, an education to develop their talents. Great Society programs like elementary and secondary education, financial aid for college, job training, and much of the health care effort were designed to put them on their own feet, not on the taxpayer's back.

There were also Americans who, largely through no fault of their own, were unable to take care of themselves. For them, the Great Society sought to provide either money or the services that money could buy, so they could live at a minimum level of human dignity. Among these were the poor children, the permanently disabled, and the elderly.

Did the Great Society programs fail? Many who come at them with the political hindsight of the contemporary right think so. But—

Ask the 11 million students who have received loans for their college education whether the Higher Education Act failed.

Ask the 4 million blacks who registered to vote in eleven Southern states and the 6,000 blacks who held elective public office in 1984 whether the Voting Rights Act failed.

Ask the 8 million children who have been through Head Start whether the Poverty Program failed.

Ask the millions of Americans who have enjoyed the 14,000 miles of scenic trails, 7,200 miles of scenic rivers, 45 new national parks, 83 million acres of wilderness areas, and 833 endangered species of plants, animals, and birds that have been preserved—ask them whether the 278 conservation and beautification laws, including the Wilderness Act of 1964, the Endangered Species Preservation Act of 1966, and the Scenic Trails System and Wild and Scenic Rivers Acts of 1968 failed.

Ask the 2 million senior citizens who were raised above the poverty level by the minimum payment requirements of the Social Security Act amendments of 1966 whether that legislation failed.

Ask the millions of visitors whether the laws establishing the Kennedy Center and Hirschorn Museum failed.

Ask the 400 professional theater companies, the 200 dance companies, and the 100 opera companies that have sprung up since 1965 whether the National Endowments for the Arts and Humanities failed.

Ask San Franciscans that use BART, Washingtonians that use Metro, Atlantans that use MARTA, and cities and counties that use the 56,000 buses purchased since 1966—the equivalent of our entire national fleet—whether the Urban Mass Transit Act failed.

Ask the millions of workers who gained new skills through the Manpower Development and Training Act, the Job Corps, and the National Alliance for Businessmen, whether those programs failed.

Ask the 10 million Americans living in the 3 million housing units funded by federal aid whether the Great Society Housing Acts of 1964 and 1968 failed.

What would America be like if there had been no Great Society programs?

Perhaps no better examples exist than the changes brought about by health laws, civil rights statutes, and consumer legislation.

*Health.* Without Medicare and Medicaid; the heart, cancer and stroke legislation; and forty other health bills, life expectancy would be several years shorter, and deaths from heart disease, stroke, diabetes, pneumonia, and influenza would be much higher. Since 1962, life expectancy has jumped five years, from seventy to seventy-five. Life expectancy for blacks has risen even more, with a stunning eight-year improvement for black women. This year, for the first time in America, a black baby girl at birth has a life expectancy greater than that of a white baby boy.

*Civil rights.* In 1965, when the Voting Rights Act was passed, there were 79 black elected officials in the South; now there are nearly 3,000. Nationally, the percentage of blacks registered to vote has grown from less than 30 percent to almost 60 percent. Before the Civil Rights Act of 1964, black people in large parts of this country could not sleep in most hotels, eat in most restaurants, try on clothes at department stores, or get a snack at a lunch counter. Today, this seems a foreign and distant memory. Black enrollment in higher education has tripled, and the proportion of blacks holding professional, technical, and management jobs has more than doubled.

*Consumer protection.* The Great Society's consumer legislation sought to give the individual a fair chance in the world of products sold with the aid of the best designers and marketers, money lent on notes prepared by the shrewdest lawyers and accountants, meat and poultry from chemically fed animals, thousands of products from baby cribs that choked to refrigerator doors that couldn't be pushed open from the inside. So the Great Society gave birth to the Truth in Packaging, Truth in Lending, Wholesome Meat, Wholesome Poultry, and Product Safety Acts. And if you want to know why it's so hard to open a Tylenol bottle, blame the Great Society's child safety legislation. Auto and Highway Safety Acts gave us seat belts, padded dash boards, and a host of automobile design changes.

Has America changed?

- When Lyndon Johnson spoke at the University of Michigan in 1964, he noted that 8 million adult Americans had not finished five years of school, 20 million had not finished eight years, and 54 million had not completed high school. Today, only 3 million have not completed five years, 8 million have not completed 8 years, and 28 million have not completed high school.
- Infant mortality has been cut by more than half, from 26 deaths per 1,000 live births in 1963 to 10.9 in 1983.

- More than 30,000 schools have received funds under the Elementary and Secondary Education Act to teach remedial math and reading to disadvantaged students.
- Thanks to Highway Beautification, 600,000 billboards have been removed from highways and 10,000 junkyards have been cleaned up.

And what of the overall impact of the Great Society on poverty in America? In 1960, 22 percent of the American people lived below the official poverty level. When Lyndon Johnson left office in 1969, that had dropped to 13 percent. Despite the relatively flat economy of the 1970s, the official poverty level did not rise. Indeed, by 1979 it was still about 12 percent. But, and this is a but we must repeat again and again, if we count the income effects of the Great Society service programs, such as those for health care, job training, aid to education, and rehabilitation for the handicapped, by the mid-1970s the poverty rate had been reduced to less than 7 percent. The early 1980s have sadly seen the rate rise up again.

And the Great Society has been invaluable to President Reagan, not just as a political whipping boy, but as the key to his attack on inflation. President Reagan was able to drive down inflation with a sledgehammer because of the cushions Lyndon Johnson's Great Society provided: liberalization of welfare, food stamps and unemployment compensation; Medicaid and Medicare; community health centers; work training; housing; and a host of other programs. Ronald Reagan taught us that we can rapidly wring inflation out of the economy because the remnants of a compassionate, interventionist government are there not only to keep the mobs off the streets, but to keep most needy families at a minimum living standard and adequately fed.

I've always felt that Lyndon Johnson died convinced that the civil rights programs, notably the Voting Rights Act, marked his administration's finest hours. He certainly spent his political capital generously to enact these programs. To me, the Great Society's achievements with older Americans have also been remarkable. The combination of Medicare, Medicaid's support of nursing homes (forty-three cents of each Medicaid dollar goes to them), minimum Social Security benefits, senior citizen centers and food programs, and improved Veterans Administration benefits, along with private-sector retirement plans, virtually eliminated poverty among the elderly in America. As LBJ used to say, much remains to be done; I believe a great deal of our energies and resources in the future must be devoted to poor children and single-parent families.

I've given many examples of the successes of the Great Society. What of its shortcomings?

Did we legislate too much? Perhaps. We seemed to have a law for everything. Fire safety. Water safety. Pesticide control for the farm. Rat control for the ghetto. Bail reform. Immigration reform. Medical libraries. Presidential disability. Juvenile delinquency. Safe streets. Tire safety. Age discrimination. Fair housing. Corporate takeovers. International monetary reform. Sea grant colleges. When we discovered that poor students needed a good lunch, we devised legislation for a school lunch program. When we later found out that breakfast helped them learn better, we whipped up a law for a school breakfast program. When a pipeline exploded, we proposed the Gas Pipeline Safety Act.

When my son Joe swallowed a bottle of aspirin, President Johnson sent Congress a Child Safety Act. When it was too hard for citizens to get information out of the government, we drafted a Freedom of Information Act. When we needed more doctors, or nurses, or teachers, we legislated programs to train them.

Did we stub our toes? Of course.

We made our mistakes, plenty of them. In health, our Great Society quest to provide access to health care for the elderly and the poor led us to accede to the demands of hospitals and physicians for open-ended cost-plus and fee-for-service payments. As a result, with Medicare and Medicaid, we adopted inherently wasteful and inefficient reimbursement systems. Incidently, we recognized the danger of exploding health care costs in 1968, but Congress denied President Johnson's request to change Medicare's payment system.

There were too many narrow categorical grant programs created in health, education, and social services. It's one thing to embark upon a program to help states educate millions of poor children, or to provide scholarships so that any American with the brains and talent can go to college. It's quite another to set curriculum priorities from Washington with funds that must be spent on specific subjects of education, such as environmental or ethnic studies or metric education.

The struggle for civil rights left us deeply and often unjustifiably suspicious of the motives and intentions of institutional and middle America. It influenced our attitudes about consumer safety, occupational health, environmental protection, and transportation. It undermined our trust in the states.

As a result, many federal laws were written in far too much detail. And regulation writers cast aside the great American common-law principle that every citizen is presumed to obey, the law. Quite the contrary, we wrote laws and regulations on the theory that each citizen would seek to circumvent them. We became victims of the self-defeating and self-fulfilling premise that, unless we were protected by a law or regulation, we were vulnerable. As regulations got into too many nooks and crannies of American life, they created testy resistance and needlessly invited ridicule. But we should remember that the massive influx of regulations that so irritated Americans came not during the Johnson years, but the decade that followed. It was the seventies, not the sixties, that brought us 6,000 schedule codes under Medicare, pages and pages of regulations under the Occupational Health and Safety legislation, hundreds of pages of education regulations.

At times we may have lost sight of the fact that these laws—hundreds of them—were not an end in themselves. Often we did not recognize that government could not do it all. And, of course, there were overpromises. But they were based on high hopes and great expectations and fueled by the frustration of seeing so much poverty and ignorance and illness amidst such wealth. We simply could not accept poverty, ignorance, and hunger as intractable, permanent features of American society. There was no child we could not feed; no adult we could not put to work; no disease we could not cure; no toy, food, or appliance we could not make safer; no air or water we could not clean. But it was all part of asking "not how much, but how good; not only how to create wealth, but how to use it, not only how fast we (were) going, but where we [were] headed."

This twentieth anniversary of the Great Society is not a time for giving up on those precious goals to which so many of us devoted so much of our energy and our lives. It is not even a time for hunkering down. The Great Society is alive and well —in Medicare and Medicaid; in the air we breathe and the water we drink, in the rivers and lakes we swim in; in the schools and colleges our students attend; in the medical miracles from the National Institutes of Health; in housing and transportation and equal opportunity. We can build on the best of it, and recognize our mistakes and correct them.

We must once again join our talents and experience to make our government a responsive servant of the people. For a democratic government to respond means to lead, to forge the claims of narrow groups on the anvil of government to serve the needs of all of our people, to know the special importance of protecting the individual in the modern bureaucracy, to recognize the fundamental right of each person to live in human dignity.

That was what the Great Society at its best did. It converted the hopes and aspirations of all kinds of Americans into a political force that brought out much of the good in each of us. The result was a social revolution in race relations that even a bloody civil war could not achieve; a revolution in education that opened college to any American with the ability and ambition to go; a revolution in health that provided care for all the elderly and many of the poor; a sea change in the relationship of consumers to big corporate sellers and lenders; a born-again respect for our land and air and water that is still gaining momentum.

The achievements of the Great Society did not come easily. As everyone in this room knows, that kind of work in government is hard, often frustrating, sometimes exasperating. But the rewards are far greater for those in a democracy who work persistently to build and shape government to serve the people, than for those who tear it apart or lash out in despair and frustration because the task is too much for them. I deeply believe that the Great Society teaches that we can succeed in that work of building and shaping. Like G. K. Chesterton, "I do not believe in a fate that befalls people however they act. But I do believe in fate that befalls them unless they act."

Too many of us, including many of our young Americans and some in government, don't try because the tasks seem too difficult, sometimes impossible. Of course those who govern will make mistakes, plenty of them. But we must not fear failure. What we should fear above all is the judgment of God and history if we, the most affluent people on God's earth, free to act as we wish, choose not to govern justly, not to distribute our riches fairly, and not to help the most vulnerable among us—or worse if we choose not even to try. Whatever historians of the Great Society say twenty years later, they must admit that we tried, and I believe they will conclude that America is a better place because we did.

## NOTES

1. Some statistics in this address are taken from papers prepared for this conference by professionals in fields on which the Great Society touched: Donald M. Baker, Counsel for Labor, Committee on Education and Labor, U.S. House of Representatives, and General Counsel. Office of Economic Opportunity, 1964–1969; Michael C. Barth, Vice President, ICF Incorporated, a Washington, D.C., consulting firm, an expert in economics and income maintenance programs; Livingston Biddle, former Chairman of the National Endowment For the Arts; Ernest L. Boyer, former U.S. Commissioner of Education and now President of the Carnegie Foundation for the Ad-

vancement of Teaching; Richard Cotton, an attorney with the Washington office of Dewey, Ballantine, Bushby, Palmer & Wood and an expert in environmental and energy issues; Karen Davis, economist and Chair, Department of Health Policy and Management at the Johns Hopkins University School of Public Health; Representative Henry B. Gonzalez, Chairman, Subcommittee on Housing and Community Development, Committee on Banking, Finance, and Urban Affairs, U.S. House of Representatives; Representative James J. Howard, Chairman, Committee on Public Works and Transportation, U.S. House of Representatives; David Swankin, a public-interest attorney in the Washington, D.C., law firm of Swankin and Turner and former Executive Director of the President's Committee on Consumer Interests, forerunner to the White House Office of Consumer Affairs; Ray Marshall, professor of economics at the LBJ School of Public Affairs and Secretary of Labor during the Carter administration, and William L. Taylor, Director of the Center for National Policy Review at Catholic University and David Tatel, attorney with the Washington, D.C., law firm of Hogan and Hartson and director of the HEW Office for Civil Rights during the Carter administration, both experts in civil rights. The text of the speech represents the views of Mr. Califano, for which he assumes complete responsibility.

# POSTSCRIPT

## Did the Great Society Fail?

Murray is the best-known conservative social policy intellectual in the United States. His *Losing Ground: American Social Policy, 1950–1980* (Basic Books, 1984) was sponsored into a best-seller by the Manhattan Institute (a right-wing think tank) and became required reading for the Reagan administration staffers. The book uses statistical evidence to demonstrate that the Great Society welfare programs made the situation worse for the American underclass. Like former president Bush's press secretary, Marlin Fitzwater, Murray argues that the conditions in south central Los Angeles that produced the riots in 1992 were "a product of the reforms of a quarter century ago."

Murray is not without his critics. Christopher Jenks disputes Murray's analysis in *Rethinking Social Policy: Race, Poverty and the Underclass* (Harvard University Press, 1992). Jenks believes, for example, that a single parent may provide a more desirable environment for raising children then a welfare mother forced into an unreliable marriage. But Murray believes that only through a tight-knit nuclear family will the social problems of a poverty-ridden underclass be resolved.

While conservatives believe that the Great Society has gone too far, and while radicals argue that the reforms never extended beyond surface changes, a third group (liberals) defends both the thrust and outcome of President Johnson's social programs. Califano has given us a spirited defense of the Great Society's accomplishments, listing the hundreds of bills pouring forth from Congress concerning mass transportation, public housing, the environment, education, consumer protection, health care, and civil rights programs.

Did the Great Society succeed? Certainly Califano is correct in arguing that Johnson's programs benefited many middle-class families in areas of health, education, and consumer protection. The elderly also got big boosts in social security payments and an improved health care package. Finally, where would African Americans be today without the Voting Rights Act of 1965?

Where Califano and Murray disagree is in the efforts of the job-training and welfare programs to eliminate hard-core poverty in the large cities. Murray believes that these programs created new problems. But Califano defends the goals and accomplishments of the Great Society.

Three books are essential to the understanding of the Johnson years: Nicholas Lemann, *The Promised Land: The Great Black Migration and How It Changed America* (Alfred A. Knopf, 1991); Allen J. Matusow, *The Unravelling of America: A History of Liberalism in the 1960's* (Harper & Row, 1984); and John Morton Blum, *Years of Discord: American Politics and Society, 1961–1974* (W. W. Norton, 1991).

# ISSUE 15

## Could the United States Have Prevented the Fall of South Vietnam?

**YES: Harry G. Summers, Jr.,** from *On Strategy: A Critical Analysis of the Vietnam War* (Presidio, 1982)

**NO: George C. Herring,** from "America and Vietnam: The Unending War," *Foreign Affairs* (Winter 1991/1992)

### ISSUE SUMMARY

**YES:** Military analyst Harry G. Summers, Jr., attributes the United States' failure in Southeast Asia to a strategic blunder on the part of President Lyndon Johnson and the Congress, who could have effectively mobilized American public opinion in support of the government's policies by issuing a formal declaration of war against North Vietnam.

**NO:** Professor of history George C. Herring argues that American policymakers exaggerated the strategic importance of Vietnam and deluded themselves about the United States' power.

At the end of World War II, imperialism was coming to a close in Asia. Japan's defeat spelled the end of her control over China, Korea, and the countries of Southeast Asia. Attempts by the European nations to reestablish their empires were doomed. Anti-imperialist movements emerged all over Asia and Africa, often producing chaos.

The United States faced a dilemma. America was a nation conceived in revolution and was sympathetic to the struggles of Third World nations. But the United States was afraid that many of the revolutionary leaders were Communists who would place their countries under the control of the expanding empire of the Soviet Union. By the late 1940s the Truman administration decided that it was necessary to stop the spread of communism. The policy that resulted was known as containment.

Vietnam provided a test of the containment doctrine in Asia. Vietnam had been a French protectorate from 1885 until Japan took control during World War II. Shortly before the war ended, the Japanese gave Vietnam its independence, but the French were determined to reestablish their influence in the area. Conflicts emerged between the French-led nationalist forces of South Vietnam and the Communist-dominated provisional government of the Democratic Republic of Vietnam (DRV), which was established in Hanoi in August 1945. Ho Chi Minh was the president of the DRV. An avowed

Communist since the 1920s, Ho had also become the major nationalist figure in Vietnam. As the leader of the anti-imperialist movement against French and Japanese colonialism for over 30 years, Ho managed to tie together the Communist and Nationalist movements in Vietnam.

A full-scale war broke out in 1946 between the Communist government of North Vietnam and the French-dominated country of South Vietnam. After the Communists defeated the French at the battle of Dien Bien Phu in May 1954, the latter decided to pull out. At the Geneva Conference the following summer, Vietnam was divided at the 17th parallel pending elections.

The United States became directly involved in Vietnam after the French withdrew. In 1955 the Republican president Dwight Eisenhower refused to recognize the Geneva Accords but supported the establishment of the South Vietnamese government. Its leader was Ngo Dinh Diem, an authoritarian Catholic who was more popular with U.S. politicians than he was with the Buddhist peasants of South Vietnam, who resented his oppressive rule. In 1956 Diem, with U. S. approval, refused to hold elections, which would have provided a unified government for Vietnam in accordance with the Geneva agreement. The Communists in the south responded by again taking up the armed struggle. The war continued for another 19 years.

Both President Eisenhower and his successor, John F. Kennedy, were anxious to prevent South Vietnam from being taken over by the Communists, so economic assistance and military aid were provided. Kennedy supported the overthrow of the Diem regime in October 1963 and hoped that the successor government would establish an alternative to communism. It did not work. Kennedy himself was assassinated three weeks later. His successor, Lyndon Johnson, changed the character of American policy in Vietnam by escalating the air war and increasing the number of ground forces from 21,000 in 1965 to a full fighting force of 550,000 at its peak in 1968.

The next president, Richard Nixon, adopted a new policy of "Vietnamization" of the war. Military aid to South Vietnam was increased to ensure the defeat of the Communists. At the same time, American troops were gradually withdrawn from Vietnam. South Vietnamese president Thieu recognized the weaknesses of his own position without the support of U. S. troops. He reluctantly signed the Paris Accords of January 1973.

Once U.S. soldiers were withdrawn, Thieu's regime was doomed. In the spring of 1975 a full-scale war broke out, and the South Vietnamese government collapsed. Could the United States have prevented a North Vietnamese victory? In the following selections, Harry G. Summers, Jr., an Army officer who served in Vietnam, claims that the outcome would have been different had the Johnson administration formally declared war on North Vietnam. Such a policy, says Summers, would have resulted in a mobilization of public opinion and solidifying of the national will in support of the government's program. George C. Herring, on the other hand, believes that a succession of American presidents misapplied the containment policy to an inherently unstable situation in Vietnam with disastrous results.

YES **Harry G. Summers, Jr.**

# THE NATIONAL WILL

## THE PEOPLE

One of the more simplistic explanations for our failure in Vietnam is that it was all the fault of the American people—that it was caused by a collapse of national will. Happily for the health of the Republic, this evasion is rare among Army officers. A stab-in-the-back syndrome never developed after Vietnam.

By an ironic twist of fate, the animosity of the Officer Corps was drained off to a large extent by General William C. Westmoreland. On his shoulders was laid much of the blame for our Vietnam failure. According to a 1970 analysis, "For the older men, the villains tend to be timorous civilians and the left-wing press; for the younger men, they are the tradition-bound senior generals and the craven press. For one group, it is the arrogance of McNamara; for the other the rigidity of Westmoreland." Those then "younger men" now make up the majority of the Army's senior officers. For example, the Vietnam experience of the Army War College Class of 1980 was mostly at the platoon and company level.... [P]lacing the blame on General Westmoreland was unfair, but, unfair or not, it did spare another innocent victim—the American people.

The main reason it is not right to blame the American public is that President Lyndon Baines Johnson made a conscious decision not to mobilize the American people—to invoke the national will—for the Vietnam war. As former Assistant Secretary of Defense for Public Affairs Phil G. Goulding commented, "In my four-year tour [July 1965–January 1969] there was not once a significant organized effort by the Executive Branch of the federal government to put across its side of a major policy issue or a major controversy to the American people. Not once was there a 'public affairs program'... worthy of the name." Having deliberately never been built, it could hardly be said that the national will "collapsed." According to his biographer, President Johnson's decision not to mobilize the American people was based on

From Harry G. Summers, Jr., *On Strategy: A Critical Analysis of the Vietnam War* (Presidio, 1982), pp. 11–19, 21–31. 

his fears that it would jeopardize his "Great Society" programs. As he himself said:

> ... History provided too many cases where the sound of the bugle put an immediate end to the hopes and dreams of the best reformers: The Spanish-American War drowned the populist spirit; World War I ended Woodrow Wilson's New Freedom; World War II brought the New Deal to a close. Once the war began, then all those conservatives in the Congress would use it as a weapon against the Great Society....
>
> And the generals. Oh, they'd love the war, too. It's hard to be a military hero without a war. Heroes need battles and bombs and bullets in order to be heroic. That's why I am suspicious of the military. They're always narrow in their appraisal of everything. They see everything in military terms.

What the military needed to tell our Commander-in-Chief was not just about battles and bombs and bullets. They needed to tell him that, as Clausewitz discovered 150 years earlier, "it would be an obvious fallacy to imagine war between civilized peoples as resulting merely from a rational act on the part of the Government and to consider war as gradually ridding itself of passion." They needed to tell him that it would be an obvious fallacy to commit the Army without first committing the American people. Such a commitment would require battlefield competence and clear-cut objectives to be sustained, but without the commitment of the American people the commitment of the Army to prolonged combat was impossible....

After World War II this connection between the Army and the people was weakened in the name of insuring more rapid response to threats of American security. For the first time in our history a large standing military was maintained in peacetime and our reserve forces declined in importance. The unwitting effect of this was the creation of a neo–18th century–type Army answerable more to the Executive than to the American people. In June 1950, the President—without asking the Congress for a declaration of war—committed this Army to combat in Korea. The reaction to this action in the Congress should have warned us, as General Weyand put it, that the American people take a jealous and proprietary interest in the commitment of their Army.

During what General Matthew Ridgway called "The Great Debate" on the Korean war (the 1951 Joint Senate Armed Forces and Foreign Affairs Committee Hearings), one of the major topics was the issue of Constitutional control over the military. In their findings the committee emphasized that "the United States should never again become involved in war without the consent of the Congress." They were particularly concerned that the Korean war not set a precedent for the commitment of the Army without congressional consent.

Presaging what was to follow in the Vietnam war, the military witnesses did not see the criticality of this point. For example, Senator Wayne Morse of Oregon asked General MacArthur, "Do you believe that we should have declared war against the Koreans or against the Chinese?" MacArthur answered that we were in fact practicing war—a limited war to which he objected but a war nonetheless. When asked about the constitutionality of the war he replied that "the actions of the United Nations might well be regarded as [the] declaration of war." Senator Harry P. Cain of Washington later raised the same question and MacArthur answered, "I have never given special consideration to the *technical question* of whether a declaration of war should be made or not."

Senator Cain later asked then Secretary of Defense George Marshall, "Tell me what modern day factors require a formal declaration of war against our enemies?" General Marshall agreed it was an important question but evaded the issue and laid the blame on the complications of collective action. During the questioning of General of the Army Omar Bradley (then Chairman of the Joint Chiefs of Staff) by Senator William Knowland of California and Senator Cain, General Bradley said, "Someone might question whether technically or not [the Korean war] was a war because normally Congress declares war and I don't believe Congress has declared a war.... The question of when you declare a war in this case, how you do it, and how you explain to the people the exact nature of it I don't know."

It is often forgotten that the attempt to fight without mobilizing the American people and without a declaration of war by the Congress almost came to grief in Korea. As General Maxwell D. Taylor wrote:

> The national behavior showed a tendency to premature war-weariness and precipitate disenchantment with a policy which had led to a stalemated war. This experience, if remembered, could have given some warning of dangers ahead to the makers of the subsequent Vietnam policy. Unfortunately, there was no thorough-going analysis ever made of the lessons to be learned from Korea, and later policy makers proceeded to repeat many of the same mistakes.

With all the warnings that the Korean war provided about the importance of mobilizing the national will and legitimizing this mobilization through a declaration of war, how could we go so wrong in Vietnam? Part of the answer is in the temper of the times.

The Vietnam war coincided with a social upheaval in America where the old rules and regulations were dismissed as irrelevant and history no longer had anything to offer. There were those who proclaimed it a new age—the "Age of Aquarius." Even the term sounds banal today, but in the mid-1960s respected speakers at Leavenworth and Carlisle were warning the Army that we were entering a new phase—"post-industrial society," "Consciousness Three"—and "relevancy" was the watchword....

Like the flower children, the Army and the military establishment went through its own version of the Age of Aquarius. We thought the rules for taking America to war were hopelessly old-fashioned and out of date. Like society, we became confused between form and substance. Legalistic arguments that the form of a declaration of war was out of date may have been technically correct, but they obscured the fact that this form was designed to be an outward manifestation of a critical substance—the support and commitment of the American people.

A formal declaration of war was seen as a useless piece of paper, in much the same light as many saw the marriage certificate. In the 1960s and early 1970s, there were many, especially among the trendy and sophisticated, who saw marriage as an antiquated institution. By avoiding marriage they thought they could avoid the trauma of divorce, just as some thought that by avoiding a declaration of war they could avoid the trauma of war. But thousands of years of human nature and human experience are not so easily changed. By the late 1970s, it had become obvious that formal institutions had societal value. This reaction was summed up by *Washington Post* writer Judith Martin in her "Miss Manners" column. Some wrote questioning the worth of a marriage certificate, since it was just a piece of paper. She replied, "Miss Manners has a whole safety deposit box full of pieces of paper."

Pieces of paper *do* have value. A marriage certificate—or a declaration of war—legitimizes the relationship in the eyes of society and announces it to the world. It focuses attention, provides certain responsibilities, and creates impediments to dissolution. While neither a marriage certificate nor a declaration of war are guarantees for staying the course, these legal forms are of immense value to society.

But in the early 1960s, we were under the delusion that we could disregard not only the *form* of a declaration of war but also its *substance*—the mobilization of the American people. Secretary of Defense Robert S. McNamara was quoted as saying:

> The greatest contribution Vietnam is making—right or wrong is beside the point—is that it is developing an ability in the United States to fight a limited war, to go to war without the necessity of arousing the public ire.

But "right or wrong" was not beside the point and neither was the intangible of "public ire." Vietnam reinforced the lessons of Korea that there was more to war, even limited war, than those things that could be measured, quantified and computerized. A bitter little story made the rounds during the closing days of the Vietnam war:

> When the Nixon Administration took over in 1969 all the data on North Vietnam and on the United States was fed into a Pentagon computer—population, gross national product, manufacturing capability, number of tanks, ships, and aircraft, size of the armed forces, and the like.
>
> The computer was then asked, *"When will we win?"*
>
> It took only a moment to give the answer: *"You won in 1964!"*

The story had a bite, for by every quantifiable measurement there was simply no contest between the United States, the most powerful nation on the face of the earth, and a tenth-rate backward nation like North Vietnam. Yet there was one thing that did not fit into the computer—national will, what Clausewitz calls the moral factor. We have seen earlier that President Johnson deliberately avoided mobilizing the national will so as not to jeopardize his Great Society programs. The North Vietnamese, after their experience with the French, had every reason to believe that American morale could be our weak strategic link. Knowing they did not have the military means to defeat us, they concentrated on this weakness. It was not a new strategy. "When we speak of destroying the enemy's forces," Clausewitz wrote, "we must emphasize that nothing obliges us to limit this idea to physical forces: The moral element must also be considered."

The failure to invoke the national will was one of the major strategic failures of the Vietnam war. It produced a strategic vulnerability that our enemy was able to exploit. Consider this explanation of Tet 1968, written by Clausewitz 150 years earlier:

> Not every war need be fought until one side collapses. When the motives and tensions of war are slight we can imagine that the very faintest prospect of defeat might be enough to cause one side to yield. If from the very start the other side feels that this is probable, it will obviously concentrate on bringing about this probability rather than take the long way round and totally defeat the enemy.

## THE CONGRESS

One of the continuing arguments about the Vietnam war is whether or not a formal declaration of war would have made any difference. On the one hand there are those who see a declaration of war as a kind of magic talisman that would have eliminated all our difficulties. On the other hand there are those who see a declaration of war as a worthless anachronism. The truth is somewhere in between. A declaration of war is a clear statement of *initial* public support which focuses the nation's attention on the enemy. (Continuation of this initial public support is, of course, contingent on the successful prosecution of war aims.) As we will see, it was the lack of such focus on the enemy and on the political objectives to be obtained by the use of military force that was the crux of our strategic failure.

Further, a declaration of war makes the prosecution of the war a shared responsibility of both the government and the American people.... [W]ithout a declaration of war the Army was caught on the horns of a dilemma. It was ordered into battle by the Commander-in-Chief, the duly elected President of the United States. It was sustained in battle by appropriations by the Congress, the elected representatives of the American people. The legality of its commitment was not challenged by the Supreme Court of the United States. Yet, because there was no formal declaration of war, many vocal and influential members of the American public questioned (and continue to question) the legality and propriety of its actions.

This dilemma needs to be understood. It transcends the legal niceties over the utility of a declaration of war. It even transcends the strategic military value of such a declaration. It should not be dismissed as a kind of sophisticated "stab in the back" argument. As will be seen, the requirement for a declaration of war was rooted in the principle of civilian control of the military, and the failure to declare war in Vietnam drove a wedge between the Army and large segments of the American public.

It is not as if we did not know better. We knew perfectly well the importance of maintaining the bond between the American people and their soldiers in the field, and that this bond was the source of our moral strength....

By requiring that a declaration of war be made by the representatives of the people (the Congress), rather than by the President alone, the Founding Fathers sought to guarantee this substance and insure that our armed forces would not be committed to battle without the support of the American people. Ironically, President Johnson seemed to know that. In a peculiar passage in light of what was to follow, he said:

> I believed that President Truman's one mistake in courageously going to the defense of South Korea in 1950 had

> been his failure to ask Congress for an expression of its backing. He could have had it easily, and it would have strengthened his hand. I made up my mind not to repeat that error...

Like President Truman in 1950, President Johnson could probably have had a declaration of war in August 1964 after the Gulf of Tonkin incidents when two American destroyers were attacked by North Vietnamese patrol boats. Instead of asking for a declaration of war, however, President Johnson asked Congress for a resolution empowering him to "take all necessary measures to repel an armed attack against the forces of the United States and to prevent further aggression." This Southeast Asia Resolution (better known as the Gulf of Tonkin resolution) passed the Senate by a vote of 88–2, and the House by a unanimous voice vote of 416–0.

Commenting on this resolution, Senator Jacob Javits of New York acknowledged congressional complicity on Vietnam.

> The language of the Gulf of Tonkin resolution was far more sweeping than the congressional intent. In voting unlimited presidential power most members of Congress thought they were providing for retaliation for an attack on our forces; and preventing a large-scale war in Asia, rather than authorizing its inception....
>
> Whatever President Johnson's position, however, Congress had the obligation to make an institutional judgment as to the wisdom and the propriety of giving such a large grant of its own power to the Chief Executive...
>
> ... The power of decision... had not been stolen. It had been surrendered.

All this may have been avoided by a declaration of war, but there was a kind of Catch-22 working against it. When the President could have had it he didn't think he needed it, and when he needed it he couldn't have it. As the distinguished historian Arthur M. Schlesinger, Jr. commented, "[President] Johnson could certainly have obtained congressional authorization beyond the Tonkin Gulf resolution for a limited war in Vietnam in 1965. He might even, had he wished (but no one wished), have obtained a declaration of war." The reason why neither the President nor the Congress (nor the military either, for that matter) seemed to think a declaration of war was necessary and why the President deliberately did not seek to mobilize public support for such a proposal was that initially no one envisioned a 10-year war, the massive commitment of American ground troops, nor the ground swell of American opposition. It was hoped that the use of U.S. tactical air power in South Vietnam, the "Rolling Thunder" air campaign against North Vietnam, and the limited use of U.S. troops to protect air bases and logistics installations would cause the North Vietnamese to halt their aggression.

By the spring of 1965, it was obvious that such a limited response was not effective, and the decision was made to commit U.S. ground combat troops to the war. Rather than go back to the Congress and ask for a declaration of war, "efforts were made to make the change as imperceptible as possible to the American public..." In retrospect this was a key strategic error. Failure to make this crucial political decision led to fear of making the political decision to mobilize the reserves. Failure to mobilize the reserves led to failure of the military leadership to push for strategic concepts aimed at halting North Vietnamese aggression and led to campaigns against the symptoms of the aggression—the insurgency in the South—rather than against the aggressor itself.... [W]hy [was] a declaration of war not requested prior to the commitment of U.S. ground combat forces[?]

One reason was that it would have seemed ludicrous for a great power like the United States to declare war on a tiny country like North Vietnam. War sanctions, both foreign and domestic, were deemed too massive to be appropriate. Another reason was the desire not to risk a Korea-style intervention by threatening Chinese security. There was also the danger that a formal declaration of war against North Vietnam might have triggered the implementation of security guarantees by China and the Soviet Union. Yet another reason may have been the fear that Congress would not approve such a declaration. This refusal would have caused an immediate halt to U.S. efforts in South Vietnam (a preferable result, given the final outcome). A final reason may have been our use of the enemy's terminology to describe the nature of the war. In his analysis of our failure to declare war, University of California Professor Chalmers Johnson commented:

> [The label "People's War"] made it harder for a counterinsurgent state, such as the United States, to clarify for its own citizens exactly whom it was fighting when it defended against a people's war. Steeped in the legalistic concept that wars are between states, the American public became confused by its government's failure to declare war on North Vietnam and thereby identify the *state* with which the United States was at war....

While there is no evidence the military insisted on a declaration of war at the time, General Westmoreland did say in his autobiography that:

> President Johnson erred in relying on the Gulf of Tonkin resolution as his authority from the Congress to do what he deemed necessary in Southeast Asia. When dissent developed in 1966 and 1967, he would have been well advised to have gone back to the Congress for reaffirmation of the commitment to South Vietnam, a vote either of confidence or rejection.... President Johnson... should have forced the Congress to face its constitutional responsibility for waging war.

As a matter of practical politics General Westmoreland's recommendation was simply not feasible. A declaration of war undoubtedly would have been obtainable in 1964 and may even have been possible in the spring of 1965, but by the time the protests started in 1966–1967 even a statement of continued congressional support, much less a declaration of war, would have been a difficult if not impossible endeavor. It was made more difficult because President Johnson was caught up in a contradiction of his own making. Stirring up the American people in support of the war would have been the surest way to insure continued congressional support, but as we have seen, this was precisely what President Johnson did not want to do.

Instead of seeking further congressional support for the war, President Johnson took the opposite tack and fell back on his authority as President. In March 1966, the Legal Advisor to the Department of State told the Senate Committee on Foreign Relations:

> There can be no question in present circumstances of the President's authority to commit U.S. Forces to the defense of South Vietnam. The grant of authority to

the President in Article II of the Constitution extends to the actions of the United States currently undertaken in Vietnam.

Emphasizing this point in a news conference on 18 August 1967, President Johnson said, "We stated then, and we repeat now, we did not think the [Gulf of Tonkin] resolution was necessary to do what we did and what we're doing."

The only other time a declaration of war was politically feasible was when Richard M. Nixon assumed the Presidency in January 1969. He could have demanded that Congress either affirm our commitment with a declaration of war, giving him authority to prosecute the war to its conclusion, or reject the commitment, allowing him to immediately withdraw all American troops from Vietnam. But President Nixon had foreclosed this option with his campaign promises to bring the war to a close. Within weeks after assuming office, "Johnson's war" had become "Nixon's war." Like President Johnson, he fell back on his position as Commander in Chief as authority to prosecute the war.

Commenting on this, the Senate Committee on Foreign Relations said:

> The issue to be resolved is the proper locus within our constitutional system of the authority to commit our country to war. More, perhaps, than ever before, the Executive and Congress are in disagreement as to where that authority properly lies. It is the Executive's view, manifested in both words and action, that the President, in his capacity as Commander in Chief, is properly empowered to commit the Armed Forces to hostilities in foreign countries. It is the committee's view—*conviction* may be the better word—that the authority to initiate war, as distinguished from acting to repel a sudden attack, is vested by the Constitution in the Congress and in the Congress alone....
>
> From the Executive's standpoint, repeal of the Tonkin resolution will in no way impair what it believes to be its authority to conduct the present war. The Executive branch has already... disavowed a reliance on the Gulf of Tonkin resolution as authority or support for its conduct of the war in Indochina. From the standpoint of the committee, on the other hand, repeal of the Tonkin resolution will leave the Executive in the legal position of continuing to conduct an unauthorized war... The committee does not regard the Tonkin resolution as a valid legal authorization for the war in Indochina. This being the case, repeal of the resolution will not create but simply confirm and clarify the existence of a legal vacuum.

Into this so-called "legal vacuum" fell the U.S. Army, caught in the middle between the executive and the legislative branches. This was a dangerous position for both the Army and for the Republic. It was dangerous for the Army because in failing to mobilize the national will the United States lost what Clausewitz called the strength of the passions of a people mobilized for war. Instead of the passions of the American people strengthening and supporting us, the more vocal and passionate voices were too often raised in support of our enemies.

More importantly, it was dangerous for the Republic. The Army became the focus of anti-war sentiment. While such sentiment is not unusual in American history, and there has been public dissent against many of our wars, this dissent was usually directed primarily against the government rather than against the military. During the Vietnam war, however, many of the protestors focused their attention on the military itself and attempted to subvert it through public demonstrations, underground newspapers, teach-ins and infiltration. For example, the so-called "American Servicemen's Union" called for soldiers to disobey their orders and to refuse to fight in Vietnam. By attacking the *executors* of U.S. Vietnam policy rather than the *makers* of that policy, the protestors were striking at the very heart of our democratic system—the civilian control of the military. As former Chief of Staff General Fred C. Weyand commented:

> During the Vietnam war there were those —many with the best of intentions— who argued that the Army should not obey its orders and should refuse to serve in Vietnam. But their argument that soldiers should obey the "dictates of their conscience" is a slippery slope indeed. At the bottom of this slope is military dictatorship.

In the later stages, when the Vietnam war became a partisan political issue, the Army was placed in the untenable position of becoming involved in domestic politics solely because it was obeying its orders. As General Westmoreland observed:

> I recognized that it was not the job of the military to defend American commitment and policy. Yet it was difficult to differentiate between pursuit of a military task and such related matters as public and congressional support and the morale of the fighting man, who must be convinced that he is risking death for a worthy cause. The military thus was caught in between.

This impasse continued as long as U.S. troops were committed to Vietnam. It was not until November 1973 that Congress, over the President's veto, passed the War Powers Resolution in an attempt to increase congressional control. The purpose of the Resolution was:

> ... To fulfill the intent of the framers of the Constitution of the United States and insure that the collective judgment of both the Congress and the President will apply to the introduction of United States Armed Forces into hostilities, or into situations where imminent involvement in hostilities is clearly indicated by the circumstances, and to the continued use of such forces in hostilities or in such situations.

The Resolution requires the President to consult with the Congress before military forces are committed. Military involvement can continue for 60 days, and for another 30 days thereafter if the President certifies in writing that the safety of the force so requires. Unless Congress specifically authorizes it by a declaration of war, resolution or legislation, the involvement cannot be continued beyond the 90 days. As one observer noted:

> The law forces Congress to take a decision after two or at the most three months of confrontation. A vote to continue operations signifies the sharing of responsibility with the Executive; a vote to terminate signifies an assumption of responsibility by Congress alone.

Although the War Powers Resolution is a step toward solving the legal issues involved, it does not necessarily solve the moral and psychological issues so important to the Army. It raises the appalling specter of taking soldiers into combat and then being forced to disengage under fire because congressional approval was not forthcoming. As Senator Thomas F. Eagleton of Missouri warned:

> The President, under this measure, could deploy [troops] wherever he wanted,

> tomorrow. There is a 60-day period but the troops are there. They are deployed, being shot at, dying, and the flag is committed...

Practical political concerns will probably provide a safeguard against this first shortcoming. After the experience with Vietnam, no President is liable to commit the Army unless he is reasonably sure the mood of the Congress and the Nation will support such an involvement....

We saw earlier that the congressional safeguard of a declaration of war had fallen out of fashion after World War II. But fashions change. Testifying before the Senate Foreign Relations Committee in March 1980 on the Iranian crisis, the distinguished scholar and diplomat George F. Kennan argued that the correct U.S. response should have been a declaration of war. Not only would it have given the President clear-cut military authority, but it also would have provided nonmilitary options—e.g., internment of Iranian citizens, seizure of funds. U.S. public concern would have been fixed and focused, and a clear signal would have been sent to the international community.

As columnist William F. Buckley observed:

> To declare war in this country would require a researcher to inform the President and Congress on just how to go about doing it. Declaring war is totally out of style. The post-Hiroshima assumption being that the declaration of war brings with it the tacit determination to use every weapon necessary in order to win that war. Thus we didn't go to war against North Korea, North Vietnam, or Cuba. But...
>
> To declare war is not necessarily to dispatch troops, let alone atom bombs. It is to recognize a juridically altered relationship and to license such action as is deemed appropriate. It is a wonderful demystifier... [leaving] your objective in very plain view.

... [O]ne of the primary causes of our Vietnam failure was that we did not keep our "objective in very plain view." If a declaration of war could have accomplished that one task it would have been worth the effort.

# NO

## George C. Herring

# AMERICA AND VIETNAM: THE UNENDING WAR

It has been an article of faith among many Americans that the nation's defeat in Vietnam was self-inflicted. The United States failed, they allege, because it did not use its power wisely or decisively—the civilians forced the military to fight with one hand tied behind its back. In addition, some argue, a hostile and hypercritical media and a near-treasonous antiwar movement turned public opinion against the war, forcing Presidents Johnson and Nixon to scale back U.S. involvement just when victory was within grasp. Such arguments imply, if they do not state outright, that the United States could have prevailed had it used its military power without limit and suppressed domestic dissent. They have provided the basis for numerous "lessons," some of them applied with a vengeance in the Persian Gulf.

This revisionist view of the war is fundamentally flawed. It accepts as a given what can never be more than mere speculation. There is no way to know whether the war could have been won if it had been fought differently. More important, to attribute U.S. failure to an errant strategy and lack of will oversimplifies a very complex problem and provides at best a partial explanation.

The strategy applied by President Johnson and his secretary of defense, Robert McNamara, was without question doomed to failure. The theory was that if the United States gradually increased the level of military pain it would reach a point where the Vietnamese communists would decide that the costs were greater than the potential gain. The theory turned out to be wrong. The level of pain Hanoi was prepared to endure was greater than Washington could inflict.

To jump to the conclusion, however, that the unrestricted use of American power could have produced victory in Vietnam at acceptable cost raises troubling questions. We can never know whether a bombing campaign of the sort advocated by the Joint Chiefs of Staff in Vietnam, and actually applied in the Gulf War, would have forced Hanoi to accept a settlement on U.S. terms, but there is ample reason to question whether it would have. The technology of 1991 was not available in 1965, and in any event North Vietnam was not vulnerable to air power in the way Iraq was vulnerable. The capacity of air power to cripple a preindustrial society was in fact quite limited. Even if the United States had destroyed the cities and industries of North Vietnam, there is considerable evidence to suggest that the Vietnamese were prepared to fight on, underground if necessary.

Invasion of enemy sanctuaries in Laos, Cambodia and North Vietnam might have made General William C. Westmoreland's attrition strategy more workable, but such steps would also have raised the costs of the war far out of proportion to the stakes and at a time when American resources were already stretched thin. Neither intensified bombing nor escalation of the ground war would have solved what was always the central problem—the political viability of South Vietnam.

The reasons why President Johnson refused to expand the war must also be considered. He feared that if the United States pushed North Vietnam to the brink of defeat, the Soviet Union, China or both might intervene, broadening the conflict to dangerous proportions, perhaps even to the level of nuclear confrontation. Whether Johnson's fears were justified can never be known, of course, but he would have been foolish in 1965–67 to have dismissed them out of hand. Destruction of North Vietnam would have been counterproductive in terms of the larger U.S. goal of containing China. In any event there was no reason for Johnson to push the war to the brink of a nuclear confrontation as long as he assumed that American goals could be achieved with less risk. And even if the United States had been able to militarily subdue North Vietnam without provoking outside intervention, it would still have faced the dangerous and costly task of occupying a hostile nation along China's southern border while simultaneously suppressing an insurgency in South Vietnam.

In terms of public opinion, there is no question but that after 1967 disillusionment with the war placed major constraints on policymakers, and the antiwar movement and U.S. media played a part in this. Critics of the war exposed error and self-deception in official statements, stimulating public doubt about the trustworthiness and wisdom of government and its leaders. Antiwar demonstrations also affected public opinion indirectly, contributing to the rise of domestic strife that fed a general, pervasive war-weariness, which in turn stimulated pressures for de-escalation and withdrawal. As for the media, reporting of the war was sometimes sensationalized and often ahistorical and ethnocentric. The early misreporting of the 1968 Tet offensive has been well documented, and after Tet the media undoubtedly became more critical of the war.

Still, the impact of the antiwar movement and the media on public opinion has been exaggerated. Careful studies of the polls indicate that until very late a majority of Americans considered the antiwar movement more obnoxious than the war. Thus in a perverse sort of way, and to a point, antiwar demonstrations may have strengthened support for the war. There is no persuasive evidence that it was the media that turned public opinion against the war; many social scientists contend that media content generally reinforces rather than changes existing views. In any event the antiwar movement and the media had much less impact on public opinion than the growing cost of the war in terms of lives lost and taxes paid. In this regard it is instructive to note that trends in popular support for the Vietnam War follow almost exactly those for the Korean War, where there was no antiwar movement and media coverage was generally uncritical.

The problem with all such explanations is that they are too ethnocentric. They reflect the persistence of what British writer D. W. Brogan once called "the illusion of American omnipotence," the belief that the difficult we do tomorrow, the impossible may take awhile. When failure occurs it must be our fault, and we seek scapegoats in our midst: the poor judgment of our leaders, the media, the antiwar movement. The flaw in this approach is that it ignores the other side of the picture. The sources of America's frustration and ultimate failure must also be found in the local circumstances of the war: the nature of the conflict, the weakness of America's ally and the strength of its adversary.

The Vietnam War posed extremely difficult challenges for Americans. It was fought in a climate and on a terrain that were singularly inhospitable: thick jungles, foreboding swamps and paddies, rugged mountains, insufferable heat and humidity. The climate and terrain neutralized America's technological superiority and control of the air. Needless to say those who had endured the land for centuries had a distinct advantage over outsiders, particularly when the latter came from a highly industrialized and urbanized environment.

In the beginning, at least, it was a people's war, where people rather than territory were the primary objective. Yet Americans as individuals and as a nation could never really bridge the vast cultural gap that separated them from all Vietnamese. Not knowing the language or culture, they had difficulty at times even distinguishing between friend and foe. Their mission was at best morally ambiguous and, however benevolent their intentions, Americans often found themselves on the wrong side of Vietnamese nationalism. In this context America's lavish and even reckless use of airpower and firepower was counterproductive, destroying, in the immortal words of the defender of Ben Tre, the very society the United States was purporting to save.

More important perhaps was the formless, yet lethal, nature of warfare in Vietnam, a war without distinct battlelines or fixed objectives, where traditional concepts of victory and defeat were blurred. This type of war was particularly difficult for Americans schooled in the conventional warfare of World War II and Korea. And there was always the gnawing—but fundamental—question, first raised by John F. Kennedy: how can we tell if we are winning? The only answer that could be devised was the notorious body count, as grim and corrupting as it was ultimately unreliable as a measure of success.

Even more important in explaining the U.S. failure was the unequal balance of forces it inherited in Vietnam. In South Vietnam, Americans attempted a truly formidable undertaking on a very weak foundation. The country to which they committed themselves in 1954 lacked many of the essential ingredients for nationhood. Indeed there was hardly a less promising place in the world to conduct an experiment in nation-building. Vietnam's economy had been devastated by the first Indochina war. The French had destroyed the traditional political order, and their departure left a gaping vacuum —no firmly established political institutions, no native elite willing to work with the United States and capable of exercising effective leadership. Southern Vietnam was rent by a multitude of conflicting ethnic, religious and political forces. When viewed from this perspective, there were probably built-in limits to what the United States could have accomplished there.

For nearly twenty years, Americans struggled to establish a viable nation in the face of internal insurgency and external invasion, but the rapid collapse of South Vietnam after U.S. military withdrawal in 1973 suggests how little was really accomplished. The United States could never find leaders capable of mobilizing the disparate population of southern Vietnam—the fact that it had to look for them suggests the magnitude of the problem. Washington launched a vast array of ambitious and expensive programs to promote sound government, win the hearts and minds of the people, and defeat the insurgents. When its client state was on the verge of collapse in 1965 the United States filled the vacuum with its own combat forces. Ironically—and tragically—the more it did, the more it induced dependency among those it was trying to help. Consequently, right up to the fall of Saigon in 1975, the South Vietnamese elite expected the United States to return and rescue them from defeat. This is not to make the South Vietnamese scapegoats for U.S. failure. It is rather to suggest that, given the history of southern Vietnam and the conditions that prevailed there in 1954, the creation of a viable nation by an outside power may have been impossible.

From beginning to end the United States also drastically underestimated the strength, determination and staying power of its adversary. This is not to suggest that the North Vietnamese and the National Front for the Liberation of South Vietnam were superhuman. They made colossal blunders and paid an enormous price for their success. They have shown a far greater capacity for making war than for nation-building. Still, in terms of the local balance of forces, they had tremendous advantages. They were tightly mobilized and regimented and deeply committed to their goals. They skillfully employed the strategy of protracted war, already tested against France, perceiving that the Americans, like the French, would become impatient and, if they bled long enough, might weary of the war. "You will kill ten of our men, but we will kill one of yours," Ho Chi Minh once remarked, "and in the end it is you who will tire." The comment was made to a French general on the eve of the first Indochina war, but it is an accurate commentary on the second as well.

America's fatal error, therefore, was to underestimate its foe. U.S. policymakers rather casually assumed that the Vietnamese, rational beings like themselves, would know better than to stand up against the most powerful nation in the world. It would be like a filibuster in Congress, Johnson once predicted: enormous resistance at first, then a steady whittling away, then Ho Chi Minh hurrying to get it over with. Years later Henry Kissinger still confessed surprise that his North Vietnamese counterparts were fanatics. Since their own goals were limited and from their standpoint more than reasonable, Americans found it difficult to understand the total unyielding commitment of the enemy, the willingness to risk everything to achieve an objective.

The circumstances of the war thus posed a dilemma that Americans never really understood, much less resolved. Success would probably have required the physical annihilation of North Vietnam, but given the limited American goals this would have been distasteful and excessively costly. It ran a serious risk of Soviet and Chinese intervention and would have been counterproductive by creating a vacuum into which China would flow. The only other way was to establish a viable South Vietnam, but given the weak foundation from which America worked and the cultural gap, not to mention the strength of the internal revolution, this was probably beyond its capacity. To put it charitably, the United States may have placed itself in a classic no-win situation....

* * *

For Vietnam the principal legacy of the war was continued human suffering. The ultimate losers were the South Vietnamese. Many of those who remained in Vietnam endured poverty, oppression, forced labor and "reeducation" camps. More than 1.5 million so-called boat people fled the country after 1975. Some perished in flight; others languished in squalid refugee camps in Southeast Asia. Between 750,000 and one million eventually resettled in the United States. The popular stereotype of the Vietnamese-American was one of assimilation and overachievement. In reality many remained unassimilated and lived near or below the poverty line, depending on minimum-wage jobs or welfare. The new immigrants also endured alienation, encountered prejudice from Americans for whom they were a living reminder of defeat, and suffered from the popular image of the successful Asian, which implied that the unsuccessful had only themselves to blame.

Even for the winners victory was a bittersweet prize. The Hanoi regime attained—at least temporarily—its goal of hegemony in Indochina, but at enormous cost. In time it was bogged down in its own "Vietnam" in Cambodia, for a decade waging a costly and ineffectual counterinsurgency against stubborn Cambodian guerrillas. Its long-standing goal of unifying Vietnam was achieved in name only. Historic differences between north and south were exacerbated during three decades of war, and even the most heavy-handed methods could not force the freewheeling and resilient south into a made-in-Hanoi mold. Most mortifying for many Vietnamese, long after the end of the war their country remained dependent on the Soviet Union....

Although the United States emerged physically unscathed, the Vietnam War was among the most debilitating in its history. The economic cost has been estimated at $167 billion, a raw statistic that does not begin to measure its impact. The war triggered the inflation that helped to undermine America's position in the world economy. It also had a high political cost, along with Watergate, increasing popular suspicion of government, leaders and institutions. It crippled the military, at least for a time, and temporarily estranged the United States from much of the rest of the world.

Nowhere was the impact of Vietnam greater than on the nation's foreign policy. The war destroyed the consensus that had existed since the late 1940s, leaving Americans confused and deeply divided on the goals to be pursued and the methods used. From the Angolan crisis of the mid-1970s to Central America in the 1980s to the Persian Gulf in 1990, foreign policy issues were viewed through the prism of Vietnam and debated in its context. Popular divisions on the gulf crisis derived to a large extent from the Vietnam experience, and the

Gulf War was fought on the basis of its perceived lessons.

Much like World War I for the Europeans, Vietnam's greatest impact was in the realm of the spirit. As no other event in the nation's history, it challenged Americans' traditional beliefs about themselves, the notion that in their relations with other people they had generally assumed a benevolent role, the idea that nothing was beyond reach. It was a fundamental part of a much larger crisis of the spirit that began in the 1960s, raising profound questions about America's history and values. The war's deep wounds still fester among some of its 2.7 million veterans, for whom victory in the Persian Gulf reinforced rather than erased bitter memories. The persisting popularity of Vietnam novels, television shows and films suggests the extent to which the war is still etched in the nation's consciousness and will probably continue to be so despite the Persian Gulf....

* * *

In light of the dramatic events of the last two years Americans may be tempted to view the Vietnam War as an anomaly. The collapse of the Soviet Union and its empire and the demise of communism leave the government of Vietnam an apparent anachronism, one of a handful of regimes clinging to a discredited doctrine. In this context it would be easy for Americans to regard the Vietnam War as little more than a tactical defeat in what turned out to be a strategic victory, a lost battle in a Cold War eventually won. In the larger scheme of post-World War II history, Vietnam might come to be seen as unimportant or even irrelevant.

Americans would err grievously to view their longest and most divisive war in such terms. Whether the United States in fact won the Cold War is at best arguable. In any event it remains important for Americans to understand why their nation intervened in Vietnam and why ultimately it failed. Morality and legality aside, by wrongly attributing the conflict in Vietnam to world communism, Americans drastically misjudged the conflict's origins and nature. By intervening in what was essentially a local struggle, they placed themselves at the mercy of local forces, a weak client and a determined adversary. What might have remained a local conflict with primarily local implications was elevated into a major international conflict with enormous human costs that are still being paid. Along with Afghanistan, Vietnam should stand as an enduring testament to the pitfalls of interventionism and the limits of power, something that may be more vital than ever to keep in mind after the deceptively easy military victory in the Persian Gulf.

# POSTSCRIPT

## Could the United States Have Prevented the Fall of South Vietnam?

The Vietnam conflict continues to attract a tremendous amount of attention: On college campuses, many students express deep interest in the war, which predates their births, as do many of their teachers, a number of whom came of age in the Vietnam era, some as soldiers, some as student protesters, some as disinterested bystanders. Moreover, national policymakers, including President Bill Clinton, Senator Bob Kerry (D-Nebraska), and Congressman Newt Gingrich (R-Georgia), have on more than one occasion employed Vietnam as a touchstone to explain their own programs and policies. Not surprisingly, Southeast Asia seems to serve as a frequent backdrop for recent foreign policy decisions.

George Herring challenges the assumptions behind containment theory that guided the policies of every president from Truman through Johnson concerning Vietnam. This critique is further documented in Herring's *America's Longest War*, 2d ed. (John Wiley, 1986). The 13-part television series first broadcast on PBS is now widely available on videocassette for classroom use. Stanley Karnow, *Vietnam: A History* (Viking Penguin, 1983) and Stephen Cohen, ed., *Vietnam: Anthology and Guide to a Television History* (Alfred A. Knopf, 1983) are printed supplements to the televised series. Both are criticized by Norman Podhoretz in "Vietnam: The Revised Standard Version," *Commentary* (April 1984).

Harry Summers's essay is representative of a body of work that seeks to explain why the United States, the most powerful nation in the world, failed to win a military victory over what most considered to be a third-rate nation. Political scientist Guenter Lewy was one of the first scholars to explore Pentagon military records on the Vietnam conflict. In *America in Vietnam* (Oxford University Press, 1978), Lewy denies the claims of antiwar activists that the United States carried out a policy of genocide, and he blames television for its "one-dimensional coverage of the conflict." At the same time, Lewy is highly critical of General William Westmoreland's attempt to fight a conventional war of attrition against an unconventional enemy who insisted on waging a guerrilla conflict. Other analyses of American military policy in Southeast Asia include Bruce Palmer, Jr., *The 25-Year War* (University Press of Kentucky, 1984) and Gary Hess, "The Military Perspective on Strategy in Vietnam," *Diplomatic History* (1986).

Twenty years after the collapse of the government of South Vietnam, scholars maintain a fascination with the many issues associated with the war. For a fuller understanding of the Vietnam conflict, see David Halberstam,

*The Best and the Brightest* (Random House, 1972); Theodore Draper, *Abuse of Power* (Viking, 1967); Townsend Hoopes, *The Limits of Intervention* (David McKay, 1970); Leslie Gelb and Richard Betts, *The Irony of Vietnam: The System Worked* (Brookings Institution, 1979); Larry Berman, *Planning a Tragedy: The Americanization of the War in Vietnam* (W. W. Norton, 1982); Loren Baritz, *Backfire: A History of How American Culture Led Us into Vietnam and Made Us Fight the Way We Did* (William Morrow, 1985); and Marilyn B. Young, *The Vietnam Wars, 1945–1990* (Harper Collins, 1991). Francis Fitzgerald's Pulitzer Prize–winning *Fire in the Lake: The Vietnamese and the Americans in Vietnam* (Little, Brown, 1972) places the war against the backdrop of the culture of Indochina, while Myra MacPherson, *Long Time Passing: Vietnam and the Haunted Generation* (Doubleday, 1984) analyzes the war's impact on American society. A number of anthologies examine the conflict in Southeast Asia from a number of different perspectives. Three of the best are Harrison E. Salisbury, ed., *Vietnam Reconsidered: Lessons From a War* (Harper & Row, 1984); Jeffrey P. Kimball, ed., *To Reason Why: The Debate About the Causes of U. S. Involvement in the Vietnam War* (McGraw-Hill, 1990); and Andrew J. Rotter, ed., *Light at the End of the Tunnel: A Vietnam War Anthology* (St. Martin's Press, 1991).

# ISSUE 16

## Was Martin Luther King, Jr.'s Leadership Essential to the Success of the Civil Rights Movement?

**YES: Vincent Gordon Harding,** from "Beyond Amnesia: Martin Luther King, Jr., and the Future of America," *Journal of American History* (September 1987)

**NO: Clayborne Carson,** from "Martin Luther King, Jr.: Charismatic Leadership in a Mass Struggle," *Journal of American History* (September 1987)

**ISSUE SUMMARY**

**YES:** Professor of religion and social transformation Vincent Gordon Harding stresses the point that Martin Luther King, Jr., promoted a forceful and singular vision that went well beyond desegregation campaigns to include demands for an end to racism, excessive materialism, and war as keys to the future security of the United States and the rest of the world.

**NO:** Associate professor of history Clayborne Carson concludes that the civil rights struggle would have followed a similar course of development, even had King never lived, because its successes depended upon mass activism, not the actions of a single leader.

On a steamy August day in 1963, Martin Luther King, Jr., mounted a podium constructed in front of the Lincoln Memorial in Washington, D. C., and, in the studied cadence of a preacher, delivered his famous "I Have a Dream" speech. For many Americans, black and white, King's speech represented the symbolic climax of the civil rights movement. The Civil Rights Act of 1964 and the Voting Rights Act of 1965 were merely denouement.

Actually, there was more that was symbolic at the March on Washington than King's electrifying oration. The call for the march had been issued by A. Philip Randolph, a long-time civil rights activist, who had threatened in 1941 to stage a similar protest march to bring attention to the economic inequality suffered by African Americans. Randolph's presence at the head of the march reflected a realization of *his* dream. Moreover, several of the speakers that day paid homage to W. E. B. Du Bois, the godfather of the twentieth-century black protest movement in the United States. An embittered exile from the land of his birth, Du Bois had died the previous day (at the age of 95) in Ghana, West Africa. The presence of Randolph and Du Bois, in flesh and spirit, served as a reminder that the movement to extend full civil and political rights to black Americans on a basis of equality was not confined to the 1950s and 1960s. For decades, African Americans had endured an enforced second-class citizenship. But in the 1940s and 1950s, following constitutional victories spearheaded by the National Association for the Advancement of Colored People in the areas of housing, voting, and education, black Americans awakened to the possibilities for change in their status. These victories coincided with the rise of independent nations in Africa, led by black leaders such as Kwame Nkrumah, which encouraged pride in the African homeland among many black Americans. Finally, the nonviolent direct action movement, pioneered by interracial organizations such as the Congress of Racial Equality (CORE) and individuals like A. Philip Randolph, James Farmer, and Martin Luther King, Jr., issued a clarion call to blacks and their white supporters that full equality was around the corner.

So much has been said and written about Martin Luther King, Jr.'s role in the civil rights movement that it is virtually impossible to separate the image of King from the protests for desegregation and political and economic equality of the 1950s and 1960s. However, is it appropriate to focus attention solely on King's leadership? Does this not do a disservice to the many other leaders and organizations that contributed to the movement's success? What of the roles played by the rank-and-file participants who did not enjoy a leadership position in one of the civil rights organizations, but without whose support little progress would have been possible?

Both of the following essays were originally presented in 1986 at a symposium in Washington, D. C., entitled, "Martin Luther King, Jr.: The Leader and the Legacy." Professor Vincent Harding locates King's greatness in the years after the march in Selma and the Voting Rights Act of 1965, when King turned his attention to the problems of the poor, including those in the urban North, and to a critique of the ongoing warfare in Southeast Asia. These challenges, Harding insists, not only addressed matters of interest to African Americans but also outlined a visionary hope for all mankind.

Clayborne Carson criticizes King's almost mythical image and feels that bestowing praise solely upon King for civil rights successes takes credit away from the black movement as a whole. Carson prefers to focus upon the valuable role played by local leaders and the mass activism of the southern campaigns. There were, after all, other tactical and ideological inspirations for the civil rights protest than those supplied by King. While not denying King's significance, Carson reminds his readers that sustained protests occurred in many southern communities in the 1960s where Martin Luther King had little or no involvement.

# YES Vincent Gordon Harding

## BEYOND AMNESIA: MARTIN LUTHER KING, JR., AND THE FUTURE OF AMERICA

In the 1970s, as a fascinating variety of voices began to press the nation to decide where it stood concerning the memory and meaning of Martin Luther King, Jr., and as we instinctively sought an easy way to deal with the unrelenting power of this disturber of all unjust peace, a black poet perhaps best reflected our ambivalence. Carl Wendell Hines wrote:

> Now that he is safely dead
> let us praise him
> build monuments to his glory
> sing hosannas to his name.
> Dead men make
> such convenient heroes; They
> cannot rise
> To challenge the images
> we would fashion from their lives.
> And besides,
> it is easier to build monuments
> than to make a better world.

Then as the voices of artists and family and millions of black people (and their votes, and their nonblack allies) began to build, the sad wisdom of Hines's words seemed to sharpen and to cut deeper at every moment. For it became increasingly clear that most of those who were leading the campaign for the national holiday [to commemorate King] had chosen, consciously or unconsciously, to allow King to become a convenient hero, to try to tailor him to the shape and mood of mainstream, liberal/moderate America.

From Vincent Gordon Harding, "Beyond Amnesia: Martin Luther King, Jr., and the Future of America," *Journal of American History*, vol. 74, no. 2 (September 1987).  Notes omitted.

Symbolic of the direction given the campaign has been the unremitting focus on the 1963 March on Washington, the never-ending repetition of the great speech and its dream metaphor, the sometimes innocent and sometimes manipulative boxing of King into the relatively safe categories of "civil rights leader," "great orator," harmless dreamer of black and white children on the hillside. And surely nothing could be more ironic or amnesiac than having Vice-President George Bush, the former head of the Central Intelligence Agency, the probable White House overseer of Contra actions, speaking words in King's honor. Or was it more ironic to watch the representatives of the Marine Corps, carrying fresh memories from the invasion of Grenada and from their training for Libya and for Nicaragua, playing "We Shall Overcome," while the bust of the prince of nonviolence was placed in the Capitol rotunda, without a word being spoken about nonviolence?

* * *

It appears as if the price for the first national holiday honoring a black man is the development of a massive case of national amnesia concerning who that black man really was. At both personal and collective levels, of course, it is often the case that amnesia is not ultimately harmful to the patient. However, in this case it is very dangerous, for the things we have chosen to forget about King (and about ourselves) constitute some of the most hopeful possibilities and resources for our magnificent and very needy nation. Indeed, I would suggest that we Americans have chosen amnesia rather than continue King's painful, uncharted, and often disruptive struggle toward a more perfect union. I would also suggest that those of us who are historians and citizens have a special responsibility to challenge the loss of memory, in ourselves and others, to allow our skills in probing the past to become resources for healing and for hope, not simply sources of pages in books or of steps in careers. In other words, if as Hines wrote, Martin King "cannot rise to challenge" those who would make him a harmless black icon, then *we* surely can—assuming that we are still alive.

Although there are many points at which our challenge to the comfortable images might be raised, I believe that the central encounters with King that begin to take us beyond the static March-on-Washington, "integrationist," "civil rights leader" image are located in Chicago and Mississippi in 1966. During the winter of that year King moved North. He was driven by the fires of Watts and the early hot summers of 1964 and 1965. Challenged and nurtured by the powerful commitment of Malcolm X to the black street forces, he was also compelled by his own deep compassion for the urban black community—whose peculiar problems were not fundamentally addressed by the civil rights laws so dearly won in the South. Under such urgent compulsion, King left his familiar southern base and stepped out on very unfamiliar turf. For Hamlin Avenue on Chicago's blighted West Side was a long way from the marvelous, costly victories of Selma, St. Augustine, and Birmingham, and Mayor Richard Daley was a consummate professional compared to the sheriffs, mayors, and police commissioners of the South. But King had made his choice, and it is one that we dare not forget.

By 1966 King had made an essentially religious commitment to the poor, and he was prepared to say:

> I choose to identify with the underprivileged. I choose to identify with the poor. I choose to give my life for the hungry. I choose to give my life for those who have been left out of the sunlight of opportunity. I choose to live for and with those who find themselves seeing life as a long and desolate corridor with no exit sign. This is the way I'm going. If it means suffering a little bit, I'm going that way. If it means sacrificing, I'm going that way. If it means dying for them, I'm going that way, because I heard a voice saying, "Do something for others."

We understand nothing about the King whose life ended in the midst of a struggle for garbage workers if we miss that earlier offering of himself to the struggle against poverty in America, to the continuing battle for the empowerment of the powerless—in this nation, in Vietnam, in South Africa, in Central America, and beyond.

In a sense, it was that commitment that took him from Chicago to Mississippi in the late spring of 1966, as he responded to the attempted assassination of James Meredith, taking up with others that enigmatic hero's "march against fear." There on the highways of the Magnolia State we have a second crucial encounter with the forgotten King. He was an embattled leader, the King who was challenged, chastened, and inspired by the courageous, foolhardy Young Turks of the Student Nonviolent Coordinating Committee. He was attentive to those veterans of the struggle who raised the cry for "Black Power," who made public the long simmering challenge to King's leadership, who increasingly voiced their doubts about the primacy of nonviolence as a way of struggle, and who seemed prepared to read whites out of the movement. Perhaps the most important aspect of the Meredith March for King's development was the question the young people raised in many forms: "Dr. King, why do you want us to love white folks before we even love ourselves?" From then on the issues of black self-love, of black and white power, and of the need to develop a more militant form of nonviolence that could challenge and enlist the rising rage of urban black youth were never far from King's consciousness. Along with his deepening commitment to the poor, those were the subjects and questions that did much to shape the hero we have forgotten.

One of the reasons for our amnesia, of course, is the fact that the forgotten King is not easy to handle now. Indeed, he never was. In 1967, after spending two hectic weeks traveling with the impassioned black prophet, David Halberstam, a perceptive journalist, reported that

> King has decided to represent the ghettos; he will work in them and speak for them. But their voice is harsh and alienated. If King is to speak for them truly, then his voice must reflect theirs; it too must be alienated, and it is likely to be increasingly at odds with the rest of American society.

Halberstam was right, but only partly so. After the Selma marches of 1965, King's voice did sound harsher in its criticism of the mainstream American way of life and its dominant values—including the assumption that the United States had the right to police the world for "free enterprise." Not only did the white mainstream object to such uncompromising criticism from a "civil rights leader" who was supposed to know his place, but respectable black people were increasingly uncomfortable as well. For some of them were making use of the fragile doorways that the freedom movement had helped open. Others, after years of frustration, were finally being promoted into the positions of responsibility and higher earnings that their skills and experience should have earlier made available. Too often, King was considered a threat to them as well, especially as his commitment to the poor drove him to increasingly radical assessments of the systemic flaws in the American economic order, an order they had finally begun to enjoy.

But Halberstam, a man of words, saw only part of the picture. King did more than *speak* for the ghettos. He was committed to mobilizing and organizing them for self-liberating action. That was his deeper threat to the status quo, beyond words, beyond alienation. That was what King's friend Rabbi Abraham Heschel surely understood when he introduced King to an assembly of rabbis in these words: "Martin Luther King is a voice, a vision and a way. I call upon every Jew to harken to his voice, to share his vision, to follow in his way. The whole future of America will depend on the impact and influence of Dr. King."

Part of what we have forgotten, then, is King's vision, beyond the appealing dream of black and white children holding hands, beyond the necessary goal of "civil rights." From the outset, he held a vision for all America, often calling the black movement more than a quest for rights—a struggle "to redeem the soul of America." By the end of his life, no one who paid attention could mistake the depth and meaning of that vision. At the convention of the Southern Christian Leadership Conference (SCLC) in 1967, King announced, "We must go from this convention and say, 'America, you must be born again... your whole structure must be changed.'" He insisted that "the problem of racism, the problem of economic exploitation, and the problem of war are all tied together." These, King said, were "the triple evils" that the freedom movement must address as it set itself to the challenge of "restructuring the whole of American society." This was the vision behind the call he issued in his final public speech in Memphis on April 3, 1968: "Let us move on in these powerful days, these days of challenge to make America what it ought to be. We have an opportunity to make America a better nation."

That final speech was delivered to a crowd of some two thousand persons, mostly black residents of Memphis who had come out in a soaking rain to hear King and to support the garbage workers' union in its struggle for justice. King's challenge to his last movement audience reminds us that he also carried a large and powerful vision concerning the role of black people and others of the "disinherited" in American society. His vision always included more than "rights" or "equal opportunity." On December 5, 1955, at the public meeting that launched the Montgomery bus boycott and Martin Luther King, Jr., into the heart of twentieth century history, King had announced,

> We, the disinherited of this land, we who have been oppressed so long, are tired of going through the long night of captivity. And now we are reaching out for the daybreak of freedom and justice and equality.

As a result of that decision and that movement, King said,

> when the history books are written in the future somebody will have to say "There

> lived a race of people, of black people, fleecy locks and black complexion, a people who had the moral courage to stand up for their rights, and thereby they injected a new meaning into the veins of history and of civilization." And we're gonna do that. God grant that we will do it before it's too late.

From beginning to end, the grand vision, the magnificent obsession never left him, the audacious hope for America and its disinherited. Only in the light of that dual vision can we understand his voice, especially in its increasing alienation from the mainstream, in its urgent movement beyond the black and white civil rights establishment. In his last years, the vision led him to call repeatedly for "a reconstruction of the entire society, a revolution of values." Only as we recapture the wholeness of King's vision can we understand his conclusion in 1967 that "something is wrong with capitalism as it now stands in the United States." Only then can we grasp his word to his co-workers in SCLC: "We are not interested in being integrated into *this* value structure. Power must be relocated." The vision leads directly to the voice, calling for "a radical redistribution of economic and political power" as the only way to meet the real needs of the poor in America.

When our memories allow us to absorb King's vision of a transformed America and a transforming force of black people and their allies, then we understand his powerful critique of the American war in Vietnam. After he struggled with his conscience about how open to make his opposition, after he endured intense pressure to be quiet from Washington and from the civil rights establishment, King's social vision and his religious faith stood him in good stead. He spoke out in a stirring series of statements and actions and declared:

> Never again will I be silent on an issue that is destroying the soul of our nation and destroying thousands and thousands of little children in Vietnam.... the time has come for a real prophecy, and I'm willing to go that road.

Of course, King knew the costly way of prophets—as did the rabbi who called us "to follow in his way." We must assume that neither the black prophet nor his Jewish brother was speaking idle words, opening up frivolous ways. Rather those were visions, voices, and ways not meant to be forgotten.

Indeed, in a nation where the gap between rich and poor continues to expand with cruel regularity, where the numbers of black and Hispanic poor vie with each other for supremacy, where farmers and industrial workers are in profound crisis, where racism continues to proclaim its ruthless American presence, who can afford to forget King's compassionate and courageous movement toward justice? When the leaders of the country spew reams of lies to Congress and the people alike, in public and private statements, when the official keepers of the nation's best hopes seem locked in what King called "paranoid anti-communism," when we make cynical mercenaries out of jobless young people, sacrificing them to a rigid militarism that threatens the future of the world, do we dare repress the memory of a man who called us to struggle bravely toward "the daybreak of freedom and justice and equality"? Dare we forget a man who told us that "a nation that continues year after year to spend more money on military defense than on programs of social uplift is approaching spiritual death"?

Clearly, we serve our scholarship and our citizenship most faithfully when we move ourselves and others beyond amnesia toward encounters with the jagged leading edges of King's prophetic vision. When we do that we recognize that Martin King himself was unclear about many aspects of the "way" he had chosen. In his commitment to the poor, in his search for the redistribution of wealth and power in America, in his relentless stand against war, in his determination to help America "repent of her modern economic imperialism," he set out on a largely uncharted way. Still, several polestars pointed the way for him, and they may suggest creative directions for our personal and collective lives.

As King searched for a way for Americans to press the nation toward its best possibilities, toward its next birth of freedom and justice, he held fast to several basic assumptions. Perhaps it will help to remember them:

1. He seemed convinced that in the last part of the twentieth century, anyone who still held a vision of "a more perfect union" and worked toward that goal had to be prepared to move toward fundamental, structural changes in the mainstream values, economic and political structures, and traditional leadership of American society.
2. King believed that those who are committed to a real, renewed war against poverty in America must recognize the connections between our domestic economic and political problems and the unhealthy position that we occupy in the military, economic, and political wards of the global community. In other words, what King called "the triple evils of racism, extreme materialism and militarism" could be effectively fought only by addressing their reality and relationships in our life at home and abroad.
3. Unlike many participants in current discussions of poverty and "the underclass" in American society, King assumed that his ultimate commitment was to help find the ways by which the full energies and angers of the poor could be challenged, organized, and engaged in a revolutionary process that confronted the status quo and opened creative new possibilities for them and for the nation. Surely this was what he meant when he said,

   > the dispossessed of this nation—the poor, both white and Negro—live in a cruelly unjust society. They must organize a revolution against that injustice, not against the lives of... their fellow citizens, but against the structures through which the society is refusing to lift... the load of poverty.

4. By the last months of his life, as King reflected on the developments in the freedom movement since its energies had turned northward and since some of its participants had begun to offer more radical challenges to the policies of the federal government at home and abroad, he reached an inescapable conclusion. The next stages of the struggle for a just American order could no longer expect even the reluctant support from the national government that the movement had received since Montgomery. Now, he said, "We must formulate a program and we must fashion the new tactics which do not count on government good will, but instead serve to compel unwilling

authorities to yield to the mandates of justice."

5. Defying most of the conventional wisdom of black and white America, King determined to hold fast to both of his fundamental, religiously based commitments: to the humanizing empowerment and transformation of the poor and of the nation and to the way of nonviolence and creative peace making. His attempt to create a Poor People's Campaign to challenge—and, if necessary, to disrupt —the federal government on its home ground was an expression of this wild and beautiful experiment in creating nonviolent revolution. Planning for a massive campaign of civil disobedience carried on by poor people of all races, aided by their unpoor allies, King announced, "We've got to make it known that until our problem is solved, America may have many, many days, but they will be full of trouble. There will be no rest, there will be no tranquility in this country until the nation comes to terms with [that problem]."

For those who seek a gentle, nonabrasive hero whose recorded speeches can be used as inspirational resources for rocking our memories to sleep, Martin Luther King, Jr., is surely the wrong man. However, if there is even a chance that Rabbi Heschel was correct, that the untranquil King and his peace-disturbing vision, words, and deeds hold the key to the future of America, then another story unfolds, another search begins. We who are scholars and citizens then owe ourselves, our children, and our nation a far more serious exploration and comprehension of the man and the widespread movement with which he was identified.

Recently, the Afro-American liberation theologian Cornel West said of King, "As a proponent of nonviolent resistance, he holds out the only slim hope for social sanity in a violence-prone world." What if both the black theologian and the Jewish scholar-mystic are correct? What if the way that King was exploring is indeed vital to the future of our nation and our world? For scholars, citizens, or celebrants to forget the real man and his deepest implications would be not only faithless, but also suicidal. For in the light of the news that inundates us every day, where else do we go from here to make a better world?

# NO

Clayborne Carson

# MARTIN LUTHER KING, JR.: CHARISMATIC LEADERSHIP IN A MASS STRUGGLE

The legislation to establish Martin Luther King, Jr.'s birthday as a federal holiday provided official recognition of King's greatness, but it remains the responsibility of those of us who study and carry on King's work to define his historical significance. Rather than engaging in officially approved nostalgia, our remembrance of King should reflect the reality of his complex and multifaceted life. Biographers, theologians, political scientists, sociologists, social psychologists, and historians have given us a sizable literature of King's place in Afro-American protest tradition, his role in the modern black freedom struggle, and his eclectic ideas regarding nonviolent activism. Although King scholars may benefit from and may stimulate the popular interest in King generated by the national holiday, many will find themselves uneasy participants in annual observances to honor an innocuous, carefully cultivated image of King as a black heroic figure.

The King depicted in serious scholarly works is far too interesting to be encased in such a didactic legend. King was a controversial leader who challenged authority and who once applauded what he called "creative maladjusted nonconformity." He should not be transformed into a simplistic image designed to offend no one—a black counterpart to the static, heroic myths that have embalmed George Washington as the Father of His Country and Abraham Lincoln as the Great Emancipator.

One aspect of the emerging King myth has been the depiction of him in the mass media, not only as the preeminent leader of the civil rights movement, but also as the initiator and sole indispensible element in the southern black struggles of the 1950s and 1960s. As in other historical myths, a Great Man is seen as the decisive factor in the process of social change, and the unique qualities of a leader are used to explain major historical events. The King myth departs from historical reality because it attributes too much to King's exceptional qualities as a leader and too little to the impersonal, large-scale social factors that made it possible for King to display his singular abilities on

From Clayborne Carson, "Martin Luther King, Jr.: Charismatic Leadership in a Mass Struggle," *Journal of American History*, vol. 74, no. 2 (September 1987), pp. 448–454. 

a national stage. Because the myth emphasizes the individual at the expense of the black movement, it not only exaggerates King's historical importance but also distorts his actual, considerable contribution to the movement.

A major example of this distortion has been the tendency to see King as a charismatic figure who single-handedly directed the course of the civil rights movement through the force of his oratory. The charismatic label, however, does not adequately define King's role in the southern black struggle. The term *charisma* has traditionally been used to describe the godlike, magical qualities possessed by certain leaders. Connotations of the term have changed, of course, over the years. In our more secular age, it has lost many of its religious connotations and now refers to a wide range of leadership styles that involve the capacity to inspire—usually through oratory—emotional bonds between leaders and followers. Arguing that King was not a charismatic leader, in the broadest sense of the term, becomes somewhat akin to arguing that he was not a Christian, but emphasis on King's charisma obscures other important aspects of his role in the black movement. To be sure, King's oratory was exceptional and many people saw King as a divinely inspired leader, but King did not receive and did not want the kind of unquestioning support that is often associated with charismatic leaders. Movement activists instead saw him as the most prominent among many outstanding movement strategists, tacticians, ideologues, and institutional leaders.

King undoubtedly recognized that charisma was one of many leadership qualities at his disposal, but he also recognized that charisma was not a sufficient basis for leadership in a modern political movement enlisting numerous self-reliant leaders. Moreover, he rejected aspects of the charismatic model that conflicted with his sense of his own limitations. Rather than exhibiting unwavering confidence in his power and wisdom, King was a leader full of self-doubts, keenly aware of his own limitations and human weaknesses. He was at times reluctant to take on the responsibilities suddenly and unexpectedly thrust upon him. During the Montgomery bus boycott, for example, when he worried about threats to his life and to the lives of his wife and child, he was overcome with fear rather than confident and secure in his leadership role. He was able to carry on only after acquiring an enduring understanding of his dependence on a personal God who promised never to leave him alone.

Moreover, emphasis on King's charisma conveys the misleading notion of a movement held together by spellbinding speeches and blind faith rather than by a complex blend of rational and emotional bonds. King's charisma did not place him above criticism. Indeed, he was never able to gain mass support for his notion of nonviolent struggle as a way of life, rather than simply a tactic. Instead of viewing himself as the embodiment of widely held Afro-American racial views, he willingly risked his popularity among blacks through his steadfast advocacy of nonviolent strategies to achieve radical social change.

He was a profound and provocative public speaker as well as an emotionally powerful one. Only those unfamiliar with the Afro-American clergy would assume that his oratorical skills were unique, but King set himself apart from other black preachers through his use of traditional black Christian idiom to advocate unconventional political ideas. Early in his life King became disillusioned with the unbridled emotionalism associated with his father's religious fundamentalism, and, as a thirteen year old, he questioned the bodily resurrection of Jesus in his Sunday school class. His subsequent search for an intellectually satisfying religious faith conflicted with the emphasis on emotional expressiveness that pervades evangelical religion. His preaching manner was rooted in the traditions of the black church, while his subject matter, which often reflected his wide-ranging philosophical interests, distinguished him from other preachers who relied on rhetorical devices that manipulated the emotions of the listeners. King used charisma as a tool for mobilizing black communities, but he always used it in the context of other forms of intellectual and political leadership suited to a movement containing many strong leaders.

Recently, scholars have begun to examine the black struggle as a locally based mass movement, rather than simply a reform movement led by national civil rights leaders. The new orientation in scholarship indicates that King's role was different from that suggested in King-centered biographies and journalistic accounts. King was certainly not the only significant leader of the civil rights movement, for sustained protest movements arose in many southern communities in which King had little or no direct involvement.

In Montgomery, for example, local black leaders such as E. D. Nixon, Rosa Parks, and Jo Ann Robinson started the bus boycott before King became the leader of the Montgomery Improvement Association. Thus, although King inspired blacks in Montgomery and black residents recognized that they were fortunate to have such a spokesperson, talented local leaders other than King played decisive roles in initiating and sustaining the boycott movement.

Similarly, the black students who initiated the 1960 lunch counter sit-ins admired King, but they did not wait for him to act before launching their own movement. The sit-in leaders who founded the Student Nonviolent Coordinating Committee (SNCC) became increasingly critical of King's leadership style, linking it to the feelings of dependency that often characterize the followers of charismatic leaders. The essence of SNCC's approach to community organizing was to instill in local residents the confidence that they could lead their own struggles. A SNCC organizer failed if local residents became dependent on his or her presence; as the organizers put it, their job was to work themselves out of a job. Though King influenced the struggles that took place in the Black Belt regions of Mississippi, Alabama, and Georgia, those movements were also guided by self-reliant local leaders who occasionally called on King's oratorical skills to galvanize black protestors at mass meetings while refusing to depend on his presence.

If King had never lived, the black struggle would have followed a course of development similar to the one it did. The Montgomery bus boycott would have occurred, because King did not initiate it. Black students probably would have rebelled—even without King as a role model—for they had sources of tactical and ideological inspiration besides King. Mass activism in southern cities and voting rights efforts in the deep South were outgrowths of large-scale social and political forces, rather than simply consequences of the actions of a single leader.

Though perhaps not as quickly and certainly not as peacefully nor with as universal a significance, the black movement would probably have achieved its major legislative victories without King's leadership, for the southern Jim Crow system was a regional anachronism, and the forces that undermined it were inexorable.

To what extent, then, did King's presence affect the movement? Answering that question requires us to look beyond the usual portrayal of the black struggle. Rather than seeing an amorphous mass of discontented blacks acting out strategies determined by a small group of leaders, we would recognize King as a major example of the local black leadership that emerged as black communities mobilized for sustained struggles. If not as dominant a figure as sometimes portrayed, the historical King was nevertheless a remarkable leader who acquired the respect and support of self-confident, grass-roots leaders, some of whom possessed charismatic qualities of their own. Directing attention to the other leaders who initiated and emerged from those struggles should not detract from our conception of King's historical significance; such movement-oriented research reveals King as a leader who stood out in a forest of tall trees.

King's major public speeches—particularly the "I Have a Dream" speech—have received much attention, but his exemplary qualities were also displayed in countless strategy sessions with other activists and in meetings with government officials. King's success as a leader was based on his intellectual and moral cogency and his skill as a conciliator among movement activists who refused to be simply King's "followers" or "lieutenants."

The success of the black movement required the mobilization of black communities as well as the transformation of attitudes in the surrounding society, and King's wide range of skills and attributes prepared him to meet the internal as well as the external demands of the movement. King understood the black world from a privileged position, having grown up in a stable family within a major black urban community; yet he also learned how to speak persuasively to the surrounding white world. Alone among the major civil rights leaders of his time, King could not only articulate black concerns to white audiences, but could also mobilize blacks through his day-to-day involvement in black community institutions and through his access to the regional institutional network of the black church. His advocacy of nonviolent activism gave the black movement invaluable positive press coverage, but his effectiveness as a protest leader derived mainly from his ability to mobilize black community resources.

Analyses of the southern movement that emphasize its nonrational aspects and expressive functions over its political character explain the black struggle as an emotional outburst by discontented blacks, rather than recognizing that the movement's strength and durability came from its mobilization of black community institutions, financial resources, and grass-roots leaders. The values of southern blacks were profoundly and permanently transformed not only by King, but also by involvement in sustained protest activity and community-organizing efforts, through thousands of mass meetings, workshops, citizenship classes, freedom schools, and informal discussions. Rather than merely accepting guidance from above, southern blacks were resocialized as a result of their movement experiences.

Although the literature of the black struggle has traditionally paid little attention to the intellectual content of black politics, movement activists of the 1960s made a profound, though often ignored, contribution to political thinking. King may have been born with rare potential, but his most significant leadership attributes were related to his immersion in, and contribution to, the intellectual ferment that has always been an essential part of Afro-American freedom struggles. Those who have written about King have too often assumed that his most important ideas were derived from outside the black struggle—from his academic training, his philosophical readings, or his acquaintance with Gandhian ideas. Scholars are only beginning to recognize the extent to which his attitudes and those of many other activists, white and black, were transformed through their involvement in a movement in which ideas disseminated from the bottom up as well as from the top down.

Although my assessment of King's role in the black struggles of his time reduces him to human scale, it also increases the possibility that others may recognize his qualities in themselves. Idolizing King lessens one's ability to exhibit some of his best attributes or, worse, encourages one to become a debunker, emphasizing King's flaws in order to lessen the inclination to exhibit his virtues. King himself undoubtedly feared that some who admired him would place too much faith in his ability to offer guidance and to overcome resistance, for he often publicly acknowledged his own limitations and mortality. Near the end of his life, King expressed his certainty that black people would reach the Promised Land whether or not he was with them. His faith was based on an awareness of the qualities that he knew he shared with all people. When he suggested his own epitaph, he asked not to be remembered for his exceptional achievements—his Nobel Prize and other awards, his academic accomplishments; instead, he wanted to be remembered for giving his life to serve others, for trying to be right on the war question, for trying to feed the hungry and clothe the naked, for trying to love and serve humanity. "I want you to say that I tried to love and serve humanity." Those aspects of King's life did not require charisma or other superhuman abilities.

If King were alive today, he would doubtless encourage those who celebrate his life to recognize their responsibility to struggle as he did for a more just and peaceful world. He would prefer that the black movement be remembered not only as the scene of his own achievements, but also as a setting that brought out extraordinary qualities in many people. If he were to return, his oratory would be unsettling and intellectually challenging rather than remembered diction and cadences. He would probably be the unpopular social critic he was on the eve of the Poor People's Campaign rather than the object of national homage he became after his death. His basic message would be the same as it was when he was alive, for he did not bend with the changing political winds. He would talk of ending poverty and war and of building a just social order that would avoid the pitfalls of competitive capitalism and repressive communism. He would give scant comfort to those who condition their activism upon the appearance of another King, for he recognized the extent to which he was a product of the movement that called him to leadership.

The notion that appearances by Great Men (or Great Women) are necessary preconditions for the emergence of major movements for social change reflects not only a poor understanding of history, but also a pessimistic view of the possibilities for future social change. Waiting for the Messiah is a human weakness that is unlikely to be rewarded more than once in a millennium. Studies of King's life offer support for an alternative optimistic belief that ordinary people can collectively improve their lives. Such studies demonstrate the capacity of social movements to transform participants for the better and to create leaders worthy of their followers.

# POSTSCRIPT

## Was Martin Luther King, Jr.'s Leadership Essential to the Success of the Civil Rights Movement?

By 1966, despite the many successes associated with his direct action campaigns in the South, Martin Luther King, Jr.'s prominence had begun to decline. The civil rights victories had failed to produce a nation free from segregation and political intimidation. A "white backlash" had begun to block further gains, and growing black nationalist trends were producing a call for "Black Power." By the time of his assassination in April 1968, King's philosophy was being challenged by younger, more radical blacks who saw nonviolent direct action as an obsolete strategy. The answer, they believed, lay not in "black and white together" but rather in efforts by black citizens to initiate control within their own communities where their actions would not be undermined or co-opted by the "white power structure."

The literature on King and the civil rights movement is extensive. August Meier, Elliott Rudwick, and Francis L. Broderick, eds., *Black Protest Thought in the Twentieth Century,* 2d ed. (Bobbs-Merrill, 1971) presents a collection of documents that places the activities of the 1950s and 1960s in a larger framework. The reflections of many of the participants of the movement are included in Howell Raines, *My Soul Is Rested: The Story of the Civil Rights Movement in the Deep South* (G. P. Putnam, 1977). Detailed studies of King include David L. Lewis, *King: A Critical Biography* (Praeger, 1970); Stephen B. Oates, *Let the Trumpet Sound: The Life of Martin Luther King, Jr.* (Harper & Row, 1982); David J. Garrow's Pulitzer Prize–winning *Bearing the Cross: Martin Luther King, Jr., and the Southern Christian Leadership Conference* (William Morrow, 1986); and Adam Fairclough, *To Redeem the Soul of America: The Southern Christian Leadership Conference and Martin Luther King, Jr.,* (University of Georgia Press, 1987). For an understanding of two prominent civil rights organizations, see August Meier and Elliott Rudwick, *CORE: A Study in the Civil Rights Movement, 1942–1968* (Oxford University Press, 1973) and Clayborne Carson, *In Struggle: SNCC and the Black Awakening of the 1960s* (Harvard University Press, 1981). The black nationalist critique of King and the nonviolent direct action campaign is effectively presented in Malcolm X and Alex Haley, *The Autobiography of Malcolm X* (Grove Press, 1964) and Peter Goldman, *The Death and Life of Malcolm X* (Harper & Row, 1974). Finally, the texture of the civil rights movement is captured brilliantly in Henry Hampton's documentary series "Eyes on the Prize."

# ISSUE 17

## Will History Forgive Richard Nixon?

**YES: Joan Hoff-Wilson,** from "Richard M. Nixon: The Corporate Presidency," in Fred I. Greenstein, ed., *Leadership in the Modern Presidency* (Harvard University Press, 1988)

**NO: Stanley I. Kutler,** from "Et Tu, Bob?" *The Nation* (August 22/29, 1994)

### ISSUE SUMMARY

**YES:** According to professor of history Joan Hoff-Wilson, the Nixon presidency reorganized the executive branch and portions of the federal bureaucracy and implemented domestic reforms in civil rights, welfare, and economic planning, despite its limited foreign policy successes and the Watergate scandal.

**NO:** Professor and political commentator Stanley I. Kutler argues that President Nixon was a crass, cynical, narrow-minded politician who unnecessarily prolonged the Vietnam War to ensure his reelection and implemented domestic reforms only when he could outflank his liberal opponents.

In late April 1994, ex-president Richard M. Nixon, age 81, died in a coma in a hospital in New York City. Twenty years before, Nixon became the only U.S. president forced to resign from office.

Richard Milhous Nixon was born in Yorba Linda in Orange County, California, on January 9, 1913, the second of five children. When he was nine his family moved to Whittier, California. His mother encouraged him to attend the local Quaker school, Whittier College, where he excelled at student politics and debating. He earned a tuition-paid scholarship to Duke University Law School and graduated third out of a class of twenty-five in 1937. He returned to Whittier and for several years worked with the town's oldest law firm.

Nixon had hopes of joining a bigger law firm, but World War II intervened. He worked in the tire rationing section for the Office of Price Administration in Washington, D.C., before joining the navy as a lieutenant, junior grade, where he served in a Naval Transport Unit in the South Pacific for the duration of the war. Before his discharge from active duty, Republicans asked him to run for a seat in California's 12th congressional district in the House of Representatives. He won the primary and defeated Jerry Vorhees, a nationally known, New Deal, Democratic incumbent, in the general election of 1946. In that year the Republicans gained control of Congress for the first time since 1930.

Nixon's campaign against Vorhees foreshadowed tactics that he would successfully employ in subsequent campaigns. He accused Vorhees of accepting money from a communist-dominated political action committee. This tactic, known as "red-baiting," was effective in the late 1940s and early 1950s because the American public had become frightened of the communist menace. In 1950 Nixon utilized similar tactics in running for the U.S. Senate against Congresswoman Helen Gahagan Douglas. He won easily.

Young, energetic, a vigorous campaign orator, and a senator from the second largest state in the Union with impeccable anticommunist credentials, Nixon was chosen by liberal Republicans to become General Dwight Eisenhower's running mate in the 1952 presidential election. In the election Eisenhower and Nixon overwhelmed the Democrats. Nixon became the second-youngest vice president in U.S. history and actively used the office to further his political ambitions.

The 1960 presidential campaign was one of the closest in modern times. Nixon, who was considered young for high political office at that time, lost to an even younger Democratic senator from Massachusetts, John F. Kennedy. Out of 68 million votes cast, less than 113,000 votes separated the two candidates.

In 1962 Nixon was persuaded to seek the governorship of California on the premise that he needed a power boost to keep his presidential hopes alive for 1964. Apparently, Nixon was out of touch with state politics. Governor Pat Brown defeated him by 300,000 votes.

Nixon then left for New York City and became a partner with a big-time Wall Street legal firm. He continued to speak at Republican dinners, and he supported Barry Goldwater of Arizona for the presidency in 1964. After Goldwater's decisive defeat by Lyndon B. Johnson, Nixon's political fortunes revived yet again. In March 1968 Johnson announced he was not going to run again for the presidency. Nixon took advantage of the opening and won the Republican nomination.

During the 1968 presidential campaign Nixon positioned himself between Democratic vice president Hubert Humphrey, the liberal defender of the Great Society programs, and the conservative, law-and-order third-party challenger Governor George Wallace of Alabama. Nixon stressed a more moderate brand of law and order and stated that he had a secret plan to end the war in Vietnam. He barely edged Humphrey in the popular vote, but Nixon received 301 electoral votes to 191 for Humphrey. Wallace received nearly 10 million popular votes and 46 electoral college votes.

This background brings us to Nixon's presidency. Was Nixon an effective president? In the first selection Professor Joan Hoff-Wilson argues that Nixon achieved a number of domestic policy successes in the areas of civil rights, welfare, economic planning, and in the reorganization of the executive branch and some federal agencies. Professor Stanley I. Kutler maintains that President Nixon was a crass, cynical, narrow-minded bigot who implemented policy changes for strictly political reasons.

# YES

Joan Hoff-Wilson

## RICHARD M. NIXON: THE CORPORATE PRESIDENCY

Richard Milhous Nixon became president of the United States at a critical juncture in American history. Following World War II there was a general agreement between popular and elite opinion on two things: the effectiveness of most New Deal domestic policies and the necessity of most Cold War foreign policies. During the 1960s, however, these two crucial postwar consensual constructs began to break down; and the war in Indochina, with its disruptive impact on the nation's political economy, hastened their disintegration. By 1968 the traditional bipartisan, Cold War approach to the conduct of foreign affairs had been seriously undermined. Similarly, the "bigger and better" New Deal approach to the modern welfare state had reached a point of diminishing returns, even among liberals.

In 1968, when Richard Nixon finally captured the highest office in the land, he inherited not only Lyndon Johnson's Vietnam war but also LBJ's Great Society. This transfer of power occurred at the very moment when both endeavors had lost substantial support among the public at large and, most important, among a significant number of the elite group of decision makers and leaders of opinion across the country. On previous occasions when such a breakdown had occurred within policy- and opinion-making circles—before the Civil and Spanish American Wars and in the early years of the Great Depression—domestic or foreign upheavals had followed. Beginning in the 1960s the country experienced a similar series of failed presidents reminiscent of those in the unstable 1840s and 1850s, 1890s, and 1920s.

In various ways all the presidents in these transitional periods failed as crisis managers, often because they refused to take risks. Nixon, in contrast, "[couldn't] understand people who won't take risks." His proclivity for risk taking was not emphasized by scholars, journalists, and psychologists until after he was forced to resign as president. "I am not necessarily a respecter of the status quo," Nixon told Stuart Alsop in 1958; "I am a chance taker." Although this statement was made primarily in reference to foreign affairs, Nixon's entire political career has been characterized by a series of personal and professional crises and risky political policies. It is therefore not surprising that as president he rationalized many of his major foreign and domestic initiatives as crises (or at least as intolerable impasses) that could be resolved only by dramatic and sometimes drastic measures.

A breakdown in either the foreign or domestic policy consensus offers both opportunity and danger to any incumbent president. Nixon had more opportunity for risk-taking changes at home and abroad during his first administration than he would have had if elected in 1960 because of the disruptive impact of war and domestic reforms during the intervening eight years. Also, he inherited a wartime presidency, with all its temporarily enhanced extralegal powers. Although the Cold War in general has permanently increased the potential for constitutional violations by presidents, only those in the midst of a full-scale war (whether declared or undeclared) have exercised with impunity what Garry Wills has called "semi-constitutional" actions. Although Nixon was a wartime president for all but twenty months of his five and one-half years in office, he found that impunity for constitutional violations was not automatically accorded a president engaged in an undeclared, unsatisfying, and seemingly endless war. In fact, he is not usually even thought of, or referred to, as a wartime president.

Periods of war and reform have usually alternated in the United States, but in the 1960s they burgeoned simultaneously, hastening the breakdown of consensus that was so evident by the time of the 1968 election. This unusual situation transformed Nixon's largely unexamined and rather commonplace management views into more rigid and controversial ones. It also reinforced his natural predilection to bring about change through executive fiat. Thus a historical accident accounts in part for many of Nixon's unilateral administrative actions during his first term and for the events leading to his disgrace and resignation during his second.

The first few months in the Oval Office are often intoxicating, and a new president can use them in a variety of ways. But during the socioeconomic confusion and conflict of the late 1960s and early 1970s, some of the newly appointed Republican policy managers (generalists) and the frustrated holdover Democratic policy specialists (experts) in the bureaucracy unexpectedly came together and began to consider dramatic policy changes at home and abroad. Complex interactions between these very different groups produced several significant shifts in domestic and foreign affairs during the spring and summer of 1969. A radical welfare plan and dramatic foreign policy initiatives took shape.

The country had elected only one other Republican president since the onset of FDR's reform administrations thirty-six years earlier. Consequently, Nixon faced not only unprecedented opportunities for changing domestic policy as a result of the breakdown in the New Deal consensus, but also the traditional problems of presidential governance, exacerbated in this instance by bureaucratic pockets of resistance from an unusual number of holdover Democrats. Such resistance was not new, but its magnitude was particularly threatening to a distrusted (and distrustful) Republican president who did not control either house of Congress. Nixon's organizational recommendations for containing the bureaucracy disturbed his political opponents and the liberal press as much as, if not more than, their doubts about the motivation behind many of his substantive and innovative suggestions on other domestic issues such as welfare and the environment.

Because much of the press and both houses of Congress were suspicious of him, Nixon naturally viewed administrative action as one way of obtaining significant domestic reform. Moreover, some of his initial accomplishments in administratively redirecting U.S. foreign policy ultimately led him to rely more on administrative actions at home than he might have otherwise. In any case, this approach drew criticism from those who already distrusted his policies and priorities. Nixon's covert and overt expansion and prolongation of the war during this period reinforced existing suspicions about his personality and political ethics. In this sense, liberal paranoia about his domestic programs fueled Nixon's paranoia about liberal opposition to the war, and vice versa. By 1972, Nixon's success in effecting structural and substantive change in foreign policy through the exercise of unilateral executive power increasingly led him to think that he could use the same preemptive administrative approach to resolve remaining domestic problems, especially following his landslide electoral victory....

## FOREIGN POLICY SCORECARD

It was clearly in Nixon's psychic and political self-interest to end the war in Vietnam as soon as possible. Although he came to office committed to negotiate a quick settlement, he ended up prolonging the conflict. As a result, he could never build the domestic consensus he needed to continue the escalated air and ground war (even with dramatically reduced U.S. troop involvement) and to ensure passage of some of his domestic programs. For Nixon (and Kissinger) Vietnam became a symbol of influence in the Third World that, in turn, was but one part of their geopolitical approach to international relations. Thus the war in Southeast Asia had to be settled as soon as possible so as not to endanger other elements of Nixonian diplomatic and domestic policy.

Instead, the president allowed his secretary of state to become egocentrically involved in secret negotiations with the North Vietnamese from August 4, 1969, to January 25, 1972 (when they were made public). As a result, the terms finally reached in 1973 were only marginally better than those rejected in 1969. The advantage gained from Hanoi's agreement to allow President Nguyen Van Thieu to remain in power in return for allowing North Vietnamese troops to remain in South Vietnam can hardly offset the additional loss of twenty thousand American lives during this three-year-period—especially given the inherent weaknesses of the Saigon government by 1973. On the tenth anniversary of the peace treaty ending the war in Vietnam, Nixon admitted to me that "Kissinger believed more in the power of negotiation than I did." He also said that he "would not have temporized as long" with the negotiating process had he not been "needlessly" concerned with what the Soviets and Chinese might think if the United States pulled out of Vietnam precipitately. Because Nixon saw no way in 1969 to end the war quickly except through overt massive bombing attacks, which the public demonstrated in 1970 and 1971 it would not tolerate, there was neither peace nor honor in Vietnam by the time that war was finally concluded on January 27, 1973; and in the interim he made matters worse by secretly bombing Cambodia.

The delayed ending to the war in Vietnam not only cast a shadow on all Nixon's other foreign policy efforts but also established secrecy, wiretapping, and capricious personal diplomacy as standard operational procedures in the conduct of foreign policy that ultimately carried over into domestic affairs. Despite often duplicitous and arbitrary actions, even Nixon's strongest critics often credit him with an unusual number of foreign policy successes.

Although fewer of his foreign policy decisions were reached in a crisis atmosphere than his domestic ones, Nixon's diplomatic legacy is weaker than he and many others have maintained. For example, the pursuit of "peace and honor" in Vietnam failed; his Middle Eastern policy because of Kissinger's shuttling ended up more show than substance; his Third World policy (outside of Vietnam and attempts to undermine the government of Allende in Chile) were nearly nonexistent; détente with the USSR soon foundered under his successors; and the Nixon Doctrine has not prevented use of U.S. troops abroad. Only rapprochement with China remains untarnished by time because it laid the foundation for recognition, even though he failed to achieve a "two China" policy in the United Nations. This summary is not meant to discredit Richard Nixon as a foreign policy expert both during and after his presidency. It is a reminder that the lasting and positive results of his diplomacy may be fading faster than some aspects of his domestic policies.

## OUTFLANKING LIBERALS ON DOMESTIC REFORM

Presidents traditionally achieve their domestic objectives through legislation, appeals in the mass media, and administrative actions. During his first administration Nixon offered Congress extensive domestic legislation, most of which aimed at redistributing federal power away from Congress and the bureaucracy. When he encountered difficulty obtaining passage of these programs, he resorted more and more to reform by administrative fiat, especially at the beginning of his second term. All Nixonian domestic reforms were rhetorically linked under the rubric of the New Federalism. Most competed for attention with his well-known interest in foreign affairs. Most involved a degree of the boldness he thought necessary for a successful presidency. Most increased federal regulation of nondistributive public policies. Most were made possible in part because he was a wartime Republican president who took advantage of acting in the Disraeli tradition of enlightened conservatism. Most offended liberals (as well as many conservatives), especially when it came to implementing certain controversial policies with legislation. Many were also undertaken in a crisis atmosphere, which on occasion was manufactured by individual members of Nixon's staff to ensure his attention and action.

In some instances, as political scientist Paul J. Halpern has noted, Nixon's longstanding liberal opponents in Congress "never even bothered to get the facts straight" about these legislative and administrative innovations; the very people who, according to Daniel Moynihan, formed the "natural constituency" for most of Nixon's domestic policies refused to support his programs. It may well have been that many liberals simply could not believe that Nixon would ever do the right thing except for the wrong reason. Thus they seldom took the time to try to determine whether any of his efforts to make the 1970s a decade of reform were legitimate, however politically motivated. Additionally, such partisan opposition made Nixon all the more willing to reorganize the executive branch of government with or without congressional approval.

My own interviews with Nixon and his own (and others') recent attempts to rehabilitate his reputation indicate that Nixon thinks he will outlive the obloquy of Watergate because of his foreign policy initiatives—not because of his domestic policies. Ultimately, however, domestic reform and his attempts at comprehensive reorganization of the executive branch may become the standard by which the Nixon presidency is judged.

**Environmental Policy**

Although Nixon's aides cite his environmental legislation as one of his major domestic achievements, it was not high on his personal list of federal priorities, despite polls showing its growing importance as a national issue. White House central files released in 1986 clearly reveal that John Ehrlichman was initially instrumental in shaping the president's views on environmental matters and conveying a sense of crisis about them. Most ideas were filtered through him to Nixon. In fact Ehrlichman, whose particular expertise was in land-use policies, has been described by one forest conservation specialist as "the most effective environmentalist since Gifford Pinchot." Ehrlichman and John Whitaker put Nixon ahead of Congress on environmental issues, especially with respect to his use of the permit authority in the Refuse Act of 1899 to begin to clean up water supplies before Congress passed any "comprehensive water pollution enforcement plan."

"Just keep me out of trouble on environmental issues," Nixon reportedly told Ehrlichman. This proved impossible because Congress ignored Nixon's recommended ceilings when it finally passed (over his veto) the Federal Water Pollution Control Act amendments of 1972. Both Ehrlichman and Whitaker agreed then and later that it was "budget-busting" legislation designed to embarrass the president on a popular issue in an election year. Statistics later showed that the money appropriated could not be spent fast enough to achieve the legislation's stated goals. The actual annual expenditures in the first years after passage approximated those originally proposed by Nixon's staff.

**Revamping Welfare**

Throughout the 1968 presidential campaign Nixon's own views on welfare remained highly unfocused. But once in the Oval Office he set an unexpectedly fast pace on the issue. On January 15, 1969, he demanded an investigation by top aides into a newspaper allegation of corruption in New York City's Human Resources Administration. Nixon's extraordinary welfare legislation originated in a very circuitous fashion with two low-level Democratic holdovers from the Johnson administration, Worth Bateman and James Lyday. These two bureaucrats fortuitously exercised more influence on Robert Finch, Nixon's first secretary of health, education and welfare, than they had been able to on John W. Gardner and Wilbur J. Cohn, Johnson's two appointees. Finch was primarily responsible for obtaining Nixon's approval of what eventually became known as the Family Assistance Program (FAP).

If FAP had succeeded in Congress it would have changed the emphasis of

American welfare from providing services to providing income; thus it would have replaced the Aid to Families with Dependent Children (AFDC) program, whose payments varied widely from state to state. FAP called for anywhere from $1,600 (initially proposed in 1969) to $2,500 (proposed in 1971) for a family of four. States were expected to supplement this amount, and in addition all able-bodied heads of recipient families (except mothers with preschool children) would be required to "accept work or training." However, if a parent refused to accept work or training, only his or her payment would be withheld. In essence, FAP unconditionally guaranteed children an annual income and would have tripled the number of children then being aided by AFDC.

A fundamental switch from services to income payments proved to be too much for congressional liberals and conservatives alike, and they formed a strange alliance to vote it down. Ironically, FAP's final defeat in the Senate led to some very impressive examples of incremental legislation that might not have been passed had it not been for the original boldness of FAP. For example, Supplementary Security Income, approved on October 17, 1972, constituted a guaranteed annual income for the aged, blind, and disabled.

The demise of FAP also led Nixon to support uniform application of the food stamp program across the United States, better health insurance programs for low-income families, and an automatic cost-of-living adjustment for Social Security recipients to help them cope with inflation. In every budget for which his administration was responsible—that is, from fiscal 1971 through fiscal 1975—spending on all human resource programs exceeded spending for defense for the first time since World War II. A sevenfold increase in funding for social services under Nixon made him (not Johnson) the "last of the big spenders" on domestic programs.

**Reluctant Civil Rights Achievements**

Perhaps the domestic area in which Watergate has most dimmed or skewed our memories of the Nixon years is civil rights. We naturally tend to remember that during his presidency Nixon deliberately violated the civil rights of some of those who opposed his policies or were suspected of leaking information. Nixon has always correctly denied that he was a conservative on civil rights, and indeed his record on this issue, as on so many others, reveals as much political expediency as it does philosophical commitment. By 1968 there was strong southern support for his candidacy. Consequently, during his campaign he implied that if elected he would slow down enforcement of federal school desegregation policies.

Enforcement had already been painfully sluggish since the 1954 *Brown v. Board of Education* decision. By 1968 only 20 percent of black children in the South attended predominantly white schools, and none of this progress had occurred under Eisenhower or Kennedy. Moreover, the most dramatic improvement under Johnson's administration did not take place until 1968, because HEW deadlines for desegregating southern schools had been postponed four times since the passage of the 1964 Civil Rights Act. By the spring of 1968, however, a few lower court rulings, and finally the Supreme Court decision in *Green v. Board of Education,* no longer allowed any president the luxury of arguing that freedom-of-choice plans were adequate for rooting out racial discrimination, or that de facto segregation caused by residential patterns was not as unconstitutional as *de jure* segregation brought about by state or local laws.

Despite the real national crisis that existed over school desegregation, Nixon was not prepared to go beyond what he thought the decision in *Brown* had mandated, because he believed that de facto segregation could not be ended through busing or cutting off funds from school districts. Nine days after Nixon's inauguration, his administration had to decide whether to honor an HEW-initiated cutoff of funds to five southern school districts, originally scheduled to take place in the fall of 1968 but delayed until January 29, 1969. On that day Secretary Finch confirmed the cutoff but also announced that the school districts could claim funds retroactively if they complied with HEW guidelines within sixty days. This offer represented a change from the most recent set of HEW guidelines, developed in March 1968, which Johnson had never formally endorsed by signing.

At the heart of the debate over various HEW guidelines in the last half of the 1960s were two issues: whether the intent of the Civil Rights Act of 1964 had been simply to provide freedom of choice or actually to compel integration in schools; and whether freedom-of-choice agreements negotiated by HEW or lawsuits brought by the Department of Justice were the most effective ways of achieving desegregation. Under the Johnson administration the HEW approach, based on bringing recalcitrant school districts into compliance by cutting off federal funding, had prevailed. Nixon, on the other hand, argued in his First Inaugural that the "laws have caught up with our consciences" and insisted that it was now necessary "to give life to what is in the law." Accordingly, he changed the emphasis in the enforcement of school desegregation from HEW compliance agreements to Justice Department actions—a legal procedure that proved very controversial in 1969 and 1970, but one that is standard now.

Nixon has been justifiably criticized by civil rights advocates for employing delaying tactics in the South, and particularly for not endorsing busing to enforce school desegregation in the North after the April 20, 1971, Supreme Court decision in *Swann v. Charlotte-Mecklenburg Board of Education.* Despite the bitter battle in Congress and between Congress and the executive branch after *Swann,* the Nixon administration's statistical record on school desegregation is impressive. In 1968, 68 percent of all black children in the South and 40 percent in the nation as a whole attended all-black schools. By the end of 1972, 8 percent of southern black children attended all-black schools, and a little less than 12 percent nationwide. A comparison of budget outlays is equally revealing. President Nixon spent $911 million on civil rights activities, including $75 million for civil rights enforcement in fiscal 1969. The Nixon administration's budget for fiscal 1973 called for $2.6 billion in total civil rights outlays, of which $602 million was earmarked for enforcement through a substantially strengthened Equal Employment Opportunity Commission. Nixon supported the civil rights goals of American Indians and women with less reluctance than he did school desegregation because these groups did not pose a major political problem for him and he had no similar legal reservations about how the law should be applied to them.

## MIXING ECONOMICS AND POLITICS

Nixon spent an inordinate amount of time on domestic and foreign economic matters. Nowhere did he appear to reverse himself more on views he had held before becoming president (or at least on views others attributed to him), and nowhere was his aprincipled pragmatism more evident. Nixon's failure to obtain more revenue through tax reform legislation in 1969, together with rising unemployment and inflation rates in 1970, precipitated an effort (in response to a perceived crisis) to balance U.S. domestic concerns through wage and price controls and international ones through devaluation of the dollar. This vehicle was the New Economic Policy, dramatically announced on August 15, 1971, at the end of a secret Camp David meeting with sixteen economic advisers. Largely as a result of Treasury Secretary Connally's influence, Nixon agreed that if foreign countries continued to demand ever-increasing amounts of gold for the U.S. dollars they held, the United States would go off the gold standard but would at the same time impose wage and price controls to curb inflation. The NEP perfectly reflected the "grand gesture" Connally thought the president should make on economic problems, and the August 15 television broadcast dramatized economic issues that most Americans, seldom anticipating long-range consequences, found boring.

When he was not trying to preempt Congress on regulatory issues, Nixon proposed deregulation based on free-market assumptions that were more traditionally in keeping with conservative Republicanism. The administration ended the draft in the name of economic freedom and recommended deregulation of the production of food crops, tariff and other barriers to international trade, and interest rates paid by various financial institutions. Except for wage and price controls and the devaluation of the dollar, none of these actions was justified in the name of crisis management. In general, however, political considerations made Nixon more liberal on domestic economic matters, confounding both his supporters and his opponents.

Nixon attributes his interest in international economics to the encouragement of John Foster Dulles and his desire as vice-president in the 1950s to create a Foreign Economic Council. Failing in this, he has said that his travels abroad in the 1950s only confirmed his belief that foreign leaders understood economics better than did American leaders, and he was determined to remedy this situation as president. Nixon faced two obstacles in this effort: Kissinger (because "international economics was not Henry's bag"), and State Department officials who saw "economic policy as government to government," which limited their diplomatic view of the world and made them so suspicious or cynical (or both) about the private sector that they refused to promote international commerce to the degree that Nixon thought they should. "Unlike the ignoramuses I encountered among economic officers at various embassies in the 1950s and 1960s," Nixon told me, "I wanted to bring economics to the foreign service."

Because of Nixon's own interest in and knowledge of international trade, he attempted as president to rationalize the formulation of foreign economic policy. After 1962, when he was out of public office and practicing law in New York, he had specialized in international economics and multinational corporations —definitely not Henry Kissinger's areas of expertise. In part because they were not a "team" on foreign economic policy and in part because Nixon bypassed the NSC almost entirely in formulating his New Economic Policy, Nixon relied not on his national security adviser but on other free-thinking outsiders when formulating foreign economic policy.

Next to John Connally, Nixon was most impressed with the economic views of Peter G. Peterson, who, after starting out in 1971 as a White House adviser on international economic affairs, became secretary of commerce in January 1972. Although Connally and Peterson appeared to agree on such early foreign economic initiatives as the NEP and the "get tough" policy toward Third World countries that nationalized U.S. companies abroad, as secretary of commerce Peterson ultimately proved much more sophisticated and sensitive than the secretary of the treasury about the United States' changed economic role in the world. In a December 27, 1971, position paper defending Nixon's NEP, Peterson remarked that the new global situation in which the United States found itself demanded "shared leadership, shared responsibility, and shared burdens... The reform of the international monetary systems," he said, must fully recognize and be solidly rooted in "the growing reality of a genuinely interdependent and increasingly competitive world economy whose goal is mutual, shared prosperity —not artificial, temporary advantage." At no point did Peterson believe, as Connally apparently did, that "the simple realignment of exchange rates" would adequately address the economic realignment problems facing the international economy.

In 1971 Nixon succeeded in establishing an entirely new cabinet-level Council on International Economic Policy (CIEP), headed by Peterson. This was not so much a reorganization of functions as it was an alternative to fill an existing void in the federal structure and to provide "clear top-level focus on international economic issues and to achieve consistency between international and domestic economic policy." For a variety of reasons—not the least of which was Kissinger's general lack of interest in, and disdain for, the unglamorous aspects of international economics—the CIEP faltered and finally failed after Nixon left office. Its demise seems to have been hastened by Kissinger's recommendation to the Congressional Commission on Organization of Foreign Policy that it be eliminated, despite the fact that others, including Peterson, testified on its behalf. The CIEP was subsequently merged with the Office of the Special Trade Representative.

* * *

Even with Nixon's impressive foreign and domestic record, it cannot be said that he would have succeeded as a managerial or administrative president had Watergate not occurred. Entrenched federal bureaucracies are not easily controlled or divested of power even with the best policy-oriented management strategies. That his foreign policy management seems more successful is also no surprise: diplomatic bureaucracies are smaller, more responsive, and easier to control than their domestic counterparts. Moreover, public concern (except for Vietnam) remained minimal as usual, and individual presidential foreign policy initiatives are more likely to be remembered and to appear effective than domestic ones. Nonetheless, the real importance of Nixon's presidency may well come to rest not on Watergate or foreign policy, but on his attempts to restructure the executive branch along functional lines, to bring order to the federal bureaucracy, and to achieve lasting domestic reform. The degree to which those Nixonian administrative tactics that were legal and ethical (and most of them were) became consciously or unconsciously the model for his successors in the Oval Office will determine his final place in history.

Although Nixon's corporate presidency remains publicly discredited, much of it has been privately preserved. Perhaps this is an indication that in exceptional cases presidential effectiveness can transcend popular (and scholarly) disapproval. What Nixon lacked in charisma and honesty, he may in the long run make up for with his phoenixlike ability to survive disaster. Nixon has repeatedly said: "No politician is dead until he admits it." It is perhaps an ironic commentary on the state of the modern presidency that Richard Nixon's management style and substantive foreign and domestic achievements look better and better when compared with those of his immediate successors in the Oval Office.

# NO

**Stanley I. Kutler**

## ET TU, BOB?

There is nothing quite like H.R. Haldeman's diaries, published recently during the official period of mourning for Richard Nixon. They are repulsive almost beyond belief, yet therein lies their importance. Ostensibly designed to record the doings of a great man, they devastate Nixon's reputation. Truly Haldeman has proved Mark Antony's observation that the good that men do is buried with their bones; the evil they do lives long after them. The diaries appeared three weeks after Nixon's death as a nearly 700-page book, unveiled first on a two-part *Nightline* program, which predictably focused on Nixon's racial and ethnic slurs. Soon thereafter came the CD-ROM, which included a "complete" version of the diaries (60 percent more material than in the book) and some added attractions, including "home" movies (developed at government expense), photos, bios of key and bit players and an amazing apologia in the form of an unsent 40,000-plus-word letter to James Neal, who prosecuted Haldeman. Like Antony, Haldeman had motives other than praising Caesar.

The diaries reflect two men in an "intense one-on-one relationship," men who were not, according to Haldeman's widow, personal friends. Since Nixon had few close friends, this means very little. The two often dined alone on the presidential yacht and then went to the President's sitting room to chat. The President would drink his '57 Lafite-Rothschild and serve Haldeman the California "Beaulieu Vineyard stuff." And Haldeman would have to read aloud Nixon's *Who's Who* entry. Maybe he was supposed to savor that instead.

The tapes revealed Nixon's shabbiness; the diaries underline his shallowness. The recurring themes of the diaries are simple: getting re-elected, getting even. Nixon was consumed with P.R., constantly prodding Haldeman on how to spin stories, how to protect his image and, almost comically, how to deny that the President was interested in such things. Haldeman, the old advertising executive, usually relished the game, yet he must have found it tiresome as well. P.R., he noted, "would work a lot better if he would quit worrying... and just be President." Impossible; for Nixon it was all.

Altogether, the picture is not pretty. It is mostly warts and little face, and certainly not the one Nixon had in mind as he took his leave. Shortly after

Haldeman died last fall, Nixon asked Haldeman's family to delay publication, ostensibly so as not to interfere with the promotion of his own book. What a hoot it would have been if Nixon, appearing on the *Today* show, had had to confront some of the juicier items from his trusted aide's diaries. In any event, Haldeman said that he hoped his book—which fleshes out and expands the daily notes that have been available for some time—would "once and for all" put the Nixon years into perspective. It certainly helps, but probably not as he intended.

Nixon always knew that Haldeman's diaries were potential dynamite. Archibald Cox subpoenaed the files on May 25, 1973, but the President had taken control of the diaries and put them with his papers, which eventually went to the National Archives (over his protests, to be sure). In 1980, Haldeman cut a deal with the Archives, deeding the diaries to the public (meaning he always intended for them to be seen, contrary to *Nightline*'s and his wife's assertions) in exchange for the Archives' agreement to keep them closed for a decade, later extended for several more years. Haldeman then promptly filed suit against the government, claiming (falsely) that he had been unlawfully deprived of access to his property in the intervening years. But the court refused to get involved "in the niceties of Fifth Amendment doctrine" since the case revolved around one question: Why did Haldeman leave his diaries in the White House when he was dismissed on April 30, 1973?

The government nailed Haldeman when it introduced Oval Office conversations for May 2 and 9, 1973 (Haldeman had "left" the White House but he returned—to listen to tapes!), in which Nixon and Haldeman typically concocted a scenario for future spin. In brief, Nixon would claim the materials as his own and cloak them with executive privilege: "Your notes belong to the President," Nixon told him. Haldeman finished the thought: "And fortunately, they're . . . in your possession; they're not in mine." In those days, we had few illusions about Nixon and his aide. District Judge John Garrett Penn said that Haldeman could have avoided the dispute had he claimed the diaries as his own at the outset, or had he made photocopies when he viewed the materials. The conflict, the judge ruled, was entirely Haldeman's fault. "He could have obviated this entire conflict; he chose another route solely for his own protection, and should not now be given a forum to complain that he did not choose wisely." He may not have chosen wisely as far as Nixon is concerned—but Haldeman will do well by his heirs.

* * *

Most reactions to the diaries have concentrated on long-familiar Nixon slanders of Jews and blacks. The reluctance to confront the policy and institutional concerns of the diaries is somewhat understandable, for if the mainstream media honestly surveyed this material, they would impeach themselves for their insipid attempts to peddle revisionist views of Nixon in the wake of his death. The diaries clearly reveal the President's extraordinary cynicism, as well as his lack of knowledge of both domestic and foreign policy. No single work so effectively exposes Nixon as a mean, petty, vindictive, insecure—even incompetent—man, and all this from one who professed to admire him; from a man Nixon even said he "loved." Could it have been intentional?

Haldeman himself spent the past two decades portraying himself as a selfless, self-effacing, dedicated servant to the President. But the myth of Haldeman as Stevens the butler in *Remains of the Day*—just a passive vessel for Nixon's commands—is misleading. Haldeman was an old-fashioned Southern California reactionary, weaned on his family's nativist and patriotic views and supported by a plumbing fortune. Nixon correctly perceived him as a "son-of-a-bitch" and used him as a "Lord High Executioner."

Unintentionally, I would guess, Haldeman has provided us with wonderful comic moments. After the Thomas Eagleton nomination fiasco in 1972, Spiro Agnew, either with inspired wit or sheer meanness, asked Dr. Joyce Brothers to second his own nomination—as if to receive psychological certification of his sanity. Nixon issued a presidential order directing Agnew to rescind the invitation. Then there are Great Moments of Protocol: Who would ride in the President's golf cart, Bob Hope or Frank Sinatra? Finally, Nixon wanted a White House reception to honor Duke Ellington and told Haldeman to invite other jazz notables, including Guy Lombardo. "Oh well," the knowing Haldeman sighed.

Haldeman's diaries show that he spent either hours or "all day" with the President. Sometimes Haldeman recorded Nixon's thoughts on substantive policy such as China or the settlement of the Vietnam War. But usually the subjects were relentlessly repetitive, as were the homilies that Nixon dispensed. And yet Haldeman faithfully recorded and preserved the President's words. During the 1972 campaign, Haldeman and John Ehrlichman spent inordinate amounts of time listening to the President repeatedly go over matters such as his prospects in every state, who would be dismissed, who would be moved and how enemies would be punished. Apparently even "two of the finest public servants," as Nixon characterized them when he dismissed them, could not abide the monotony of it all without sarcasm. "Why did he buzz me?" Haldeman asked Ehrlichman in a note written during one of the President's soliloquies. Like a schoolchild answering a passed message, Ehrlichman sketched several answers:

> "He had an itchy finger."
>
> "Also there was a chair unoccupied."
>
> "Also he has been talking about not just reordering the chaos, and he would like you to understand that point."

Supposedly, Nixon wanted someone to keep the "routine baloney" away from him; it "bores and annoys him," Haldeman noted. Yet Haldeman often wearily complained about the tedium, as when he noted that the "P had the morning clear, unfortunately, and called me... for over four hours as he wandered through odds and ends...."

Aside from the President's behavior, the most significant revelations surround Henry Kissinger. From the outset, Nixon and Haldeman recognized Kissinger as a devious, emotionally unstable person. The President saw him as a rival for public acclaim, ever anxious to magnify himself for the contemporary and historical record. Nixon did not entirely trust Kissinger's briefings. Most surprising, however, was Haldeman's intimate involvement in the management of foreign policy as the President regularly shared his thoughts and views on Kissinger with his Chief of Staff.

In the pathology of the Nixon White House, perhaps the sickest subject involved what Haldeman repeatedly called the "K-Rogers flap," which he blamed equally on Kissinger's "unbelievable ego" and Secretary of State William Rogers's pique. We long have understood Kissinger's pre-inaugural coup that enabled him and Nixon to bypass the State Department bureaucracy; yet what Kissinger wanted was the place for himself. Haldeman relentlessly portrays Kissinger as a mercurial, temperamental infant, constantly concerned with his standing and status; Nixon considered Kissinger "obsessed beyond reason" with Rogers.

Nixon and Kissinger appear more as adversaries than as allies. In November 1972, miffed at Kissinger's media attempts to grab the lion's share of credit for the China opening, Nixon instructed Haldeman to tell Kissinger that he had tapes of their conversations! Nixon warned Haldeman that *Time* might "needle us [and] go for K as the Man of the Year, which would be very bad, so we should try to swing that around a different way." Students of Vietnam policy have an interesting task in sorting out responsibility for the protracted peace negotiations. Kissinger expressed to Haldeman his fear that Nixon wanted to "bug out" and not carry through on long-term negotiations. Kissinger well knew that message would get back to Nixon and steel him against any appearances of being "soft."

Haldeman's diaries substantially confirm the criticism of Kissinger's detractors, especially Seymour Hersh's biting analysis of the Nixon-Kissinger foreign policies in *The Price of Power.* Appearance was often substituted for substance, and at times, as in the SALT negotiations, Kissinger seemed entirely out of his element. What then does this say of the President of the United States —who similarly was unconcerned with substance and seemed most bent on preventing Kissinger from getting too much praise? Certainly, Adm. Elmo Zumwalt had it right when he said that two words did not apply to the Vietnam peace accords: peace and honor. Kissinger's frantic search for a Shanghai Communiqué in 1972 would have bordered on the comic had it not been so fraught with obsequiousness toward his new friends and cynicism toward Nixon's longtime Taiwanese patrons.

Everything had a political calculus. In December 1970, Nixon, Kissinger and Haldeman considered a Vietnam trip the next spring in which the President would make "the basic end of the war announcement." Kissinger objected, saying that if we pulled out in 1971 there could be trouble (ostensibly for the Thieu regime) that the Administration would have to answer for in the 1972 elections. Kissinger urged Nixon to commit only to withdrawing all troops by the end of 1972. Another year of casualties seemed a fair exchange for the President's electoral security.

Billy Graham's choicer remarks about Jews and their "total domination of the media" have been prominently reported. Let's take Graham at his word and agree that some of his best friends are Jews. In the guise of God's messenger, Graham was a Nixon political operative, dutifully reporting back to the White House on what Lyndon Johnson had said about George McGovern, George Wallace's intentions on resuming his presidential bid in 1972, Graham's efforts to calm down Martha Mitchell, plans to organize Christian youth for Nixon, his advice to Johnny Carson to be a little biased in Nixon's favor if he wanted to be helpful and the Shah of Iran's remark that the President's re-election had saved civilization. When Nixon's tapes were first revealed in April 1974, a chastened Graham complained about Nixon's "situational ethics" and lamented that he had been "used." Used once, used again, he could not resist the limelight of preaching at Nixon's funeral.

* * *

John Ehrlichman has maintained that Nixon would be remembered as the great domestic policy President of the twentieth century. (Guess who was Nixon's domestic adviser?) That notion, too, is a chapter in the current drive for revisionism. Well, it won't wash, unless one accepts the view that whatever was accomplished happened in spite of Richard Nixon. His Administration publicly advocated policies that the President clearly didn't believe in. Consider:

- School desegregation: Haldeman noted that Nixon was "really concerned... and feels we have to take some leadership to try to reverse Court decisions that have forced integration too far, too fast." Nixon told Attorney General John Mitchell to keep filing cases until they got a reversal. Nixon proposed getting a right-wing demagogue into some tough race and have him campaign against integration—and he "might even win." He fired Leon Panetta, then a mid-level Health, Education and Welfare functionary, who was doing too much in behalf of school desegregation. (Panetta wouldn't quit, so Nixon announced his "resignation.")
- "[Nixon] was very upset that he had been led to approve the IRS ruling about no tax exemption for private schools, feels it will make no votes anywhere and will badly hurt private schools...."
- "About Family Assistance Plan, [President] wants to be sure it's killed by Democrats and that we make big play for it, but don't let it pass, can't afford it."
- "On welfare, we have to support HR 1 until the election. Afterward, we should not send it back to Congress." "On HR 1 there's some concern that if we hang too tight on the passage of it, that it may actually pass and defeat our Machiavellian plot. Our Congressional tactic overall has got to be to screw things up."
- "He's very much concerned about handling of the drug situation; wants the whole thing taken out of HEW. He makes the point that they're all on drugs there anyway."
- Nixon agreed to continue an I.B.M. antitrust action but urged Haldeman "to make something out of it so we can get credit for attacking business."
- "The P was also very upset about the DDT decision. Ruckleshaus has announced a ban on it. He [Nixon] thinks we should get this whole environment thing out of E and [John] Whitaker's hands because they believe in it, and you can't have an advocate dismantle something he believes in. He also wanted [Fred] Malek to check on who Ruckleshaus has on his staff in terms of left-wing liberals."
- Nixon "made the point that he feels deeply troubled that he's getting sucked in too much on welfare and environment and consumerism."

Liberals cringed in 1968 when Nixon promised to appoint judges who would favor the "peace forces" as opposed to the "criminal forces." Nixon, of course, like all Presidents, sought appointments to mirror his (and his constituency's) wishes. After the Senate rejected his nomination of G. Harrold Carswell for the Supreme Court in 1970, Nixon briefly flirted with nominating Senator Robert Byrd, knowing the Senate would be unlikely to reject one of its own. When Hugo Black resigned from the Court in 1971, Nixon, feverishly backed by Pat Buchanan, pushed for Virginia Congressman Richard Poff, once an ardent backer of segregation. Nixon happily recognized that this would only roil the waters again. Poff had the good sense to withdraw, whereupon Nixon raised Byrd's name again. Why not? Byrd was a former Klansman and "more reactionary than [George] Wallace," Nixon said, obviously relishing a chance to embarrass the Senate.

Following this, Nixon warmed to Mitchell's inspired concoction of nonentities: Herschel Friday (a fellow bond lawyer) and Mildred Lilley, an obscure local California judge who was meant only to be a sacrificial lamb. "The theory on the woman is that the ABA is not going to approve her, and therefore, he'll let her pass and blame them for it," Haldeman wrote. (This was the same American Bar Association committee that had endorsed the unqualified Carswell, Haldeman failed to note.) Nixon wanted Lewis Powell, but for the other open seat the White House tendered an offer to Senator Howard Baker, who called in his answer half an hour too late and was displaced by William Rehnquist in a coup led by Richard Moore, friend and aide to John Mitchell. A rare moment as the President caught Haldeman by surprise.

Everyone seemed happy, Nixon said, except his wife, who had been campaigning for a woman. That is the only time Haldeman recorded the President taking Mrs. Nixon seriously. The diaries are filled with Nixon and Haldeman's shared disdain for the First Lady; for example, Nixon could spare but a few moments for her 60th birthday party and then he hid out in his office.

* * *

Almost from the day that Nixon assumed office, he was off and running for 1972. Teddy Kennedy preoccupied him; in 1969, Nixon and his staff saw the battle over the antiballistic missile as the opening salvo of the 1972 campaign against Kennedy. Even after Chappaquiddick, Nixon seriously believed that Kennedy was a threat. He instigated Ehrlichman's own investigation of the incident and repeatedly told Haldeman that they couldn't let the public forget Chappaquiddick. He encouraged Charles Colson, who had agents follow Kennedy in Paris and photograph him with various women.

Vietnam was small potatoes compared with the amount of time the President and his aide plotted strategy and dirty tricks against political enemies. The Boys of '72 knew their way around this territory without much help In Nixon's 1962 gubernatorial campaign, they had established a bogus Democratic committee to mail cards to registered Democrats expressing concern for the party under Pat Brown. A Republican judge convicted them of campaign law violations and held that the plan had been "reviewed, amended and finally approved by Mr. Nixon personally," and that Haldeman similarly "approved the plan and the project."

In July 1969, Nixon directed Haldeman to establish a "dirty tricks" unit with the likes of Pat Buchanan and Lyn Nofziger. "Hardball politics," Haldeman later called it. Nixon regularly urged that the I.R.S. investigate Democratic contributors and celebrity supporters. He also wanted a review of the tax returns of all Democratic candidates "and start harassment of them, as they have done of us." He wanted full field investigations of Clark Clifford and other doves; he ordered mailings describing Edmund Muskie's liberal views to be sent throughout the South; and one basic line of his Watergate counteroffensive was to expose Democratic Party chairman Larry O'Brien's tax problems and his allegedly unsavory list of clients.

Alas, Haldeman has little new to offer on Watergate. He claims that the diaries are unexpurgated and complete on this score. That may be stretching the truth. The Watergate section contains long, discursive comments about the activities of many principals, but they are merely summaries Haldeman compiled from contemporary documents and his own choice memories. The entries focus on the complicity of just about everyone but H.R. Haldeman. When read together with the lengthy letter that Haldeman allegedly wrote (and did not send) in 1978 to the prosecutor, the implication is that he and Nixon were guilty only of a "political containment"—he was no party to a conspiracy to obstruct justice and he committed no perjury. He knew that the burglars had been given "hush money," but he insisted it was not a cover-up. It is a little late in the day for such a defense; furthermore, his own words demolish it.

The diaries expand on the finger-pointing that emerged from the tape revelations twenty years ago. Now we clearly see how Nixon, Haldeman and Ehrlichman sought to make Mitchell their fall guy, and how they coddled John Dean for so long to keep him in camp. In the letter to prosecutor James Neal, Haldeman turned from Mitchell to establish the outlines of a Dean conspiracy theory, one that has become fashionable among the former President's men in recent years.

From the outset, Haldeman knew the significance of the Watergate break-in. The day after, he called it "the big flap over the weekend," and he immediately knew that the Committee to Re-elect the President was involved. If so, that meant the White House, for John Mitchell and Jeb Magruder reported directly to Haldeman and his aides on campaign activity. Eventually, the True Campaign Chairman—the President himself—knew what happened there. Two days later, Haldeman reported that Nixon "was somewhat interested" in the events. Interested enough that we have eighteen and a half minutes of deliberately erased tape. Later that same day, June 20, Haldeman noted that Watergate "obviously bothered" Nixon and they discussed it "in considerable detail." But he gives us none.

Haldeman is fudging here. Tapes released two years ago, which cover Watergate conversations for June 1972—we previously had only the notorious "smoking gun" tape of June 23—reveal extensive conversations, beginning with the first attempt to concoct a containment or cover-up scenario on June 20. (Once again, the media missed this story as they made much ado about Nixon's remark that Liddy was "a little nuts.") Using the C.I.A. to thwart the F.B.I. was not a one-time occurrence on June 23; the two men repeatedly tried to stifle the investigation under the cover of national security, even after C.I.A. Director Richard Helms ended his cooperation. In these tapes, Haldeman seems to sense the futility of their efforts: "We got a lid on it and it may not stay on," he told the President on June 28. For nearly a year—not just in his last month as Chief of Staff—Haldeman knew that Watergate was trouble.

Significantly, Haldeman omits any mention of the President's offer of cash to him and Ehrlichman in April 1973 —after Ehrlichman ominously said, "I gotta start answering questions." When the President asked if they could use cash, Haldeman reacted with a blend of fury and sarcasm. "That compounds the problem," he said. "That really does." For good reason, Nixon needed their silence. But the President's insensitivity knew no bounds. After he announced Haldeman's resignation, he asked his departing aide to check out reaction to the speech. Probably for the only time, Haldeman refused a direct request. But in fact, he spent several more months listening to tapes to prepare for Nixon's defense.

The thousands of hours of taped conversations that Nixon fought so long to suppress will eventually be made public. Does anyone believe they will exonerate him or enhance his historical reputation? In the meantime, Haldeman's diaries take the lid off the Oval Office for the first four years of Nixon's presidency. What he has shown beyond dispute is that the Nixon of the Watergate years—furtive, manipulative and petty; often weak, sometimes comic and, above all, dishonest—was consistent with the behavior patterns of the earlier years. No Old Nixon; no New Nixon: There was one and only one.

# POSTSCRIPT

## Will History Forgive Richard Nixon?

Professor Joan Hoff-Wilson is one of the few professional historians to render a positive evaluation of President Nixon. She places him in the context of the late 1960s and early 1970s, when support for big government, New Deal, Great Society programs had dimmed and the bipartisan, anticommunist foreign policy consensus has been shattered by the Vietnam War. She gives him high marks for vertically restructuring the executive branch of the government and for attempting a similar reorganization in the federal bureaucracy.

Unlike most defenders of Nixon, Professor Hoff-Wilson considers Nixon's greatest achievements to be domestic. Though he was a conservative, the welfare state grew during his presidency. In the area of civil rights, between 1968 and 1972, affirmative action programs were implemented, and schools with all black children in the southern states declined from 68 percent to 8 percent. Even on such Democratic staples as welfare, the environment, and economic planning, Nixon had outflanked the liberals.

Hoff-Wilson has fleshed out her ideas in much greater detail in *Nixon Reconsidered* (Basic Books, 1994). British conservative cabinet minister and historian Jonathan Aitken has also written a favorable and more panoramic view of the former president entitled *Nixon: A Life* (Regnery Gateway, 1993).

Historian Stephen E. Ambrose's three-volume biography *Nixon* (Simon & Schuster, 1987, 1989, 1991) also substantiates Hoff-Wilson's emphasis on Nixon's domestic successes. Ambrose's evaluation is even more remarkable because he was a liberal historian who campaigned for George McGovern in 1972 and had to be talked into writing a Nixon biography by his publisher. In domestic policy, Ambrose told *The Washington Post* on November 26, 1989, Nixon "was proposing things in '73 and '74 he couldn't even make the front pages with—national health insurance for all, a greatly expanded student loan operation, and energy and environmental programs." With regard to foreign policy, both Ambrose and Aitken disagree with Hoff-Wilson; they consider Nixon's foreign policy substantial and far-sighted. In the second volume of his biography, *Nixon: The Triumph of a Politician, 1962–1972* (Simon & Schuster, 1989), Ambrose concludes that the president was "without peer in foreign relations where 'profound pragmatic' vision endowed him with the potential to become a great world statesman."

Professor Stanley I. Kutler accepts none of the revisionists' premises. In *The Wars of Watergate: The Last Crisis of Richard Nixon* (Alfred A. Knopf, 1990), Kutler focuses on both the negative side of Nixon's personality and his abuse of presidential power. In his review of *The Haldeman Diaries*, Kutler finds further substantiation for his view that Nixon was a narrow-minded, bigoted, self-calculating individual who took no action in his career that was not politically motivated. Unlike other writers who saw a "new" Nixon emerge as president, Kutler maintains that there was only one Nixon—a man possessed with a "corrosive hatred that decisively shaped" his behavior and career.

Neither Ambrose nor Kutler accept the view that Nixon was a corporate executive who reorganized government to enhance decision making. Both would agree that Nixon loved intrigue, conspiracies, and surprise. At the same time Kutler argues that Nixon went much further than any of his predecessors in abusing presidential power by siccing the Internal Revenue Service (IRS) on potential enemies, impounding funds so that the Democrat-controlled Congress couldn't implement its legislative programs, and finally covering up and lying for over two years about the Watergate scandal.

Clearly, historians will be disputing the Nixon legacy for a long time. Two works have tried to place Richard Nixon within the context of his times. Liberal historian Herbert S. Parmet, the first to gain access to Nixon's prepresidential papers, has published *Richard Nixon and His America* (Little, Brown, 1990). Less thoroughly researched in primary sources but more insightful is *New York Times* reporter Tom Wicker's *One Of Us: Richard Nixon and the American Dream* (Random House, 1991).

In order to gain a real feel for the Nixon years, you should consult contemporary or primary accounts. Nixon himself orchestrated his own rehabilitation in *RN: The Memoirs of Richard Nixon* (Grosset & Dunlop, 1978); *The Real War* (Warner Books, 1980); *Real Peace* (Little, Brown, 1984); *No More Vietnams* (Arbor House, 1985); and *In the Arena: A Memoir of Victory, Defeat and Renewal* (Simon & Schuster, 1990). Nixon's own accounts should be compared with former national security adviser Henry Kissinger's memoirs *White House Years* (Little, Brown, 1979). *The Haldeman Diaries: Inside the Nixon White House* (Putnam, 1994), which is the subject of Kutler's review essay, is essential for any undertaking of Nixon. Haldeman's account fleshes out the daily tensions of life in the Nixon White House and adds important details to the Nixon and Kissinger accounts. Other primary accounts include *The Nixon Presidency: Twenty-Two Intimate Perspectives of Richard M. Nixon*, vol. 6, in the series *Portraits of American Presidents* (University Press of America, 1987), which contains a series of discussions with former officials of the Nixon administration conducted by the White Burkett Miller Center for the Study of Public Affairs at the University of Virginia.

Two of the best review essays on the new historiography about our 37th president are "Theodore Draper: Nixon, Haldeman, and History," *The New York Review of Books* (July 14, 1994) and Sidney Blumenthal, "The Longest Campaign," *The New Yorker* (August 8, 1994).

# CONTRIBUTORS TO THIS VOLUME

## EDITORS

**LARRY MADARAS** is a professor of history and political science at Howard Community College in Columbia, Maryland. He received a B.A. from the College of the Holy Cross in 1959 and an M.A. and a Ph.D. from New York University in 1961 and 1964, respectively. He has also taught at Spring Hill College, the University of South Alabama, and the University of Maryland at College Park. He has been a Fulbright Fellow and has held two fellowships from the National Endowment for the Humanities. He is the author of dozens of journal articles and book reviews.

**JAMES M. SoRELLE** is an associate professor of history at Baylor University in Waco, Texas. He received a B.A. and an M.A. from the University of Houston in 1972 and 1974, respectively, and a Ph.D. from Kent State University in 1980. He has also taught at Ball State University, and, in addition to introductory courses in American history, he teaches upper-level sections in African American, urban, and late nineteenth- and twentieth-century U.S. history. His scholarly articles have appeared in *Houston Review, Southwestern Historical Quarterly,* and *Black Dixie: Essays in Afro-Texan History and Culture in Houston* (Texas A&M University Press, 1992), edited by Howard Beeth and Cary D. Wintz. He also has contributed entries to *The Handbook of Texas, The Oxford Companion to Politics of the World,* and *Encyclopedia of the Confederacy.*

## STAFF

Mimi Egan Publisher
Brenda S. Filley Production Manager
Libra Ann Cusack Typesetting Supervisor
Juliana Arbo Typesetter
Lara Johnson Graphics
Diane Barker Proofreader
David Brackley Copy Editor
David Dean Administrative Editor
Richard Tietjen Systems Manager

## AUTHORS

**DAVID H. BENNETT** is a professor in the Maxwell School of History at Syracuse University in Syracuse, New York. He has received several Outstanding Teacher awards, and he is the author or coauthor of numerous publications, including *Demagogues in the Depression: American Radicals and the Union Party, 1932–1936* (Rutgers University Press, 1969).

**BARTON J. BERNSTEIN** is a professor of history at Stanford University in Stanford, California. He has edited several works on the Truman administration and the atomic bomb, and he is the author of *Hiroshima and Nagasaki Reconsidered: The Atomic Bombings of Japan and the Origins of the Cold War, 1941–1945* (General Learning Press, 1975).

**GARY DEAN BEST** is a professor of history at the University of Hawaii in Hilo, Hawaii. He is a former fellow of the American Historical Association and of the National Endowment for the Humanities, and he was a Fulbright Scholar in Japan in 1974–1975. His publications include *Herbert Hoover: The Postpresidential Years, 1933–1964*, 2 vols. (Hoover Institute Press, 1983).

**JOHN BODNAR** is a professor of history at Indiana University at Bloomington. His publications include *Workers' World: Kinship, Community, and Protest in an Industrial Society, 1900–1940* (Johns Hopkins University Press, 1982) and *Remaking America: Public Memory, Commemoration, and Patriotism in the Twentieth Century* (Princeton University Press, 1992).

**McGEORGE BUNDY** is a professor emeritus of history at New York University in New York City. He is a former president of the Ford Foundation, and he was a special assistant to the president for national security under Presidents John F. Kennedy and Lyndon B. Johnson. His publications include *The Strength of Government* (Harvard University Press, 1968) and *Danger and Survival* (Random House, 1988).

**JOSEPH A. CALIFANO, JR.**, is a lawyer and partner in the law firm Dewey, Ballantine, Bushby, Palmer, and Wood in Washington, D.C., and the chair of the board for the Kennedy School of Government at Harvard University. He received an LLB from Harvard University in 1955.

**WILLIAM G. CARLETON** was a professor emeritus of history and political science at the University of Florida in Gainesville, Florida. His publications include *The Revolution in American Foreign Policy* (Random House, 1967), and his most important essays have been published in the collection *Technology and Humanism* (Vanderbilt University Press, 1970).

**CLAYBORNE CARSON** is a professor of history at Stanford University in Stanford, California. He is also a senior editor of the Martin Luther King, Jr., papers project at the university's Martin Luther King, Jr., Center for Nonviolent Social Change, which published in 1992 the first volume of a 14-volume edition of King's speeches, sermons, and writings. His publications include *In Struggle: SNCC and the Black Awakening of the 1960s* (Harvard University Press, 1981) and *Malcolm X: The FBI File* (Carroll & Graf, 1991).

**ALFRED D. CHANDLER, JR.**, is the Straus Professor Emeritus of Business History at the Harvard Business School. He has reconceptualized the field of business history with such books as his Pulitzer Prize–winning *The Visible Hand: The Managerial Revolution to American Business* (Harvard University Press, 1977). He is also the author of *Strategy and Structure: Chapters in the History of the American Industrial Enterprise* (MIT Press, 1962), which won the Newcomen Book Award, and *Scale and Scope: The Dynamics of Industrial Capitalism* (Harvard University Press, 1990), which won the Association of American Publishers Award.

**STANLEY COBEN** is a professor of history at the University of California, Los Angeles. He is best known for his research on the American Red Scare of the early 1900s, and he is the author of *A. Mitchell Palmer: Politician* (Columbia University Press, 1963).

**CARL N. DEGLER** is the Margaret Byrne Professor Emeritus of American History at Stanford University in Stanford, California. He is a member of the editorial board for the Plantation Society, and he is a member and a former president of the American History Society and of the Organization of American Historians. His book *Neither Black Nor White: Slavery and Race Relations in Brazil and the United States* (University of Wisconsin Press, 1972) won the 1972 Pulitzer Prize for history.

**W. E. B. DU BOIS** (1868–1963), widely considered to be the most prominent black intellectual of the twentieth century, was a founding member of the National Association for the Advancement of Colored People (NAACP) and the first African American to receive a Ph.D. from Harvard University. His historical works include *The Suppression of the Atlantic Slave Trade to the United States of America, 1638–1870* (1896) and *Black Reconstruction* (Harcourt Brace, 1935).

**ERIC FONER** is the DeWitt Clinton Professor of History at Columbia University in New York City. He is the author of several books and articles on the Civil War and Reconstruction eras, including *Free Soil, Free Labor, Free Men: The Ideology of the Republican Party Before the Civil War* (Oxford University Press, 1970) and *Nothing But Freedom: Emancipation and Its Legacy* (Lousiana State University Press, 1983). He is also the author of *Tom Paine and Revolutionary America* (Oxford University Press, 1976). He received a Ph.D. in history from Columbia University in 1969.

**SHERNA BERGER GLUCK** is a lecturer in oral history at California State University, Long Beach, and the editor of *From Parlor to Prison: Five American Suffragists Talk About Their Lives* (Hippocrene Books, 1976).

**ERNEST S. GRIFFITH** (1896–1981), an editor and writer, was a professor of political science and political economy in the School of International Service at the American University in Washington, D.C. He also held academic appointments at Harvard University and Syracuse University, and he served as the director of the legislative reference service at the Library of Congress.

**OSCAR HANDLIN** is the Carl M. Loeb Professor of History at Harvard University in Cambridge, Massachusetts, where he has been teaching since 1941. A Pulitzer Prize–winning historian, he has written or edited more than 100 books, including *Liberty and Power, 1600–1760* (Harper & Row, 1986) and *Liberty in Expansion* (Harper & Row, 1989), both coauthored with Lilian Handlin.

**VINCENT GORDON HARDING** is a professor of religion and social transformation in the Iliff School of Theology at the University of Denver in Denver, Colorado. He has been a scholar-activist in movements for peace and justice during the last three decades, and he was the first director of the Martin Luther King, Jr., Center for Nonviolent Social Change. His publications include *The Other American Revolution* (Center for Afro-American Studies, 1980) and *There Is a River: The Black Struggle for Freedom in America* (Harcourt Brace Jovanovich, 1981).

**LOUIS R. HARLAN** is the Distinguished University Professor of History Emeritus at the University of Maryland in College Park, Maryland. His publications include *Separate and Unequal: Public School Campaigns and Racism in the Southern Seaboard States, 1901–1915* (University of North Carolina Press, 1958) and *Booker T. Washington: The Wizard of Tuskegee* (Oxford University Press, 1983), which won the 1984 Pulitzer Prize for biography, the Bancroft Prize, and the Beveridge Prize.

**GEORGE C. HERRING** is the Alumni Professor of History at the University of Kentucky in Lexington, Kentucky. His research has focused on the United States' involvement in Vietnam, and he is the author of *America's Longest War: The United States and Vietnam, 1950–1975*, rev. ed. (McGraw-Hill, 1986).

**JOAN HOFF-WILSON** is a professor of history at Indiana University in Bloomington, Indiana, and a coeditor of the *Journal of Women's History*. She is a specialist in twentieth-century American foreign policy and politics and in the legal status of American women, and she has received numerous awards, including the Berkshire Conference of Women Historians' Article Prize and the Stuart L. Bernath Prize for the best book on American diplomacy. She has published several books, including *Herbert Hoover: The Forgotten Progressive* (Little, Brown, 1975) and *Without Precedent: The Life and Career of Eleanor Roosevelt* (Indiana University Press, 1984), coedited with Marjorie Lightman.

**HENRY KISSINGER,** a distinguished scholar, diplomat, and writer, was the secretary of state to Presidents Richard Nixon and Gerald Ford. He has published two volumes of memoirs from those years: *The White House Years* (Little, Brown, 1979) and *Years of Upheaval* (Little, Brown, 1982).

**STANLEY I. KUTLER** is the E. Gordon Fox Professor of American Institutions at the University of Wisconsin–Madison and the editor of *Reviews in American History*. His publications include *The American Inquisition: Justice and Injustice in the Cold War* (Farrar, Strauss & Giroux, 1984) and *The Wars of Watergate: The Last Crisis of Richard Nixon* (Alfred A. Knopf, 1990).

**BRUCE LAURIE** is a professor of history at the University of Massachusetts–Amherst. His publications include *Working People of Philadelphia: 1800–1850* (Temple University Press, 1980).

**FRANKLIN A. LEIB** is a professor of history at Stanford University in Stanford, California.

**WILLIAM E. LEUCHTENBURG** is the William Rand Kennan Professor of History at the University of North Carolina, Chapel Hill, and a former president of the American Historical Association and of the Organization of American Historians. His publications include *Franklin D. Roosevelt and the New Deal, 1932–1940* (Harper & Row, 1963), which won the Bancroft Prize and the Francis Parkman Prize, and *In the Shadow of FDR: From Harry Truman to Ronald Reagan* (Cornell University Press, 1985).

**ELAINE TYLER MAY** is a professor of American studies and history at the University of Minnesota in Minneapolis, Minnesota. Her publications include *Great Expectations: Marriage and Divorce in Post-Victorian America* (University of Chicago Press, 1983).

**CHARLES MURRAY** is a Bradley Fellow at the American Enterprise Institute in Washington, D.C., a privately funded public policy research organization. His publications include *In Pursuit of Happiness and Good Government* (Simon & Schuster, 1988).

**SANDRA L. MYRES** (1933–1991), a specialist in western history and women's history, was a professor of history at the University of Texas at Arlington, where she taught for 28 years.

**MARTIN J. SHERWIN** is the Walter S. Dickson Professor of History at Tufts University in Medford, Massachusetts, and the director of the university's Nuclear Age History and Humanities Center. His book *A World Destroyed: The Atomic Bomb and the Grand Alliance* (Random House, 1977), a runner-up for the 1977 Pulitzer Prize in history, received the Stuart L. Bernath Book Prize from the Society of Historians of American Foreign Relations and the American History Book Prize from the National Historical Society.

**KENNETH M. STAMPP** is the Morrison Professor Emeritus of History at the University of California, Berkeley. He has written numerous books on southern history, slavery, and the Civil War, including *Slavery in the Ante-Bellum South* (Alfred A. Knopf, 1956); *And the War Came: The North and the Secession Crisis, 1860–1861* (Lousiana University Press, 1970); and *America in 1857: A Nation on the Brink* (Oxford University Press, 1990). He is also the general editor of *Records of Ante-Bellum Southern Plantations from the Revolution Through the Civil War* (University Publications of America, 1985).

**CHRISTINE STANSELL** is a professor of history at Princeton University in Princeton, New Jersey. Her best known publication is *City of Women: Sex and Class in New York, 1790–1860* (Random House, 1986).

**HARRY G. SUMMERS, JR.,** holds the rank of colonel in the U.S. Army and serves on the faculty of the U.S. Army War College. He was an infantry squad leader in the Korean War and a battalion and corps operations officer in the Vietnam War, and he received two Purple Hearts. His articles on military strategy have appeared in *Military Review* and *Navel Institute Proceedings.*

**JON C. TEAFORD** is a professor of history at Purdue University in West Lafayette, Indiana. His publications include *The Twentieth Century American City: Problem, Promise, and Reality* (Johns Hopkins University Press, 1986) and *The Rough Road to Renaissance: Urban Revital-*

*ization in America* (Johns Hopkins University Press, 1990).

**JOHN TIPPLE** is a professor of history at California State University, Los Angeles.

**WILLIAM APPLEMAN WILLIAMS** (1921–1990) was a professor of history at Oregon State University in Corvallis, Oregon, and considered to be the dean of the New Left school of diplomatic historians. His publications include *The Roots of the Modern American Empire* (Random House, 1969) and *Empire as a Way of Life: An Essay on the Causes and Character of America's Predicament* (Oxford University Press, 1980).

# INDEX